RESTORING NATURE

RESTORING NATURE

Perspectives from the Social Sciences and Humanities

EDITED BY
PAUL H. GOBSTER AND R. BRUCE HULL

ISLAND PRESS
Washington, D.C. • Covelo, California

Library of Congress Cataloging-in-Publication Data

Restoring nature : perspectives from the social sciences and humanities
/ Paul H. Gobster and R. Bruce Hull, editors.
    p. cm.
Includes bibliographical references and index.
    ISBN 1-55963-767-6 (cloth : alk. paper) — ISBN 1-55963-768-4 (pbk. :
alk. paper)
    1. Environmental sciences—Philosophy. 2. Restoration ecology. 3.
Environmental management. I. Gobster, Paul H. II. Hull, R. Bruce.
    GE300 .R47 2000
    363.7—dc21

                                            00-009375

Printed on recycled, acid-free paper

Manufactured in the United States of America
10 9 8 7 6 5 4 3 2 1

Dedicated to all those who are taking responsibility
for their local natural environments

CONTENTS

PART II. CONFLICT OVER WHICH NATURE TO RESTORE

PART III. MAKING RESTORATION HAPPEN: PROCESS AND IMPLEMENTATION

PART IV. MAKING AND MAINTAINING RESTORED ENVIRONMENTS

ACKNOWLEDGMENTS

Many of the efforts leading to the publication of this book were funded in part by the USDA Forest Service, North Central Research Station. We are grateful to John Dwyer, project leader of North Central's "Natural Environments for Urban Populations" Research Work Unit in Chicago, for his foresight and encouragement. Robert Gronski of the University of Missouri assisted us in organizing the series of sessions at the 7th International Symposium on Society and Resource Management (ISSRM), from which the contributions to this volume were drawn. Reid Helford of Whitman College was instrumental in helping us carry the spirit of those sessions into this book with his expert audio- and videotaping of the presentations. As colleagues, chapter contributors, and friends, both Reid and David Robertson of Virginia Tech have done much to help shape our ideas and improve the content of this book. We wish them the best on their professional journeys. Bill Jordan has also gone beyond his role as a chapter contributor in encouraging this book's production and in shaping our ideas about restoring nature through many long discussions since the ISSRM sessions and through his editorship of the journal *Ecological Restoration* over the years. We hope others will continue with us the dialogue started in this book through involvement in the New Academy for Nature and Culture, which he leads. Finally, we thank Lucy Burde and Janine Benyus at the North Central Research Station and Barbara Dean and Barbara Youngblood at Island Press for their valuable editorial guidance.

Introduction

RESTORING NATURE: HUMAN ACTIONS, INTERACTIONS, AND REACTIONS

Paul H. Gobster

Bill Jordan has eloquently called it a loss of innocence. Ecological restorationists and their critics, speaking more bluntly from the trenches of battle, have labeled it an assault, a travesty, a misguided campaign, and an insidious plot. Always the optimist, John Dwyer, project leader at our Forest Service research office in Chicago, saw it as a challenge and an opportunity to learn.

Regardless of one's viewpoint, the conflict that erupted in the spring of 1996 and became known as the Chicago restoration controversy has left an indelible mark on the region's environmental community and has forever changed the way those involved will think about restoration. Its implications extend far beyond Chicago; since its inception, the controversy has provided a springboard for discussion and debate that has reached national and international audiences. Although the controversy has raised important biological and ecological issues, the pivotal issues have been social ones, exposing questions that are usually ignored or downplayed by researchers and managers dealing with ecological restoration and natural area management. *Restoring Nature* is an attempt to bring these human dimensions of restoration to the forefront. In this book, Bruce Hull and I, along with the contributing authors, hope to capture the stories, the ideas, and—most of all—the lessons from these restoration experiences.

1

In the first part of this Introduction, I describe the Chicago restoration controversy. As we suggested, many of the contributors to this book use the controversy as a touchstone for their discussions, so this background helps provide necessary context. The anatomy of the controversy also helped us organize the individual contributions to this volume. In the rest of the Introduction I describe the evolution of our thoughts in developing the book, the goal and objectives we hope to achieve, and how the individual chapters contribute to those purposes. I conclude with a brief postscript of sorts reflecting on the progress (or lack thereof) that has occurred since we began working toward this book.

The Chicago Restoration Controversy

In attempting to understand the Chicago restoration controversy, I soon learned that many of the salient "facts" were relative and subject to interpretation (as I suppose they are in most controversies). Restorationists and their critics debated what was a tree and what was brush, what was native and what was exotic, and, ultimately, what was natural and what was an artifact of human meddling in the environment. Even those on the same side and even scientists who were objectively studying the controversy had different interpretations and explanations of issues. What one focused on was dependent on one's perspective. As a social science researcher in the USDA Forest Service whose training fell largely within the area of environmental psychology, I tended to see the controversy in terms of a clash in values. Reid Helford, who was studying the controversy through the lens of sociology, countered, "It's really more about the structure and process of social and political relationships—who's got the power and who doesn't."

I concluded that the only proper way to introduce the controversy to the readers of this book was to write a personal account of how I saw it and how it affected me, fully acknowledging my own perspective and interpretation. Chapters by Helford and by Joanne Vining, Elizabeth Tyler, and Byoung-Suk Kweon provide additional background and perspective on the controversy as it pertains to their research. For those wishing to read other, often quite different perspectives, see articles by Debra Shore (1997) and Alf Siewers (1998).

For me, the controversy began in earnest on Monday, May 13, 1996. On my desk when I entered my office at the North Central Research Station of the Forest Service that morning was the front page of that Sunday's *Chicago Sun-Times,* one of Chicago's two major newspapers. The lead story, headlined in one-inch type, read "Half Million Trees May Face the Ax: DuPage Clears Forest Land to Create Prairies." The reporter, Raymond Coffey, described a developing conflict concerning the Forest Preserve District of DuPage County, a regional land management agency in west suburban Chicago, where a ten-year, $11.6 million Natural Areas Management Program was under development to restore 7,000 acres of land holdings to the oak savanna and tallgrass prairie conditions that existed in the Chicago region before European settlement.

This was a relatively new venture for DuPage and surrounding county forest preserve districts, whose land managers had traditionally considered a forest as a closed-canopy system and a preserve as a place where natural area management was largely hands-off. Restoration in the forest preserves had in fact historically meant planting trees and preventing fires, so when a citizens group called ATLANTIC—Alliance to Let Nature Take Its Course—complained that instead the district was now cutting trees and setting fires, it became a ready-made news story. Raymond Coffey, who was principally an editorial columnist, would go on to write more than thirty columns over the next two and a half years, blasting restoration efforts throughout the Chicago region from what seemed like every angle possible, with sensationalistic titles such as "Prairie People Compile Tree 'Hit List,'" "Forest Preserve District Is Picking Our Poison," "Smoking Out the County's Tree-Burning Plan," and "Guru's Forest Restoration Plans Read More Like Destruction."

The controversy in DuPage led the forest preserve board to declare a temporary moratorium on restoration activity in the county, but this was just the tip of the iceberg. By early fall of that year, restoration activity in preserves within the city of Chicago, under the management of the Forest Preserve District of Cook County, had also come under attack by citizens from surrounding neighborhoods. After a contentious public hearing, the Cook County Forest Preserve Board joined DuPage in placing a moratorium on all restoration activity in their county's forest preserves.

In the following months, additional hearings, workshops, conference sessions, radio talk shows, Web sites, newsletters, and consistent coverage by the regional and local newspapers kept the controversy in the public eye. Volunteer restoration groups, public land managers, and established environmental organizations fought back against neighborhood critics and animal rights groups (e.g., The Voice for Wildlife), the latter of whom had refocused their agenda on the controversy. New groups formed—Trees for Life and Friends of the Forest Preserves among them—each touting their anti- or pro-restoration messages. A college class was even developed around it—The Controversy over Ecological Restoration—at Chicago's DePaul University.

The May 12 article and media coverage in the weeks and months following it hit our office like bombshells. As an urban outpost of the Forest Service in metropolitan Chicago, we had long assisted local park and forest preserve districts by helping to answer management questions about people's perceptions and use of urban forest environments. Ecological restoration seemed to be a natural extension of our involvement in urban forestry, and in recent years we had become quite active in assisting with regional efforts at ecological restoration. We were charter members of a newly formed coalition of organizations called Chicago Wilderness, whose aims were to protect and restore biodiversity in a project area that encompasses the six-county Chicago metropolitan region and reaches into southeastern Wisconsin and northwestern Indiana. We were also helping to fund, through a congressional pass-through, a restoration research and demonstration project at Swallow Cliff Woods forest preserve in southern Cook County. Herb Schroeder, an environmental psychologist in our office, had begun studying the motivations and values of restoration volunteers. A number of us had spent free time volunteering in ecological restoration workdays in our local preserves. Thus, on both a professional and a personal level, we believed that restoration was generally consistent with our roles as research employees of the Forest Service and with our values as individuals.

Given this context, these attacks on restoration programs and initiatives surprised us. But what really struck us was the criticism leveled at individuals we knew personally. The Chicago office of The Nature Conservancy (TNC) has been instrumental in the development and execution of Chicago Wilderness, and two individuals at TNC were especially affected. Laurel Ross was a longtime friend and research cooperator, and she and Steve Packard had sought our advice on launching a number of major restoration initiatives in recent years. Ross, sincere and behind-the-scenes, and Packard, charismatic and outgoing, had been active in restoration efforts since the late 1970s. Working in partnership with the Forest Preserve District of Cook County and with other restorationists, they had built the North Branch Prairie Project and TNC's Volunteer Stewardship Network into nationally recognized restoration programs that now included dozens of sites and thousands of volunteers.

In many ways they saw Chicago Wilderness as their magnum opus: a program going far beyond pragmatic aspects of land protection and restoration. With globally significant ecosystems residing within a metropolitan region of 9 million people, protection and restoration efforts would need to be aimed as much at the social aspects of restoration as at the physical and technical ones. From planting wildflowers in one's backyard so that the seeds could be harvested for dispersal in the forest preserves, to supporting bond issues that would acquire new lands, successful implementation of the Chicago Wilderness project would require no less than a new paradigm of participation in nature. As a result of this broad-based change in view, "Chicagoans will feel patriotic about their native landscape," Packard would say. "Cab drivers will point out our savanna and prairie preserves to out-of-town visitors with the same pride they now feel when pointing out the Sears Tower."

So it moved me deeply to see a heavily burdened Ross and Packard, who had given so much of their personal and professional lives to the cause of restoration in Chicago, face this barrage of criticism after coming so far. These people are the good guys, I wanted to shout, not the enemy that others were making them out to be. The situation they were facing reminded me of the movie *The China Syndrome,* in which investigative reporter Kimberly Wells (played by Jane Fonda) and veteran nuclear engineer Jack Godell (played by Jack Lemmon) are thwarted by the pro-nuclear establishment in their attempts to expose a cover-up of serious construction and maintenance flaws at a nuclear power plant that nearly result in a meltdown. In the final scene, after Godell is killed by plant security agents, Wells provokes one of his co-workers into revealing the truth on camera to the media gathered outside the plant: "There's gonna be an investigation this time. And the truth will come out and people will know my friend Jack Godell wasn't a lunatic, he was a hero. . . . Jack Godell was a hero. . . ."

In their thwarted attempts to reveal what they saw as the truth in the Chicago restoration controversy, Ross and Packard seemed to me much like the Fonda and Lemmon characters (although Packard is still very much alive). Indeed, the comparison was particularly fitting because when *The China Syndrome* hit movie theaters in 1979, Packard and his early band of followers were using the practice of restoration to prevent a real-life meltdown in the Chicago-area forest preserves. Instead of construction and maintenance flaws, they were attempting to raise awareness of the problems posed by fire suppression and invasive exotics. Continuous fire suppression in the Chicago region since the time of European settlement has transformed the landscape from a diverse mixture of tallgrass prairie, open oak woodlands, savanna, and other ecosystems into one where closed forest ecosystems of sugar maples and other hardwoods increasingly dominate unmanaged forest preserves and other natural areas. Remnant pre-European-settlement oaks still remain in uncut areas, but their regeneration without some type of active management is uncommon. European settlers also introduced many new plants to the region, and some, such as the shrub European buckthorn (*Rhamnus cathartica*), have taken hold in many forest areas. While it was originally planted as a hedgerow by early settlers, its popularity as an ornamental increased with the suburbanization of the region. With its wide adaptability to conditions and its seed readily spread by birds and mice, buckthorn can now be found almost everywhere, and in many forest preserves it is a dominant plant growing below the canopy layer.[1]

These powerful forces have dramatically changed the landscape: they have literally changed the nature of nature in the Chicago region. In most places, the prairie and savanna have long been erased or hidden from view to the casual observer. As a Midwesterner nearly all my life, I grew up accepting these changes without question, but now even the woods I played in as a child in suburban Milwaukee have become nearly impenetrable due to buckthorn, and when I take my own young children there to visit they refuse to go in. In seeing these changes and learning about the restoration efforts around Chicago,

I began to develop an appreciation for these heritage landscapes and their possibilities for renewal.

I also became aware that turning back the clock requires a dedicated, intensive human effort that includes periodic burning, cutting and girdling of woody vegetation, herbicide application, seeding, and other activities. By practicing their craft through small-scale experiments and watching how the landscape responded, Packard and his growing group of restorationists pioneered new techniques that have now become accepted by many credentialed environmental scientists, although he and other volunteers for the most part wore a distinctly nonacademic badge of expertise. The full story of Packard's discoveries and the concomitant rise of the volunteer restoration movement in the Chicago area has been captured by William K. Stevens in his book *Miracle under the Oaks: The Revival of Nature in America,* as well as in articles by Packard (e.g., 1988) and Ross (e.g., 1994).

Now all the "progress" they had made was being questioned, criticized, and—what most restorationists feared—reversed as the moratoria on restoration left the buckthorn and other vegetative denizens to flourish unabated. But despite our sympathy for the restorationists, I and others in our office were becoming increasingly dismayed by their responses to their critics, both within and beyond the public eye. At a Chicago Wilderness meeting held shortly after publication of Coffey's May 12 article, for example, a prominent member of the steering committee called critics "a bunch of loonies." Others claimed the opposition was "just the deer people" looking for a way to expand their animal rights agenda, or "just a NIMBY thing" limited to a few neighborhood enclaves near certain preserves. Many restoration proponents saw opponents as misguided and misinformed, and calls rang out for increased political education within the restoration community and environmental education for those members of the public who were less than fully aboard the restoration bandwagon. "Informed people will not resist" was one of the bulleted phrases on a handout distributed by a forest preserve naturalist at a conference talk on "Public Education for Restoration: Why Are We Cutting Down All Those Trees?"

As an employee of the USDA Forest Service, whose mission in part is to harvest timber to meet the nation's demand for fiber, I was all too familiar with the argument that the public needed to be better educated so they would see that cutting trees is good for the forest. To continue the cinematic analogy, this was a movie I'd seen before, and I was increasingly uncomfortable with how the plot was unfolding.

How could the situation be improved? What could be done to facilitate an understanding of the issues and concerns involved? Public forums held to date had seemed only to worsen relations between factions. For our office, which focused on the social science aspects of urban forests, the controversy was a likely topic to study, and I wondered if perhaps a more systematic assessment would help. Were the opponents truly "just the deer people," or did their concerns extend beyond animal rights? Was the opposition "just a NIMBY thing" limited to a few neighborhood enclaves near certain preserves, or was it more widespread? These were empirical questions that could be readily explored and answered, and we were in the perfect position to do so.

The Natural Areas Conference, a national gathering of natural area managers and researchers, was being held in Chicago that October. With the conference fast approaching, I modified my original presentation idea, offering instead a preliminary effort to examine the restoration controversy from a social science perspective. To explore the scope of issues being raised in opposition to restoration, I analyzed opponents' views as expressed in newspaper articles and letters to the editor, transcripts of hearings and radio interviews, and newsletter articles and fact sheets put out by groups on both sides of the controversy (for more on the study, see Gobster 1997). Surprisingly, I found little in the way of blanket disapproval of restoration. In fact, critics often lauded the basic goals of restoration in protecting and enhancing urban nature. Instead, it was the specific practices people objected to, which I documented as including:

- removal of trees and brush: the killing of healthy trees and large as well as small "brush"; defining too many tree species as "alien" or "exotic";
- herbicide use: types being used; how, when, and at what strength they were being applied; the qualifications of those who applied them;
- prescribed fire: effects on air quality; safety of nearby homes; danger to wildlife; and
- removal of deer: justification for control; concern over methods used.

These practice-related concerns revealed *what* critics objected to. I also identified a number of process- and context-based concerns that related to *how* and *where* restoration was being carried out. These included:

- lack of information on activities where opponents felt out of the loop with regard to activities and in some cases where they felt information was withheld or activities concealed from the public;
- lack of involvement in decision making where opponents desired and felt the right to have a greater voice in decisions;
- insufficient planning for restoration where restoration was being conducted without good plans, both at a particular site and for the forest preserve system in general; and
- questionable use of volunteers where concerns existed as to whether or not the volunteers from private groups working on public lands were receiving sufficient training and supervision.

Finally, I attempted to identify the kinds of values that people expressed in relation to *why* restoration should not occur. These values all seemed to relate to fundamental ideas about the meaning of nature and included the following concerns:

- functional: the loss of air quality, privacy and solitude, and shade and cooling through prescribed burning and tree and brush removal;
- economic: the fear that restoration would increase taxes and reduce property values of homes near where trees were removed;
- recreation and wildlife: the loss of shady recreation sites and habitat for some species;
- aesthetic: restoration would harm the wooded character of the forest preserves and impose a radically different idea of what is beautiful; and
- symbolic: where some felt that restoration was an attempt to control nature and impose an arbitrary point in time to which nature should be turned back.

The range of issues and values evidenced through this research convinced me that the opponents' concerns were not narrowly conceived, and that there were some serious questions the restoration community needed to address if their programs were to gain wider public acceptance. Although I didn't know it at the time, these what, how, where, and why questions would later assist Bruce and me in selecting and structuring material for this book.

To elicit a more defensible answer to the NIMBY question than my qualitative pilot study had, Sue Barro, a social scientist in our office, and Alan Bright of Washington State University added some questions related to the controversy to a survey they were about to mail out, which was aimed at determining metropolitan Chicago residents' perceptions, attitudes, and knowledge about biodiversity. The results of that quantitative survey, with its statistically representative sampling scheme, verified my study's conclusion: while a large majority of Cook County residents (90 percent) thought that restoring natural areas in the Chicago area was a good idea, most (75 percent) felt it should not be done if it required cutting down mature trees, losing some existing wildlife habitat, or using herbicides (Barro and Bright 1998). More importantly, the study also provided concrete evidence that such feelings were widespread among metropolitan residents, not just localized to those living near the forest preserves.

While I believed we had found the answers to the empirical questions about the breadth and depth of the opposition, these did not seem to be the answers the restorationists wanted to hear. When presenting the findings of my pilot study at forums where restoration proponents were present, I was often questioned about the validity of my methods, and I increasingly felt the need to preface my remarks by saying that I was reporting on what I had found, not advocating a point of view. Barro and Bright's work was also critiqued in a letter published in *Restoration & Management Notes*, with the writer reinterpreting the authors' findings, saying they indicated public "indifference" and "widespread ignorance" (Osmund 1999, 3; see also reply by Barro and Bright 1999). More significantly, I believed our office was perceived by the restoration community as a turncoat of sorts. In a conversation with me, one prominent restorationist implied that I had done a disservice to the restoration community by legitimating the views of the critics. And our Forest Service project leader, John Dwyer, said that when he mentioned, in a meeting of restoration proponents, that their dismissal of opponents' concerns might be perceived as arrogant, the room got so quiet "you could hear a pin drop."

Were we asking the right questions in our attempts to understand the nature of the conflicts and the causes of concern? Were we providing answers to questions in ways that could be used constructively to help resolve the controversy? Ironically, just as we wondered about the naturalist who coined the slogan "Informed people will not resist," we were now wondering how our own messages were being received and interpreted.

Putting the "Constructive" into Constructivism

As a research office, we had in some ways fulfilled what I believed was our obligation to provide answers to questions people had been asking about the restoration controversy. But I also believed that our research could do more, not only to help resolve the controversy but also to help develop a more productive dialogue about managing nature in metropolitan Chicago and beyond.

To this end, in 1997 our office sponsored additional cooperative research related to the controversy, including a study on environmental values and emotions headed by Joanne Vining, an environmental psychologist from the University of Illinois at Urbana–Champaign, and a study on expertise and public involvement by Reid Helford, who at the time was a doctoral student in sociology at Loyola University–Chicago. Combining that research with the more broad-based work we were already conducting in-house and with cooperators, which related to people's experiences and involvement in natural area planning, design, and management, we were beginning to build a critical mass of knowledge on the social aspects of restoration.

One way to begin to bring this information together into a coherent and useful story, I thought, would be to do a session on restoration at the upcoming 1998 International Symposium on Society and Resource Management (ISSRM), a broad-based and well-attended biennial forum for discussing issues of social science and resource management. John Dwyer suggested that I raise the session idea with Bruce Hull, a colleague in the College of Natural Resources at Virginia Tech who was doing related work in a different part of the country. As a longtime research cooperator with our office, Bruce was known for his groundbreaking work in scenic beauty modeling in the 1980s and more recently for his research on urban nature experience. His new work dealt with understanding how different people construe nature—an issue I was beginning to struggle with in my own work, both on the restoration controversy and on an urban park restoration project.

Our first phone conversation was an eye-opener. Bruce talked about a couple of studies he was involved in that looked at how residents of rural communities in Virginia viewed forested landscapes in terms of concepts such as ecological health and integrity. These concepts, he said, are socially constructed in that their meaning depends on the socially acquired knowledge and life experience of the perceiver. Such concepts can thus mean very different things depending on whether the person expressing them is a longtime resident, an ecologist, a forest pathologist, or a timber sale manager. He had found that many local residents tended to see ecological health or integrity as visual signs of care. This meaning differs from how various experts tend to construe health and integrity, and it is this variability in meanings between and within experts and stakeholder communities that has become a major source of conflict in natural resources management.

I was aware of the recent debates on the social construction of nature (e.g., Cronon 1995, Soule and Lease 1995), and while I found them academically interesting, to date most of the treatments I'd seen were more antagonistic than helpful in terms of what they provided to managers and other practitioners. With the restoration controversy still raging back in Chicago, I wasn't sure if constructivist approaches were going to further burn rather than begin to mend any bridges.

Bruce's take, however, was refreshingly different. While he'd embraced the constructivist paradigm, he also saw it as a tool for achieving better planning and management of natural areas. "We're putting the 'constructive' into constructivism," he enthusiastically said of his work with graduate students David Robertson and Angelina Kendra, and described one example of how they'd been applying landscape architect Joan Nassauer's ideas about "cues to care" (1995) in helping to identify socially meaningful indicators of forest health and integrity. Bruce went on to describe work by other social scientists in the eastern and western United States who'd been looking at similar issues about the meanings of nature in wilderness and wildland settings. I thought back on my pilot study of the Chicago controversy, in which I had concluded that behind many of the concerns expressed by restoration opponents was a deeper set of values related to the meaning of nature that seemed to fundamentally separate them from proponents. Together we realized this was one of the essential stories underlying the restoration controversy that could be further explored in the ISSRM symposium session I'd proposed to Bruce. From that first call, Bruce was committed to helping in the effort.

The Restoration and Management of Nature:
The Conference

With Bruce signed on as a co-organizer for the symposium session, things began to move and expand. With my emphasis on restoration, the Chicago controversy, and urban settings and with Bruce's on nature, its management, and rural and wildland settings, we had the breadth and depth to make for a compelling ISSRM discussion.

We set as the goal for our session "to provide a constructive body of knowledge on the social aspects of restoring and managing nature that will lead toward the clarification and resolution of environmental problems." In developing our proposal, we found it necessary to define for ourselves and for the conference review committee just what our topic encompassed. Restoration was an ambiguous concept, with meanings as varied as one's disciplinary or professional orientation. Surely ecological restoration was a central component of what we wanted to include, but even within this boundary there was much debate and discussion as to what should qualify as a restoration (Jordan 1995). Because the social aspects of restoration linked many otherwise disparate issues and concerns, we believed that a broad definition would best satisfy our interests and those we hoped to attract as speakers and audience. Thus we defined restoration as "intentional human practices to actively manage areas for their desired natural qualities." This expansive definition embraced the spectrum of settings we wished to include as subjects of discussion, from wilderness areas, national forests, and geological features to rural agricultural lands, metropolitan parks and forests, and vacant urban land.

If restoration was an ambiguous term, then "nature" was even harder to nail down. Bruce, with his constructivist bent ever-cautioning me on the varied meaning of words we often accept uncritically, opted to leave nature as a socially defined and negotiated term. To borrow an explanation from Neil Evernden in his book *The Social Creation of Nature* (1992):

> It is fair to say that before the word was invented, there was no nature. That is not, of course, to suggest there were not the entities and phenomena we now attribute to nature, but rather to say that people were not conscious of there being any such entity as "nature." For nature is, before all else, a category, a conceptual container that permits the user to conceive of a single, discernible "thing" (89).

We also worked at more explicitly structuring our inquiry, to begin to provide a means for answering the important what, how, where, and why questions about restoration efforts. In doing this, we established the following objectives for the session: (1) to develop a conceptual foundation for the understanding of restoration issues, (2) to illustrate important issues and conflicts inherent in natural area restoration and management, (3) to provide examples of potential solutions to conflicts and controversies, and illustrate a variety of methodological and disciplinary perspectives in the social sciences and humanities, and (4) to examine case studies from a wide range of settings and locations.

With this goal, definitions, and objectives framing our view, we set out to more fully develop our proposal. While Bruce's ideas about the construction of nature formed an important conceptual piece of the puzzle, a key aspect we still lacked was one dealing with the moral and ethical foundations for restoring nature. Those in philosophy and the humanities had built an important body of work on this topic in recent years, both in academic journals such as *Environmental Ethics* and in *Restoration & Management Notes* (now *Ecological Restoration*), the principal forum of written communication for restoration practitioners, and we hoped to shine the light of those arguments onto our questions and issues in the social sciences. Knowing we would not reach many of these people through our normal conference channels, we sent invitations to prominent writers on the philosophy of natural area restoration and management, asking for their participation. To our surprise, we quickly received several affirmative replies.

By the fall of 1997 the conference was falling into place. We contacted others we knew who were working on issues related to our topic and invited their participation. Through word of mouth and the formal call for papers, we attracted additional interest. As we worked with Robert Gronski of the University of Missouri, who was coordinating the sessions for the symposium, our initial idea of a single session soon expanded to six sessions comprising twenty-eight individual presentations. The actual sessions, held under the theme "The Restoration and Management of Nature" at the University of Missouri in May 1998, were well attended and, we believed, highly successful. (For a more detailed synopsis of the sessions and abstracts of individual papers, see Gobster and Hull 1999.) Given this success, we decided to continue our work to produce this volume.

Restoring Nature: The Book

The papers we selected from our symposium sessions for this volume deal with four interrelated themes: (1) philosophical issues that help us understand why society should or should not support restoration activities, (2) conceptual issues and studies that help us understand the source of conflicts over restoration projects, (3) case studies of process and implementation that suggest ways in which restoration conflicts might be resolved, and (4) case studies of stewardship that suggest how volunteers and local residents can help make and maintain restored environments. Although Parts I and II of the book deal more with conceptual issues and problems and Parts III and IV deal more with applied principles and lessons, we encouraged our authors to not limit themselves to one approach. We asked the philosophers to relate their ideas about such things as nature–culture dualism and hyperreality to real-world problems in the restoration and management of nature. Likewise, we asked the social science contributors to tie their case-specific findings to broader theories and concepts.

As mentioned at the beginning of this Introduction, we also encouraged the contributing authors to use the Chicago restoration controversy as a touchstone for discussion of ideas and issues where it was appropriate. To further facilitate the development of common ground and the synthesis of ideas, we circulated drafts of the chapters and asked contributors within each section of the book to review each other's chapters. Thanks to these strategies as well as the participation of contributors in the symposium sessions, we think the book provides a good integration and cross-referencing of ideas among the different chapters.

Finally, in attempting to make the book interesting and useful to practitioners as well as researchers, students, and others involved in restoration and natural area management, we aimed to present a diverse range of ideas, case study settings, methodological approaches, and disciplinary perspectives. The remainder of this Introduction is a brief summary of how this diversity is captured by the various contributors to the book.

Philosophy and Rationale of Restoration

The introductory session of our theme area presentations at the ISSRM featured a debate of sorts about the moral and ethical questions regarding the practice of restoration. Underlying many of these questions is the issue of whether restoration corrupts "natural value"—that is, the value of nature independent of human concerns and desires.

We capture and expand upon this debate here. As a longtime proponent of restoration, William Jordan III, editor of *Ecological Restoration* and president of the New Academy for Nature and Culture, questions the nature–culture dichotomy upon which much of our environmental history and philosophy is built, and offers the practice of restoration as a way of reestablishing a relationship between humans and nature. In this opening essay, Jordan extends his ideas about community with nature to the topic of wilderness and argues that restoration provides a unique way for humans to "re-wild" the landscape, in turn creating positive natural value.

Diametrically opposed to Jordan's ideas is Eric Katz, a philosopher from the New Jersey Institute of Technology and a proponent of preserving natural value by maintaining a clear identity of nature apart from human intervention.

In his essay Katz extends his arguments against restoration, which began with publication of his often-cited paper "The Big Lie: Human Restoration of Nature" (1992), and responds to recent critiques of restoration by Robert Elliot (1997), Donald Scherer (1995), and William Throop (1997). Using examples as diverse as ballet performance and wolf reintroduction, Katz compellingly argues that restoring nature is philosophically misguided.

Katz's arguments, particularly one that casts restoration as an unjustifiable form of human domination over nature, are the subject of a systematic reply by Andrew Light, a philosopher from New York University. In refuting Katz's arguments, Light builds a logical case that participation in restoration can create a relationship between humans and the natural world that has a positive value and that can exist despite Katz's strict nature–culture dichotomy. Light argues that Katz's uncompromising ideal of natural value principles restricts the utility of environmental philosophy in addressing real-world problems, and he suggests that a more pragmatic approach can help direct philosophy toward more immediately pressing and productive questions about conducting restorations.

Cheryl Foster, a philosopher from the University of Rhode Island, concludes this section by addressing questions about restoration from an environmental aesthetics perspective. While she sees the nature–culture dichotomy as a tired distinction that is ultimately not very helpful in resolving environmental problems, she cautions us against what she sees as a pervasive trend in modern American culture toward the aesthetics of hyperreality, which can result in humans unquestioningly accepting models or copies of nature as nature. In looking at the topic of geological restorations, Foster argues that we might be able to build a more reasoned case for deciding when restoration is appropriate by discriminating between what is trivial and what is serious appreciation of nature, and by recognizing both the narrative (cognitive) and ambient (perceptual) properties of the environment.

Conflict over Which Nature to Restore

While the authors in the first section show us the philosophical floor plan upon which decisions about restoration can be built, contributors to Part II give us a set of guidelines and cautions about human agency. Central to this discussion is the conflict between differing ideas of how we define nature and, consequently, how we determine who gets to participate in decisions about restoration and management. Bruce Hull and David Robertson, social scientists from Virginia Tech, explain how key restoration-related concepts such as naturalness, health, and integrity not only are normative but have multiple and competing definitions. The understanding and ultimate resolution of these conflicting definitions is critical because such concepts lie at the interface of ecological science and public policy for restoration. In arguing for a more public ecology, the authors provide a set of guidelines for understanding and using environmental knowledge in making restoration decisions.

Whitman College sociologist Reid Helford examines the nature of conflict in the Chicago restoration controversy from a sociological perspective, and sees expertise and the public understanding of science as critical elements underlying the issues being debated. Helford, whose chapter stems from his doctoral research at Loyola University–Chicago, shows how expertise is used as a dividing line to present restorationists as expert knowers of nature and exclude those with other forms of knowledge and experience from the decision-making process. The conflict is exacerbated, Helford argues, because restorationists also cast themselves as grassroots activists whose campaign to save nature is value-laden and emotional. How restorationists and their critics differentially see these dual messages of value-free science and value-laden activism is at the heart of the controversy.

Environmental psychologist Joanne Vining and urban planner Elizabeth Tyler, both of the University of Illinois at Urbana–Champaign, and landscape architect Byoung-Suk Kweon of Texas A&M University also examine the Chicago restoration controversy, in their case from a psychological perspective. Using an analysis of the controversy as a basis for developing a list of arguments for and against restoration and a hypothetical scenario of the conflict, the researchers probe the environmental values and emotions of people not directly involved in the conflict. Like the Barro and Bright (1998) work mentioned earlier, Vining et al. show how conflicts can arise due to differences in values and perceptions.

In the final chapter in this section, Andrew Light, in his second contribution to the volume, addresses the potential of professionalization (certification, formal training, regulation) as a means of resolving some of the internal and external conflicts observed by Helford and Vining et al. His concern, as an environmental philosopher, is that professionalization and certification will close the content of the language of restoration, restricting how restoration is defined and in turn narrowing the ranks of who is considered a restorationist. This, Light warns, could harm what he sees as one of restoration's key values, its inherent democratic potential.

Making Restoration Happen: Process and Implementation

The final two sections of the book deal with how managers can make restoration projects succeed given the constraints and considerations discussed in previous chapters. The first of these sections presents planning and design approaches to resolving conflicts that can impede restoration efforts. Paul Gobster and Susan Barro, social scientists with the USDA Forest Service's North Central Research Station in Chicago, lead off the discussion with a case study of urban park restoration in Chicago. The study demonstrates the diversity of issues and stakeholder interests in urban nature and emphasizes the process of negotiation and the dynamics between planners and designers and stakeholder interests. The authors suggest that proactive, participatory planning may provide a way to resolve conflicts by integrating the values and expertise that exist within professional and public groups.

Landscape architect Robert Ryan of the University of Massachusetts, on the other hand, shows how conflicts might be reduced through design. In a study of restoration projects in Michigan, Ryan examines how people's knowledge and experience can affect their attachment to restoration sites and, in turn, their feelings about restoration management activities. Using the findings from his study and other work on environmental preferences, Ryan outlines a four-step process for integrating diverse public values and perceptions into restoration site planning and design.

In the final selection in Part III, social scientist Mark Brunson of Utah State University looks at a planning process called the Limits of Acceptable Change (LAC) and examines how it can be used to make decisions about the restoration of nature given an understanding and acceptance of how nature is socially constructed. Brunson sees the LAC process as a useful planning method in that it readily accounts for a continuum of ideas on what "nature" and "natural" are, a factor that routinely bogs down other planning systems that assume a nature–culture dichotomy. Brunson discusses how the LAC process can be used as a collaborative planning tool to help stakeholders work through management solutions when goals are in conflict.

Making and Maintaining Restored Environments

Environmental psychologist Herbert Schroeder of the USDA Forest Service's North Central Research Station in Chicago leads off the last section of the book, which focuses on maintaining restored environments, by examining the inner psyche of restorationists—their motives, their values, and how they perceive nature. Looking at how volunteer restorationists express themselves through newsletters aimed at those in their own group, Schroeder uncovers a rich set of themes about how restorationists view themselves and their craft. Schroeder also shows how metaphors used by restorationists, particularly those that equate restoration with war, might inadvertently heighten conflicts in situations such as the Chicago restoration controversy.

Landscape architects Robert Grese and Jane Buxton and environmental psychologist Rachel Kaplan, all of the University of Michigan, and Robert Ryan also study the psychological benefits of volunteers, in their case with a more structured survey. The authors uncover a core set of motivations that attract people to restoration as an activity, and distinguish it from motivations that attract people to other types of leisure activities. Together with Schroeder's work, this chapter helps us understand the unique and often profound benefits that participation in restoration can yield; more pragmatically, this knowledge can help managers gain insights into maintaining and expanding the ranks of volunteers.

Anthropologist Carol Raish of the USDA Forest Service's Rocky Mountain Research Station in Albuquerque concludes this section with a different perspective on how environments can be maintained and sustained, in her cases for periods that span centuries. By looking at the worldviews, traditional knowledge, and resource management practices of traditional and indigenous groups in northern New Mexico, Raish provides examples of how restorationists might integrate different ways of knowing and managing the land into the goals of restoration projects.

In the concluding chapter, Bruce Hull and David Robertson draw from the ideas presented in this book and from their own experience as social scientists as they address how we as researchers, practitioners, decision makers, and citizens can help to set goals for restoration and management. "What is possible? What is acceptable? What can be maintained? And why do it?" are the four questions to which the authors direct their attention, and in so doing they provide signposts that communities of stakeholders can use in reaching restoration and management goals.

Conclusion

It is now early November 1999 as I complete the final edits on this Introduction. Although the heat of the Chicago restoration controversy has subsided from what it was three years ago, rapprochement seems unlikely anytime soon, and restorationists and their critics are in some ways more at odds with each other than ever. In Cook County, there is still a full moratorium on restoration activity at some key sites, and at other sites it proceeds under a lengthy set of restrictions applied with careful scrutiny and supervision. Earlier this fall, concern over restoration activities around Chicago spread north to Lake County, where citizens and public officials called into question the cutting of trees to expand a wetland project on forest preserve land. Farther away, restoration logging activities in the Shawnee National Forest in southern Illinois and Coconino National Forest in Arizona raised similar concerns in wilder contexts. In different locations and ecosystems, and with different stakeholders, it seems increasingly clear to me that some fundamental issues underlie the way restoration is currently being practiced and justified within the context of society's concerns.

Yet my contact with restored nature this fall also tells me, on a personal level, that there exist values in restoration that transcend these persistent and expanding concerns of society. As I gaze out at the waves of geese washing over the vast Horicon Marsh in central Wisconsin and think back on how, in the 1910s, this land was drained and unsuccessfully farmed, then abandoned, and now reclaimed, I dwell on the promise that restoration can bring. As I

marvel at the twelve-foot-long root structure of a big bluestem plant on display at a new exhibit on restoration at Chicago's Field Museum of Natural
History, I think back on the sea of grass that gave Illinois its nearly forgotten
moniker of the Prairie State. As I absorb with all my senses the beauty of the
restored savanna at Bunker Hill forest preserve near my home—a beauty after
which we named our first daughter, Savanna—I cannot help but know the
goodness in restoration.

Restoring Nature is an attempt to work through the ambivalence that exists
within all of us as we come to terms with our places in and responsibilities to
nature and society. With Bruce Hull and the contributors to this volume, we
hope you as a reader will help us build on the efforts we have begun here.

Note

1. This is the majority view of 'landscape history in the Chicago region, the view
   currently espoused by most ecologists and land managers in the region and the
   one that forms the basis of Chicago Wilderness's *An Atlas of Biodiversity* (1998) and
   draft *Biodiversity Recovery Plan* (1999). However, given the rich diversity of ecological communities and their shifting patterns across the pre-European-settlement landscape, sketchy knowledge of pre-European-settlement land cover and
   disturbance patterns, and abrupt post-European settlement land cover change due
   to logging and grazing as well as fire suppression, there is considerable uncertainty
   as to what a given parcel of land might have looked like in the 1830s. This uncertainty, particularly as to whether certain sites were closed forest or more open and
   savanna-like, by itself constitutes one of the major disagreements in the controversy. Thus, while my general characterization of the pre-European-settlement
   landscape emphasizes prairie and savanna components, I am aware of this uncertainty and its implications. For a minority view on this debate, see Mendelson et
   al. (1992) and Mendelson (1998).

References

Barro, S. C., and A. D. Bright. 1998. "Public Views on Ecological Restoration: A Snap-
   shot from the Chicago Area." *Restoration & Management Notes* 16(1): 59–65.
Barro, S. C., and A. D. Bright. 1999. "Reply: Appearances—and Science." *Ecological
   Restoration* 17(1–2): 3–4.
Chicago Wilderness. 1998. *An Atlas of Biodiversity*. Chicago: Chicago Region Biodi-
   versity Council.
Chicago Wilderness. 1999. *Biodiversity Recovery Plan* (September 1999 draft). Chicago:
   Chicago Region Biodiversity Council.
Coffey, R. 1996. "Half Million Trees May Face the Ax: DuPage Clears Forest Land to
   Create Prairies." *Chicago Sun-Times* May 12.
Cronon, W., ed. 1995. *Uncommon Ground: Toward Reinventing Nature*. New York: W. W.
   Norton.

Elliot, R. 1997. *Faking Nature: The Ethics of Environmental Restoration.* London and New York: Routledge.

Evernden, N. 1992. *The Social Creation of Nature.* Baltimore: Johns Hopkins University Press.

Gobster, P. H. 1997. "The Chicago Wilderness and Its Critics, III. The Other Side: A Survey of the Arguments." *Restoration & Management Notes* 15(1): 32–37.

Gobster, P. H., and B. Hull. 1999. "The Restoration and Management of Nature: A Conference and Forthcoming Book Explore Restoration from the Perspectives of the Social Sciences and Humanities." *Ecological Restoration/North America* 17(1–2): 44–51.

Jordan, W. R. III. 1995. "'Restoration' (The Word)." *Restoration & Management Notes* 13(2): 151–152.

Katz, E. 1992. "The Big Lie: Human Restoration of Nature." *Research in Philosophy and Technology* 12: 231–241.

Mendelson, J. 1998. "Restoration from the Perspective of Recent Forest History." *Transactions of the Wisconsin Academy of Sciences, Arts and Letters* 86: 137–148.

Mendelson, J., S. P. Aultz, and J. D. Mendelson. 1992. "Carving Up the Woods: Savanna Restoration in Northeastern Illinois." *Restoration & Management Notes* 10: 127–131.

Nassauer, J. I. 1995. "Messy Ecosystems, Orderly Frames." *Landscape Journal* 14(2): 161–170.

Osmund, D. 1999. "The Public and Restoration: Support—or Indifference." *Ecological Restoration/North America* 17(1–2): 3.

Packard, S. 1988. "Just a Few Oddball Species: Restoration and Rediscovery of the Tallgrass Savanna." *Restoration & Management Notes* 6: 13–22.

Ross, L. M. 1994. "Illinois' Volunteer Corps: A Model Program with Deep Roots in the Prairie." *Restoration & Management Notes* 12(1): 57–59.

Scherer, D. 1995. "Evolution, Human Living and the Practice of Ecological Restoration." *Environmental Ethics* 17: 359–379.

Shore, D. 1997. "The Chicago Wilderness and Its Critics, II. Controversy Erupts over Restoration in the Chicago Area." *Restoration & Management Notes* 15(1): 25–31.

Siewers, A. 1998. "Making the Quantum-Culture Leap—Reflections on the Chicago Controversy." *Restoration & Management Notes* 16(1): 9–15.

Soule, M. E., and G. Lease, eds. 1995. *Reinventing Nature? Responses to Postmodern Deconstruction.* Washington, DC: Island Press.

Stevens, W. K. 1995. *Miracle under the Oaks: The Revival of Nature in America.* New York: Pocket Books.

Throop, W. 1997. "The Rationale for Environmental Restoration." In *The Ecological Community,* edited by R. S. Gottlieb, 39–55. New York and London: Routledge.

❖ *Part I* ❖

PHILOSOPHY
AND RATIONALE OF
RESTORATION

❧ Chapter 1 ❧

RESTORATION, COMMUNITY, AND WILDERNESS

William R. Jordan III

When the history of environmentalism in the twentieth century is written, perhaps the most striking fact about it, leaping out at the historians of the new century as an oversight almost beyond comprehension, will be its neglect of the practice of ecological restoration.

Restoration, after all, is not a new idea. Indeed, the notion of helping land recover from the effects of human use dates back at least to biblical times, in the fallowing of land. The active rehabilitation of ecosystems was a common theme of reforestation efforts in the Middle Ages, and of the practice of game management and forestry since the nineteenth century. The notion of re-creating ecosystems for aesthetic purposes is grounded in traditions of landscape design that date back to the work of naturalistic landscape designers such as Capability Brown in England and Thomas Jefferson in the United States, and reached a high level of both achievement and self-awareness in the work of designers like Frederick Law Olmsted and Jens Jensen during the decades leading up to and into the twentieth century. Beyond this, the practice of restoration in the fully modern sense—that is, the deliberate and active re-creation or restoration of historic landscapes or ecosystems defined in terms of the science of ecology—dates back at least to the pioneering work of Edith Roberts at Vassar College during the 1920s and the landmark work at the University of Wisconsin–Madison Arboretum, which began a decade later.[1]

Despite this history, there remains the overwhelming fact of neglect. Environmentalism is, of course, a wide and diverse movement, if indeed it may be called a coherent movement at all. And yet we may say that, at least until very recently, the various schools of environmental thought have to a considerable extent been united in their neglect of restoration, their skepticism about its value, and their wariness of its political implications. One after the other, for the better part of a century, environmentalists of various persuasions have walked past this work, failing to recognize its value either as a conservation strategy or as a context for negotiating the relationship between our own species and the rest of nature.

The reasons for this are no doubt complex and will provide good hunting for the environmental historians of the next generation or two. Here I venture a few suggestions, even if they are at this point little more than hypotheses, recording them because they clearly raise fascinating, important, and even urgent questions in the areas of the social sciences and humanities.

To begin with, we might suppose that the conservationists who in a sense invented ecological restoration early in the twentieth century—by linking the practices of land rehabilitation and landscape design with the then new science of ecology—failed to discover its value at least partly because of their more or less utilitarian perspective. From their perspective, restoration, with its emphasis on the full complement of species and functions (including apparently "useless" ones), seemed impractical, even self-indulgent—a kind of boutique conservation. On the other hand, to the environmentalists of the past generation, with their emphasis on the intrinsic value of nature and the rights of other species, the notion of restoration has seemed both presumptuous and politically dangerous, since the promise of restoration can be—and has been—used to undermine arguments for the preservation of existing natural or historic landscapes. At the same time, scientists for many years overlooked restoration because they saw it as applied ecology, intellectually derivative from basic research and contributing little to it.[2] And social scientists and humanists overlooked it for the good reason that, until very recently, it was not a conspicuous, widely recognized, or storied part of environmental perception and culture.

At bottom perhaps, linking all these, is an assumption of a deep metaphysical distinction between nature and culture, between humans and what we take to be everything else. This makes nature and culture fundamental categories of thought, and from this perspective restoration is either invisible or repellent because it violates these basic categories, falling into the area of metaphysical ambiguity in which the anthropologist Mary Douglas located the grounds of taboo.[3] Partly artificial and partly natural, the restored landscape is not exactly either. It is, rather, a landscape of ambiguity—the very place, we might suppose, where established identities are challenged and where relationship and community begin—yet a place where it seems we have been ill equipped either to recognize these opportunities or to take advantage of them.

In planning this essay, I knew that the opening section of this volume was to be an extension of a debate I participated in at the International Symposium on Society and Resource Management in Columbia, Missouri, in May 1998, with Eric Katz questioning the value of restoration, Andrew Light and me in our various ways defending it, and Cheryl Foster bringing in a different perspective to our nature-culture debate. At that symposium, being somewhat familiar with Eric's critique of restoration, I believed I knew what I had to say in response: that by adopting a negative view of restoration, Eric not only marginalized restoration but also precluded hope for community with nature.

My idea was that community depends on exchange—the purely economic exchange of goods and services that characterizes any ecological community, but also, at least for humans, the more perilous process of exchanging gifts—that is, taking and giving back under the pretext that the exchange is purely voluntary and free of self-interest.[4] Without this—in fact, without both kinds of exchange—there can be no community. Furthermore, restoration is— or at least can be—our gift back to nature. The restored ecosystem is something that we offer nature in return for what nature has given us, or what, if you prefer, we have taken from it. Moreover, it represents what is in a sense our best gift—the one that comes closest to being commensurate with what nature offers us.[5] Thus, I wanted to suggest that in marginalizing restoration and dwelling on the inadequacies of the gift the restorationist offers nature, critics like Eric Katz and Robert Elliot were effectively precluding community with nature.[6]

Since the aims of environmentalism, at least since Aldo Leopold, have often been defined in terms of community with nature, I believed that this was an important criticism. After making this argument at the symposium, however, I was surprised that Eric dismissed it out of hand. "But I don't *want* everything in nature to be part of the human community," he told me. In fact, he goes on, in the chapter following this one, to make the case for another value—that of wilderness—which he believes is compromised by community. And after thinking this over, I realized that between us we were actually arguing two sides of an environmental orthodoxy—an orthodoxy, however, that I began to believe was curiously contradictory.

On the one hand, we have an environmentalism that never tires of reminding us of the ecological axiom that everything is connected to everything else: quoting John Muir's line that everything in the world is hitched together, or Leopold's argument that we should learn to think of land as "a community to which we belong."[7] But on the other hand, we find ourselves making the case for wilderness conceived as nature more or less separate from humans, arguing for its preservation, insisting on its intrinsic value, and—even in the context of restoration—idealizing its value as something independent of humans, self-sustaining, self-organizing, untainted by self-consciousness, and so forth.

In other words, we have what looks like a contradiction at the heart of environmental thinking, or at least two quite distinct conceptions of the value of the natural landscape. This might confuse anyone who took the trouble to look at these two parts of the environmental message side by side. And, just conceivably, the contradictory character of this message—calling for community one minute and for the apparently very different ideal of wilderness the next—might help account for the limited effectiveness of environmental rhetoric. Which, after all, is it going to be? Or can we have both? How might the conflict between these two values be resolved? And finally, what, if anything, might restoration have to contribute to resolving it?

As I have indicated, my own thinking about restoration has been concerned almost exclusively with its implications for the first of these two ideals—community. The idea that the creation of community is the primary and defining task of environmentalism has underlain all my thinking and writing in this area. My emphasis has been on the value of restoration as a context for negotiating the relationship between humans and the rest of nature conceived as community—that is, as a way of building the human community, desperately weakened by centuries of modern "isms"—Puritanism, rationalism, nationalism, liberalism, individualism, and, of course, modernism generally—and then somehow expanding it to include the larger biotic community.[8]

In doing this I have made the case along the lines outlined above, arguing that restoration has a critical role to play in this process, not only as a way of actively conserving what cannot simply be preserved but also as a way of knowing the natural (or, more accurately, the "given") landscape, of testing and refining our ideas about it, of intensifying and raising our awareness of it and the value we place on it, of participating in its economy, of exchanging gifts with it (an act that is precluded by preservationism), and, finally—and crucially—of coming to terms with the inadequacy of what we offer back to nature in return for what we take from it.

In particular, I make the case that restoration has value precisely because it entails the loss of innocence, the idealization of harmlessness that is inherent in the paradigm of preservation, forcing us to confront the shame of creation that, others have argued, is inseparable from communion with it.

Basically, if what we want is community—and communion—with nature, I have argued that restoration provides a way of achieving it, in part because it implicates the practitioner in the highly problematic process of gift exchange. But I have paid far less attention to the values of wilderness and wildness, or even simply otherness or givenness, all of which are clearly values worth defending. Confronted by Eric Katz's argument that restoration might help create community with the landscape, but that in doing so it compromises its value as wilderness, I find myself forced to pay more attention to these values and their relationship to community.

What are we to make of this? Do we face a dilemma here, a choice between community on the one hand or wilderness and the wild on the other? Are these really competing and mutually exclusive values? Or do they overlap or intersect in such a way that we can have both at the same time?

Thinking Through the Contradiction

Briefly, in what follows I will take for granted that at least a measure of restoration, as an attempt to compensate for novel or outside influences on a landscape, is in principle essential to landscape conservation. I will also take for granted that restoration is—or can be—a valuable context in which to create community or to negotiate the relationship between the human community and the larger biotic community. I will argue, however, that neither of these—neither the management of the landscape to compensate for novel influences on it, nor the development of this process of compensatory management, or restoration, as a way of building community—is the same thing as domestication. I will argue, rather, that the restored ecosystem can be wild, that community quite properly *includes* the wild, and that in the hands of the best practitioners, restoration is an ongoing dialogue with nature as given, as self-organizing, and as unpredictable—in other words, as wild.

Let's take up these points one at a time.

First, contrary to what critics of restoration sometimes imply, restoration is not—or need not be—domestication. It does, of course, involve manipulation of a landscape and is a form of agriculture, at least so far as techniques are concerned. But so far as its ends are concerned, restoration is, quite literally, agriculture in reverse. If the gardener or farmer in some sense takes charge of the landscape, the restorationist does just the opposite, relinquishing his or her hold on it in an attempt to turn it back over to itself, or, more accurately, to let it be—and to help it become—what it used to be before he or she or we arrived in it. This does not necessarily imply that the model for a restoration project must be a landscape that is "natural" or wild or free of human influence, but only that it be a landscape shaped by forces—including human beings—other than ourselves, however we choose to define that term. It may be a coral reef that owes essentially nothing to human influence; it may be a tallgrass prairie that reflects centuries of burning by humans (but not Europeans); or it may be a deliberately designed and intensively managed landscape like Thomas Jefferson's garden at Monticello, or the peach orchard on the battlefield at Gettysburg, or a mowing meadow in France that dates back to medieval times.[9]

But when the model landscape or ecosystem is wild or natural, like a coral reef, or includes elements of wildness or naturalness, like a prairie, then restoration amounts to a deliberate attempt to liberate the landscape from management (although only as far as this can be done without jeopardizing species and processes), which is exactly the opposite of the aims of the more traditional forms of agriculture. Restoration involves not only the reintroduction of complex assemblages of species but also, in its most ambitious form, a quite deliberate and highly self-conscious attempt to "re-wild" the landscape. In the case of the prairies, this aspiration is powerfully dramatized by the deliberate reintroduction of fire, itself an archetypal symbol of wildness.[10]

In fact, the rediscovery of fire as an element in the ecology of prairies and other ecosystems, and the development of fire as a management technique, were early achievements of restorationists, foresters, and game managers that provoked controversy (and in some areas continue to do so), surely at least in part because they involve a kind of intimate collaboration with what is wild, unruly, and even chaotic in nature.[11] And, of course, the burning of the prairies and savannas of the Midwest, the pine flatwoods of the Southeast, or the forests of Yellowstone and other wilderness areas in the West are not the only examples of restorationists' attempts to re-wild the landscape they work with. Restorationists also reintroduce floods and droughts to ecosystems. They reintroduce insects and, on occasion, diseases. They reintroduce predators like wolves that have been extirpated by farmers or ranchers, and when necessary they take on the role of predator themselves, killing deer, rabbits, burros, and invasive exotic plants, both acknowledging and acting out the radical violence that is the essence of the wild. Where the chaotic and disruptive forces of nature cannot be reintroduced deliberately, restorationists simply wait for them and then take advantage of them, as they did recently after Hurricane Andrew, which swept exotic vegetation from Key Biscayne in southern Florida, clearing the ecological slate for the reintroduction of native species. Another example, achingly emblematic of the ambiguity of the restorationist's relationship with nature, is the painstaking attempt being made by restorationists at the International Crane Foundation in central Wisconsin to find ways of raising young cranes without domesticating them, so that they can eventually join wild populations—a tricky process that has involved attempts to imitate parent birds, even to the point of dressing in costume and, clumsily, offering them flying lessons.

It is true that all this is done according to a plan, and that in this sense the restorationist compromises what some prefer to regard as the wild, unreflexive innocence of nature. But it is also true that the whole process is—or at least can be—done in a spirit of setting free, in an attempt not to control the forces of nature but rather to act in concert with them. Hence, restorationists, many of whom are also gardeners in the more traditional sense, commonly distinguish between these two aspects of their work. "I'm not a gardener," Robert Betz will proclaim, standing on one of the prairies in suburban Chicago that he has weeded and tended for twenty years. "Oh, I'd never do that," another says. "That's just gardening."

The difference lies in the attempt not merely to imitate the patterns and forms and structure of nature, but also to accommodate and at times even to participate in its processes, including those that are most turbulent, unpredictable, wild, and—like fire and flood—even dangerous. Restoration is, in this sense, the deliberate opposite of domestication—it is a letting go, or at least an attempt to let go. It may be that in attempting this act of release the restorationist confronts the wild more directly than the mere observer, and pays wildness a more profound tribute. In any event, the result, when a project is successful, is a wild thing, containing as much freedom of movement as is possible, given the space and circumstances. Thus, there are no bison on the Curtis Prairie at the University of Wisconsin–Madison Arboretum, but there is fire. And on bigger prairies farther west, in Kansas and Nebraska, there are bison as well, and there the fire and the bison interact, in ways not yet understood, to make a prairie.[12]

This is quite different from the outcome of more traditional forms of gardening, with their goal of creating an ordered and simplified ecosystem, tailored to human needs and interests, and traditionally separated by a wall from the rest of nature—the wild—as restorationists, if not their critics, are well aware. And the feel of the whole enterprise is different, too—a matter that should be of considerable interest to scholars in the humanities and social sciences who are interested in the kinds of relationships humans can form with landscapes and with other species. If the restored landscape is not wilderness exactly, or at least is not wilderness yet, it eventually will be as natural processes resume and a measure of wildness and self-creation reasserts itself. In the meantime, plenty of the wild remains, as it always does in nature in the weeds in the garden, in the undiscovered precincts in back lots, and in the flora in our own gut. The restorationist is, perhaps, peculiarly close to this wildness.

This aspect of the ethos and sensibility of restoration is nicely expressed by New York City restorationist Cindy Goulder in a poem:

VOLUNTEER REVEGETATION SATURDAY

After all the stabbing at
slick clay soil in the rain,
and all the hands, backs,
eyes, knees, working the plants in
in the mud,

and after passing pots, picks,
spades, cups, bagels, chuckles, shovels,
and so many how-to's and
how-come's and
all too simple explanations,
the last thing we did was
back out,
driving live stakes into the
ground as we went,
erasing our own
route in.

If it is the path
that makes the garden,
and the garden that
civilizes the wild,
we are disengardening now,
turning on our past
and our pioneering ways
to make amends for the
scythe that went too far,
to say a thank you
audaciously
for the future.[13]

A Constituency for Wilderness

But—it is true—most restoration projects are carried out on a small scale. Even if they reach the scale of a few thousand acres, as a few have in recent years, and even if they are wild in certain respects, they still represent wilderness only in miniature, a symbolic or ceremonial wilderness. And since the quality of an ecosystem and its capacity for self-organization are scale-dependent, this is a serious flaw. We can find wildness anywhere. But wilderness we rightly think of as big—big enough to more or less look after itself.

What does the restorationist have to contribute here? First, the obvious—scaling up by devising new methods, forms of ecological jujitsu like burning vegetation or using birds to disperse plant seeds into restoration areas. An excellent example is the technique prairie restorationists in the Midwest call successional restoration—not plowing old-field sod under before planting, but merely throwing seed of prairie plants into the sod and raking it in. The process is slower but much cheaper than traditional means of tillage and, given time, the results can be even better. Time, in effect, is spent instead of money; patience is invested instead of capital; and the success of the process lends plausibility to 10,000-acre projects like those currently under way at the Neal Smith Wildlife Refuge near Des Moines or at Midewin National Tallgrass Prairie south of Chicago.

Equally important, however, is the value of restoration as a way of building a constituency for the natural (or historic) landscape and for the conservation of wilderness.

The environmentalism of the past generation has placed a high priority on wilderness preservation, but has had only limited success in actually achieving it on an adequate scale. Despite notable successes, it is probably fair to say (and I suspect that few environmentalists would argue the point) that environmentalism has generally failed to provide a plausible basis for the conservation of large natural areas in a crowded and increasingly democratic world. Traditionally, preserves were hunting parks, the prerogatives of the wealthy and privileged, and something of this exclusivity survives today in our culture of nature. In the political and economic sphere, it survives in an environmentalism that idealizes remote—and, for most, inaccessible—wilderness areas as the quintessence of nature. And at a personal level, it survives in a culture that provides only an extremely limited repertory of ways for contacting nature—ways, I mean, that engage only a limited range of human interests, talents, and abilities. The result—unintended, of course—is a kind of psychological elitism that accommodates those inclined by nature to the experiences of observation and appreciation, but has less to offer the mechanics, nurturers, healers, hunters, gatherers, artists, craftsmen, pilots, planners, leaders, and ditch-diggers among us. (At a personal level, of course, it leaves those parts of each of us unsatisfied.) And, as a result, it offers the basis for a constituency for conservation that is both smaller and perhaps, in a psychological sense, thinner than that offered by the conservationism of the first half of the twentieth century, with its grounding in hands-on activities such as hunting, fishing, and farming.

Ecologically, this is dangerous for any ecosystem that depends, as most now do, at least to some extent on human effort, even if this is only the effort of forbearance and protection. But it is also dangerous in the social, political, and psychological spheres as well. Considered at the deepest level—that of religion, defined as the discipline of creating and maintaining relationships at the spiritual level, which environmentalism properly is—it amounts to attempting to create a religion based exclusively on the practice of contemplative prayer, without ritual and without what Luther called "works" as a context for redemption into community. This is not absolutely bad. There is nothing bad about contemplative prayer. In fact, that kind of experience is important for everyone. For most, however, it provides an inadequate basis for a relationship and a way of life.

It is precisely this, I suspect, that defines the limit of what modern environmentalism can achieve in its attempt to "preserve" classic landscapes. Environmental groups characteristically call for the preservation of large areas, citing ideas and research from disciplines such as landscape ecology and conservation biology indicating that large areas are necessary to provide a measure of sustainability and independence from human influence. (I say a measure of independence because complete independence is not only impossible but also incompatible with an ecologically grounded environmental sensibility or ethic.) Thus the conservation group Wild Earth recently published a plan calling for the setting aside of vast areas in North America—including, for example, roughly a third of Florida—as wilderness preserves.[14] This may be called for, spiritually as well as ecologically. But it is one thing to formulate such plans, and another to realize them. To do that it will be necessary to enlist a constituency commensurate with such a program—that is, a constituency as broad and as deep as the constituency for, say, Disneyland, professional sports, popular fashion, or Hollywood movies.

And these comparisons with various performing arts are suggestive. A fundamental weakness of preservation as a paradigm for conservation is that, as a non-act, it provides only a weak base for the development of the performance and ritual that will be needed to explore and articulate the terms of our relationship with particular landscapes, to create values related to these relationships, and to generate emotional commitment to them. As an overt, complex, fascinating, and even at times inherently dramatic act, restoration can become not only a form of recreation but also ultimately a performing art, a way of creating community and other transcendent values such as meaning, beauty, and the sacred. It is, moreover, a comprehensive act, one that does not displace traditional activities such as birding, backpacking, and botanizing, but incorporates them and adds to them, expanding the repertory of experiences and techniques available to environmentalists in carrying out their work on behalf of the natural landscape and the diversity, wildness, and even otherness—or givenness—that it represents.

In this way it provides what seems to me a plausible basis for the creation of the large, deeply committed constituency that will be needed to ensure conservation of large natural—or wilderness—areas. It does this, moreover, with the material close at hand—the landscapes that most people actually inhabit, the urban parks, rights-of-way, stream corridors, and vacant lots of the urban and suburban landscape that have, or can be made to have, a powerful symbolic relationship with larger and more remote wilderness areas. Restoration, in fact, is a kind of ecological junkpicking. And this has obvious social implications for the inner cities, for example, and for the suburbs. This spinning of environmental straw into gold is tremendously encouraging and dramatizes, in a way that wilderness experience by itself does not, the hopeful idea that humans can influence even complex ecosystems in positive ways and, by extension, do belong on this planet—a notion that much of the environmentalist rhetoric of recent decades has left very much in doubt.[15]

So far as more "pristine" natural areas are concerned, restoration is important for at least three reasons. First, it provides an alternative to the consumptive use of remote natural areas (including low-impact activities such as backpacking and birding). Second, it creates a constituency for conservation of such areas—real wilderness areas. And third, it can actually result in the upgrading of natural areas, or to their expansion on an environmentally significant scale. With restoration rather than preservation as a model, millions of people will spend more time creating intimate wild places in their own neighborhoods and less time visiting—and consuming—nature in remote wilderness areas. In the process they will get closer to nature than they would hiking or driving through a national park, and they will be helping to build local community rather than weaken it by investing time and resources in vacations and first or second homes in the country. Such people may be expected to support conservation of larger, wilder areas because they will understand them. They will also feel less compulsion to consume these wild areas by attempting to inhabit them. Such areas will then be left relatively undisturbed, and will be available for their best possible use as places for vision quests, spiritual retreats, study, the making of films, and other works of art—and, of course, as models for restoration projects.

Wilderness and Community

Finally, I would like to make an observation about the nature of wilderness itself and its relationship to community and to the practice of restoration. In thinking about restoration and the way it may be said to compromise wilderness, we should keep in mind that it is in the very nature of wilderness to be compromised. Wilderness is the unknown. It owes little or nothing to humans, and it is perhaps dangerous to them. Wilderness is always a frontier that advances as human knowledge and understanding progress. In fact, the commonplace idea of wilderness is really a somewhat bowdlerized idea of nature, entertained by people who have ensured themselves considerable freedom from the conditions of real wilderness. Aldous Huxley pointed this out many years ago in an essay on the romantic environmentalists of the nineteenth century,[16] and the sentimentality he saw in the Wordsworthian nature–culture of his time certainly survives in the environmentalism of our own time.

The wild landscape we idealize as environmentalists is really a relatively comfortable wilderness, and this perhaps compromises its value in a psychological and spiritual sense much more than the fact that it may have been to some extent restored and turned back into the wild. For real wilderness, we will always have to go out to the frontier, into the truly uncharted country. For us, now and in the future, this will mean following the trajectory of exploration outward into the depths of the oceans and into outer space, and inward to the inner city, to encounters with other cultures, and to the exploration of our own inner selves.

And it is here, I think, that we finally reach a perspective from which we can resolve the contradiction between wilderness and community—not by keeping them apart, but by finding the element of wilderness in the experience of community. This, however, calls for a change in the way we think about community. Community, we tend to think, is comfortable, pleasant, tame—the opposite of the wild. What we overlook are the more troubling aspects of community—the challenge to the ego and even the identity of the individual that it entails, the imposition on others that is inseparable from community, and the loss of innocence that is the cost of membership in community. These matters tend to be underplayed in a liberal culture, which typically articulates values in terms of individual rights, and in doing so softens— and ultimately trivializes—community and its institutions. But they are evident in the deliberate violation of categories that Mary Douglas describes as a route to the real, the sacred, and the communal. They are evident in the experiences of liminality, *communitas,* and anti-structure that the anthropologist Victor Turner found at the heart of the experience of community.[17] They are evident in classic rituals of initiation into community, which involve the ritualized death of the self. And they are evident in rituals of communion, which characteristically involve both killing and eating—transforming the violence of what mythologist Joseph Campbell called "the deed of life" into an act of communion. This is brought about through the alchemy of ritual sacrifice, in which the sacrificer not only confronts the appalling fact that life feeds on death, that our food consists entirely of the bodies of our brother and sister creatures, but also self-consciously participates in this universal scandal of nature and creation and, in the process, achieves communion with it. Strikingly, the communion is bidirectional. The sacrificer achieves communion with the prey by killing and eating it and, at the same time, achieves communion with his or her companions by eating *with* them.

Thus, at the very heart of community, in the experiences of liminality and anti-structure, we find the wild. In traditional societies, where the crisis of life typically was encountered in the killing of individual animals or, less dramatically, of plants, this took the form of the ritual killing of a single, representative individual in the context of ritual sacrifice. Today, perhaps what is needed is something more—a way of dealing with the monstrosity and shame of killing not just individuals but entire ecological communities. Restoration, as I see it, is important because it provides a context in which to do this. It is the resurrection—always incomplete and in part imaginary—that makes the killing not merely an end in itself but a first step into communion. Properly conceived, it not only compensates for our crimes against nature but also implicates us in them, providing a context for confronting the monstrous fact—the heart of the wild, perhaps—that life and creation always depend on destruction.

Restoration, then, is perhaps one way to resolve the contradiction between community and wilderness—not by keeping them apart but by revealing the wildness at the heart of both.

Notes

1. Dave Egan, "Historic Initiatives in Ecological Restoration," *Restoration & Management Notes* 8, no. 2 (1990): 83–90.
2. For an exploration of the value of restoration as a technique for basic ecological research, see William R. Jordan III, Michael E. Gilpin, and John D. Aber, *Restoration Ecology: A Synthetic Approach to Ecological Research* (Cambridge: Cambridge University Press, 1987).
3. Mary Douglas, *Purity and Danger: An Analysis of the Concepts of Pollution and Taboo* (New York: Routledge, 1966). Also see my short essay linking Douglas's ideas with restoration, "The Prairie and the Pangolin," *Ecological Restoration* 17, no. 3: 105–106.
4. This conception of community is actually contained in the word itself, as sociologist David McCloskey at Seattle University has pointed out to me. Etymologically, the word is a compound derived from the Latin *cum* (with) and *munus,* which means an exchange (or, more remotely, a change) at successive levels as a relationship is intensified: first, a duty; second, a gift; and finally, a sacrifice—that is, the giving of the gift in a way that ritually acknowledges and compensates for its inadequacy, resolving in make-believe terms a tension that cannot be resolved in literal terms.
5. I am drawing here from Mary Douglas's work; from Marcel Mauss, *The Gift: The Form and Reason for Exchange in Archaic Societies* (New York: W. W. Norton, 1990); and from Lewis Hyde, *The Gift: Imagination and the Erotic Life of Property* (New York: Random House, 1979).
6. See Eric Katz, this volume. See also his paper, "The Ethical Significance of Human Intervention in Nature," *Restoration & Management Notes* 9, no. 2 (1991): 90–96. Another persistent critic is the Australian environmental philosopher Robert Elliot, most recently in the provocatively titled *Faking Nature* (New York: Routledge, 1997).
7. This widely quoted comment appears in the foreword to Leopold's *A Sand County Almanac* [Oxford: Oxford University Press, 1949 (1981 edition)], viii.
8. I explore this theme in more detail in my forthcoming book, *The Sunflower Forest: Ecological Restoration and the New Communion with Nature.*
9. The idea that restoration is necessarily concerned with the re-creation of "natural" or "wilderness" areas reflects the fact that the idea of restoration took shape in New World settings, principally in the United States, Canada, and Australia, and that it was inspired in part by a desire to return dramatically altered landscapes to some semblance of their precontact condition, which was often understood—or misunderstood—to be essentially free of human influence. A growing body of

scholarship has made it clear in recent years that this conception of the precontact landscape is to a considerable extent a romantic fantasy that, among other things, seriously downplays the roles of indigenous peoples in shaping the landscapes in which they live [see, for example, William M. Denevan, "The Pristine Myth: The Landscape of the Americas in 1492," and other essays in "The Americas Before and After 1492: Current Geographical Research," *Annals of the Association of American Geographers* 80, no. 3 (1992)]. In any event, as the work of practitioners in other parts of the world has made clear, there is nothing about the idea of restoration that requires the goal of a restoration project to be a natural or even a healthy landscape—all it has to be is historic. In fact, far from resisting the discovery of the human influence on pre-Columbian landscapes, many restorationists have welcomed these insights and have even contributed to them in various ways. The contention that restoration implies a nature-culture dualism rests on the same rather parochial reading of what this form of land management is all about, and is discredited when we find restorationists self-consciously reenacting fires historically set by Indians, or restoring a landscape originally designed by Frederick Law Olmsted in New York's Central Park.

10. For up-to-date accounts of the craft of restoration as it is practiced on the prairies of the Midwest, written with the authority and perspective of practitioners, see Stephen Packard and Cornelia F. Mutel, eds., *The Tallgrass Restoration Handbook: For Prairies, Savannas and Woodlands* (Washington, DC: Island Press, 1997).

11. Stephen J. Pyne, *Fire in America: A Cultural History of Wildland and Rural Fire* (Princeton: Princeton University Press, 1982), and other books on the history and culture of fire by the same author.

12. For overviews see Henry F. Howe, "Dominance, Diversity and Grazing in Tallgrass Restoration," *Ecological Restoration* 17, nos. 1 and 2 (1999): 59–66; and Colleen Davison and Kelly Kindscher, "Fire, Grazing and Mowing on Tallgrass Prairies," *Ecological Restoration* 17, no. 3 (1999): 136–143.

13. Originally published in *Restoration & Management Notes* 14, no. 1 (1996): 62. Reproduced with the permission of the author. Copyright 1999 by Cindy Goulder.

14. Reed F. Noss, Michael A. O'Connell, and Dennis D. Murphy, *The Science of Planning: Habitat Conservation under the Endangered Species Act* (Washington, DC: Island Press, 1997), 182. For further discussion of this plan, also see Reed F. Noss and Allen Y. Cooperider, *Saving Nature's Legacy: Protecting and Restoring Biodiversity* (Washington, DC: Island Press, 1994).

15. Until very recently, little had been written about the experience of restoration from the perspective of the practitioner. For excellent accounts of the practice and experience of restoration, see William K. Stevens, *Miracle under the Oaks: The Revival of Nature in America* (New York: Pocket Books, 1995); Stephanie Mills, *In Service of the Wild: Restoring and Reinhabiting Damaged Land* (Boston: Beacon Press, 1995); and Freeman House, *Totem Salmon: Life Lessons from Another Species* (Boston: Beacon Press, 1999).

16. Aldous Huxley, "Wordsworth in the Tropics." In *Collected Essays* (New York: Bantam, 1960), 1–10.

17. Victor Turner, *The Ritual Process: Structure and Anti-structure* (Ithaca: Cornell University Press, 1969).

꙰ *Chapter 2* ꙰

ANOTHER LOOK AT RESTORATION: TECHNOLOGY AND ARTIFICIAL NATURE

Eric Katz

Why is the restoration and management of nature a philosophical issue? Why, indeed, should any environmental policy be a matter of concern for philosophers? The obvious reason is that any human activity is subject to ethical analysis and justification—we need to see what values are promoted or retarded by particular policies. But even more basic than the ethical analysis is the philosophical search for meaning. What is the essential character of a given human activity? What does it mean to say that we humans are restoring natural ecosystems? What are we doing when we restore the natural world? In asking these questions, I am not seeking a detailed description of the science and technology of the restoration process—I am seeking the philosophical meaning of the restoration of nature.

In this essay I reexamine the restoration and management of nature, reviewing and expanding arguments I have made previously concerning the distinction between human interventions in nature and the unmodified continuation of natural processes. I argue that the presence of human intentionality creates a clear distinction between human artifacts and natural entities, and that this distinction has important consequences for understanding the meaning and value of policies of environmental restoration and management.

The mistaken idea that the technological restoration of nature is equivalent to natural value is a result of the human belief that we wield supreme power in our dealings with the natural world. Our knowledge, our science, and our technology, we seem to believe, can do anything, correct any problem, heal any wound. The ancient Greeks had a word for this: hubris, the excessive pride that comes from an uncritical belief in one's own superiority. The mistaken belief that restoration policies can replace natural value by the creation of functionally equivalent natural systems is an expression of human hubris regarding our technological power and mastery of the natural world.

In a policy framework that justifies and advocates the restoration of nature, humanity will face no moral limits to its attempts to modify, manage, manipulate, and dominate the natural world, for humanity will believe that it has the power to make nature whole. But if, instead, we recognize the importance of natural value unmodified by human technology, the value of a nature free from human intentionality, we will understand the limits of our knowledge and power. We will understand that there is a realm of value with which we should not interfere, a realm of value that ought to be protected and preserved. We cannot be the masters of nature, molding nature to our wishes and desires, without destroying the value of nature. The realization of this truth is the cure for human hubris, the acceptance of the limitations of human power.

In the first part of this essay, I review my previously published arguments and defend the idea that there is a dualism between human artifacts and natural entities. I discuss the importance of origin, historical continuity, and authenticity for a proper evaluation of artifacts and natural processes. I illustrate this philosophical discussion with a consideration of cases involving the reintroduction of wolves into wilderness areas. In the second part of this essay, I critically review some recent philosophical literature on the ethics of ecological restoration. I argue that these attempts to justify some types of restoration and management policies will lead to a general weakening of the environmentalist goal of the preservation of nature.

Nature versus Artifact: Origin, Historical Continuity, and Authenticity

In several previously published essays (Katz 1992a, Katz 1992b, Katz 1993, Katz 1995; collected in Katz 1997), I argued that ecological restorations (and to a certain extent, policies of natural resource management) do not actually restore or manage natural systems. Once a system has been created, designed, or managed by human technology and science, it is no longer a natural system—it is now an artifact, a product of human intention and design. I argued that there is a fundamental ontological difference—that is, a fundamental difference in the essential character—of natural entities and human artifacts. Artifacts exist only because of human intention and design. Artifacts are the physical manifestation of human purpose imposed on the world of nature. An artifact would not be conceived, designed, or created unless it was thought to promote some human purpose. This is completely unlike the origin of natural entities. Natural entities, of course, do not exist through any process of design or purpose—unless we want to raise a whole host of theological questions, which I think it is better to avoid.[1]

Based on the fundamental difference between artifacts and naturally occurring entities, I questioned the meaning of ecological restoration and the policies of sustainable forestry, and I used the provocative phrase "the big lie" to characterize the policy of the restoration of nature (Katz 1992a). Once we see that the introduction of human intentionality and purpose fundamentally changes the character of a natural system, we cannot say that we are restoring nature. Instead, we are creating artifactual systems—or, at best, hybrid systems of natural entities and artifacts—that are designed to achieve some set of human purposes or benefits. These human benefits may be significant and important, and thus the policies of restoration and management may be justified, but they should not be characterized as the restoration of nature. The danger in misunderstanding the meaning of these environmental polices is an increased humanization of the natural world, the limitless expansion of human power to mold and manipulate the natural world.

Let's explore this argument in a little more detail, anticipating and responding to some objections. First, there is the question of dualism. In the following chapter, my friend and colleague Andrew Light calls me "an admitted nature–culture dualist," and others have likewise criticized me for allegedly advocating a radical separation between humanity and nature. Isn't there a unity and harmony between humanity and nature? Don't humanity and nature exist in an interdependent relationship? But I do not advocate—nor does my argument imply—a complete dualism of humanity and nature. To use the old Earth Day rhetoric, I do know that humanity is "a part" of the natural world and not "apart" from it. I really do know that humans are biological beings who are dependent in very crucial ways on a functioning biosphere to survive and prosper. Humanity is, in its primary being, a part of the natural world. But human artifacts are not a part of nature. There is a radical distinction between human artifacts and naturally occurring entities.

I believe this distinction is so clear that I am often perplexed by people who claim there is no distinction. The most general form of the counterargument is that since humans are the products of natural evolution, and since artifacts are the products of human thought and skills that are themselves evolutionary products, then artifacts are as natural as human beings (see, e.g., Scherer 1995). But this argument blurs important distinctions—for example, it makes everything natural. It also obscures the manner in which entities are produced in the world. Artifacts are the result of human intentions. Natural entities are not. What could be clearer?

This dualism is not absolute, for naturalness and artifactuality exist along a spectrum of various kinds of entities. Things can be more or less natural, more or less artifactual. A wooden chair is more natural than a plastic chair, because it is more closely related to the naturally produced material that forms its basic structure. The plastic chair is further from its original material or source. But both chairs are definitely artifacts, essentially different from naturally occurring entities—from, for example, a fallen tree on which I sit in the forest. Why are the chairs different? Because they are the result of human intention. We could stand around and watch nonhuman nature at work forever, and we would never see it produce a chair. Although humans are biological beings, the products of an evolutionary process, what we humans do—the things we create, build, make, imagine—are all artifactual, with a source outside the realm of naturally occurring entities, processes, and systems. Our artifacts, our culture, would not exist if we humans had not intentionally interfered with and molded the natural world. Nature alone could not create the world in which we now find ourselves.

Why is this dualism important for an understanding of restoration policy? Once we recognize that there is a distinction between human artifactual creations and naturally occurring systems, we will tend to evaluate the different kinds of entities and systems differently. In addition, we will begin to redefine, or at least redescribe, exactly what restorationists and natural resource managers are doing.

What is it within the artifact–natural entity distinction that is crucial? Three aspects of the creation process are important: origin, historical continuity, and what I call authenticity. All three features are also present in the creation of human artworks, so it is appropriate that Robert Elliot, in his original essay on this topic, "Faking Nature" (1982), used the analogy between restorations and art forgeries to illustrate key value decisions, and in my work I have built on Elliot's comparisons.[2]

When considering any work of human art, its origin is of primary importance. We want to know who the artist was (or is), what influenced his or her work, and perhaps what the social, political, economic, and historical conditions were during the time period in which the artist worked. A work of art that appeared similar to the given one but had different origins would be valued differently. The same is true of historical continuity. A work of art that was damaged and then repaired would have a different value than the same work of art if it had endured through time without any damage. Combining these features creates the condition of authenticity—the work of art we see today really is the same work of art that was created by a particular artist in the past, unmodified by subsequent historical events.

My major modification of Elliot's original argument focused on dynamic works of art such as ballet or opera, since these works, I believe, are more similar to the dynamic processes of natural systems (Katz 1992a). Nevertheless, the crucial features of origin, historical continuity, and authenticity are still determining factors in the value of the artistic creation. A ballet modified by the original choreographer is viewed differently from a ballet modified by someone else. George Balanchine, for example, frequently modified and updated his works for the New York City Ballet. (In almost all cases, these changes were seen as improvements, the modifications of a more mature artist.) Now Balanchine is dead and can no longer modify his works; thus when Peter Martins, the current Ballet-Master-in-Chief of the City Ballet, makes changes, all those balletomanes who appreciate Balanchine are appalled.[3] But at least Martins was educated and danced in the Balanchine tradition. Consider a complete outsider—say, a Broadway musical or rock-show choreographer—changing Balanchine's *Nutcracker.* Surely this would be an outrageous attack on the ballet's authenticity—even if the resulting ballet were enjoyable to watch (see also Katz 1996).

When we shift back to the restoration or re-creation of natural systems, we must still focus on origins, historical continuity, and authenticity. The major difference is that in the case of human artworks, we are dealing with situations in which one human (or group of humans) is replaced in the creative process with another human (or group), but in the case of the restoration of natural systems, there was no original artist or designer. Here the lack of authenticity, the interruption of historical continuity, and the change of origin come about because we add human intentionality. We interrupt the natural development of an area and modify it to meet human goals, ideals, or designs. We mold the natural system to meet our needs—whether these be economic, political, scientific, cultural, or aesthetic. We modify nature and turn it into an artifact. When we consider the authenticity of a natural system, the presence or absence of human intentionality is the key determining factor of its value and ontological character.

Let's consider a series of cases. These cases illustrate the difference between natural changes in a system and human-induced artifactual changes; they also show that the differences between artifacts and natural entities are relative, that they exist along a spectrum of more or less natural and more or less artifactual. The cases concern the reintroduction of wolves into Yellowstone National Park, a designated wilderness area. Is the reintroduction of wolves into Yellowstone the restoration of nature? Consider a range of cases, some actually true, some merely possible:

(1) Wild wolves, never captured or bred by humans, migrate on their own from Canada into Yellowstone and establish several distinct packs in different regions of the park.

(2) Some Canadian wolves are captured by U.S. scientists and released into Yellowstone, where they establish several distinct packs in different regions of the park.

(3) Some Canadian wolves are captured by U.S. scientists, bred extensively in captivity, and then released into Yellowstone, where they establish several distinct packs in different regions of the park.

(4) Good wolf specimens from several zoological parks are bred together and the offspring released into Yellowstone, where they establish several distinct packs in different regions of the park.

(5) Using the most recent genetic engineering techniques, several wolves are cloned and then bred in captivity, and their offspring are released into Yellowstone, where they establish several distinct packs in different regions of the park.

Now imagine that on the ground, the ecological consequences of all five cases are indistinguishable. All five cases lead to the flourishing of wolves in the park and thus the reintroduction of natural predation into the wilderness area—a result that all environmentalists (of a preservationist bent) would find satisfactory.

But are all the cases the same? Are they of equal value? Isn't it obvious that the essential characters of the cases are different? In case (1) there is absolutely no human intervention. Case (2) introduces a minimal amount of human intervention, and the degree of human control and manipulation increases dramatically as we move down to case (5). Our intuitions about the value of these different cases rest entirely on our response to the level of human intervention, manipulation, and control of the natural processes involved. These intuitions reveal an important truth about the essence of the restoration process: the level of human interference and intervention changes our perception, meaning, and value of wild nature, natural entities, and natural processes. Recognizing this point should cause us to change our evaluation of policies that seek to restore, manage, and control the natural environment.

Rationalizing Restoration: A Critique of Three Recent Views

What is actually going on when we do ecological restoration? We are creating artifactual systems that resemble nature, but they are not an authentic nature because of the presence of human intentionality (and human technology and science). Does this make restoration bad? Is it an evil policy? It would be impossible to make any blanket generalization. Clearly, ecological restoration, when it is advocated by committed environmentalists, is designed to improve the world.

But I am concerned that a favorable analysis and justification of restoration will lead to environmental policies in which restoration will be abused. Elliot's original work on restoration was meant to counter a position he called the "restoration thesis" (he now calls it the "replacement thesis")—a position advocated by the developers and despoilers of natural areas. Proponents of the restoration thesis claim that since it is possible to restore a damaged natural area so that it is just as valuable as before it was damaged, then there is no reason not to develop the area—for example, by strip-mining (Elliot 1982, Elliot 1997). Thus any analysis of the ethics of restoration that lends support to the practice also lends support to policies that justify the degradation and destruction of natural areas. This point cannot be overemphasized: the justification of restoration policies in general will lend support to anyone who wishes to develop (and hence, degrade or destroy) a natural area. The developer can always claim that after the initial destruction of the natural area, it can be restored to a state that is as good as the original.

Consider some important recent work on the philosophy of restoration. Donald Scherer has argued that the functional equivalence of an ecological restoration to the original ecosystem is all that matters in the determination of value (Scherer 1995, 364). But the idea of "functional equivalence" makes a mockery of the idea of the preservation of natural value—and thus even more the idea of the restoration of natural value. As I have argued elsewhere, a criterion of functional ecological equilibrium leaves one susceptible to "the substitution problem" (Katz 1985). Ecological function is a standard applied to holistic systems, not to the individuals who live in and make up the systems. Individuals can be replaced as long as the overall functioning of the system is maintained. As long as our only concern is the ecological function of the system, then we may simply substitute more ecologically efficient components—provided that we have sufficient knowledge. This criterion eliminates any direct argument for the preservation of natural entities within the system. As long as ecological function is maintained, individuals may be replaced or destroyed. We do not even have to replace an original species or individual with a natural entity. We could design a technological equivalent to a natural species that is more ecologically efficient—flowers that are not eaten by deer, or a robotic predator to control the deer population (Katz 1985). Thus the substitution problem shows that the idea of functional equivalence cannot be used as the standard for a positive evaluation of an ecological restoration, for we can create a system that is functionally equivalent without restoring or preserving anything that was part of the original system.

William Throop, in a more subtle argument, has attempted to solve what he calls the "paradox" of restoration—the inability to reproduce those values connected to the historical properties of an entity or system (Throop 1997). He claims that we can produce values that are similar enough even though the historical properties are lost. Throop claims that "restoration can approximate the pattern of components and processes that was originally brought about in a more wild fashion. If this pattern acquires value from its having been brought about *largely by nature,* then such value is returned through restoration even though the historical property is not" (Throop 1997, 51, my emphasis). Throop seems to have in mind cases such as Steve Packard's controlled burning and replanting of grassland savannas in the Midwest—where, after the initial intervention, natural processes are permitted to run their course (Packard 1988; see Katz 1997, 100–101). This type of restoration cannot produce or restore the wildness of the natural area—for Throop defines wildness as entities or processes that have not been recently altered or significantly controlled by humans (Throop 1997, 48). In my terminology, this type of restoration fails the test of authenticity, but for Throop it does offer the compromise of creating a less humanized environment—the restoration occurs largely through natural processes. For Throop, this compromise can lend support to the idea that some ecological restoration is an effective tool of environmental policy.

And finally, even Robert Elliot has recently softened his objection to all restorations. In his 1997 book *Faking Nature,* he claims that restoration, especially when it is concerned with the rehabilitation of damaged systems, can help to maximize value in the world, even when the value of the restored system is not the value that would be equivalent to the original undisturbed system. Elliot's argument is based on a detailed typology of various kinds of restorations. Two sets of distinctions are crucial to his position—the difference between tokens and types, and the difference between extrinsic and intrinsic restorations (Elliot 1997, 100–111). A token-restoration attempts to restore the precise object or ecosystem; a type-restoration merely restores or re-creates an object or system of a similar type. In the realm of environmental policy, where ecological restorations are used to repair the damage caused by the interference in or development of a natural area, we are dealing with type-restoration, for the original natural area will often be so badly damaged that it is only possible to restore a similar type of system. The restoration or replacement thesis to which Elliot objects is thus a principle of environmental policy involving type-restoration.

The second distinction, between extrinsic and intrinsic restorations, concerns the methodology of token-restorations. An extrinsic restoration merely removes features that have been added to the original object or system: we remove dirt or varnish from a painting, or exotic species from an ecosystem. But an intrinsic restoration adds material to a damaged object or system: we patch a wall or reintroduce a species into an area where it has become extinct. Elliot sees little wrong with extrinsic restoration projects, and even says that token-restoration can be justified as a means of achieving type-preservation of rare ecosystems.

But what is actually being preserved or restored in these cases? Not, as Elliot claims, the natural value of these entities or systems. (Nor, as Throop admits, is the wildness value—the value outside of human influence—being restored.) Elliot argues that a restoration, if properly done (if it uses "natural designs and is constituted by natural objects") "may possess considerable intrinsic value," and surely more than the degraded system it replaces (Elliot 1997, 108). But clearly this value is artifactually produced; it is not natural value at all. Elliot even abandons his primary position, the importance of origins and historical continuity. In discussing cases of restoration that follow natural design, he writes that "we can legitimately think of the restored ecosystem as exhibiting a continuity with the natural past, despite the fact that the continuity has been artificially achieved" (Elliot 1997, 160). So for Elliot, artificial restoration can be a legitimate natural continuity. But such a view appears to be a perversion of both language and policy, substituting an artifactual reality for the preservation of natural processes. Saying it is a natural continuity does not make it so.

It is clear, I hope, that these recent analyses of ecological restoration fail to address the central issue raised by my argument: the presence of human intentionality in the intervention into natural processes changes the fundamental character and meaning of those processes. The basic problem with the arguments of Scherer, Throop, and Elliot (in his 1997 book) is that they morally rationalize policies that do not yield authentic restorations, and thus they give support to those who wish to employ the restoration or replacement thesis. What I am most concerned with—from an ethical perspective, from the perspective of an advocate of policy—is that once a general policy of restoration is justified, it will be used not only by right-thinking committed environmentalists but also by those who wish to continue to degrade and damage natural environments. The degraders and destroyers of natural ecosystems will have a perfect excuse for their activities: they can claim that they can restore the damaged ecosystem to its pre-existing state, or to a state that is functionally equivalent and as valuable as the original. In the policy goals of these destroyers and abusers of nature, restoration policy will always be "the big lie."

Toward Preserving Natural Value

What about cases in which human intentionality is absent? Can there be a natural restoration of nature? How do we evaluate situations in which nature restores itself? The late Australian philosopher Richard Sylvan claimed that my argument and analysis expanded the notion of an artifact too far (Sylvan 1994, 20). According to Sylvan, not all restoration is artifactual, since nature itself can act to restore an ecosystem and in time wash out human influence. I agree. We can have cases in which, after an initial human intervention has degraded a

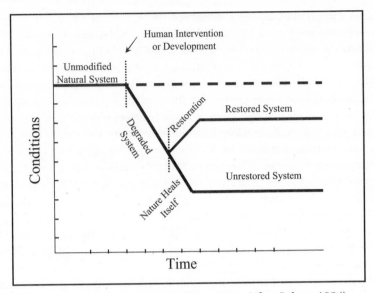

Figure 2.1. Nature versus Restoration Time Line (after Sylvan 1994).

natural system, nature is left to heal itself. But in these cases, the natural progression of nature has been interrupted, and the resulting system, after a time, will be different from the system that would have existed had no human interference occurred. The time lines that represent the processes of nature will be different (see Figure 2.1, my modification of Sylvan 1994, 17). Thus, the initial human intervention—in this case, the action that degrades the natural system—radically changes the character of the natural processes. We may not want to call the resulting system an artifact of human intentionality and purpose, and yet the system is not equivalent to undisturbed nature. Humanity has interjected itself into the natural processes of the system.

The belief that nature is so powerful that it can heal itself no matter what humanity does to it is simply the mirror image of the belief that we humans can control, heal, and restore the natural world. Once again, these beliefs morally rationalize our desire to intervene in natural processes to further human interests. We are transfixed by visions of power, human and natural, and we believe that we can harness both kinds of power for the promotion and development of human good. Thus the goal of my argument is simple, clear, and direct: it is necessary to emphasize the artifactuality of all human-induced restorations because of the danger of human hubris. If we humans think that we can restore nature, then we will believe that we are omnipotent in our ability to affect, mold, and heal the natural world. We will have no need for any particular part of the natural world, any particular ecosystem, bioregion, or species—for they all can be restored, replaced, or modified according to human design. And thus we arrive at the moral imperative that underlies the philosophical analysis of restoration policy. The chief ethical point is that if we think restorations are a desirable goal of environmental policy, then we will believe that there are no limits to our power and ambition to develop, degrade, restore, and manage the natural world. Nature itself—a nature unmodified by human intention, knowledge, technology, and power—will lose its value. The ideal of preserving a nature free of human manipulation will no longer offer a restraint to human action. We will create for ourselves a totally artifactual world, a world in which the presence of human intentionality is inescapable. Natural value will no longer exist, and we will live in a world that is totally human.

Notes

1. Did God design the world and all the natural entities therein? Perhaps. But note that even if we consider the natural world to have been designed by God, it would still be fundamentally different from a world created by human design for human purposes. We cannot assume that God designed the world for human good.
2. It may be that the pejorative terminology of forgeries, fakes, and lies has obscured the philosophical points being made. I am not accusing ecological restorationists of being purposeful deceivers or perpetrators of fraud. The point, as I will explain later in this chapter, is to see that the same factors that make us devalue an art forgery also apply to the restoration of a natural ecosystem.
3. The authenticity of ballet (as of all dynamically performed art) is in itself an interesting philosophical issue. Since every performance of a ballet is literally different, how does one judge an authentic performance? In my view, we have to start with the steps. Balanchine, for example, choreographed specific ballets for particular individual dancers; however, when another, different dancer performs the ballet, we still consider it authentic because the steps remain the same. The interpretation of the steps is open to change, depending on the ideas of the dancer and the current ballet director. But if Martins changes the steps, then we no longer have an authentic Balanchine ballet. Similarly, we can have an infinite number of interpretive readings of Hamlet's soliloquy from an infinite number of actors, but once we change the words, we no longer have an authentic Shakespeare play.

References

Elliot, R. 1982. "Faking Nature." *Inquiry* 25: 81–93.

Elliot, R. 1997. *Faking Nature: The Ethics of Environmental Restoration*. London and New York: Routledge.

Katz, E. 1985. "Organism, Community, and the 'Substitution Problem.'" *Environmental Ethics* 7: 241–256.

Katz, E. 1992a. "The Big Lie: Human Restoration of Nature." *Research in Philosophy and Technology* 12: 231–241.

Katz, E. 1992b. "The Call of the Wild: The Struggle Against Domination and the Technological Fix of Nature." *Environmental Ethics* 14: 265–273.

Katz, E. 1993. "Artefacts and Functions: A Note on the Value of Nature." *Environmental Values* 2: 223–232.

Katz, E. 1995. "Imperialism and Environmentalism." *Social Theory and Practice* 21: 271–285.

Katz, E. 1996. "The Problem of Ecological Restoration." *Environmental Ethics* 18: 222–224.

Katz, E. 1997. *Nature as Subject: Human Obligation and Natural Community.* Lanham, MD: Rowman & Littlefield.

Packard, S. 1988. "Just a Few Oddball Species: Restoration and the Rediscovery of the Tallgrass Savanna." *Restoration & Management Notes* 6(1): 13–22.

Scherer, D. 1995. "Evolution, Human Living and the Practice of Ecological Restoration." *Environmental Ethics* 17: 359–379.

Sylvan, R. 1994. "Mucking with Nature." Unpublished manuscript, no date. (Subsequently published in *Against the Mainstream: Critical Environmental Essays.* Canberra: Research School of Social Sciences, Australian National University.)

Throop, W. 1997. "The Rationale for Environmental Restoration." In *The Ecological Community,* edited by R. S. Gottlieb, 39–55. New York and London: Routledge.

❧ Chapter 3 ❧

ECOLOGICAL RESTORATION AND THE CULTURE OF NATURE: A PRAGMATIC PERSPECTIVE

Andrew Light

Most environmental philosophers have failed to understand the theoretical and practical importance of ecological restoration. I believe this failure is primarily due to the mistaken impression that ecological restoration is only an attempt to restore nature itself, rather than an effort to restore an important part of the human relationship with nonhuman nature. In investigating this claim, I will first discuss the possibility of transforming environmental philosophy into a more pragmatic discipline, one better suited to contributing to the formation of sound environmental policies, including ecological restoration. Specifically, I will advocate an alternative philosophical approach to the ideas about the value of ecological restoration raised by Eric Katz and other philosophers who claim that restored nature can never reproduce the actual value of nature. I will make this contrast more explicit and further argue that Katz's views in particular are not sufficiently sensitive to the values at work in the variety of projects falling within the category of ecological restoration. We need a more practically oriented philosophical contribution to discussions of ecological restoration policies than environmental philosophers have provided so far. A richer description of the ethical implications of restoration will identify a large part of its value in the revitalization of the human culture of nature.

Before reaching this conclusion, however, I will briefly consider an alternative framework for environmental philosophy as a whole.

Environmental Philosophy: What and for Whom?

Two underlying questions that I believe still confound most environmental philosophers are "What is our discipline actually for?" and, consequently, "Who is our audience?" So far, most work in environmental ethics has been concerned with describing the nonanthropocentric value of nature—that is, the value of nature independent of human concerns and reasons for valuing nature—and determining the duties, obligations, or rights that follow from that description. But one can easily wonder whether such work is directed only toward other environmental philosophers as a contribution to the literature on value theory or whether it has a broader aim. Certainly, given the history of the field—formally beginning in the early 1970s with the work of thinkers as diverse as Arne Naess, Val Plumwood, Holmes Rolston, Peter Singer, and Richard Sylvan, all concerned with how philosophers could make some sort of contribution to the resolution of environmental problems—one would think that the aspirations of environmental philosophy would be greater than simply continuing an intramural discussion about the value of nature.

But if environmental philosophy is more than a discussion among philosophers about natural value, to what broader purposes and audiences should it reach? Taking a cue from the content and expected readership of this book, I pose at least four responses. Environmental philosophy might serve as (1) a guide for environmental activists searching for ethical justifications for their activities in defense of other animals and ecosystems, (2) an applied ethic for resource managers, (3) a general tool for policy makers, helping them to shape more responsible environmental policies, and (4) a beacon for the public at large, attempting to expand their notions of moral obligation beyond the traditional confines of anthropocentric (human-centered) moral concerns.

Environmental philosophy should, of course, aim to serve all of these purposes and groups, although I think that most importantly we should focus our energies on guiding policy makers and the public. My rationale is this: If the original reason that philosophers established this field was to make a philosophical contribution to the resolution of environmental problems (consistent with other professionals' response to environmental concerns in the early 1970s), then the continuation—indeed, the urgency—of those problems demands that philosophers do all they can to actually help change present policies and attitudes involving environmental problems. If we talk only to each other about value theory, we have failed as environmental professionals. But if we can help convince policy makers to formulate better policies and make the case to the public at large to support these policies for ethical reasons, then we can join other environmental professionals in making more productive contributions to the resolution of environmental problems.

As it now stands, however, the current focus in environmental philosophy on describing the nonanthropocentric value of nature often ends up separating environmental philosophy from other forms of environmental inquiry. One prime example of this disconnection from practical considerations is that many environmental philosophers do not think of restoration ecology in a positive light. My friend and colleague Eric Katz comes near the top of the list of these philosophers; his chapter in this volume is the latest in a series of articles in which he argues that ecological restoration does not result in a restoration of nature and, in fact, may even create a disvalue in nature. Robert Elliot is another influential thinker in this camp, although his views have moderated significantly in recent years. Katz, Elliot, and others maintain that if the goal of environmental philosophy is to describe the non-human-centered value of nature and to distinguish nature from human appreciation of it, then presumably nature cannot be the sort of thing that is associated with human creation or manipulation. Thus, if restorations are human creations, argue philosophical critics such as Katz, they can never count as the sort of thing that contains natural value.

In this view, restorations are not natural—they are artifacts. To claim that environmental philosophers should be concerned with ecological restoration is therefore to commit a kind of category mistake: it is to ask that they talk about something that is not part of nature. But to label ecological restorations a philosophical category mistake is the best-case scenario in this view; at worst, restorations represent the tyranny of humans over nature and should not be practiced at all. Katz has put it most emphatically in arguing that "the practice of ecological restoration *can only* represent a misguided faith in the hegemony and infallibility of the human power to control the natural world" (Katz 1996, 222, my emphasis).

I have long disagreed with claims like this one. My early response to such positions was to simply set them aside in my search for broader ethical and political questions useful for a more public discussion of policies concerning ecological restoration (e.g., Light and Higgs 1996). But I now think it is dangerous to ignore the arguments of Katz and Elliot, for at least two reasons. First, their arguments represent the most sustained attempt yet to make a philosophical contribution to the overall literature on restoration and thus ought to be answered by philosophers also interested in restoration. Second, the larger restoration community is increasingly coming to believe that the sorts of questions being addressed by Katz and Elliot are the only kind of contribution that philosophy as a discipline can make to discussions of restoration. And since Katz has explicitly rejected the idea that ecological restoration is an acceptable environmental practice, the restoration community's assumption that environmental ethicists tend to be hostile to the idea of ecological restoration is a fair one. Given this disjunction, there would be no ground left for a philosophical contribution to public policy questions concerning ecological restoration, since none of these issues would count as moral or ethical questions.[1]

I believe that philosophers can make constructive contributions to ecological restoration and to environmental issues in general by helping to articulate the normative foundations for environmental policies in ways that are translatable to the public. But making such contributions requires doing environmental philosophy in some different ways. Specifically, it requires a more public philosophy, one focused on making the kinds of arguments that resonate with the moral intuitions most people carry around with them every day. Such intuitions usually resonate more with human-centered notions of value than with abstract nonanthropocentric conceptions of natural value.

Environmental pragmatism is my term for the view that makes it plausible for me to make this claim about the importance of appealing to human motivations in valuing nature. By this I do not mean an application of the traditional writings of the American pragmatists—Dewey, James, and Pierce, for example—to environmental problems. Instead, I simply mean the recognition that a responsible and complete environmental philosophy includes a public component with a clear policy emphasis (see, for example, Light 1996a, 1996b, 1996c). It is certainly appropriate for philosophers to continue their search for a true and foundational nonanthropocentric description of the value of nature. But environmental philosophers would be remiss if they did not also try to make other, perhaps more appealing ethical arguments that may have an audience in an anthropocentric public. Environmental pragmatism in my sense is agnostic concerning the existence of nonanthropocentric natural value. It is simply a methodology permitting environmental philosophers to endorse a pluralism allowing for one kind of philosophical task inside the philosophy community—searching for the "real" value of nature—and another task outside of that community—articulating a value for nature that resonates with the public and therefore has more impact on discussions of projects such as ecological restorations that may be performed by the public.

This approach modifies the philosophical contribution to questions about restoration ecology in a positive way. As mentioned, many philosophers have criticized ecological restoration because it is a human intervention into natural processes. In contrast, I have argued that such projects as the prairie restorations at the University of Wisconsin–Madison Arboretum would be fully supported by a pragmatic environmental philosophy (Light 1996b). Restoration makes sense because on the whole it results in many advantages over mere preservation of ecosystems that have been substantially damaged by humans. More significantly, this pragmatic approach exposes other salient ethical issues involving the practice of ecological restoration beyond the discussion of natural value, such as whether there are moral grounds that justify encouraging public participation in restoration (see Light and Higgs 1996). It is therefore the duty of the pragmatic environmental philosopher to become involved in debates with practitioners about what the value of restoration is in human terms, rather than to keep the discussion restricted to a private debate among philosophers on whether restored nature is really nature. In the rest of this chapter, I will both offer a specific critique of Katz's claims about the value of restoration, a critique that does not rely on a pragmatist foundation for environmental philosophy, and discuss some pragmatic issues that contribute to a fuller philosophical analysis of the practice and ethics of ecological restoration.

Ecological Restoration: A Preliminary Distinction

Following the project described above, in previous work I have outlined some preliminary distinctions that paint a broader picture of the philosophical terrain up for grabs in restoration than that presented by Katz and Elliot. Specifically, in response to Elliot's early critique of restoration (1982), I have tried to distinguish between two categories of ecological restoration that have differing moral implications.

Elliot begins his seminal article on restoration, "Faking Nature," by identifying a particularly pernicious kind of restoration—restoration that is used to rationalize the destruction of nature. On this claim, any harm done to nature by humans is ultimately repairable through restoration, so the harm should be discounted. Elliot calls this view the "restoration thesis" and states that "the destruction of what has value [in nature] is compensated for by the later creation (re-creation) of something of equal value" (Elliot 1976, 82). Elliot rejects the restoration thesis through an analogy based on the relationship between original and replicated works of art and nature. Just as we would not value a replication of a work of art as much as we would the original, we would not value a replicated piece of nature as much as we would the original, such as some bit of wilderness. Elliot's argument that the two sorts of value choices are similar is persuasive.

In responding to Elliot's (1982) criticisms of the value of restoration, I suggested a distinction implicit in his analysis of restoration to help us think through the value of ecological restoration (Light 1997). The distinction is based on an acknowledgment Elliot makes in his 1982 article (and expands upon in his 1997 book): "Artificially transforming an utterly barren, ecologically bankrupt landscape into something richer and more subtle may be a good thing. That is a view quite compatible with the belief that replacing a rich natural environment with a rich artificial one is a bad thing" (Elliot 1982, 87).

Following Elliot's lead that some kinds of restoration may be beneficial, I distinguished between two sorts of restorations: (1) malicious restorations, such as the kind described in the restoration thesis, and (2) benevolent restorations, or those undertaken to remedy a past harm done to nature although not offered as a justification for harming nature. Benevolent restorations, unlike malicious restorations, cannot serve as justifications for the conditions that would warrant their engagement.

If this distinction holds, then we can claim that Elliot's original target was not all of restoration, but only a particular kind of restoration, namely malicious restorations. While there is mixed evidence to support the claim that Elliot was originally going after only malicious restorations in his first work on the topic, the distinction is nonetheless intuitively plausible. The sorts of restorations undertaken at the Wisconsin Arboretum or as part of the Chicago Wilderness effort, for example, are certainly not offered as excuses or rationales for the destruction of nature. In contrast, the restorations involved in mountaintop mining projects in rural West Virginia can definitely be seen as examples of malicious restorations. Mountaintop mining—where tops of mountains are destroyed and dumped into adjacent valleys—is in part rationalized through a requirement that the damaged streambeds in the adjacent valleys be restored. The presumed ability to restore these streambeds is used as a justification for allowing mountaintop mining, making this practice a clear instantiation of Elliot's restoration thesis. The upshot of this malicious-benevolent distinction is that one may be able to grant much of Elliot's claim that restored nature is not original nature while still not denying that there is some kind of positive value to the act of ecological restoration in many cases. Even if benevolent restorations are not restorations of original nature, and hence more akin to art forgeries than to original works of art, they can still have some kind of positive content.

The idea that many restorations can have positive content may be developed more by pushing the art analogy a bit further. If ecological restoration is a material practice like making a piece of art (fake or not), why isn't it like art restoration rather than art forgery? After all, we know that some parallels can be drawn between restoration projects and mitigation projects. A mitigation often involves the wholesale creation of a new ecosystem designed to look like a bit of nature that may have absolutely no historical continuity with the natural history of the land on which it is placed. For example, in order to meet an environmental standard that demands no net loss of wetlands, some environmental managers will sanction the creation of a wetland to replace a destroyed one on a piece of land where there had been no wetland. Conversely, a restoration must be tied to some claim about the historical continuity of the land on which the restoration is taking place. In some cases, this might simply entail linking original pieces of nature together to restore the integrity of the original ecosystem without creating a new landscape altogether (as in the case of the Wildlands Project to link the great western parks in the United States and Canada with protected corridors). In that sense, a restoration could be more like repairing a damaged work of art than like creating a fake one.[2]

The possibility of having benevolent restorations does much to clear the way for a positive philosophical contribution to questions of restoration. Katz, however, unlike Elliot, denies the positive value of any kind of restoration. For him, a restoration can only be malicious because all restorations represent evidence of human domination and arrogance toward nature. But surprisingly, even though Katz draws on Elliot's work in formulating his own position, he seems to ignore the fact that Elliot's original description of the restoration thesis was primarily directed against particular kinds of restorations. In his earliest and most famous article on restoration, "The Big Lie: Human Restoration of Nature," Katz acknowledged that while Elliot claimed that the restoration thesis mostly was advocated as a way of undermining conservation efforts by big business, he (Katz) was surprised to see environmental thinkers (such as forest biologist Chris Maser) advocating "a position similar to Elliot's 'restoration thesis.'" This position, as Katz interprets it, is that "restoration of damaged nature is seen not only as a practical option for environmental policy but also as a moral obligation for right-thinking environmentalists" (1997, 96). But Maser's position is not the restoration thesis as Elliot defines it. Katz never shows that Maser, or any other restoration advocate whom he analyzes, actually argues for restoration as a rationale for destruction of nature. He never demonstrates that those in the restoration community endorse restorations for malicious reasons. If in fact they do not, then what is wrong with restoration, in Katz's view?

Katz Against Restoration

Just as Elliot's original target of the restoration thesis has faded from philosophical memory, Katz's original target has also been somewhat lost in the years since he began writing on this topic in 1992. At first, Katz seemed most concerned with the arguments of fellow environmental ethicists like Paul Taylor and Peter Wenz, who advocated variously "restitutive justice" and a "principle of restitution" as part of our fulfillment of possible human obligations to nature. If we harmed nature, according to Taylor and Wenz, we should have to compensate it. Restoration would be part of a reasonable package of restitution. According to Katz, in these views humans have an "*obligation* and *ability* to repair or reconstruct damaged ecosystems" (1997, 95, my emphasis). But I think it is crucial here to note the argument Katz is actually taking on and the objection he proceeds to make.

As Katz describes it, there are actually two separable questions to put to Taylor, Wenz, and other advocates of restoration: (1) Do we have an obligation to try to restore damaged nature? and (2) Do we have the ability to restore damaged nature? Katz argues quite forcefully that we do not have the ability to restore nature because what we actually create in ecological restorations are humanly produced artifacts—not nature, nonanthropocentrically conceived. Based on this claim, he assumes that the first question—whether we have an obligation to try to restore nature—is moot. Katz's logic is simple: we do not have an obligation to do what we cannot in actuality do.

But even if we were to grant Katz his position that it is impossible to restore nature, we may still have moral obligations to try to restore nature. How can this be true? There are a number of reasons, but before fully explicating this view, we need to first better understand Katz's arguments.

Katz's chapter in this volume reviews and expands upon several arguments he has made against restoration over the years. In examining his papers on this topic,[3] I have identified five separable but often overlapping arguments he has made against both the idea that we can restore nature and the practice of trying to restore it. I call these arguments KR1–5. They are listed below in the order they arise in his work, each accompanied by an example of supporting evidence from Katz's various papers on restoration.

KR1. The Duplicitous Argument
"I am outraged by the idea that a technologically created 'nature' will be passed off as reality" (1997, 97).[4]

KR2. The Arrogance (or Hubris) Argument
"The human presumption that we are capable of this technological fix demonstrates (once again) the arrogance with which humanity surveys the natural world" (1997, 97).

KR3. The Artifact Argument
"The re-created natural environment that is the end result of a restoration project is nothing more than an artifact created for human use" (1997, 97).[5]

KR4. The Domination Argument
"The attempt to redesign, recreate and restore natural areas and objects is a radical intervention in natural processes. Although there is an obvious spectrum of possible restoration[s] . . . all of these projects involve the manipulation and domination of natural areas. All of these projects involve the creation of artifactual realities, the imposition of anthropocentric interests on the

processes and objects of value. Nature is not permitted to be free, to pursue its own independent course of development" (1997, 105).[6]

KR5. The Replacement Argument
"If a restored environment is an adequate replacement for the previously existing natural environment [which for Katz it can never be], then humans can use, degrade, destroy, and replace natural entities and habitats with no moral consequence whatsoever. The value in the original natural entity does not require preservation" (1997, 113).[7]

I disagree with all of these arguments and have articulated what I hope are thorough responses of them elsewhere. Here I will focus on KR4, the domination argument, which is perhaps the one that arises most often throughout all of Katz's restoration papers. It is arguably the case that one can answer all of Katz's arguments by conceding one important premise of all of his claims as long as KR4 can be independently answered. KR4 also is interesting to me because his original articulation of it involved a very slim admission that there is some sort of difference between various kinds of restoration projects. Even though these differences are not ultimately important for Katz, he still nonetheless acknowledged them, and they give me a space in which I can critique his position.

In addition, I believe that KR1–3 and KR5 can be ignored in rejecting Katz's position as long as we are prepared to concede for now one important premise of all of his arguments. This is Katz's ontological assumption (a claim concerning the nature or essence of a thing) that humans and nature can be meaningfully separated so as to definitively argue that restored nature is an artifact, a part of human culture, rather than a part of nature. As Katz has admitted in an as yet unpublished public forum on his work, he is a nature-culture dualist. This means that for Katz, nature and culture are separate things entirely.[8] If one rejects this overall ontological view, then one may reject most of Katz's objections to restoration. But it is incredibly difficult to disprove another philosopher's ontology, let alone get him or her to concede this point.[9] Thus, even though I disagree with it, I will accept Katz's underlying assumption that restored nature does not reproduce nature.

But even if I grant this point that restored nature is not really nature, KR4 is still false because it is arguably the case that restoration does not dominate nature in any coherent sense but instead often helps nature to be free of just the sort of domination that Katz is concerned about. The reasoning here is straightforward enough. If I can show that restorations are valuable for nature, even if I concede that they do not re-create nature, then the various motivations for restoration will distinguish whether a restoration is duplicitous (KR1) or arrogant (KR2). A benevolent restoration, for example, would not risk KR1 or KR2 because in principle it is not trying to fool anyone, nor is it necessarily arrogant. Further, and more simply, conceding Katz's ontological claim about the distinction between nature and culture eliminates the significance of KR3—since we no longer care whether what is created is an artifact—as well as KR5, since we have given up hope that a restoration could ever actually serve as a replacement for "real" nature.

Now, back to the domination argument. KR4 is a claim that could hold even for a view that conceded Katz's nature–culture distinction. The reason, following Katz, would be that even a failed attempt to duplicate natural value—or create something akin to nature while conceding that in principle real nature can never be restored by humans—could still count as an instance of domination as Katz has defined it. An attempt at restoration, according to Katz's logic, would still prohibit nature from ever being able to pursue its own development. The reason is that for Katz, restoration is always a substitute for whatever would have occurred at a particular site without human interference. The idea is that even if humans can produce a valuable landscape of some sort on a denuded acreage, this act of production is still an instance of domination over the alternative of a natural evolution of this same acreage, even if a significant natural change would take ten times as long as the human-induced change and would be arguably less valuable for the species making use of it. Still, one can muster several arguments against KR4 (I will provide four) and still play largely within Katz's biggest and most contentious assumption about the ontological status of restored nature. After going through these arguments, we will see that these claims can lead to a new philosophical context for the evaluation of restoration, which I believe in the end also undermines the other KR arguments.

1. We can imagine cases in which nature cannot pursue its own interests (however one wishes to understand this sense of nature having interests) because of something we have done to it. For example, many restorations are limited to bioactivation of soil that has become contaminated by hazardous industrial waste. If restoration necessarily prohibits nature from being free, as KR4 maintains, then how do we reconcile this claim with the relative freedom that bioactivation makes possible? Restoration need not determine exactly what grows in a certain place, but may in fact simply be the act of allowing nature to again pursue its own interests rather than shackling it to perpetual human-induced trauma. In many cases of restoration, this point can be underscored when we see how anthropogenically damaged land (or soil) can be uniquely put at risk of invasion by anthropogenically introduced exotic plants. South African ice plant, an exotic in southern California that destroys the soil it is introduced into, is highly opportunistic and can easily spread onto degraded land, thus ensur-

ing that native plants will not be able to reestablish themselves. I highlight here this contentious native–exotic distinction because I suspect that given Katz's strong nature–culture distinction, he would necessarily have to prefer a landscape of native plants over a landscape of exotics where the existence of the exotics is a result of an act of human (cultural) interference in nature. Allowing nature to pursue its own interests, given prior anthropogenic interference, thus involves at least as strong a claim to protect it from further anthropogenic risk through restoration practices as does the case Katz makes for leaving it alone.

2. Even if we do agree with Katz that restorations produce only artifacts, can't it still be the case that the harm we cause nature still requires us to engage in what Katz would term "attempted restorations"? It simply does not follow from the premise that something is more natural when it is relatively free of human interference that we must therefore always avoid interfering with nature (this is actually a point that Katz finally recognizes in a later paper, "Imperialism and Environmentalism"). It is a classic premise of holism in environmental ethics (the theory that obligations to the nonhuman natural world are to whole ecosystems and not to individual entities, a view that Katz endorses) that some interference is warranted when we are the cause of an imbalance in nature. For example, hunting of white-tailed deer is thought to be permissible under holism since humans have caused that species' population explosion. If such interventions are permissible to help "rectify the balance of nature," then why are there not comparable cases with the use of restoration as an aid to the original, real nature? We can even imagine that such cases would be less controversial than holistic defenses of hunting.

There are cases where restoration, even if it results in the production of an artifact, does not lead to the domination described by Katz. Imagine a case in which the restoration project is one that will restore a corridor between two wilderness preserves. If there is positive natural value in the two preserves that is threatened because wildlife is not allowed to move freely between them, then restoration projects that would restore a corridor (by removing roads, for example) would actually be not only morally permissible but also possibly ethically required depending on one's views of the value of the nature in the preserves. This is not restoration as a second best to preservation or a distraction from preservation; it is restoration as an integral and critical part of the maintenance of natural value. So even if we agree with Katz that humans cannot really restore nature, it does not follow that they ought not to engage in restoration projects that actually repair the damage caused by past domination rather than further that domination.

Given objections like the two discussed so far, it is important to try to

get a better handle on exactly what sort of damage is caused by domination in the sense described by Katz. It turns out that the worst damage to
nature for Katz is domination that prevents the "self-realization" of nature:

> The fundamental error is thus domination, the denial of
> freedom and autonomy. Anthropocentrism, the major con-
> cern of most environmental philosophers, is only one species
> of the more basic attack on the preeminent value of self-real-
> ization. From within the perspective of anthropocentrism,
> humanity believes it is justified in dominating and molding
> the nonhuman world to its own human purposes (1997,
> 105).

Thus, the problem with restoration is that it restricts natural self-realization in order to force nature onto a path that we find more appealing.

3. With this clarification, we can then further object to Katz that his sense
   of restoration confuses restoration with mitigation. The force of the
   charge of domination is that we mold nature to fit our own human purposes. But most restorationists would counter that it is nonanthropocentric nature that sets the goals for restoration, not humans. While there is
   indeed some subjectivity in determining what should be restored at a particular site (which period do we restore to?) and uncertainty about how
   we should do it (limitations in scientific and technical expertise), we cannot restore a landscape any way we wish and still have a good restoration
   in scientific terms. If Katz's objection is that when we restore a denuded
   bit of land, we are at least making something that fits our need to have
   more attractive natural surroundings—an argument he often makes—we
   can reply that because of the constraints on restoration (as opposed to mitigation), the fact that we find a restored landscape appealing is only contingently true. It is often the case that what we must restore to is not the
   preferred landscape of most people. The controversy over the Chicago
   Wilderness project is a good example of this: many local residents see
   restoration activities as destroying the aesthetically pleasing forests that
   now exist in order to restore the prairie and oak savanna ecosystems that
   were present prior to European settlement. But philosophically, because a
   restored landscape can never necessarily be tied only to our own desires
   (since our desires are not historically and scientifically determined in the
   same way that the parameters of a restoration are), then those desires cannot actually be the direct cause of any restriction on the self-realization of
   nature.
4. Finally, we must wonder about this value of self-realization. Setting aside
   the inherent philosophical problems with understanding what self-realization means in the case of nature, one has to wonder how we could know

what natural self-realization would be in any particular case, and why we would totally reject a human role in helping to make it happen if we could discern it. In an analogous case involving two humans, we do not say that a human right to (or value of) self-realization is abrogated when a criminal who harms someone is forced to pay restitution. Even if the restitution is forced against the will of the victim, and even if the compensation in principle can never make up for the harm done, we would not say that somehow the victim's self-realization has been restricted by the act of restitution by the criminal. Again, there seems to be no clear argument here for why the moral obligation to try to restore has been diminished by Katz's arguments that we do not have the ability to really restore nature or pass off an artifact as nature.

Restoring Environmental Philosophy

If I am justified in setting aside the rest of Katz's arguments (KR1–3 and KR5) by accepting his claim that humans cannot restore real nature, what sort of conclusions can we draw about the role of philosophy in sorting out the normative issues involved in restoration? As it turns out, Katz gives us an insight that is helpful in figuring out the next step.

After explaining the harm we do to nature in the domination we visit upon it through acts of restoration, Katz briefly assesses the harm that we do to ourselves through such actions:

> But a policy of domination transcends the anthropocentric subversion of natural processes. A policy of domination subverts both nature and human existence; it denies both the cultural and natural realization of individual good, human and nonhuman. Liberation from all forms of domination is thus the chief goal of any ethical or political system (1997, 105).

Although not very clearly explained by Katz, this intuition represents a crucial point for proceeding further. In addition to connecting environmental philosophy to larger projects of social liberation, Katz here opens the door to a consideration of the consequences of restoration on humans and human communities. As such, Katz allows an implicit assertion that there is a value involved in restoration that must be evaluated in addition to the value of the objects that are produced by restoration.

But the problem with drawing this conclusion is that this passage is also perhaps the most cryptic in all of Katz's work on restoration. What does Katz mean by this claim? How exactly does restoration deny the realization of an individual human, or cultural, good? This claim can be made understandable only by assuming that some kind of cultural value connected to nature is risked through the act of dominating or otherwise causing harm to nature. But what is this value?

I think the value Katz is alluding to here, although he never explores it seriously, is related to the part of human culture that is connected to external, nonhuman nature. This is not simply a suggestion that we humans are part of nature; it also points out that we have a relationship with nature that exists on moral as well as physical terrain in such a way that our actions toward nature can reciprocally harm us. If this is the view implicit in this claim, then it is still consistent with much of the rest of Katz's larger views about the value of nature. We have a relationship with nature even if we are separable from it. I will accept this basic tenet of Katz's argument: we do exist in some kind of moral relationship with nature. And without fully explicating the content of that relationship, it seems that Katz is right in assuming that somehow our actions toward nature morally implicate us in a particular way. In the same sense, when we morally mistreat another human, we not only harm them but harm ourselves (by diminishing our character, by implicating ourselves in evil—however you want to put it). Katz is suggesting that our relationship with nature has a determinant effect on our moral character—or, perhaps more accurately, this suggestion is necessary for Katz's comment to make sense, even though he never expresses it himself.

If this assumption is correct, and if there is any truth in the arguments I have put forward so far that there can be some kind of positive value to our interaction with nature, then doing right by nature will have the same reciprocal effect of morally implicating us in a positive value as occurs when we do right by other persons. Perhaps Katz would agree. He would disagree, however, with the suggestion I would want to add: that there is some part of many kinds of restorations (if not most kinds) that contains positive value. Aside from the other suggestions I have already made concerning the possible positive content of restoration, one can also consider that the relationship with nature that is implied in Katz's view has a moral content in itself that is not reducible to the value of fulfilling this relationship's concomitant obligations. The relationship between humans and nature imbues restoration with a positive value even if it cannot replicate natural value in its products. But understanding this point will require some explanation.

Consider that if I have a reciprocal relationship with another human (in which I do right by them and they do right by me), then, to generalize Katz's view, there is a moral content to both of our actions that implicates each of us as persons. Each of us is a better person morally because of the way we interact with each other in the relationship. But the relationship itself, or rather just the fact of the existence of the relationship, has a moral content of its own (or what we could call a normative content, meaning that the relationship can be assessed as being in a better or worse state) that is independent of the fulfill-ment of any obligations.

If this point of the possible separation between the value of a relationship and the value of the fulfillment of obligations does not follow intuitively, imag-ine a case in which two people act according to duty toward each other with-out building a relationship of substantive normative content between them. For example, I have a brother with whom I am not terribly close. While I always act according to duty to him—I never knowingly do harm to him, and I even extend special family obligations to him—I do not have a substantive relationship with him that in itself has a normative content. Thus, if I do not speak to him for a year, nothing is lost because there is no relationship to maintain or that requires maintenance for normative reasons. But if my brother needed a kidney transplant, I would give him my kidney unhesitat-ingly out of a sense of obligation—something I would not feel obliged to do for someone outside my family—even though I still do not feel intimately comfortable around him in the same way I do with my closest friends. (It isn't necessarily a disvalue, only a sense of indifference, a lack of closeness.) Our relationship as persons has no positive value for me—as distinct from my rela-tionships with friends, which include a sense of intimate affection and care for each other. Thus I can have interaction with another person, even interaction that involves substantial components of obligation and duty (and, in Katz's terms, I will never put myself in a position to dominate the other person) but still not have a relationship with that person that involves any kind of positive value or that has normative standards of maintenance.

I don't think I have any obligation to have a relationship with normative content with my brother, even though my mother would like it if I did. But if I did have that kind of a relationship with him, it would have a value above and beyond the moral interaction I have with him now (the obligations I have to him, which can be iterated) that aids in a determination of our moral char-acters.[10] If we had a relationship with normative content, there would be a positive or negative value that could be assessed if I lost touch with him or ceased to care about his welfare. (I could very well claim that it would be bet-ter for me to have such a relationship with him, but this would require an additional argument.)

Consider further: If I wanted to rectify or create anew a substantive nor-mative relationship with my brother, like the relationship I have with several close friends, how would I do it? One thing I could do would be to engage in activities with him—the same sorts of activities (let's call them material interactions) that I do with my friends now. I might work with him to put up a fence or help him plant his garden. I might begin to talk over my personal and professional problems with him. I might go on a long journey with him that demanded some kind of mutual reliance, such as white-water rafting or visiting a foreign city where neither of us spoke the native language. In short, although there are, of course, no guarantees, I could begin to have some kind of material relationship with him as a prelude to having some kind of substantive normative relationship with him. Many factors might limit the success of such a project: for one thing, the distance between the two of us—he lives in our hometown of Atlanta and I live in New York. So if I were really serious about this project of building a relationship between us that had value independent of the value of the fulfillment of our mutual obligations to each other, I'd have to come up with ways around these interfering factors. Importantly, though, I couldn't form a substantive normative relationship with him merely by respecting his right of self-realization and autonomy as a person; I would have to somehow become actively involved with him.

When we compare the case of the estranged brother to that of nature, many parallels arise. We know that we can fulfill obligations to nature in terms of respecting its autonomy and self-realization as a subject (in Katz's terms) without ever forming a substantive normative relationship with it. Assuming also that a kind of relationship with nature is possible according to Katz's scheme (for this is in part what we harm when we dominate nature), it is fair to say that a relationship consisting of positive normative value with nature is compatible with Katz's overall view of the human-nature relationship. Because he says so little about what our positive relationship to nature could be, he is in no position to restrict it a priori. We also know that, as in the case of the estranged brother, we need some kind of material bridge in order to create a relationship with nature.

How do we build that bridge? Suggesting ways to overcome the gap between humans and nature (without necessarily disvaluing it) seems in part to be the role of environmental philosophy in questions of ecological restoration. Certainly, as in the case of my brother, distance is a problem. Numerous environmental professionals have emphasized the importance of being in nature in order to care for nature. Also, acts of preservation are important for there to be nature to have a relationship with. But what about restoration? Can restoration help engender such a positive normative relationship with nature?

It seems clear to me that it can. When we engage in acts of benevolent restoration, we are bound *by* nature in the sense that we are obligated to respect what it once was attempting to realize before we interfered with it. In Katz's terms, we are attempting to respect it as an autonomous subject. But we are also bound *to* nature in the act of restoring. In addition to the substantial personal and social benefits that accrue to people who engage in benevolent forms of restoration (see chapters by Schroeder and Grese et al. in this volume), we can also say that restoration restores the human connection to nature by restoring the part of culture that has historically contained a connection to nature. This kind of relationship goes well beyond mere reciprocity; it involves the creation of a value in relationship with nature beyond obligation. While it would take further argument to prove, I believe that this kind of relationship is a necessary condition for encouraging people to protect natural systems and landscapes around them rather than trade them for short-term monetary gains from development. If I am in a normative relationship with the land around me (whether it is "real" nature or not), I am less likely to allow it to be harmed further.

Specifying the parameters of restoration that help to achieve this moral relationship with nature will be the task of a more pragmatic environmental philosophy. As mentioned at the outset of this chapter, environmental pragmatism allows for and encourages the development of human-centered notions of the value of nature. Pragmatists are not restricted to identifying obligations to nature in the existence of nonanthropocentric conceptions of value but may embrace an expression of environmental values in human terms. More adequately developing the idea of restoration in terms of the human–nature relationship is thus appropriately under the pragmatist's purview. More importantly, however, the value articulated here exists between anthropocentrism and nonanthropocentrism, fully relying on the capacities of both sides of the human–nature relationship.[11]

We can even look to Katz for help in completing this pragmatic task. We don't want restorations that try to pass themselves off as the real thing when they are actually "fakes" (KR1) or are pursued through arrogance (KR2); nor are we interested in those that are offered as justifications for replacing or destroying nature (KR5). We would not want our comparable human relationships to exhibit those properties either. But even given the legacy of inhuman treatment of each other, we know that it is possible to restore human relationships in ways that do not resemble KR1, KR2, or KR5. There is, however, one possible concern to attend to in KR3, the artifact argument. Although earlier I said that the importance of KR3 is diminished by granting Katz's nature–culture distinction, there is a way that it can still cause us problems in grounding attempts at restoration in the positive value of strengthening the human–nature relationship.

If we allow Katz's claim that what has been restored is not really nature, then he may argue that we are not restoring a cultural relationship with nature but, in a sense, only extending the artifactual material culture of humans. At best, all we can have with restoration is a relationship with artifacts, not nature. Maybe he will allow that we improve our relationships with each other through cooperative acts of restoration, but this is not the same as a restoration of a relationship with nature itself.

But it should be clear by now that Katz would be mistaken to make such an objection for several reasons, stemming in part from my earlier remarks:

1. Even if we admit that restored nature is an artifact and not real nature, restored nature can also serve as a way for real nature to free itself from the shackles we have previously placed upon it. Restoration can allow nature to engage in its own autonomous restitution. Of the different sorts of restoration projects that I have mentioned earlier, many amount to aids to nature rather than creations of new nature.

2. Even if restoration is the production of an artifact, these artifacts do bear a striking resemblance to the real thing. This is not to say that restorations can be good enough to fool us (KR1). Rather, it is simply to point out that an opportunity to interact with the flora and fauna of the sort most common in benevolent restorations will increase the bonds of care that people will have with nonrestored nature. If a denuded and abandoned lot in the middle of an inner-city ghetto is restored by local residents who have never been outside of their city, it will help them better appreciate the fragility and complexity of the natural processes of nature itself should they encounter them. The fact that restorationists are engaged in a technological process does not necessarily mean that their practices do not serve the broader purpose of restoring a relationship with nature. Similarly, while beginning some form of mediated communication with my brother (such as e-mail or regular phone calls) does not restore a fully healthy communicative relationship with him in the way that face-to-face conversation might, it still helps me get used to the idea of some form of immediate and substantive communication.

3. Finally, if Katz persists in his concern that the act of restoration reifies domination by reaffirming our power over nature through the creation of artifacts, we can say that exactly the opposite is likely the case (at least in the case of benevolent restorations) when the goal is restoring the culture of nature, if not nature itself. Restorationists get firsthand (rather than anecdotal and textbook) exposure to the actual consequences of human domination of nature. A better understanding of the problems of bioactivating soil, for example, gives us a better idea of the complexity of the harm we have caused to natural processes. In a much healthier way than Katz seems willing to admit, knowing about that harm can empower us to learn more precisely why we should object to the kinds of activities that can cause the harm in the first place. As a parallel human case, imagine a carrier of a disease that is deadly and contagious (but not, for some reason, fatal to her) who ignores warnings about taking precautions to avoid spreading the disease to other people. If that person passes on her deadly disease to others, would it not in the end benefit her to volunteer in a hospital ward full of people dying from this particular disease? If the disease were incurable, she could never restore health to its victims even if she sought to (either out of reciprocity or a desire to form helpful nor-

mative relationships with others), but the experience might teach her the importance of taking precautions against giving the disease to others. Restoration similarly teaches us the actual consequences of our actions rather than allowing us to ignore them by restricting our interaction to nature to those parts we have not yet damaged.[12]

Conclusion

In a follow-up essay to "The Big Lie" called "The Call of the Wild," which used the image of the "wildness" in the white-tailed deer population at his summer home on Fire Island to help distinguish nature from culture, Katz embraced a kind of reciprocal relationship with nature. The wild white-tailed deer, which he admitted in the essay were now quite tame, were described as ". . . members of my moral and natural community. The deer and I are partners in the continuous struggle for the preservation of autonomy, freedom, and integrity. This shared partnership creates obligations on the part of humanity for the preservation and protection of the natural world" (1997, 117). Surely we would respond that this relationship also creates obligations of benevolent restoration as well. If the deer were threatened with harm without a needed restoration of a breeding ground, for example, would Katz not be obliged to do it? And, in doing this restoration, would he not help to generate positive value in his relationship with those deer?

It seems clear that benevolent restorations of this sort are valuable because they help us restore our relationship with nature, by restoring what could be termed our culture of nature. This is true even if Katz is correct that restored nature has the ontological property of an artifact. Restoration is an obligation exercised in the interests of forming a positive community with nature and thus is well within the boundaries of a positive, pragmatic environmental philosophy. Just as artifacts can serve valuable relationship goals by creating material bridges to other subjects, artifactual landscapes can help restore the culture of nature. Further defining the normative ground of benevolent restorations should be the contribution that philosophy can make to the public consideration and practice of ecological restoration. It is a contribution directed at a larger audience, beyond the professional philosophy community, and aimed toward the practical end of helping to resolve environmental problems.[13]

Notes

1. If we accept Katz's position, a philosophical inquiry into restoration would actually be an investigation of some kinds of questions other than those legitimately posed by environmental philosophers. Since Katz argues that restored nature is only an artifact, philosophers of technology would presumably still be doing phi-

losophy when they were involved in an investigation of ecological restoration. The suggestion that Katz is trying to define certain practices as outside the field of environmental ethics is no red herring. In a public forum discussing his work at the Central Division meeting of the American Philosophical Association in Chicago in 1998, Katz stated publicly that agriculture was not the proper purview of environmental ethics. Philosophers working on questions of ethics and agriculture could be doing agricultural ethics but not environmental ethics.

2. From the early aesthetic theory of Mark Sagoff (before he ever turned to environmental questions), one can also extract the following distinction to deepen the discussion of different kinds of benevolent restorations: (1) integral restorations, or restorations that "put new pieces in the place of original fragments that have been lost," and (2) purist restorations, or restorations that "limit [themselves] to clearing works of art and to reattaching original pieces that may have fallen" (Sagoff 1978, 457). As it turns out, one can argue that integral restorations are aesthetically (and possibly ethically) worrisome, since they seem to create hybrid works of art (created by both the artist and the restorationist). But this does not really undermine the analogy with ecological restorations, since many of these restorations are more akin to purist restorations—for example, cleaning land by bioactivating soil—than to integral ones. Perhaps more common would be a subclass of purist restoration that we might call rehabilitative restoration—for example, cleaning out exotic plants that had been introduced into a site and allowing the native plants to reestablish themselves. Such activity is akin to the work of a purist art restorationist who corrects the work of a restorationist who had come before her. If a restorationist, for example, were to remove an eighteenth-century integral addition to a sixteenth-century painting, we would assume that this rehabilitative act was consistent with a purist restoration. I provide a much more thorough discussion of the import of this distinction for ecological restoration in Light (1997).

3. Katz has four main papers on restoration: "The Big Lie: Human Restoration of Nature" (1992), "The Call of the Wild: The Struggle Against Domination and the Technological Fix of Nature" (1992), "Artifacts and Functions: A Note on the Value of Nature" (1993), and "Imperialism and Environmentalism" (1993). All of these papers are collected in Katz (1997), and it is these versions that I have drawn on for this chapter.

4. Originally in "The Big Lie" (as are KR2–KR4). KR1 is restated later in "The Call of the Wild": " . . . what makes value in the artifactually restored natural environment questionable is its ostensible claim to be the original" (Katz 1997, 114).

5. KR3 is most thoroughly elaborated later in "Artifacts and Functions."

6. The domination argument is repeated in "The Call of the Wild" (Katz 1997, 115) with the addition of an imported quote from Eugene Hargrove: domination "reduces [nature's] ability to be creative." The argument is also repeated in "Artifacts and Functions" and further explicated in "Imperialism and Environmentalism." As far as I can determine, though, Katz does not really expand the argument for domination in this last paper, except to deem imperialism wrong because it makes nature into an artifact (KR3).

7. Originally in "The Call of the Wild" and repeated in "Imperialism and Environmentalism" (Katz 1997, 139).

8. The forum here is the same as the one referenced in note 1.

9. The absence of any perceptible progress in Katz's views following his debate with Donald Scherer is a case in point. Scherer spends too much time, I think, trying to advance a critique of Katz's ontology and metaphysics. The resulting debate appears intractable. See Scherer (1995) and Katz (1996).

10. On a broader scale, just as there can be a town full of decent, law-abiding citizens, those citizens may not constitute a moral community in any significant sense.

11. It is also the case that restoration will be only one of a large collection of practices available for adaptive management. Indeed, there could even be cases where something akin to mitigation (albeit a benevolent kind) rather than restoration would be justified if a claim to sustaining some form of natural value warranted it. In a project to clean up an abandoned mine site, for example, restoring the site to a landscape that was there before might not be the best choice; instead, a sustainable landscape that would help preserve an endangered species now in the area might be more appropriate. But overall, environmentalists must consider human interaction with nature to be an acceptable practice in order to begin the ethical assessment of any case of environmental management. I am indebted to Anne Chapman for pressing me to clarify this point.

12. Katz can legitimately respond that there seems to be no unique reason why people couldn't have experiences that generate a closer relationship with nature as a result of activities other than restoration. Why couldn't we just use this sort of argument to encourage more acts of preservation, or to simply promote taking more walks though nature? Such an objection would, however, miss a crucial point. Even if it can be proved that we can have these kinds of positive experiences with nature through ways other than acts of restoration (and I see no reason why we couldn't), this does not diminish the case being built here: that restoration does not necessarily result in the domination of nature. The goal of my argument is not to show that restoration provides a unique value compared with other environmental practices, but only to reject the claim that there is no kind of positive value that restoration can contribute to nature in some sense. So an objection by Katz of this sort would miss the target of our substantive disagreement. Additionally, one could argue that (1) restoration does, in fact, produce some unique values in our relationship with nature (see my other contribution to this volume for such a case in relation to the potential democratic values in restoration), and that (2) even if not unique in itself, restoration helps to improve other sorts of unique values in nature. A case for (2) could be made, for example, in Allen Carlson's work on the importance of scientific understanding for appreciating the aesthetic value of nature (Carlson 1995). Arguably, our experiences as restorationists give us some of the kinds of understandings of natural processes required for aesthetic appreciation, in Carlson's view. Importantly, this understanding is a transitive property: it gives us an ability to aesthetically appreciate not only the nature we are trying to restore but also the nature we are not trying to restore. Restoration thus can provide a unique avenue to the aesthetic appreciation of all nature, restored or not. The main point, however, should not be lost: restoration is an important component in a mosaic of efforts to revive the culture of nature.

Given that there is no reason to believe that it has other disastrous effects, restoration seems warranted within a prescribed context even if it is not a cure-all.

13. This chapter is based on a presentation originally given at a plenary session (with Eric Katz and William Jordan) of the International Symposium on Society and Resource Management, University of Missouri, Columbia, in May 1998. Subsequent versions were presented as the keynote address of the Eastern Pennsylvania Philosophy Association annual meeting, Bloomsburg University, November 1998; and at Georgia State University, the State University of New York at Binghamton, and Lancaster University in the United Kingdom. I have benefited much from the discussions at all of these occasions and especially from the helpful comments provided by Cari Dzuris, Cheryl Foster, Warwick Fox, Paul Gobster, Leslie Heywood, Bruce Hull, Bryan Norton, George Rainbolt, and Christopher Wellman.

References

Carlson, A. 1995. "Nature, Aesthetic Appreciation, and Knowledge." *The Journal of Aesthetics and Art Criticism* 53: 393–400.

Elliot, R. 1982. "Faking Nature." *Inquiry* 25: 81–83.

Elliot, R. 1997. *Faking Nature.* London: Routledge.

Katz, E. 1996. "The Problem of Ecological Restoration." *Environmental Ethics* 18: 222–224.

Katz, E. 1997. *Nature as Subject: Human Obligation and Natural Community.* Lanham, MD: Rowman & Littlefield Publishers.

Light, A. 1996a. "Environmental Pragmatism as Philosophy or Metaphilosophy." In *Environmental Pragmatism,* edited by A. Light and E. Katz, 325–338. London: Routledge.

Light, A. 1996b. "Compatibilism in Political Ecology." In *Environmental Pragmatism,* edited by A. Light and E. Katz, 161–184. London: Routledge.

Light, A. 1996c. "Callicott and Naess on Pluralism." *Inquiry* 39: 273–294.

Light, A. 1997. "Restoration and Reproduction." Unpublished manuscript presented at the Symposium on Ethics and Environmental Change: Recognizing the Autonomy of Nature, St. John's, Newfoundland, Canada, June 4–5.

Light, A., and E. Higgs. 1996. "The Politics of Ecological Restoration." *Environmental Ethics* 18: 227–247.

Sagoff, M. 1978. "On Restoring and Reproducing Art." *The Journal of Philosophy* 75: 453–470.

Scherer, D. 1995. "Evolution, Human Living, and the Practice of Ecological Restoration." *Environmental Ethics* 17: 359–379.

❧ Chapter 4 ❧

RESTORING NATURE IN AMERICAN CULTURE: AN ENVIRONMENTAL AESTHETIC PERSPECTIVE

Cheryl Foster

Environmental Aesthetic Theory and Restoration Practice

As the Chicago restoration controversy described in the Introduction to this volume has demonstrated (see also Gobster 1997; Helford, this volume; Shore 1997), individual responses to visible acts of restoration vary according to broad differences in scientific education, civic involvement, and personal values. Despite such variations in individual opinions over specific restoration projects, however, general attitudes toward restoration practices in the United States point to a widespread sensibility that is particularly American in character and disturbingly at odds with itself. In this essay I suggest that the sensibility underlying some assumptions about restoration involves an aesthetic of hyperreality—a state of affairs in which the pervasive presence of models, copies, or imitations of reality leads to acceptance of the models, copies, or imitations as reality. This sensibility permeates the cultural backdrop against which discussions about restoration take place and is thus a serious, if often hidden, dimension of those discussions.

What, precisely, does an aesthetic of hyperreality entail?

> Hyperreality points to a blurring of distinctions between the
> real and the unreal in which the prefix "hyper" signifies more

real than real, whereby the real is produced according to a model. When the real is no longer simply given (for example as a landscape or the sea), but is artificially (re)produced as "real" (for example as a simulated environment), it becomes not unreal, or surreal, but realer-than-real, a real retouched and refurbished in a "hallucinatory resemblance" with itself (Best and Kellner 1991, 119).

By way of illustration, consider a British case of geological restoration, analyzed by Keekok Lee in her article "Beauty for Ever?" Lee explores the restoration of Yew Tree Tarn in England's Lake District, a National Trust property whose natural beauty was threatened after an underground fault drained the lake (Lee 1995). A dam was constructed to keep the beauty of Yew Tree Tarn "permanent" by restoring the lake to something that looked like its original state, thus continuing the look of a landscape made famous by its association with the Romantic movement in English poetry and art. Due to the construction of the dam, the restored landscape, or perceived surface of the environment, simulated the original landscape surface in sensuous detail.

Lee, however, argues that piecemeal engineering to correct or reverse geologic processes is misguided because, while structure is more or less permanent, processes involve change, which may lead over time to changes in identity.

> To arrest or deflect geological change where it could lead to unaesthetic or less aesthetic structures amounts to treating geological formations, the products of such processes of change, as mere artifacts in the name of what is beautiful. It is, to adapt a phrase, "to pervert the course of nature" in order to serve our human purposes and ends (Lee 1995, 221–222).

Lee acknowledges that "the spirit of Romanticism has succeeded in turning the Lake District into an embodiment of the 'Englishness' of the English countryside" (Lee 1995, 219). Yet she believes that it is a philosophical error to regard works of artifice and nature as belonging to the category of cultural objects worthy of preservation and, where necessary, restoration. Restoring Yew Tree Tarn, according to Lee, places this landscape in a class more appropriately reserved for artifacts, which nature is not. Lee thus advocates a strict separation of artifice and nature when considering issues of restoration—a separation endangered by a cultural propensity for hyperreality.

Hyperreality has been called a pervasive force in the United States by theorists from many disciplines, perhaps most notably by the French philosopher Jean Baudrillard. In his travelogue *America,* Baudrillard attributes the erosion of traditional aesthetic values, based on knowledge of an object's history and context, to the omnipresence of kitsch and hyperreality in American culture, and "the disappearance of history and the real in the televisual" (Baudrillard 1993, 101). According to Baudrillard, the disappearance of a causal, historical distinction between the natural and the artifactual leads to the evaporation of any significant distinction between them at all (Baudrillard 1983, 3). American culture, for Baudrillard, both causes and is the product of this evaporation of a distinction between the natural and the artificial realms of existence.

> America ducks questions of origins; it cultivates no origin or mythical authenticity; it has no past and no founding truth. Having known no primitive accumulation of time, it lives in a perpetual present. Having seen no slow, centuries-long accumulation of a principle of truth, it lives in perpetual simulation, in a perpetual present of signs (Baudrillard 1983, 76).

Baudrillard admires rather than criticizes this aspect of American culture, noting that attempts among some Americans to embrace a more traditional notion of culture are tiresome to him: "If it is the lack of culture that is original, then it is the lack of culture one should embrace" (Baudrillard 1983, 101).

Yet Baudrillard enjoys the status of being a visitor to the United States. His stake in its environmental heritage as well as its future is that of the distant observer. Given the extent to which hyperreality forms the unconscious aesthetic sensibility of a culture with very pressing environmental challenges, American contributors to the debate surrounding restoration practice might consider the possible impediment posed by this sensibility to the successful creation of sound and sustainable environmental policies. Thus far, extensive consideration of the impact of hyperreality on restoration attitudes has been largely absent from discussion (for an exception, see Birch 1995).

Consider that even in professional philosophical discussion, we often think of natural environments as original, untouched places that avoid cultivation by human agency. But what places exist in today's world that are not in some way or other touched by human intentions or actions, if only by thoughtless accident? These are difficulties to be faced in sorting out when restoration is, if ever, an appropriate practice in environmental policy. Some principal commentators on the restoration controversy promote the idea that human manipulation of environmental processes is just a logical and empirical extension of natural processes (e.g., Hickman 1996; Jordan, this volume). Others insist that any form of deliberate intervention in environmental processes amounts to anthropocentric domination of nature and thus a form of self-delusion about what human beings can accomplish in relation to nature restoration (e.g., Birch 1995; Katz 1997a; Katz 1997b; Katz, this volume). At both of these extremes in the restoration dispute, significant presumptions about what is "natural" and what is "artifactual" lurk behind the discussion.

Such presumptions have nevertheless been explored in some detail by those in the field of environmental aesthetics. The philosopher Yuriko Saito, who has published extensively on questions of aesthetics in the environment, upholds a conceptual split between the aesthetics of art and the aesthetics of nature. "If we consider the aesthetic appreciation of nature as appreciating the *way in which* nature tells its own story through its sensuous qualities, we can account for the asymmetry between art and nature in terms of their aesthetic values" (Saito 1998, 105 [emphasis in original]). Any asymmetry in aesthetic value between art and nature, as indicated by Saito, has bearing on how ecological restoration is viewed. If nature tells a continuous, causal story through natural sensuous qualities appearing in and through the landscape surface, but that story has been interrupted over time by human action, can the natural story then be resumed (and the environment thus restored) when a sensuous landscape surface similar to that of the original environment replaces whatever interrupted the natural landscape story? Or is the restored environment something quite other than nature's own story, something staged and artifactual rather than natural in character and thus in reception?

American identity itself contains a constant clash between fascination with the idea of pure wilderness on the one hand and immersion in an environment of seamless simulation on the other (Baudrillard 1993, 104): Denali and the Grand Canyon stand at one end of public consciousness, while Disney reigns at the opposite end. Inherent in American cultural sensibility is an unresolved dichotomy of value between what is taken to be utterly natural and what is assumed to be ingeniously artifactual. Given American susceptibility to neglecting causal genesis, however, the ideas of wilderness and technological innovation, rather than the actual things themselves, often come to hold importance for American myths and legends.

Of course, it proves impossible to maintain absolute opposition between nature and artifice in the realm of value. Bifurcated, simplified, or arcadian models for aesthetic appreciation of nature and artifice do not reflect with any degree of utility the actual environments considered for or undergoing ecological restoration. We must seek a more sophisticated model for grasping the tensions pulling at us in this debate.

For example, I have suggested that many of the most visible theories within the aesthetics of the natural environment fall into one of two dichotomous categories, the narrative or the ambient (Foster 1998). Narrative approaches to nature's aesthetic value interpret the perceived environment as an index of nonperceptual stories, whether those stories be mythological, historical, or scientific in character. Ambient approaches, by contrast, read the environment as a reflection of perceptual processes that focus on the enveloping, sensuous dimension of inhabiting natural space. Narrative and ambient approaches appear to be in conflict with each other when taken in polar isolation. They can, however, form complementary aspects of a broader sensibil-

ity in environmental aesthetics, one that celebrates both nonperceptual context and sensuous form while continuing to respect the status of nature as
largely "other" to human beings.

Even so, it is possible within this sphere to trivialize the aesthetic experience of nature, as philosopher Ronald Hepburn argues in his essay "Trivial and
Serious in Aesthetic Appreciation of Nature." Hepburn presents a dichotomy
that parallels the narrative and the ambient but introduces at the same time an
ethical tone of inquiry (Hepburn 1993, 66–67). While my distinction between
the narrative and the ambient is enclosed within a larger circle of pluralistic or
even pragmatic environmental appreciation, Hepburn's distinction occupies a
linear trajectory. The midpoint between the sensuous and thought extremes
on his scale demarcates the point of serious aesthetic appreciation of nature.
An appreciation at either pole, senses only or thought only, represents the trivialization of nature (Figure 4.1).

Hepburn asserts that "an aesthetic approach to nature is trivial to the
extent that it distorts, ignores, suppresses truth about its objects, feels and
thinks about them in ways that falsify how nature really is" (Hepburn 1993,
69). Thus, any appreciation that pushes thought to the periphery in enjoying
sensuous qualities, or that ignores sensuous features in perception to contem-
plate absent facts, does not engender a comprehensive grasp of nature's aesthetic character.

Two American cases involving the restoration of geological curiosities
have particular relevance to the point about trivialization made here. They particularly lend themselves to analysis when we consider the clash of a hyperreal
aesthetic sensibility and a strict separation of artifice and nature. During the
1997 Memorial Day weekend, a sandstone arch called Eye of the Needle was
vandalized on a Montana site overseen by the Bureau of Land Management
(Earth Almanac 1998). This eleven-foot formation had stood above the Missouri River for millennia and was passed (and noted) by Meriwether Lewis
and William Clark on their journey westward in 1804 through 1806, a route

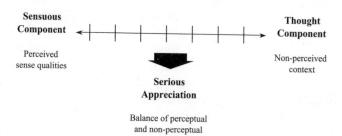

Figure 4.1. Model for Understanding the Serious Aesthetic Appreciation of
Nature (after Hepburn 1993).

now popularly traced by contemporary canoeists and others boating on the river beneath the arch. In knocking out about three feet from the very top of the arch, the vandals for all intents and purposes destroyed the very phenomenon that held significance for visitors: the chance occurrence in nature of a freestanding sandstone arch. Managers from the BLM conferred with staff of the National Park Service, the Forest Service, and others in seeking advice about restoration. Should they replace the three feet or so of rock that was knocked from the top of the arch so that the restoration would be an indistinguishable replica of the original?

Vandalism interrupted what Saito calls the "story" of this geological curiosity. Can this natural story be resumed through restoration? More importantly, should it? In the months following the act of vandalism, many people argued that the arch should be restored to appear as it had been seen by Lewis and Clark, as well as others before and after them. Eventually it was decided to leave the vandalized arch as it was but also to place a scaled-down replica of the original arch, assembled from the same kind of sandstone, near the BLM office some distance away from the actual site. Nevertheless, the fact that restoration was being seriously considered demonstrates the marked tolerance and advocacy for hyperreality: presenting as natural that which would no longer be entirely natural in origin.

The Eye of the Needle controversy can be viewed in the context of a second case involving a geological curiosity: the restoration of the Old Man of the Mountain in New Hampshire, a craggy granite profile jutting from a mountain 200 feet above a lake. Tourists flock to take pictures of it, and over time the Old Man has evolved into a symbol of New Hampshire itself, imbued with many layers of history, myth, and ritual. Restoration to repair and contravene mass wasting from the Old Man has taken place since 1915 and so provides a more extensive temporal context for consideration than the more recent case of the Eye of the Needle arch in Montana.

The original and ongoing appreciation of both landmarks possibly deemphasizes what Hepburn terms the thought component in reference to natural history. Each appears instead to stress only visual or surface qualities of the landscape, which Hepburn disparages as seeking a "fanciful likeness" between natural curiosities and human objects (i.e., an archway in one case, an old man's profile in the other). Seen this way, popular appreciation of the Eye of the Needle and the Old Man of the Mountain participates in the aesthetic trivialization of nature by ignoring geological history and processes in favor of superficial wonderment at the surface appearance of human structures, products, or forms in the natural landscape.

In addition, intervention in or restoration of either landmark may be seen to exacerbate this initial trivialization of nature through the impulse to participate in an aesthetic of hyperreality—one that marginalizes the thought component or natural history narrative in favor of simulating ambient, sensuous surface properties that once occurred naturally in each case. The cultural adherence to an aesthetic of hyperreality can thus indicate a tendency toward engaging in a trivial aesthetic appreciation of nature because such an appreciation stresses surface or ambient sense qualities at the expense of an integration of those qualities with knowledge of their historical and scientific contexts. More importantly, the prevalence of a hyperreal aesthetic in America marks the public assumption, however unconscious, of a tacit but thorough implosion of boundaries between the natural and the artificial, thus muddying the waters for reasoned reflection about restoration.

An emphasis on isolated perceptual qualities over ecological understanding in the aesthetic appreciation of natural environments might account for the alacrity with which a nonspecialist public seizes upon restoration as an option for geological curiosities, whose primary attraction is often aesthetic or perceptual (Sanders 1997), but rejects restoration where favored aesthetic features like nonnative trees will be felled to make way for native species such as prairie grasses (Gobster 1997, 33; Shore 1997, 26).

In limiting one's aesthetic appreciation to perceived surfaces without linking those surfaces to historical and scientific contexts, the narrative of time is displaced from the appearance of sense qualities in space. The resulting falsification of experience emerges through a disruption of continuity between the factual, nonperceived context and the ambient, sensuous surface. Many environmental philosophers worry about this disruption of space and time in understanding and appreciating natural environments.

Robert Elliot asserts, "[W]hat is significant about wilderness is its causal continuity with the past" (Elliot 1995, 83), while Thomas Birch, referring to hyperreality and its culture of simulation, warns, "Appropriation into this throwaway world involves throwing away the former, and other, reality in favor of a simulation that is illusory" (Birch 1995, 149).

To what extent, then, does the practice of ecological restoration exhibit a tendency toward hyperreality, toward the implosion of meaningful boundaries between nature and artifice? To explore such questions, I examine the geological restoration of the Old Man of the Mountain in light of its broad aesthetic appeal, an appeal that includes not only a "trivial" fixation on the ambient, sensuous surface of the landscape but also elements of literary, symbolic, and ritual culture. Aesthetic appreciations that move beyond spatial surfaces into an integration of surface and knowledge—space and time—are often considered to be "thicker" in character than appreciations that focus only or entirely on perceived sense qualities. Here I will address the question of how much thicker an understanding of the aesthetic—an understanding beyond the ambient surface—ought to be in determining the appropriateness of restoration, and, in light of this, discuss issues of relevance to both the Old Man of the Mountain and the Eye of the Needle.

An American Case Study: The Old Man of the Mountain in New Hampshire

The Old Man of the Mountain has come to represent New Hampshire itself, and, as we shall see, this symbolic affiliation accounts for no small part of its craggy significance. What is the Old Man of the Mountain? Spatially it occupies a 40-by-25-foot series of granite ledges, perched 200 feet above Profile Lake and the Pemigewassett River in the Franconia region of New Hampshire's White Mountains. The ledges as seen from the right angle resemble a profile or the visage of an old man—hence the affectionate name. Long enshrined in local memory through Abenaki legend, this geological curiosity was first surveyed by European settlers in 1805. Restoration efforts to prevent mass wasting of the ledges, especially the "forehead," have been continuous since 1915, when Edward Geddes designed and crafted the Bessemer steel turnbuckles and cables that would soon afterward be secured to hold the Old Man in place.

The Old Man now attracts 5 to 6 million visitors per year, serves as an official state symbol carried on New Hampshire license plates and other state insignia, and is the subject of an exhaustive Web site (www.edsanders.com). Since 1997 the Old Man and the history of its maintenance and restoration have been the main focus of a small museum in the Franconia region of New Hampshire. The museum has much to document: every year in mid-July, a restoration operation is managed by Niels Nielsen, a former bridge construction superintendent for the New Hampshire Department of Transportation, and, more recently, by Nielsen's son David and daughter-in-law Deborah. The restoration effort involves spraying bleach to kill lichen; filling cracks with wire, epoxy, and fiberglass; adjusting cables and turnbuckles; and measuring to anticipate future mass wasting via mechanical weathering and frost wedging. Scores of volunteers turn out to assist with the preparation of materials, while many others come just to watch the Nielsens descend the precipitous ledges. Damage will continue not only through mass wasting but also through human interference: in 1989 the *Manchester Union Leader* ran an article chronicling acid rain damage to the granite surface of the Old Man. Thus, preservation and restoration efforts no longer resist purely natural processes but respond directly to the side effects of human industry.

Given the popularity of the Old Man as both a symbol of New Hampshire and a significant cultural attraction, it may seem almost unpatriotic to question the process of restoration as it is required to retain the topography of the Great Stone Face (as the Old Man is sometimes called, after a Nathaniel Hawthorne story of the same name). Yet such questioning reveals much about the place of aesthetics in public consciousness. Without intervention, the shape of the Great Stone Face would have altered significantly; by now it would no longer resemble a face. Edward Geddes first defended the need for restoration of structural integrity in 1915. His turnbuckles and cables, which have been either in place or replaced by others since 1916, are readjusted annually to hoist the drooping forehead and counter the pull of gravity. Without them, the top ledge (at the very least) would have crumbled and tumbled off into the lake long ago.

Yet note this characterization of the Old Man as it appears on Gran-Net, an official Web site for attractions and events in New Hampshire: "The Profile, or the Great Stone Face, names by which it is also known, is a natural rock formation that developed millions of years ago from a series of geological events. . . . Consisting of five separate granite ledges whose natural arrangement creates a profile from the right viewing point, The Old Man of the Mountain measures about 40 feet from chin to forehead" (Gran-Net 1998).

Although the original formation owed its shape to geological processes, those same processes, in the absence of human interference, would have led to significant change, and thus the destruction of the profile itself, by this point in time. Restoration efforts, however, have been sustained and vigorously supported. As mentioned earlier, an entire museum has been devoted to those efforts. Furthermore, the profile is advertised and visited primarily as a geological curiosity, one whose surface contours resemble a human visage. Stressing this resemblance, however, seems to promote Hepburn's sense of trivialization in the aesthetic appreciation of nature, emphasizing as it does coincidental surface analogies (fanciful resemblances) rather than the pathways of natural change. In light of the practical implications of blurring a distinction between nature and artifice, we can ask: should the Old Man continue to be restored? Philosophical reflection enhances our understanding of what is at issue.

In a similar context, Thomas Birch discusses processual change and natural identity in his essay on "The Incarceration of Wildness" (1995). Birch laments the anthropomorphic tendency to confuse nature with raw material for human use. He notes that Baudrillard's "brilliant and alarming analysis of modern Western culture starkly illuminates the uses to which imperial culture puts its wild others," and goes on to underscore the presence of hyperreality as a dominant influence on American environmental culture (Birch 1995, 149). Even Baudrillard's own thinking on the impulse to control natural processes has direct relevance to the consideration of impeding geological change.

> It is no longer a question of imitation, nor of reduplication, nor even of parody. It is rather a question of substituting signs of the real for the real itself, that is, an operation to deter every real

process by its operational double, a metastable, programmatic, perfect descriptive machine which provides all the signs of the real and short circuits its vicissitudes (Baudrillard 1983, 4).

Where geological formations are the result of, and submit to, continual processual change in the alteration of topography, geological restoration defers by contrast to metastability and programmatic control, seeking aesthetic persistence through an interventionist technology.

How do considerations of processual change versus controlled metastability apply to the Old Man? From one view, the restoration of the Old Man of the Mountain can be classified as a straightforward case of arresting geologic change, as a gesture of hyperreality and domination that glosses over the conceptual fissure between natural phenomena and human products. From another view, intervention through restoration or maintenance of the profile's granite face might be taken as craft, where the object of intervention has long been removed from wilderness and has instead occupied what Michael Pollan has called the "middle landscape" (Pollan 1998).

Pollan addresses himself to a set of disused agrarian landscapes in Connecticut, landscapes that would be subject to the encroachment of either forest or development without deliberate intervention. Defying the trajectories of both nature and economic growth, Pollan argues for the preservation of a "purely cultural" agrarian landscape if only as a lesson or a reminder of human times past, times in which humanity and nature appeared to have reached some sort of accommodation. He interprets preserved agrarian landscapes as "balancing acts" that are beautiful to behold, landscapes whose aesthetic character depends on resisting the pull of wilderness in one direction and civilization in another, constituting an open-air museum of sorts. Pollan's defense of such landscapes and his rendering of the issues surrounding their maintenance have bearing on the discussion of ecological and geological restoration, for they point toward a gray area of human concern that falls somewhere between the poles of natural process and human product. This gray area requires for its appreciation both sensuous and cognitive factors, like Hepburn's midpoint, the point of serious aesthetic appreciation of nature. This suggests that what makes an aesthetic appreciation serious is not its being about nature itself per se but rather its balancing the cognitive and sensuous elements of awareness in a manner appropriate to whatever object or environment is at hand—whether that environment be wild, artificial, or something between the two.

In deference to the gray area between nature and culture, I shall ask a provocative question. Might the Old Man of the Mountain possess aesthetic value that is thicker in character than a superficial or hyperreal appreciation, and, if it does possess such value, does this then justify intervention or restoration to counter geological processes? By elucidating some nonambient dimen-

Table 4.1. Narrative Dimensions for Examining the Aesthetic Value of the Old Man of the Mountain

Literary/Cultural	Symbolic	Ritual/Totemic
Abenaki myth	License plates	Annual maintenance
Sprague painting	Gran–Net logo and claim	Historical consciousness
Webster poem	Old Man Museum	Relics
Hawthorne story	Old Man Web site	Hereditary high priests

sions, or the cognitive contexts, of the Old Man's aesthetic value, I explore possible grounds of a defense against the claim that appreciating the Old Man of the Mountain represents a trivialization of nature, where the primary source of aesthetic value lies in fanciful resemblance between a granite mountain ledge and an old man's craggy countenance. Although other categories could certainly be generated, I shall rely upon three general classes of consideration for my exploration: the literary/cultural, the symbolic, and the ritual/totemic (see Table 4.1). These same categories will then be applied, more briefly in the next section, to the case of the Eye of the Needle arch in Montana and geological curiosities more broadly, as a way of thinking through the range and depth of aesthetic values as they influence attitudes toward restoration more generally.

Literary/Cultural

Four explicit references can be made to literary and cultural invocations involving the Old Man. The earliest of these grows out of the modern version of an Abenaki myth.[1] In her recounting of the tale, Alison Friedberg concludes, "Perceived as a great omen, the valley under the stone became a peaceful gathering place for sacred tribal ceremonies and festivals, where all weapons were left behind, and participants reveled in the beauty of their civilization" (Friedberg 1996).

European settlers followed their Abenaki predecessors in paying homage to the Old Man. Artist Isaac Sprague created a drawing entitled "Profile Mountain at Franconia, New Hampshire," which was printed as a plate in a popular book from 1848, edited by William Oakes. An entry accompanying the Sprague plate at a 1998 Beinecke Library exhibition at Yale University makes note of what we might now interpret as the early seeds of hyperreal fascination in American culture.

> In the 1840's the White Mountains of New Hampshire came to compete with the "Fashionable Tour" through upstate New York to Niagara as an opportunity to seek sublime and picturesque landscapes in the United States without straying too

far from civilization. Here early Victorian travelers could indulge in the anthropomorphizing of the landscape, naming every rock and hiking to the right angle to see the "Old Man of the Mountain." Oakes' view book, with plates after Isaac Sprague, allowed them to relive the experience at home (Beinecke Library 1998).

Daniel Webster immortalized the Old Man in an ode, quoted in its entirety in several locations where information about the site is disseminated.

Men hang out their signs indicative of their respective trades.

Shoemakers hang out a gigantic shoe;

jewelers, a monster watch;

even a dentist hangs out a gold tooth;

but up in the Franconia Mountains God Almighty

has hung out a sign to show that in New England, He makes men (Sanders 1997).

Finally, and perhaps most enduringly, Nathaniel Hawthorne gave the Old Man a sustained literary tribute in his vivid and moralistic short story "The Great Stone Face" (Hawthorne 1852). Hawthorne describes the Old Man as "a work of Nature in her mood of majestic playfulness, formed on the perpendicular side of a mountain by some immense rocks, which had been thrown together in such a position as, when viewed at a proper distance, precisely to resemble the features of the human countenance" (Hawthorne 1852, 105). Oddly enough, the moral of the story features a modest young boy named Ernest who grows to manhood (and becomes a preacher) through hard work and fidelity to the natural landscape.[2] Paradoxically, Hawthorne's artistic tribute to the Old Man is itself a moral tale extolling the wisdom and wonders of natural processes.

In each of these four cases, the sensuous, ambient value of the Old Man is linked to a deeper cultural history or narrative. Beginning with Abenaki myth, artistic tributes to the serendipitous appearance of a human visage have taken root in New England consciousness. Recall Saito's exploration of the split between nature and art in aesthetic appreciation. The Old Man surely has a geological history, a story that corresponds to its shape and identity as determined and altered by natural process. Just as surely, the Old Man is also the focal point of stories (and other artistic gestures) that predate modern environmental consciousness. Given the density of human stories surrounding the Old Man, which kind of story—geological or artistic/mythical—ought to take precedence at this stage in cultural development? Such a question cannot be answered with reference to literary or cultural significance alone but must also be considered through both broader symbol and community ritual.

Symbolic

A brief summary of the ways in which the Old Man appears as a symbol of New Hampshire adds depth to the literary and cultural dimensions of aesthetic appreciation. New Hampshire license plates, for example, have featured the Old Man since early in the twentieth century, whereas postcards of its visage can be traced to the mid-nineteenth century: both forms of representation literally move and thus spread the symbolic significance of the Old Man in association with New Hampshire. The Gran-Net Web site, an information site listing events and organizations in New Hampshire, has as its logo the Old Man's profile and devotes space to introducing visitors to the Old Man and its history.

The Old Man of the Mountain Museum collects and exhibits memorabilia related to restoration efforts to keep the Old Man intact. A 1997 article from the *Manchester Union Leader* remarks, "'The Old Man of the Mountain' has inspired poetry and now stands as a symbol of New Hampshire. But despite its rich history, there has never been a place for people to see what has gone into its preservation that has spanned nearly a century" (Colquhoun 1997). The curator of the museum, Inez McDermott, claims that its most exciting exhibit is "a design by a quarry superintendent who devised the series of turnbuckles that has kept the Old Man's forehead in place since 1916" (Colquhoun 1997). In other words, the museum immortalizes precisely the sort of technological innovation that allows human ingenuity to impede geological processes. In centralizing and exhibiting artifacts from the restoration and preservation process, the museum adds thickness to the existing literary/cultural aesthetic appreciation of the Old Man. In essence, the museum celebrates neither the chance occurrence of a stone visage in nature nor the natural history that allowed such a curiosity to emerge, but rather the human response to that chance occurrence in all its forms and manifestations.

A counterpart to the museum itself is the Old Man of the Mountain Web site maintained online by Ed Sanders, a New Hampshire resident with a keen dedication to getting the message of the Old Man out into cyberspace. For those who cannot visit the Old Man or the museum, Sanders provides numerous photographs of the rock formation, its restoration over the years, and items displayed in the exhibits; facts about both its natural and social history; and references to artworks featuring the Old Man (including Webster's poem). Here we see a principle similar to that of William Oakes's Victorian view-book: pictures and information allow those who do not travel into the White Mountains to nonetheless experience the textures and activities belonging to the

Old Man. Even so, the Old Man partakes of a third level of aesthetic value, one with roots in performative rather than material culture.

Ritual/Totemic

As mentioned, local residents as well as visitors gather each year in mid-July to assist in or watch the annual maintenance (and sometimes restoration) of the Old Man's granite visage. This is no ordinary cleanup but has evolved into a full-blown ritual that is anticipated, advertised, and covered in the New Hampshire news media as well as on the Web. In this spirit, the summer intervention constitutes a civic ritual that invites a pluralistic community to gather, peacefully as in Abenaki legend, beneath the profile to celebrate local civilization. Since the Old Man functions as a symbol of New Hampshire, his presence above the gathered crowds functions not unlike totemic, symbolic, or sacred objects used in religious rituals throughout human history.

Similarly, the ritual itself relies on hereditary high priests—Niels Nielsen and his family—to oversee and implement the ritual of maintenance and restoration. Nielsen has been the recognized leader of annual efforts for decades, so much so that initial efforts to fund the eventual Old Man of the Mountain Museum began as direct contributions to Nielsen in 1984. At the dedication of the museum in 1997, Rob Thomson, commissioner of the New Hampshire Department of Resources and Economic Development, lauded Nielsen's central role in keeping the Old Man intact. "Just as the Old Man is a symbol of New Hampshire, what makes New Hampshire great is the unselfish service to the state of Niels Nielsen. His tireless dedication is one of the reasons why it's in such great shape" (Colquhoun 1997).

Thus, the values of the institution itself—both the state and the symbol of it in the Old Man—are embodied in the high priest of the civic ritual.[3] Niels Nielsen has stopped descending the granite ledges, but photographs now feature not only Nielsen's son David and his wife Deborah, but also their son Tommy, waiting in the wings to assume his "priestly" duties (Sanders 1998). The annual maintenance of the Old Man relies on the presence of a hereditary title for leadership and historical continuity, like many priesthoods or royal lineages of old.

Clearly, an historical consciousness pervades these rituals as well, a consciousness embodied in the material relics on display at the Old Man of the Mountain Museum. Thus, the identity of place connected with the Franconia region of New Hampshire, no less than the identity of the state itself, takes root in social events and material products that began in, but are no longer confined to, natural occurrences. Most urgently, as this historical consciousness gains weight and adds depth to the aesthetic appreciation of the Old Man itself, it becomes problematic to pit the natural history of the site against its cultural and civic history (recall the Yew Tree Tarn case discussed by Keekok Lee).

Here we encounter an intriguing ambiguity in connotations of the concept of restoration itself. Restoration in one way refers to replacing granite materials with look-alike epoxy filler or resisting gravity through constraint of renegade pieces of rock, thus restoring the Old Man to the state it was in before extreme mass wasting. If intervention ceased and natural processes were allowed to take over tomorrow, however, restoration comes to mean returning the Old Man site to the forces of geologic process, where frost wedging and gravity would eventually cause the visage to disappear.

Then again, restoration can be thought of in ways that avoid the polarity of natural process on the one hand and interventionist control on the other. In the Chicago restoration controversy, parts of the landscape are returned to something like their original states by felling trees and planting native prairie grass. The process is undertaken not for aesthetic reasons but to achieve an ecosystem that reflects a more sustainable balance of elements for that region. In this case, intervention functions not to impede but to revive the native features of a landscape. By contrast, maintenance of the Old Man staves off the geological processes endemic to the site. Either way, those thinkers examining the restoration debate need to take into account the cultural values that contribute to the public's views on the topic—the aesthetic sensibilities, both trivial and thick, that lurk behind support of or resistance to individual restoration initiatives.

Analysis and Considerations

In considering explanations for aesthetic value in relation to geological curiosities, it is possible first to apply the categories generated in the previous section to the case of the Eye of the Needle arch in Montana. For example, just as the Abenaki, Hawthorne, Webster, and Sprague immortalized the Old Man in their literary/cultural tributes, the explorers Lewis and Clark made note of the Eye of the Needle in their journeys westward. Similarly, the Old Man is symbolic of the tenacity of New Hampshire's people and state identity, while the Eye of the Needle arch can be interpreted as a symbolic gateway to the West, a gateway beneath which America's premier expansionist explorers passed in service to American claims on lands in the Oregon territories. Finally, the ritual/totemic function of the Old Man's annual cleaning is echoed in the recreational passage, beneath or along the Eye of the Needle arch, of Americans either on foot or in boats on the Missouri River (Earth Almanac 1998).

More broadly, both cases reveal attention paid to often hidden but powerful dimensions of aesthetic experience. Artistic and cultural value often adheres to the aura surrounding an object whose presence extends back through time and has been touched or remarked upon by famous personages from ages past. Walter Benjamin explores the aesthetic allure of aura in his famous essay "The Work of Art in the Age of Mechanical Reproduction," in which he equates the artistic values of originality and rarity with the legacy of an earlier ritual value that prized saintly relics, totemic objects, and sacred portals of divine or supernatural forces (Benjamin 1992). The aura of an object connects one, via physical or spatial presence, to persons and practices that preceded the present era. The Old Man and the Eye of the Needle depend in part for their aura upon the previous attentions of American literary, cultural, and civic heroes.

Symbolic value grows out of and feeds upon such attentions, emerging over time as a layered identity for a place and persons who dwell there. Despite latter-day acknowledgments of the Native American presence prior to European invasion, invocations of the Old Man and the Eye of the Needle arch both point toward the striving onward of European settlers in the United States. New Hampshire is the Granite State not only because of the igneous rock that pervades its White Mountains but also because its citizens are known for their resistance to excessive bureaucratic control, embodied in the state's motto, "Live Free or Die!" Similarly, the Eye of the Needle is most often cited as a place admired by explorers Lewis and Clark. Its configuration as a portal symbolizes a doorway for American claims westward to the Pacific Ocean, welcoming expansion of a dominant Anglo culture as ordered by Thomas Jefferson. Not all narratives attaching to a site suggest positive American history: in each case, an element of domination, of both wilderness and native peoples, lingers among other American myths.

Finally, the significance of both geological curiosities can be attributed in part to their synthesis of features in American civic consciousness: wilderness, individualism, and ingenuity. The Old Man continues to be not only maintained but also celebrated as a controlled aspect of nature; yet its original power flows precisely from its emergence by chance in nature, a fact manifested in contemporary advertisements and publicity for the site. In addition, it serves as a symbol of the rugged individualism on which New Hampshire prides itself. Had the decision been made to restore the Eye of the Needle to replicate its former appearance, a similar claim might have been made for it. Yet the Eye of the Needle will not, for the foreseeable future, be restored. Through this decision we can begin to collate and analyze the various observations made thus far.

Despite its emphasis on wilderness in national consciousness, America remains enamored of simulation, as was previously noted in the discussion about Baudrillard.

What is new in America is the clash of the first level (primitive and wild) and the "third kind" (the absolute simulacrum). There is no second level. This is a situation we find hard to grasp . . . it is Disneyland that is authentic here! The cinema and TV are America's reality! The freeways, the Safeways, the skylines, the speed, and deserts—these are America, not the galleries, churches, and culture. . . . (Baudrillard 1993, 104).

America emerges as a paradox, a nation whose identity conjures up images of wilderness. Both components—image and wilderness—have bearing here. In "The Machine in the Garden Revisited," a comprehensive and brilliant article on the history of nature photography in America, photographer and theorist Deborah Bright draws unswerving, well-documented attention to the influence of nature images on the development of American identity. The work of photographers like Ansel Adams, Timothy O'Sullivan, and Edward Weston not only contributed directly to popular support for the establishment of national parks, but also embedded in American consciousness visions of wilderness landscapes that most would never visit but would nonetheless embrace as emblematic of our culture (Bright 1992).

When it comes to issues in geological as well as ecological restoration, philosophers, policy makers, and managers would be wise to reckon with the depth and extent of America's paradoxical stance toward itself. At once embodying both wilderness and simulation, America relies upon the images of itself as a pioneer nation—as a community of rugged individualists forging the New World—in maintaining a sense of identity. Yet the impulse to maintain images, or social narratives, at the expense of natural processes threatens to erase the natural foundations upon which American identity is based. Geological and ecological identities shift over time through processes that operate independently of humankind. But cultural identity, resting in America as it does on a paradoxical addiction to hyperreality, exerts a powerful aesthetic pull on popular consciousness, where debates about restoration play themselves out. What can be concluded from this?

Fundamentally, geologic curiosities like the Old Man should be fully acknowledged as partly artifactual in character. At present, although the Old Man of the Mountain Museum in New Hampshire enshrines the gradual encroachment of artifactuality on the profile, public advertisements of the site appear to emphasize the natural and geological origins of the formation at the expense of stressing human intervention. The purely geological narrative has been continually interrupted since 1916, when the first cables and turnbuckles were secured. For this reason alone, the Old Man of the Mountain can no longer be considered a natural geologic curiosity. It is more like an installation of sorts, or an instantiation of Pollan's middle landscape, at this point in time.

It could nevertheless be argued that trivialization of the natural formation is avoided through the thick aesthetic appreciation of the Old Man that has emerged due to the cultural, symbolic, and ritual practices and products that have arisen in response to it over the last 150 or so years. The thickness of these accumulated tributes constitutes something like a serious aesthetic appreciation. Such an appreciation relies on cognitive as well as sensuous appreciation, although certainly not an appreciation at this stage of natural processes or nature as such. This might not matter: there is room among the various environments, wild and artificial, for the preservation of those landscapes that embody the relationship between humanity and nature as it existed during an earlier period in our cultural history. The Old Man of the Mountain may indeed be one of those landscapes.

These are, however, precisely the reasons not to restore the Eye of the Needle arch. First, it lacks the range and depth of accumulated associations that attach to the Old Man, and the question of its restoration has arisen at the end, rather than at the beginning, of the American century. Replacing three feet of sandstone to replicate the original arch would erase the traces of vandalism that have had an effect on the site. Vandalism constitutes an unfortunate but regular aspect of contemporary American culture. Perhaps more crucially, respect for natural processes, as conveyed through what Yuriko Saito and Allen Carlson identify as "nature's stories" (Carlson 1993, Saito 1998), is also becoming part of late twentieth-century American culture. Surely one way to resolve the paradox of American identity is to respect nature enough to desist from new or fresh attempts at its simulation, where simulation serves what is primarily an aesthetic, commercial, or recreational purpose. This course of action reassesses the dominance of anthropocentric utility in American culture, and it faces up to and educates the public about the less savory aspects of that culture as manifested in the destruction of the arch.

Second, restoring the Eye of the Needle arch would simulate what was originally a chance geological formation by undercutting chance altogether and replacing it with ingenuity. This course of action would defer to an ambient, sensory, or surface impression at the expense of what had been a genuine geological narrative, a narrative whose story has now been interrupted by human vandalism. Since the attraction of the arch arose from its serendipitous configuration in the first place—the trivial charm of nature's anthropomorphic whimsy—replication of the original arch through artifice would contravene the basis of its most obvious appeal: its spontaneous emergence in nature. Granted, the same can be said about the Old Man, but in that case—and this is a key consideration—the human narratives began to accumulate long before we grasped either the extent of environmental degradation through interference in natural processes or the symbolic domination inherent in the American proclivity for hyperreality, which often seeks the quick technological fix to natural inconveniences and promotes metastable opportunities for human use and enjoyment (Elliot 1994, Katz 1997b).

Third, it can be argued that the original appreciations of the Old Man and the Eye of the Needle were trivial even at their inceptions, before interventions began, and thus that such types of appreciation should not be encouraged any longer. To a large extent this is sound reasoning. Much of the touristic aesthetic attention paid to the Old Man remains trivializing and kitschy in tone, reflecting in ten-second snapshots a superficial attachment to fanciful resemblances. Constant emphasis of perceived surfaces is unlikely to promote curiosity about or acquaintance with more variegated natural history or even cultural history. Does this mean that a decision should be taken to halt the annual maintenance of the Old Man and let gravity exert its pull? Not necessarily: fascination with the Old Man may be largely trivial, but it reflects the aesthetic consciousness of an earlier age, one concretized by Abenaki myth, literary tributes, and artistic cultural products and continued in the rituals and museums of today. Again, the present Old Man resembles Pollan's middle landscape of Connecticut farms, where an open-air museum commemorates an earlier period in human and natural history.

The Eye of the Needle, by contrast, would fall directly into kitschy hyperreality were it to be restored. To avoid exacerbating the initial vandalism with a second intervention, natural processes should be allowed to continue despite the interruption. The arch in the end may attract tourist attention, but it is not a restored and maintained shrine quite yet, as the Old Man (or Yew Tree Tarn in England) seems to be. To treat the Eye of the Needle as an artifact would smack of anachronism, embracing the aesthetic values of an earlier period even though a more sophisticated aesthetic appreciation of natural environments has become possible due to an enlargement of scientific understanding.

Consider for a moment the case of a giant tree in Poland, a venerated and ancient oak thought to be about 1,000 years old. The tree has recently been fitted with branch supports and a lightning conductor to protect it from strikes and allow it to live for several more centuries (Newman 1998). The tree now enters a middle landscape phase in being so fitted, for human intervention seeks to stabilize and program elements of nature rather than let those elements interact ecosystemically (Newman 1998). As Baudrillard observes, America seeks metastability in its cultural landscape, even when that landscape invades and transforms what was natural. When we think about geological and ecological restoration, the motivations for such intervention require rigorous inspection.

Fourth, and finally, geological restoration of the Old Man resituates value away from its original natural narrative and toward an invented look of nature.

Despite the Old Man Museum and the public celebration of maintenance efforts, the Old Man continues to rely for its power on its genesis in natural history. The tolerance of the American public (as well, perhaps, as that of foreign visitors) for casually overlooking a more complex history—the fact that the Old Man has been artificially maintained since 1916—in deference to trivializing gawking cannot be underestimated. It is the same tolerance that would restore the Eye of the Needle arch quickly to forget the interruption; the same tolerance for perpetuating grossly inhuman stereotypes of female beauty in the name of economic growth; the same tolerance for digitally altering images of nature or cultural artifacts so they will fit nicely on a magazine cover or a page; the same tolerance for maintaining a pleasant, controlled appearance of nature everywhere at the expense of enduring nature's own vicissitudes.

These analyses and considerations have been undertaken in light of geological curiosities, but their relevance to issues in restoration ecology can be demonstrated. Yet the application of these analyses to ecological restoration cases can have very different consequences due to variations in intention between ecological and geological restoration projects. The American tendency toward an acceptance of hyperreality underlies several key issues in all restoration debates, such as those emerging from the Chicago Wilderness project as well as from the maintenance of the Old Man. However, while hyperreality informs our understanding of why many people accept and promote restoration of geological curiosities, it may also indicate why some of the same people reject restoration in Chicago: aesthetics.

Admiration of geological curiosities often limits itself to a sensuous surface or ambient appreciation, or it functions as an outgrowth of such appreciations. Ecological restoration, by contrast, can draw the ire of local residents because it seeks to alter an accepted aesthetic surface to bring into being an ecosystem of more native condition. In the case of the Chicago restoration controversy, many people who did not know about the scientific justifications for the project objected to the removal of trees, which left what they felt to be an open, barren landscape (Gobster 1997, 33). In this way, objectors did not empathize immediately with the aim of restoring native prairie grass to its original habitat but instead resented the removal of aesthetic features they enjoyed and even attributed to the ambience of local identity in some cases.

Despite this difference of emphasis regarding aesthetics, ecological restoration and geological restoration share other issues, which will continue to knot up into perplexing philosophical tangles unless thinkers from different fields work together to unravel them. For both varieties of restoration, there is no getting around a conceptual split between natural processes and artifactual products—especially in America, where identity is predicated upon images of untamed wilderness. Even though ecological restoration attempts to supplant current environments with more native species and arrangements, the act of restoration itself is one of anthropogenic management. It differs significantly from restoration of geological curiosities, however, in that it does not work toward any aesthetic or recreational stasis, nor does it seek to replace nature with the appearance of nature, as do many geological restorations. Ecological restoration seeks perhaps to manage for a more natural form of change, where "natural" connotes processes neither initiated nor propelled by human agency. Ecological restoration does not hold natural process in suspension so much as it winds the clock back to let succession proceed as it might have done with less interference on our part.

Some might argue that a more natural solution would, of course, be to cease land management altogether: to refuse to take on new management duties while at the same time halting projects already in hand. But this seems to me to be as unnatural for humanity as it might be natural for some ecosystems. The strict conceptual dichotomy between natural process on the one hand and artifactual product on the other may in the big empirical picture be a false dichotomy, one that oversimplifies the issues and values at stake in discussions of restoration to maintain a pristine fidelity to logic. Thinkers in the American pragmatist tradition have to some extent begun to suggest just this (Light 1996; Light, this volume; Weston 1996). What pragmatism has thus far left out, or failed to integrate in any sustained way, is a rigorous understanding of the American impulse toward hyperreality, the thoughtless blurring of boundaries between reality and simulation, nature and artifice.

If the dichotomy between nature and artifice proves to be false or overly simplified, there remains the difficulty of demonstrating the relevance of any distinction between nature and artifice in a culture predisposed to mix one with the other. For ecological as well as geological restoration, the aestheticism of American popular culture must be sorted out into its trivial and more serious (thick) dimensions, so that motivations for restoration may be viewed in light of their influence. The narrative of science can reverberate in a thick, serious aesthetic appreciation of landscape or wilderness, just as a trivial, superficial aesthetic approach to landscape or wilderness can give way to an ambient appreciation informed by history and integrated with fact.

I would argue that we ought to avoid sorting restoration disputes into tired, analytically convenient categories of nature and culture. Not much is left to be gained by citing logical truisms, whether they assert the inability of restoration efforts to replace nature due to its cultural origin (and literal inability to move back in time), or the absorption of all human cultural activity into the province of nature (which stresses the concept of nature well beyond colloquial limits). For better or worse, Americans live in a culture where nature remains idealized while culture erases its nature. The implications of hyperreality for the restoration debate remain profound and far reaching, indicating as they do an unconscious or casual acceptance of simulation and fiction in everyday American life. The cultural sensibility of hyperreality evades the neat contraries made famous by atomistic reasoning and will continue to exert a strong influence on popular attitudes, including attitudes about ecological and geological restoration, until its stranglehold on American culture is made manifest and fully critiqued.[4]

Notes

1. The disabled Chief Pemigewasset fell in love with Minerwa, the daughter of a rival Mohawk chieftain, and their union led to peace among the warring tribes. One spring, however, Minerwa was called back to the Mohawk tribe to attend to her dying father many miles away. Although a daughter's husband customarily accompanies her, Pemigewasset's disability prevented him from making the journey. He went with Minerwa as far as he could and then agreed to watch for her smoke signals when she arrived safely. He watched for the signals before returning to his tribe for the summer.

   As fall approached, Minerwa was due to return and Pemigewasset traveled with his braves to the highest cliff in the region to watch for her approach. They camped for weeks, but no smoke signals came, and even though Pemigewasset became ill as the weather worsened, he refused to leave his perch. Instead, he ordered his braves to build a shelter there for him and then leave, which they reluctantly did. Pemigewasset spent the winter there, watching for Minerwa, who never returned.

   The following spring, Pemigewasset's braves returned to the cliff top only to find their chief's bones inside the intact shelter. They turned toward home to bring sad news, but as one brave turned back to pay homage to the memory of his chief, he jumped in astonishment: molded into the peak of the cliff was the face of Pemigewasset!

2. Ernest is told by his mother of an old Indian legend that predicts the birth in their region of a child who will grow to be the "greatest and noblest personage of his time," a person whose visage will be that of the Great Stone Face. Of course, several worldly villagers return to the area after having made their fortunes, but each one disappoints until the villagers come to see that it is humble Ernest himself who has grown to resemble the face. Along the way a poet visits the village to meet Ernest (the poet who had written an ode to the Great Stone Face—Daniel Webster?!), and, in expounding on poetry, Hawthorne disparages those who "thought to show the soundness of their judgment by affirming that all the beauty and dignity of the natural world existed only in the poet's fancy" (Hawthorne 1852, 124).

3. Note here that Thomson is not an ecologist, geologist, or environmental advocate but rather a commissioner in a state department of resources and economic development. What values mix with those of aesthetics when erecting or declaring the importance of civic monuments?!

4. My heartfelt thanks go to Bruce Hull, Andre Ariew, and especially Paul Gobster

for their insightful and detailed comments on an earlier version of this chapter. I also cite with gratitude Allen Carlson, Yuriko Saito, and Ronald Hepburn, whose thoughts on the nature versus artifice dichotomy have challenged me to rethink my own position on a great many occasions.

References

Baudrillard, J. 1983. *Simulations,* translated by P. Foss, P. Patton, and P. Beitchman. New York: Semiotext[e].

Baudrillard, J. 1993. *America,* translated by C. Turner. London: Verso.

Beinecke Library. 1998. "The Sublime and the Picturesque, Part 1: Isaac Sprague, 'Profile Mountain at Franconia, New Hampshire.'" In *Scenery of the White Mountains, with Sixteen Plates from the Drawings of Isaac Sprague,* edited by W. Oakes (original published 1848). Available online at www.library.yale.edu/beinecke/sublime1.htm.

Benjamin, W. 1992. "The Work of Art in the Age of Mechanical Reproduction." In *Illuminations,* edited by W. Benjamin, translated by H. Zohn, 211–244. London: Fontana Press.

Best, S., and D. Kellner. 1991. *Postmodern Theory: Critical Interrogations.* New York: The Guilford Press.

Birch, T. 1995. "The Incarceration of Wildness: Wilderness Areas as Prisons." In *Postmodern Environmental Ethics,* edited by M. Oelschlaeger, 137–161. Albany: State University of New York Press.

Bright, D. 1992. "The Machine in the Garden Revisited: American Environmentalism and Photographic Aesthetics." *Art Journal* Summer 1992: 60–71.

Carlson, A. 1993. "Appreciating Art and Appreciating Nature." In *Landscape, Natural Beauty and the Arts,* edited by S. Kemal and I. Gaskell, 199–227.

Colquhoun, L. 1997. "Old Man of the Mountain Museum Dedicated." *Manchester Union Leader* September 26.

Earth Almanac. 1998. "Requiem for a Ruined Arch in Montana." *National Geographic* 193: 3.

Elliot, R. 1994. "Ecology and the Ethics of Environmental Restoration." In *Philosophy and the Natural Environment,* edited by R. Attfield and A. Belsey, 31–45. Cambridge: Cambridge University Press.

Elliot, R. 1995. "Faking Nature." In *Environmental Ethics,* edited by R. Elliot, 76–88. Oxford: Oxford University Press.

Foster, C. 1998. "The Narrative and the Ambient in Environmental Aesthetics." *The Journal of Aesthetics and Art Criticism* 56: 127–138.

Friedberg. 1996. *Who Is the Old Man of the Mountain?* Online material available at www.nheditions.nh.com/96editions/october96/whoisthe/index/html.

Gobster, P. H. 1997. "The Chicago Wilderness and Its Critics, III. The Other Side: A Survey of the Arguments." *Restoration & Management Notes* 15: 32–37.

Gran-Net. 1998. *The Old Man of the Mountain.* Online material available at www.grannet.com.

Hawthorne, N. 1852. "The Great Stone Face." In *The Snow Image and Twice Told Tales,* 34–58. New York: Three Sirens Press.

Hepburn, R. W. 1993. "Trivial and Serious in Aesthetic Appreciation of Nature." In *Landscape, Natural Beauty and the Arts,* edited by S. Kemal and I. Gaskell, 65–80. Cambridge: Cambridge University Press.

Hickman, L. 1996. "John Dewey's Pragmatic Naturalism." In *Environmental Pragmatism,* edited by A. Light and E. Katz, 50–72. New York: Routledge.

Katz, E. 1997a. "The Big Lie: Human Restoration of Nature." In *Nature as Subject: Human Obligation and the Natural Community,* 93–108. Lanham, MD: Rowan and Littlefield Publishers.

Katz, E. 1997b. "The Call of the Wild: The Struggle Against Domination and the Technological Fix of Nature." In *Nature as Subject: Human Obligation and the Natural Community,* 109–120. Lanham, MD: Rowan and Littlefield Publishers.

Lee, K. 1995. "Beauty for Ever?" *Environmental Values* 4: 213–226.

Light, A. 1996. "Compatabilism in Political Ecology." In *Environmental Pragmatism,* edited by A. Light and E. Katz, 161–184. New York: Routledge.

Newman, S. 1998. "Earthweek: Diary of the Planet." *Boston Globe* August 31.

Pollan, M. 1998. "Preserving a View: Should People 'Garden' a Nature Area in Order to Retain a Farm Look?" *Chicago Tribune* April 25.

Saito, Y. 1998. "The Aesthetics of Unscenic Nature." *The Journal of Aesthetics and Art Criticism* 56: 101–112.

Sanders, E. 1997. *Old Man of the Mountain Museum.* Online material available at www.edsanders.com/nh/franconia/manmuseum/index.htm.

Shore, D. 1997. "The Chicago Wilderness and Its Critics, II. Controversy Erupts over Restoration in Chicago Area." *Restoration & Management Notes* 15: 25–31.

Weston, A. 1996. "Beyond Intrinsic Value: Pragmatism in Environmental Ethics." In *Environmental Pragmatism,* edited by A. Light and E. Katz, 285–306. New York: Routledge.

✣ *Part II* ✣

CONFLICT OVER WHICH NATURE TO RESTORE

❧ Chapter 5 ❧

THE LANGUAGE OF NATURE MATTERS: WE NEED A MORE PUBLIC ECOLOGY

R. Bruce Hull and David P. Robertson

The language we use to describe nature matters. It is used by policy analysts to set goals for ecological restoration and management, by scientists to describe the nature that did, does, or could exist, and by all of us to imagine possible and acceptable conditions of environmental quality. Participants in environmental decision making demand a lot of the language and terminology used to discuss nature. We expect it to be precise and valid (i.e., we expect it to allow accurate scientific descriptions of the environment and of environmental quality). We also expect it to be powerful and fair (i.e., we expect it to help stakeholders negotiate acceptable and achievable goals for environmental management). The problem is that the language of nature is often neither precise nor value neutral. There exist multiple, conflicting, imprecise, and biased definitions of the terms used to discuss nature. These vagaries of language can cause conflict that delays or derails well-intentioned efforts to restore and manage nature. This conflict results when people use the same terms to intentionally or unintentionally mean different things or use particular definitions to suppress or promote particular values.

What nature is and what it should be are questions that touch the heart of ecological restoration and management. The goals of a restoration project are often based on decision makers' ideas (and ideals) of what is natural, healthy, or otherwise best for nature. Yet there is no simple answer to the question "What is natural?" or "What is ecologically best for nature?" Ecological theory suggests that many alternative environmental conditions are equally possible, equally natural, and equally healthy for any given place at any given point in time. There exists no single ecologically optimum or naturally best environmental condition that can serve as an objective, unequivocal goal for ecological restoration projects (e.g., Botkin 1990; Callicott 1992, 1996; Wiener 1996, Zimmerer 1994). We learn from contemporary understandings of ecology that neither nature nor science (as a way to understand nature) can tell us what Earth should look like. Yet we use the language of nature generated by ecological science to imagine and negotiate acceptable environmental conditions. Thus the constructs of ecological science necessarily serve double duty: they are both descriptive (scientific) and prescriptive (political); they are used to describe what is and to prescribe what ought to be.

The first purpose of this chapter is to examine some of the values implicit in three terms that have currency in both scientific and political venues: naturalness, health, and integrity. Environments that have more of these qualities are presumed to have more value than environments with less of these qualities. Hence, these descriptive terms also serve as prescriptive goals for environmental management. We suggest that participants who hope to compete successfully in the negotiation of restoration policies need to recognize and understand the values, biases, and uncertainties embedded in the language used to discuss and describe nature. This purpose is not too different from what Ross et al. (1997) did for ecosystem health, Shrader-Frechette (1995) for ecological integrity, Peterson (1997) for sustainable development, Takacs (1996) for biodiversity, Lele and Norgaard (1996) for sustainability, Haydon (1997) for natural, and Shrader-Frechette and McCoy (1993) for ecological science as a whole.

Society must explicitly consider which definitions of nature and environmental quality have the most utility for restoring and managing nature. We argue that currently there is insufficient attention directed to the task of constructing an environmental knowledge that functions effectively in the prescriptive arenas of policy and management. Many mechanisms already exist to operationalize and assess the validity and precision of descriptive, scientific terms, and ample discussion of these qualities can be found in the methods sections of publications in scientific journals. But rarely do we see discussed the prescriptive qualities of these terms. The challenge to all stakeholders is to help construct an environmental knowledge that is meaningful within ecological science and effective within environmental policy. Hence, the second purpose of this chapter is to discuss dimensions of environmental knowledge that may facilitate negotiation of ecological restoration goals that are socially acceptable, ecologically meaningful, and managerially relevant. This more public ecology is the responsibility of all stakeholders, and its goal is to produce a more effective environmental knowledge. This purpose is similar to (and our analysis draws heavily on) what Norton (1998) and Sagoff (1988) suggest in their critiques of ecological science and what Bryant and Wilson (1998) suggest in their more general critique of environmental science.

The audience for this book is likely to be as diverse as the public involved in environmental decision making. Many readers of this chapter will find it unsettling that there exist multiple, biased, and contradictory definitions of nature. Those readers expecting impartiality in the scientific terms used to set environmental policy will be disappointed. Other readers will be familiar with the long-standing debate about science's (in)ability to offer impartial knowledge for subsequent use in the value-laden policy-making process (e.g., Eden 1996, Lele and Norgaard 1996, Norton 1998, O'Brien 1993). Some readers will be familiar with the controversial critique that all knowledge and language about nature is socially constructed and thereby both partial and limited (e.g., Escobar 1999, Evernden 1992, Proctor 1995, Shrader-Frechette and McCoy 1993, Soper 1995), and some will be familiar with the response to this critique (e.g., Soule and Lease 1995). We have attempted to craft this chapter so that it offers something to each segment of our diverse audience.

Naturalness, Health, and Integrity

> For those who are less interested in preaching than in policy, less concerned with the philosophical ivory tower than with embattled wetlands or forests, environmental ethics must be grounded in precise science. They must also provide complex, rationally defended principles that are capable of clear, specific, practical applications. Alternative construals might produce very different restoration goals and outcomes (Shrader-Frechette 1995, 125–126).

The language of nature is a tricky thing. Recognizing the complexity of the idea of nature, authors of texts such as this one tend to preface their thoughts with cautionary statements. For instance: "Nature is perhaps the most complex word in the [English] language" is an oft-cited quotation originally penned by Raymond Williams (1976) as the first line in a six-page definition of the term nature. In a subsequent essay, titled "Ideas of Nature," Williams (1980) further explained that nature has the potential to mean many things, and it means something slightly different to most of us according to our various situations. In his instructive and illustrative prose, Williams cautioned, "[W]hen I hear that nature is a ruthless competitive struggle I remember the butterfly, and when I hear that it is a system of ultimate mutual advantage I remember the cyclone."

In this section of the chapter we will examine three ecological terms: naturalness, health, and integrity. There exists a variety (perhaps an infinite number) of ways to define each of these qualities. Each definition implicitly or explicitly reflects values and norms. We review several definitions of each term that seem most likely to conceal values and to promote conflict and confusion among stakeholders not engaged in the contemporary ecological literature where the definitions of these terms are being debated. In particular, we highlight definitions that reflect romantic notions of nature. While Romanticism reflects popular and long-standing traditions in American and European cultures (Callicott and Nelson 1998, Cronon 1995, Oelschlaeger 1991, Soper 1995), it is not the only way to define and discuss nature. Society's development and articulation of alternative visions of nature might be constrained if the key definitions used to describe environmental quality are too heavily steeped in romantic ideals and values. Such a tendency might hinder open dialogue about society's relationship with nature just at a time in Earth's history when such a discussion seems so critical.

At the conclusion of our discussion of each term, we draw attention to additional literature where ecological scientists and other scholars are currently negotiating more precise definitions.

Naturalness

We buy "All Natural" cereal, "100% Natural" soap, and "Naturally Pure" drinking water. We practice natural remedies to cure what ails us. We reside at Woodland Hills, Evergreen Ridges, and Deerfield Meadows. We make billions of visits each year to natural parks and gardens. Obviously we value what is natural. Conversely, what is artificial, human-made, or developed has negative connotations. Referring to something as unnatural or artificial is often the harshest critique one can make.

But what does it mean for something to be natural or to possess naturalness? The concepts of nature and naturalness have been aggressively deconstructed, reinvented, reconstructed, and re-created (Callicott and Nelson 1998, Cronon 1995, Escobar 1999, Proctor 1995, Soper 1995). Among the many points made by those attempting to de- and reconstruct the idea of nature is that at least three broad definitions of naturalness exist: (1) naturalness is associated with a state of the environment that existed at some previous point in time (i.e., authentic or original nature), (2) it is a state of the environment that exists in the absence of human modification (i.e., pristine or wild nature), and (3) it is associated with a slow, or "natural," rate of change. We will attempt to show that these states of nature do not offer value-free referents to guide efforts to restore or manage nature.

Previous point in time. When nature is viewed from the perspectives of disturbance ecology and geological time, the only thing constant about it is change.

The nature present at a particular place has changed over time with accidents of geological, climatic, ecological, and evolutionary history. The nature present in the area we call Chicago, for example, has existed as mown city parks, Native American burned savannas, Ice Age glaciers, Jurassic dinosaurs, abiotic bacteria, and, for the first billion years or so of the Earth's history, rocks located at a very different latitude with no life at all. Which of these natural states is better than another? Why? These questions cannot be answered without invoking values.

It seems obvious (from a human-centered view) that humans do not wish to restore nature to a condition before the evolution of life or, for that matter, to any state existing for the approximately 5 billion years before the evolution of human life. Also, we probably do not wish to restore the nature that existed during the most recent Ice Age, given that most of us are unwilling to abandon our homes and cities to glacial moraines. Rather, the state we seem to most often idealize as natural is the state that existed during the last few thousand years, when the conditions of human habitation of North America were not too different from what they are now.

Even having narrowed our preference for nature to the postglacial, the selection of which nature to use as a benchmark is further intertwined with social values. Natural history, evolutionary biology, and paleoecology show that nature is dynamic, not static: for example, species have expanded their territories at different rates and in different directions from their most recent Ice Age refugia (Brubaker 1988). Thus, even within the last few thousand years, nature has been a moving target. Perhaps even more frustrating for those wanting to find value-free criteria to help select which state of nature to use as a goal of restoration are the conclusions from disturbance ecology that most states of nature are consequences of random events and accidents of history. The characteristics of a given ecological system are sensitive to its initial conditions and to the conditions of adjacent systems, both of which are influenced by random events (Botkin 1990, Pickett et al. 1992, Pimm 1991, Shrader-Frechette 1995). Wind, ice, fire, drought, hyperactive wildlife, and human action are just a few of the many factors that can set an ecosystem along a new trajectory of change and evolution. Botkin (1990) and others have refuted the idea of a balanced nature, where nature knows best and, if just left alone, will reach some optimal or ideal state. Today, nature is understood to be constantly changing, often in random and unpredictable ways. Balanced, stable, and permanent states of nature do not exist. Instead of one nature, we find that many possible, equally likely, equally valid natures could have existed at a given place and point in time. There is no value-free basis for picking one of these many possible trajectories of change and evolution to serve as the undisputed definition of what is natural and hence serve as a value-free goal for management and policy.

One common argument for valuing the most recently evolved nature over other possible states of nature is survival of the fittest: the assumption that the survivors are better because they survived. But nature is not necessarily objectively better in its most recently evolved state than it was in any of its previous states—evolution is not progressive. The most recently evolved nature is not the best possible nature; rather, it is merely the most fitting in the context of the most recent environmental conditions. The nature that was replaced was not necessarily weak, bad, or less desirable; it just could not compete in the context of the latest (often randomly caused) environmental conditions (Gould 1980). Stated another way, evolution does not necessarily mean betterment.

Because many possible natures exist, which nature is chosen to serve as the goal of restoration requires imposing human values and preferences for one time period and one set of initial, perhaps random, conditions. Such a decision may not be arbitrary, but it will no doubt reflect the values and preferences of the decision maker.

Minimal human modification. Another way to define naturalness is as the state of nature existing before human intervention (i.e., pristine, untouched, or wild nature). We will review several reasons why this is not a value-free definition either. When viewing nature through the lenses of anthropology and environmental history, one can find evidence of extensive and prolonged human-caused change (Crumley 1994, MacLeish 1994). Species extinction, fire, agriculture, and exotic (manipulated or imported) species have been part of the North American landscape for thousands of years. Before European settlement, millions of humans inhabited the American landscape (Denevan 1992). Native agriculture and commerce were extensive, and Native Americans transformed the landscape with cities, roads, hunting, and agriculture. In most places across the American landscape, the nature encountered by Europeans was managed, not pristine. Even the earliest European explorers of this New World rarely blazed new paths; instead they followed existing trails and provisioned their parties at existing villages (Snyder 1990). Thus the North American nature that existed before European settlement had not been pristine for perhaps 10,000 years, and the nature we know today is the result of many generations of human management. The task of establishing prehuman conditions is even more problematic on other continents where anthropogenic environmental change has been of longer duration and greater intensity.

A preference for non- or prehuman nature, the state of nature existing before any human contact, requires a normative judgment that humans, as the causal agent of environmental change, are bad. But what is objectively bad about human-induced environmental change? Populations have crashed, individual organisms have suffered, and species have gone extinct prior to, and in the absence of, humans. For example, it is only due to the chance development of photosynthetic bacteria several billion years ago that oxygen-breathing creatures are able to enjoy life today. At the time of its emergence, however, reactive oxygen literally burned other components of nature out of existence, causing enormous environmental change (damage?). Why is human-caused change worse than the change caused by beaver, lightning, volcano, or oxygen? Why does human involvement necessarily soil nature's purity? Following this path of reasoning is instructive because it helps us explore some of the biases inherent in the necessary process of selecting from alternative definitions of naturalness. One answer to these questions is that wild, dehumanized nature is healthier or has more integrity than nature manipulated by humans. This argument essentially shifts the burden from naturalness to the seemingly more scientific constructs of health and integrity that, later in this chapter, we will address as equally value-laden terms.

An alternative answer to these questions is that we do not trust ourselves: technology is out of control, caution is the better part of valor, we have but one planet and thus one chance, the intelligent tinkerer saves all the pieces, Murphy's Law. How much faith humans should place in their technology is a point of important debate (Ehrenfeld 1981, Lewis 1992, Simmon 1981). How much technology is enough and how much is too much? Do we really wish to ignore these cautions and create environmental conditions that are entirely dependent upon continued advancements in human technology? Looking toward the future, critics caution us about potentially massive and unforeseen environmental consequences stemming from technologies already implemented, not to mention the potentially devastating contingencies of uncorking the biotechnology genie. In contrast, technology advocates point to the dramatic and continuing increases in the human standard of living and see no reason why the ultimate resource, human ingenuity, will not solve any and all problems as they become socially and economically significant.

Obviously, one's faith in technology influences the degree to which one is concerned about environmental change. If one has little faith in human technology, one is more likely to prefer natural conditions—those that do not depend on human technology and intervention to ensure sustainability. In addition, one may fear that unbridled reliance on technology breeds the hubris and arrogance that will ultimately lead to society's demise (see Katz, this volume). In the end, however, these deliberations reflect concerns about the role of technology in society, not concerns about naturalness. These concerns about technology may be legitimate and should be discussed explicitly, not confused with ambiguous concepts such as naturalness.

McKibben (1989) provides another reason why the absence of human intervention is not helpful as a definition for naturalness or as a goal for ecological restoration. He contends that nature (i.e., pristine nature, unmodified by humans) is dead. Global warming, acid rain, groundwater pollution, biotechnology, and human-induced species extinction/migration have altered the entire biosphere. Human enterprise has produced the end of pristine nature. Nature can no longer be thought of as an autonomous other. Land ownership fragmentation, private property rights, and the urban growth machine increasingly pierce the preservationist armor surrounding even the largest bioreserves. Like it or not, nature is now a human artifact. Science and technology currently do not have the ability to re-create and maintain areas with minimal human modification or to shelter existing environmental preserves from the consequences of ubiquitous human-caused change.

Slower rate of change. The third definition of naturalness discussed here invokes a social preference for a slower rate of change. In this definition, preference is given to slower, more "natural" rates of change because they are presumed safer. Current, human-dominated environments, it is argued, are experiencing a rate of change seen only a few times during Earth's history. The preference for a slower rate of change reflects a concern that humans are soiling their nest faster than their technology can clean it up. Essentially it is a conservative argument grounded in a respect for tradition and a preference for caution rather than for a pedal-to-the-metal, head-first rush into the future. The argument here is similar to the one above about faith in technology. It may be a valid argument, but it is an argument about the rate of change, not naturalness per se. It is an argument that should not be derailed by an ambiguous term such as naturalness.

In conclusion, naturalness is a problematic goal for restoration to the extent that it can conceal values and social preferences about other issues such as faith in technology. There are many natures, and there are many reasons to value each of them. More sophisticated discussions about the definitions of naturalness are emerging in the scientific literature and may yet produce more precise goals for ecological conservation and restoration (see Anderson 1991, Angermeier 2000, Brunson this volume).

Health

The concept of health implies that there exists an optimal, ideal, or normal state that defines what it means to be healthy (i.e., in good condition, sound of mind and body, robust, flourishing). The degree to which something is healthy is measured by the extent to which it approaches this ideal state. The effects of stress and disease are measured by how much they cause deviation from this state. Using the health of an ecosystem as a goal for restoration and management is problematic for several reasons: (1) defining an ecosystem is problematic, (2) ecosystems are not closed systems or organisms, and (3) health does not offer clear management prescriptions. In the following discussion we will show that attempts to overcome these difficulties necessitate embedding human values and social context into the definition of health (which may create a workable definition, but not a value-neutral one).

What is an ecosystem? The term ecosystem is a complex concept, with multiple definitions that have changed over the last century as the word has come into popular usage (Bocking 1994, Ross et al. 1997, Worster 1994). There are at least three very different types of definitions for ecosystem, and many variations within each type. In some contexts, ecosystem signifies the idea of interconnected parts, the web of life, Leopold's land community. In other contexts it means something of intrinsic worth, something to be valued, something that has the right to exist. A third definition for ecosystem, and the one of relevance here, refers to a place on the ground, something that has physical location and boundaries, a unit of nature.

The boundaries of this spatial unit have proved elusive and porous. They are elusive because ecologists interested in different species, different processes, and different theories will define different ecosystem boundaries. Nature exists at many spatial scales (from the microscopic to the biosphere), many temporal scales (from the diurnal to the glacial), and many organizational scales (e.g., organisms, populations, ecological processes). Which scale one chooses determines the ecological attributes one studies as well as the attributes' spatial, temporal, and organizational properties. For example, population–community ecologists tend to view ecosystems as interconnected networks of living populations existing in the context of nonliving components, whereas process-functional ecologists emphasize energy flows and nutrient cycling in their definitions of ecosystems. Nature can be conceptually organized at many scales; therefore, multiple definitions of ecosystem boundaries exist, and no one definition can be necessarily more correct or objective than another (Levin 1992; Norton 1995; Norton 1998; Ross et al. 1997; Wright, Murray, and Merrill 1998). There is no way to unequivocally define the boundaries of an ecosystem and thus no value-free definition of ecosystem health. The boundaries will reflect the conceptual system used to describe them and hence will reflect the values and ideals embedded in that conceptual system.

Ecosystems are not closed systems or organisms. Organisms, at least relative to ecosystems, are closed systems. Hence their health is more easily (but still not easily) defined. The boundaries of an organism are more clearly defined, the inputs and outputs are more obvious, and birth and death more exactly denote beginning and ending states. Also, organisms, in contrast to ecosystems, have multiple exemplifiers. For each species, multiple organisms exist that can be said to be an example of that species. Multiple exemplifiers allow calculation of average conditions or norms for acceptable ranges of key indicators of each species such as conception, rate of growth, size, blood pressure, temperature, food intake, and death. Ecosystems, in contrast, are not closed, defined, stable, clearly bounded communities with holistic properties consistent from one example to the next. Rather, ecosystems are open, multiscalar, dynamic, and transitory assemblages of biotic and abiotic elements that exist (or could exist) contingent upon accidents of environmental history, evolutionary chance, human management, and the theoretical perspective one applies to define the boundaries. As a result of these contingencies, there are no obvious, objective, measurable, normal qualities that can be used as referents to define good ecosystem health (Botkin 1990, Shrader-Frechette 1995, Shrader-Frechette and McCoy 1995, Suter 1993, Wicklum and Davies 1995).

Certainly people can develop definitions of ecosystem types. These definitions can be objective in the sense that complete agreement among all interested parties is possible, at which point these definitions can be used reliably to identify multiple examples of each type from which norms can be calculated. However, the construction of the definition and of the agreement is also clearly dependent upon the theories, values, and social context in which the definers are embedded. Ecosystems do not exist "out there" until humans agree on where to draw the line. Ecosystems are human constructions and as such reflect human value systems that should be made explicit in the values tournament of restoration and management decisions.

Health is not prescriptive. Despite the popular appeal of human health as an intuitive metaphor for ecosystem quality, closer inspection reveals that the medical profession does not measure or study health; it focuses on disease (Ickovics and Park 1998, Suter 1993). In medicine, parts of the organism are routinely sacrificed (organs removed, limbs amputated, cancer destroyed) so that the organism may live. Applying the health metaphor to ecosystem management implies that removal of organisms and species can be done for the good of the whole, which raises questions about the rights of these species and organisms (questions that have been raised by the animal rights movement). It also implies that without intervention, the ecosystem would die. However, while the invasion of an aggressive exotic species might dramatically change the biophysical characteristics of a piece of land (i.e., the cancer analogy), life will not stop. In fact, promoting the health of one ecosystem sometimes requires killing another, thriving ecosystem. Should we burn a forest to save a prairie, or do we suppress the fire to save the forest? The controversy surrounding the restoration of the Chicago Wilderness makes it clear that stakeholders have different opinions about who the patient is. Defining the patient requires invoking values.

The meaning of health depends upon which nature is being advocated. Consider the controversy over management goals for old-growth forests in the Pacific Northwest (Chase 1995). Two very different construals of health exist, one favoring a young forest, the other an old one. Both forests are considered by their advocates to be healthy. A young forest is healthy because the trees are growing quickly and are resistant to disease and insects, and because the forest floor contains little litter that might fuel a hot, tree-killing, soil-destroying burn. In contrast, an old forest is healthy when the trees are growing slowly and decaying inside, and hence providing habitat for insects and fungi, and when the forest floor contains a large accumulation of biomass that is slowly recycling nutrients. Ecologists publishing in *Forest Science* might study and use mean annual increment of tree diameter or absence of tree-destroying insects as indicators of health for the young forest. Ecologists publishing in *Conservation Biology* might study and use unimpaired cycling of energy and nutrients or abundance and diversity of insects as indicators of health for the older forest. Which constructs and processes an ecologist studies will depend upon which nature the scientist and society idealize as appropriate for the site. Many of these natures could be healthy.

In conclusion, health is a problematic goal for restoration to the extent that it can conceal values and social preferences. More sophisticated discussions about the definitions of ecological health are emerging in the scientific literature and may yet produce more precise goals for ecological conservation and restoration (e.g., Costanza 1995, Rapport et al. 1998).

Integrity

Wicklum and Davies (1995) review the ecological science and management literatures and suggest that although many definitions for ecological integrity exist, most fall into three broad categories: (1) systems have integrity when their structure or processes stay at some acceptable (i.e., defined or negotiated) level or within some range of acceptable levels, (2) systems have integrity when they are permitted to change unaffected by humans, and (3) systems have integrity when they possess organizing and self-corrective abilities that give them resilience to perturbation. We will attempt to review the values and social preferences implicit in these definitions as identified by an excellent literature on the topic (Crossley 1996, Norton 1995, Rapport et al. 1998, Shrader-Frechette 1995, Westra and Lemons 1995, Wicklum and Davies 1995).

Acceptable structures and processes. According to the first definition, an ecosystem has integrity if it exhibits acceptable structures or processes. The task then becomes defining the term acceptable, which we will argue is a social, value-laden judgment, not an objective quality of nature. Acceptable structures and process can be defined as those exhibited in ecosystems having integrity, but this merely creates a circular definition. Typically, acceptable structures and processes are defined by observing (or theoretically reconstructing) some benchmark or baseline ecosystem: "The first hurdle in recognizing change in integrity is the selection of a benchmark state against which other states can be compared" (Angermeier and Karr 1994, 693). This definition requires, then, a benchmark or basis of comparison representing the state of integrity and against which the current ecosystem conditions may be judged.

To further simplify the argument being presented, we will narrow the choice of benchmark to two different conditions: (1) a natural, authentic, or pristine condition existing prior to or with minimum human modification [the benchmark advocated by Angermeier and Karr (1994)] or (2) a desired future condition managed by humans that produces socially valued goods and services [the benchmark advocated by Regier (1993) and described by Sagoff (1988)]. The first benchmark reflects many of the ideas associated with naturalness, which, as noted above, offers at best a problematic benchmark. Using naturalness as a benchmark for integrity amounts to little more than cloaking a subjective term in scientific garb. We will say no more about it. The alternative of selecting some desired future condition is not necessarily more useful, but perhaps it has the potential to be so. It requires definitions of terms such as resilience, diversity, and the functional and evolutionary limits of desired biota that in turn define the term acceptable. These terms, as discussed below, are found to be subjective and value-laden. Because many possible future conditions exist, there is not one objectively defined, value-neutral benchmark condition.

Change unaffected by humans. The second definition of integrity requires that the ecosystem be permitted to change, but in a manner unaffected by humans. Implicit in this definition is the value-laden position that human-induced change is bad. The values inherent in this position were discussed above with respect to naturalness.

Resilience. The third definition of integrity considered here suggests that systems having integrity possess organizing and self-corrective abilities that give them resilience to perturbation. One possible interpretation of this definition requires assuming that self-organizing and self-corrective properties exist for all ecosystems, which hints at the homeostatic, organismic, nature-knows-best model of ecosystems discounted above in the discussion about health. Certainly, it can be argued that ecosystems have numerous interdependent and coevolved properties that collectively exhibit complex and hierarchical organizing properties. But it becomes difficult to objectively define which of these many organizing properties deserve value and difficult to defend why less organized states of nature are necessarily less valued. Even if ecosystems have organizing and self-corrective abilities, it still is not possible to use these criteria to select among the many possible natures that have similar self-organizing properties, any one of which could exist at the same place and point in time.

Another possible interpretation of this third definition of integrity is that ecosystems existing with minimal human influence are better than ecosystems requiring extensive inputs of nutrients, water, and human management. This definition of integrity assumes that human inputs of nutrients, water, or whatever are evaluatively bad or that an ecosystem dependent upon humans for these inputs is less valuable than an ecosystem independent of humans. Clearly these definitions invoke value judgments that assume ecosystems dependent on human inputs are less valuable than ecosystems independent of human maintenance. Certainly one could be concerned about the intergenerational equity of taking nonrenewable resources (e.g., oil) from one ecosystem and importing it (e.g., as fertilizer) into another. Likewise, one could be concerned about the change required of one ecosystem and its inhabitants (e.g., a formerly free-flowing river that is dammed) to support another ecosystem and its inhabitants (e.g., irrigated agribusiness). But these concerns are issues of equity and justice and should be discussed as such. Important debates about the distribution of resources should not be hidden behind supposedly more objective constructs such as ecosystem integrity.

In conclusion, integrity is a problematic goal for restoration to the extent that it can conceal values and social preferences. More sophisticated discussions about the definitions of ecological integrity are emerging in the scientific literature and may yet produce more precise goals for ecological conservation and restoration (e.g., Schulze 1996, Westra and Lemons 1995).

Past, Possible, and Future Natures

Which nature should be restored? For every given setting, one can choose to restore one of many possible natures, and each of the possible natures can have qualities of naturalness, health, and integrity. The choices include (1) the various past states of nature existing during the constantly changing and somewhat random history uncovered by environmental historians and paleoecologists, (2) the many other possible natures that could have existed at previous points in time given different random accidents of environmental history, and (3) the many future natures that might yet exist as the result of human- and non-human-induced change. Which of these many natures do we choose to be the one nature that defines the environmental conditions and processes that serve as goals of restoration? Which of these many natures is best? Constructs such as naturalness, health, and integrity, as well as many other forms of environmental knowledge and value, are used to help answer these questions and, for this reason, have significant influence on efforts to restore and manage nature.

How we think and talk about nature determines which nature we select as the goal of restoration projects. If we operationalize constructs such as naturalness, health, and integrity by imposing preferences for a dehumanized nature or for the nature existing immediately preceding European settlement, then we have unnecessarily restricted the number of possible natures that can be considered. Open and direct discussions about humanity's relationship with and responsibility for environmental quality have never been more critical. Many states of nature can have naturalness, health, and integrity; we should consider them all when negotiating which nature we want to live in and with.

Toward a More Public Ecology

Contemporary understandings of ecology and science suggest to us that a value-free definition of environmental quality cannot be determined by objective criteria from nature or from science as the study of nature; thus human values and preferences will necessarily be paramount. Obviously, these values and preferences cannot be judged as objectively right or wrong by comparison with some external or scientific criteria; rather, these values and preferences are competing visions and justifications for which nature should exist. In this open-for-negotiation context, this tournament of values, stakeholders need environmental knowledge that will facilitate their deliberations of possible and desirable future natures. In this section, we argue that a more public ecology—a body of environmental knowledge that is normative, contextual, multiscalar, integrative, adaptive, and accessible—is necessary for negotiating "which nature?" Adapting ideas presented in the literature on environmental knowledge, we outline below our recommendations for how each of these qualities might be applied in making more effective restoration and management decisions.

Recognize That All Environmental Knowledge Is Normative

This chapter, as well as other chapters in this book, illustrates the inevitable value-ladenness of environmental knowledge. If we are motivated (by moral, aesthetic, or ethical reasons) to protect and restore nature for nature's sake, we might attempt to develop a knowledge base that includes normative ideas such as naturalness, health, and integrity. This is evident in the constructs advanced by the paradigms of conservation biology and restoration ecology as well as in the biocentric and ecocentric ethics of environmental philosophy. Likewise, if social preferences and market values motivate us to protect and restore nature, we will develop a knowledge base that includes concepts such as sustained yield and risk to human health. This tendency is displayed by the paradigms of ecological economics and risk assessment, and within product-oriented ecological fields such as silviculture and game-species wildlife management. Recognition and acceptance of this normative aspect of environmental knowledge is a prerequisite to achieving a more public ecology.

Construct Context-Specific Knowledge

While environmental quality may be conceptualized in the abstract (as naturalness, health, or integrity), the specific goals and objectives of restoration must be determined in the context of the place-based projects to which they apply (Shrader-Frechette 1995, Shrader-Frechette and McCoy 1993, 1994). All restoration projects are unique in that both the people involved and the places where the projects occur are unique. If environmental knowledge is to have utility in environmental decision making, it must be particular to both the people using it and the places where it is used. In ecology, universal theory is nonexistent (Sagoff 1988); there are no generalized, mathematical models of ecosystem structure and process to tell us what nature looks like and how it works in real places. Therefore, the restoration and management of nature requires knowledge that is constructed in the context of the specific places involved, as well as knowledge reflecting more generalizable ecological theory (McNeely 1992, McNeely and Pitt 1985, Pimbert and Pretty 1997). In addition, stakeholders in the process should include local people, but may also include stakeholders at the regional, national, or even international levels when restoration and management decisions affect these broader communities of interest (e.g., Greater Yellowstone Ecosystem or the Chesapeake Bay Watershed).

Knowledge Must Apply at Multiple Scales

Scale is an essential and confounding issue when constructing and applying environmental knowledge. As mentioned above, scale is understood in three dimensions: spatial, temporal, and organizational. The decision about what scale to manage is not a given but must be negotiated, and the scale that is selected will influence the desired outcomes of the project. Environmental knowledge will be most useful if it reflects scales that are relevant to specific management cases. Ecological research has tended to focus on ecological factors influencing selected species over brief time horizons (years) and small sites while ignoring the ecological factors influencing less interesting species, longer time horizons (decades), and large, politically fragmented landscapes (Norton 1998, Pimm 1991). Studies conducted at larger spatial scales and longer time frames are often too general or lack sufficient detail to support decision making in land management. Thus, management decisions require information not only about the site at hand, but also about trade-offs among many potential species, located at multiple sites, over decades of periodic anthropogenic disturbances.

Integrate Knowledge Across Disciplines, Professions, and Scales

Informed environmental decision making requires the multiscalar integration of a vast array of environmental knowledge across disciplines and a diverse public. This integration is often hindered because environmental knowledge is collected, produced, and interpreted by multiple language communities (subgroups of natural scientists, social scientists, humanities scholars, environmental professionals, and citizen activists) using incompatible units of analysis. If this mixed bag of environmental knowledge is to be managerially relevant, the units of analysis in one discipline (area of inquiry) must be compatible with those of others. If environmental research is to serve environmental management, the units of analysis need to be made compatible from one study to the next regardless of the specific discipline.

Norton (1991, 1995, 1998) has consistently argued these points and has developed a place-based approach to environmental knowledge and decision making. He contends that specific places exist in the context of multiple hierarchical scales (spatial and temporal) and that for information to be meaningful and useful, it must permit aggregation or disaggregation from one scale to the next as management issues are reconceptualized according to different boundaries of space and time. He suggests that we consider management goals and outcomes from a place (home)-based perspective that looks outward to consider progressively larger scales of space and time. Norton and Hannon (1997) offer a triscalar theory that identifies three spatial scales of environmental valuation: local, community, and global. And, following Leopold, Norton (1995, 238) defines three time horizons particularly relevant to management decisions: "individual, experiential time [as experienced by the human body]; ecological time; and geological, evolutionary time." Recognition of these expansive scales of space and time is essential for meaningful discussions about sustainability and the goal of sustaining ecosystems in situations where individuals are asked to think beyond their immediate and local self-interest.

A body of environmental knowledge that is contextual, multiscalar, and integrative will be difficult to achieve, and we should not expect that it will be perfect or complete. Our knowledge of the environment will always be partial and limited. Therefore, a more public ecology must also be adaptive and capable of learning by doing.

Promote Learning with a Knowledge Base That Can Adapt

Adaptive management has been promoted as a flexible and self-conscious process of management whereby practitioners of environmental management learn about the nature of the place for which they are responsible through well-intentioned and systematic trial and error. Under a paradigm of adaptive management, landscapes become laboratories for cautious experimentation. The lessons learned through adaptive management will be documented and advanced through case studies of specific projects and places. This inductive approach to ecological knowledge will allow for the conceptualizations of places, projects, and problems to evolve as new knowledge of each is acquired. [There is a loosely organized but expansive body of literature in the field of adaptive management (Walters 1986, Walters and Holling 1990)].

Knowledge Must Be Accessible to Diverse Stakeholders

A public ecology is also about creating a language that is accessible enough to support both broad participation and meaningful deliberation in environmental decision making. Language is essential to any negotiation, and if participants are to influence the goals and outcomes of management, they will need to communicate effectively with other participants. Effective communication demands a solid understanding of what values, norms, terminologies, and methods are acceptable or unacceptable to oneself and to others. This is one of the most serious challenges that a more public ecology will face. We need to develop a language that facilitates effective communication among diverse participants, a language that is sufficiently precise to allow scientific study and sufficiently accessible to encourage broad participation (Norton 1998).

This language needs to develop in several dimensions. First, the constructs used to study and manage nature need to be explicit. As we have argued above, negotiation will be improved if the values behind these constructs are made explicit, as opposed to implicit or concealed by ambiguous or scientized terms. Second, just as terminology should not be allowed to conceal values, it should not be allowed to conceal scientific uncertainty. Terminology should include information about the uncertainty and variability inherent in any attempt to describe, predict, or understand ecological systems.

Poorly constructed terms are a problem because agreement is superficial and confusion results if people using the same term mean different things or nothing at all. Likewise, and perhaps more sinister, the constructive negotiation of goals, objectives, and outcomes is undermined if terms that conceal values or uncertainty are used (intentionally or unwittingly) to deflect and confuse a dialogue about values by making it appear to be a strictly technical or scientific issue. Most critically, we believe that the will to participate in the negotiation is stifled when stakeholders do not have a meaningful language to use to engage in productive dialogue. Scientists, nonscientists, and other contributors to environmental knowledge need to know the intentions behind the concepts being used to set environmental policy so that they can develop the trust needed to implement that policy. Helford (this volume) notes that some critics of the restoration efforts in Chicago argued that poorly defined terms gave restorationists room to make mistakes and conceal true motives.

A meaningful language of a more public ecology must reference visible features of the landscape. Participants must be able to see and evaluate environmental quality if they are to judge whether they are making progress toward their desired future conditions. Nassauer (1988, 1992, 1995, 1997) has written extensively on this topic. The visual landscape is a powerful communications tool that can educate people about ecology and land stewardship. People learn from what they see. Constructs used to evaluate environmental quality should be visible and interpretable by stakeholders. Instead of hiding ecological processes behind buffer strips, land management should lay open, display, and exhibit ongoing ecological processes and the benefits of management. Such an aesthetic would help promote an ecologically literate public, which is critical for planning an environmentally sustainable future: "If we can see that the landscape is not healthy, we might do something about it. . . . But we are unlikely to do that if we can't see it" (Nassauer 1992, 240).

Finally, a more public ecology will bridge the gap between science and policy. A more public ecology not only will exist at the interface of science and policy, but also will function as a joint product of these sometimes disparate realms. The language of a more public ecology will facilitate the flow of ideas and information in both directions, from one side to the other and back again. Constructing this bridge is the responsibility of both science and policy (Norton 1998).

Conclusion

Environmental decision making is a tournament of competing conservation agendas in which some values and beliefs are held up and exalted, others are dismissed and ignored, and still others are left implicit and unnoticed. Stakeholders compete in the tournament to advance their value systems through the science they advocate or practice, through the definitions of environmental quality they use or study, and through the management goals they champion. It is our contention that participants who hope to compete successfully in this tournament of values should understand the rules of the game, which includes understanding the language used to discuss and describe nature. In particular, participants should understand that the terms used to describe ecological conditions are value-laden.

Perusing the editorials in professional environmental science journals, one frequently encounters the lament that the public is ignoring "our science": "If only we could educate the public, they would agree that we know what is best." In this chapter we have argued that "what is best" is negotiable; neither science nor nature provides value-free directives for management, and many people are equally well qualified to participate in the negotiation about values.

We contend that ecological scientists, professional environmental managers, and involved citizens are all stakeholders with an essential role to play in developing a body of managerially relevant environmental knowledge. This more public ecology will draw on established ecological theory and existing environmental policy and ultimately must fit within that context. A more public ecology will be a more powerful ecology. It will facilitate the negotiation and construction of restoration and management goals. It will help make ecological science relevant to ecological management. It will level the playing field in the tournament of values so that participants have a better command of the rules of the game and a clear vision of what it means to succeed. It will get stalled projects out of the courts and into adaptive management, where active and well-intentioned stewardship can be practiced and valuable lessons learned sooner rather than later. Ultimately, the trials and tribulations of restoration and management projects boil down to a debate about which nature we want and why. We hope that this chapter, with its focus on ecological definitions of environmental quality and its vision of a more public ecology, will improve the quality of this debate.

Acknowledgments

We are grateful for cooperative research agreements with the North Central Research Station, which provided support for the authors to do several projects during which time this manuscript was also produced. We would also like to acknowledge Paul Angermeier and Joe Roggenbuck for constructive reviews of earlier versions of this chapter.

References

Anderson, J. E. 1991. "A Conceptual Framework for Evaluating and Quantifying Naturalness." *Biological Conservation* 5: 347–352.

Angermeier, P. L. 2000. "The Natural Imperative for Biological Conservation." *Biological Conservation* 14(2): 373–381.

Angermeier, P. L., and J. R. Karr. 1994. "Biological Integrity versus Biological Diversity as Policy Directives." *BioScience* 44(10): 690–697.

Bocking, S. 1994. "Visions of Nature and Society: A History of the Ecosystem Concept." *Alternatives* 20(3): 12–18.

Botkin, D. 1990. *Discordant Harmonies.* London: Oxford University Press.

Brubaker, L. B. 1988. "Vegetation History and Anticipating Future Vegetation Change." In *Ecosystem Management for Parks and Wilderness,* edited by J. K. Agee, 41–61. Seattle: University of Washington Press.

Bryant, R. L., and G. A. Wilson. 1998. "Rethinking Environmental Management." *Progress in Human Geography* 22(3): 321–343.

Callicott, J. B. 1992. "Aldo Leopold's Metaphor." In *Ecosystem Health: New Goals for Environmental Management,* edited by B. G. Norton, R. Costanza, and B. D. Haskell, 42–56. Washington, DC: Island Press.

Callicott, J. B. 1996. "Do Deconstructive Ecology and Sociobiology Undermine Leopold's Land Ethic?" *Environmental Ethics* 18(4): 353–372.

Callicott, J. B., and M. P. Nelson, eds. 1998. *The Great New Wilderness Debate.* Athens: University of Georgia Press.

Chase, A. 1995. *In a Dark Wood.* Boston: Houghton Mifflin.

Costanza, R. 1995. "Ecological and Economic System Health and Social Decision Making." In *Evaluating and Monitoring the Health of Large-Scale Ecosystems,* edited by D. J. Rapport, C. L. Gaudet, and P. Calow, 103–125. Berlin: Springer-Verlag.

Cronon, W., ed. 1995. *Uncommon Ground.* New York: W. W. Norton.

Crossley, J. W. 1996. "Managing Ecosystems for Integrity: Theoretical Considerations for Resource Managers." *Society and Natural Resources* 9: 465–481.

Crumley, C. L., ed. 1994. *Historical Ecology: Cultural Knowledge and Changing Landscapes.* Santa Fe: School of American Research.

Denevan, W. M. 1992. "The Pristine Myth: The Landscape of the Americas in 1492." *Annals of the Association of American Geographers* 82(3): 369–385.

Eden, S. 1996. "Public Participation in Environmental Policy: Considering Scientific, Counter-scientific and Non-scientific contributions." *Public Understanding of Science* 5: 183–204.

Ehrenfeld, D. 1981. *The Arrogance of Humanism.* London: Oxford University Press.

Escobar, A. 1999. "After Nature: Steps to an Antiessentialist Political Ecology." *Current Anthropology* 40(1): 1–30.

Evernden, N. 1992. *The Social Creation of Nature.* Baltimore: Johns Hopkins University Press.

Gould, S. 1980. *The Panda's Thumb: More Reflections in Natural History* New York: W. W. Norton.

Haydon, R. 1997. "A Look at How We Look at What Is 'Natural.'" *Natural Area News* October.

Ickovics, J. R., and C. L. Park. 1998. "Paradigm Shift: Why a Focus on Health Is Important." *Journal of Social Issues* 54: 237–244.

Lele, S., and R. B. Norgaard. 1996. "Sustainability and the Scientist's Burden." *Conservation Biology* 10(2): 354–365.

Levin, S. A. 1992. "The Problem of Pattern and Scale in Ecology." *Ecology* 73(6): 1943–1967.

Lewis, M. W. 1992. "Technophobia and Its Discontents." In *Green Delusions: An Environmentalist Critique of Radical Environmentalism,* 117–140. Durham, NC: Duke University Press.

MacLeish, W. H. 1994. *The Day Before America.* Boston: Houghton Mifflin.

McKibben, B. 1989. *The End of Nature.* New York: Anchor Books.

McNeely, J. 1992. "Nature and Culture: Conservation Needs Them Both." *Nature and Resources* 28(3): 37–43.

McNeely, J., and D. Pitt, eds. 1985. *The Human Dimension in Environmental Planning.* London: Croon Helm.

Nassauer, J. I. 1988. "The Aesthetics of Horticulture: Neatness as a Form of Care." *HortScience* 23(6): 973–976.

Nassauer, J. I. 1992. "The Appearance of Ecological Systems as a Matter of Policy." *Landscape Ecology* 6(4): 239–250.

Nassauer, J. I. 1995. "Messy Ecosystems, Orderly Frames." *Landscape Journal* 14(2): 161–170.

Nassauer, J. I. 1997. "Cultural Sustainability: Aligning Aesthetics and Ecology." In *Placing Nature: Culture and Landscape Ecology,* edited by J. I. Nassauer, 65–83. Washington, DC: Island Press.

Norton, B. G. 1991. *Toward Unity among Environmentalists.* New York: Oxford University Press.

Norton, B. G. 1995. "Ecological Integrity and Social Values: At What Scale?" *Ecosystem Health* 1(4): 228–241.

Norton, B. G. 1998. "Improving Ecological Communication: The Role of Ecologists in Environmental Policy Formation." *Ecological Applications* 8(2): 350–364.

Norton, B. G., and B. Hannon. 1997. "Environmental Values: A Place-based Theory." *Environmental Ethics* 19(3): 227–245.

O'Brien, M. H. 1993. "Being a Scientist Means Taking Sides." *BioScience* 43: 706–708.

Oelschlaeger, M. 1991. *The Idea of Wilderness: From Prehistory to the Age of Ecology.* New Haven, CT: Yale University Press.

Peterson, T. R. 1997. *Sharing the Earth: The Rhetoric of Sustainable Development.* Columbia: University of South Carolina Press.

Pickett, S. T. A., V. T. Parker, and P. L. Fiedler. 1992. "The New Paradigm in Ecology: Implications for Conservation Biology above the Species Level." In *Conservation Biology,* edited by P. L. Fiedler and S. K. Jain, 65–88. New York: Chapman and Hall.

Pimbert, M. P., and J. N. Pretty. 1997. "Parks, People, and Professionals: Putting 'Participation' into Protected Areas Management." In *Social Change and Conservation,* edited by K. B. Ghimire and M. P. Pimbert, 297–330. London: Earthscan.

Pimm, S. L. 1991. *The Balance of Nature? Ecological Issues in the Conservation of Species and Communities.* Chicago: University of Chicago Press.

Proctor, J. 1995. "Whose Nature?" In *Uncommon Ground,* edited by W. Cronon, 269–297. New York: W. W. Norton.

Rapport, D. J., C. Gaudet, J. R. Karr, J. S. Baron, C. Bohlen, W. Jackson, B. Jones, R. J. Naiman, B. Norton, and M. M. Pollock. 1998. "Evaluating Landscape Health: Integrating Goals and Biophysical Process." *Journal of Environmental Management* 53: 1–15.

Regier, H. 1993. "The Notion of Natural and Cultural Integrity." In *Ecological Integrity and the Management of Ecosystems,* edited by S. Woodley, J. Kay, and G. Francis, 3–18. Delray Beach, FL: St. Lucie Press.

Ross, N., J. Eyles, D. Cole, and A. Iannantuono. 1997. "The Ecosystem Health Metaphor in Science and Policy." *The Canadian Geographer* 41(2): 114–127.

Sagoff, M. 1988. "Ethics, Ecology, and the Environment: Integrating Science and Law." *Tennessee Law Review* 56: 77–229.

Schulze, P., ed. 1996. *Engineering within Ecological Constraints.* Washington, DC: National Academy Press.

Shrader-Frechette, K. 1995. "Hard Ecology, Soft Ecology, and Ecosystem Integrity." In *Perspectives on Ecological Integrity,* edited by L. Westra and J. Lemons, 125–145. Dordrecht, The Netherlands: Kluwer Academic Publishers.

Shrader-Frechette, K., and E. D. McCoy. 1993. *Method in Ecology: Strategies for Conservation.* New York: Cambridge University Press.

Shrader-Frechette, K., and E. D. McCoy. 1994. "Applied Ecology and the Logic of Case Studies." *Philosophy of Science* 61: 228–249.

Shrader-Frechette, K. S., and E. D. McCoy. 1995. "Natural Landscapes, Natural Communities, and Natural Ecosystems." *Forest and Conservation History* 39(3): 138–142.

Simmon, J. 1981. *The Ultimate Resource.* Princeton, NJ: Princeton University Press.

Snyder, G. 1990. *The Practice of the Wild.* New York: North Point Press.

Soper, K. 1995. *What Is Nature?* Cambridge, England: Blackwell.

Soule, M. E., and G. Lease. 1995. *Reinventing Nature: Responses to Postmodern Deconstruction.* Washington, DC: Island Press.

Suter, G. W. 1993. "A Critique of Ecosystem Health Concepts and Indexes." *Environmental Toxicology and Chemistry* 12: 1533–1539.

Takacs, D. 1996. *The Idea of Biodiversity: Philosophies of Paradise.* Baltimore: Johns Hopkins University Press.

Walters, C. J. 1986. *Adaptive Management of Renewable Resources.* New York: Macmillan.

Walters, C. J., and C. S. Holling. 1990. "Large-scale Management Experiments and Learning by Doing." *Ecology* 71: 2060–2068.

Westra, L., and J. Lemons. 1995. *Perspectives on Ecological Integrity.* Dordrecht, The Netherlands: Kluwer Academic Publishers.

Wicklum, D., and R. W. Davies. 1995. "Ecosystem Health and Integrity?" *Canadian Journal of Botany* 73: 997–1000.

Wiener, J. B. 1996. "Beyond the Balance of Nature." *Duke Environmental Law and Policy Forum* 7(1): 1–24.

Williams, R. 1976. *Keywords: A Vocabulary of Culture and Society.* New York: Oxford University Press.

Williams, R. 1980. "Ideas of Nature." In *Problems in Materialism and Culture,* edited by R. Williams, 67–85. London: NLB.

Worster, D. 1994. *Nature's Economy: A History of Ecological Ideas.* New York: Cambridge University Press.

Wright, P. G., M. P. Murray, and T. Merrill. 1998. "Ecoregions as a Level of Ecological Analysis." *Biological Conservation* 86: 207–213.

Zimmerer, K. S. 1994. "Human Geography and the 'New Ecology': The Prospect and Promise of Integration." *Annals of the Association of American Geographers* 84(1): 108–125.

❧ Chapter 6 ❧

CONSTRUCTING NATURE AS CONSTRUCTING SCIENCE: EXPERTISE, ACTIVIST SCIENCE, AND PUBLIC CONFLICT IN THE CHICAGO WILDERNESS

Reid M. Helford

In April 1996 an exciting new project was announced, an unprecedented conservation undertaking in one of the nation's most densely populated regions. Chicago Wilderness is a collaborative effort among the more than 90 organizations that make up the Chicago Region Biodiversity Council (CRBC) to protect, restore, and manage the region's natural landscapes while educating the public about the value of these lands and management activities. A central goal of Chicago Wilderness is the ecological restoration of landscapes that are considered degraded and no longer representative of their biodiverse, pre-European-settlement condition. The Volunteer Stewardship Network (VSN), working under The Nature Conservancy (TNC), a key member of the CRBC, has been actively restoring these "degraded," "overgrown" landscapes to prairies and open woodlands for as many as twenty years at some sites.

About a week before the official public announcement of the Chicago Wilderness project, a suburban resident of Cook County wrote a letter to her county commissioner expressing concerns with the limitations of the CRBC, which sought to coordinate the region's natural land management.

... I have no objections to the purported purposes of the Biodiversity Council but I do have serious concerns about the apparent exclusionary nature of its membership policy. If the purpose of this organization is to share information in order to coordinate land and wildlife management throughout the area, then it would appear that the broadest possible sphere of experience would be desirable. If, however, the purpose of the organization is to amass a number of organizations, all of whom share one limited vision of land and wildlife management and to exclude those organizations which do not share that viewpoint, then the "Biodiversity Council" could be fairly characterized as a *political action committee* [emphasis in original].[1]

Already, before it had officially begun, the CRBC was facing demands that it listen to alternative views on nature and its management. The land management activities of this coalition were now cast as more complex than just "efficiently saving nature" or "restoring ecosystems." Nature was being defined, ordered, and controlled. That, in part, is the work of conservation. The problem is, not everyone agrees on what needs to be counted or controlled. Even the naming of nature, like the simple act of identifying native and nonnative plants or defining community types, is potentially controversial. Chicago-area conservationists know this. The CRBC *is* a political action committee—a committee organized to establish the region's way of seeing, knowing, and living with its nature.

The letter writer was not alone in her sentiments. When the Chicago City Council called a hearing to review restoration practices, some members of the public expressed anger and confusion that trees were being cut down by "so-called experts" in the name of conservation. As the controversy grew, the matter was referred to the forest preserve board of Cook County, which alone includes more than one-third of the Chicago Wilderness lands. After a noisy public hearing, the board declared a moratorium on all restoration activities until the matter could be investigated. Thus, only a few months after the announcement of Chicago Wilderness, all restoration activities in Cook County were halted.

The moratorium meant an almost complete shutdown of the VSN and was a major setback for TNC and the other members of the CRBC. Meanwhile, new tree-protecting citizens groups had been organized to oppose Chicago Wilderness, and old opposition groups such as animal rights organizations, which opposed the killing of deer by land managers, had contributed their voices to the growing debate.

While the moratorium has now been largely lifted, a few sites still remain closed to restoration activity, and the controversy continues. As I write this, a federal NEPA lawsuit and two Freedom of Information Act (FOIA) suits hang over the Forest Preserve District of Cook County (FPDCC), and a prominent Chicago newspaper columnist continues to publicly attack the concepts and practices of restoration. One group, Trees for Life, now boasts more than a hundred members and prints its own T-shirts and monthly newsletters. These critics of restoration can be found at Cook County Forest Preserve Board meetings, public hearings, and even restoration sites, wearing shirts boldly emblazoned "I am a tree hugger," reminding restorationists that the "saving of nature" is a politically complex idea indeed. This chapter examines that complexity.

The Constructivist Perspective

To understand the Chicago-area controversy over ecological restoration, one must, at least temporarily, suspend judgment on the value of restoration work. Unfortunately, many restorationists and restoration supporters, some of whom are journalists and scientists, have already decided that restoration is the answer for natural lands management and have come to understand the opposition as misguided, overly emotional, uneducated, unscientific, and NIMBYist. In the process, relatively little has been learned about the critics and their concerns.[2] Restoration groups continue to defend their work while failing to understand how anyone faced with the "evidence" could not see the natural world as they do.

Symmetry and Constructivist Inquiry

How can we gain sociological insight into the views of people who think nature should be allowed to take its course when most conservationists are committed to its active management? One answer is to explore the debate symmetrically (Bloor 1976). This perspective lets us see personal and political motivations on both sides of the debate, not just science on one and emotion or politics on the other. It is an approach that asks us to suspend the everyday assumptions we use to make sense of the world. Its outcome is an account of familiar places and practices that lets us be strangers again—to see ourselves and our work reflexively. I think such "sociological strangers" (Schutz 1964) are needed in Chicago's restoration community.

Symmetry of analysis is one of the cornerstones of constructivist inquiry. It means, in the case of the Chicago restoration controversy, that I subject both restorationists and critics of restoration to the same analyses. I make no assumptions as to who is expert and who is not. I do not assume I know what is best for a healthy ecosystem and what is not. I, like a stranger to conservation science and an outsider to the local practices of restoration, explore the conflict without use of the assumptions that frame conflict participants' views of nature, each other, and their own actions in the world.

Relativism and the Social Construction of Nature

Because I am not guided by conflict participants' distinctions between expert/nonexpert or healthy/unhealthy ecosystems, for example, I leave open the possibility that many conceptualizations may be equally valid. Further, I assume that the criteria used to judge the validity of these concepts are flexible, socially contingent, and political in character. Relativism is the aspect of constructivist research that offends many social scientists, natural scientists, and environmentalists. Many of the restorationists in my study who came to understand my research approach found it necessary to demonstrate to me their firm understanding of "nature" and to cite the institutional and scientific research support for their views in order for our discussions to proceed. For these respondents, nature was not something to be socially constructed, and they believed my relativism would lead to some strange ideas about nature.

> You can't have compromise on what nature is in northeastern Illinois. I think that's really the bottom line. We talk about restoration, that's a human concept. We talk about "let nature takes its course," that's a human concept. The natural community in this area is independent and above all that. It is what it is. That's not something we can change by talking about or by agreeing that "Well, yeah, we'll agree that in this case we're gonna compromise, nature is something different here." You can't do that because it is what it is!

There is a fear, as demonstrated in the restorationist's comments above and echoed by many critics, that such a perspective might oversocialize nature and leave nothing "real" to fight for, protect, or restore. For me, however, the value of the constructivist approach does not lie in its ability to posit the historically and socially contingent character of nature. Yes, nature is socially constructed, but the power of analyses informed by this commitment is their ability to reveal the social processes surrounding these constructions—the processes that form the social relationships that simultaneously result from and maintain these social constructions of nature. From this perspective, the social construction of nature is the construction of social structure.

Making nature is inevitably the making of social relationships. And this is why land managers, volunteer restorationists, and ecologists, to name a few, might want to listen to what social scientists have to say about nature, conservation practice, and, in particular, public conflict over these natures and practices. A constructivist analysis of the Chicago controversy will place upon conservationists a large part of the responsibility for the social relationships formed through their discovery, definition, and restoration of the region's nature. In the Chicago-area conflict, it is these social relationships that need to be attended to as part of the scientific practices of saving and restoring nature.

Expertise and the Public Understanding of Science

In this analysis, I concentrate on the social relationships and processes that I call expertise—the practices that define who will properly see nature, whose experience of nature will count, and what tools will best reveal nature's true disposition. We often see these practices as just science, but they are important political activities to be explored sociologically. These expert practices do not work in just one direction—from credentialed authority to the public. As the case of the Chicago controversy will show, expert practices are an interdependent process of negotiation, however contentious, that involves the critical lay public as unequal partner in the erection of the changing boundaries (Gieryn 1983, 1994) separating expert from nonexpert, science from politics, and healthy nature from unhealthy nature.

While concern with experts has long been an important focus of sociology, the growth of constructivist perspectives has renewed interest in exploring the means and practices by which expertise is maintained and the ways in which expert knowledges are produced and consumed. Attention to these issues from scientific experts and their institutions has also been renewed as concern about the public's lack of understanding of basic scientific knowledge has grown. This interest on the part of the scientific community is often predicated on the belief that the public is unable, or unwilling, to incorporate these scientific knowledges into its understandings of the world (Wolpert 1992). Assuming this failure on the part of the public, such scientists have called for better means of reaching and educating the layperson. Indeed, several restorationists spoke to me of the importance of the Chicago Wilderness project as a means to "educate" the "average citizen" about the importance and peril of the local forest preserves. As the controversy grew, calls for public outreach and education also grew.

In contrast to this deficit model of the public, several sociologists of science (Irwin 1995, Irwin and Wynne 1996) have pursued study of the Public Understanding of Science (PUS) informed by a constructivist perspective that assumes the public does understand science and the natural world in complex ways. Constructivist studies, as I have noted earlier in the discussion of symmetric analysis, try not to hold a priori assumptions as to what is real or proper scientific knowledge. This sociological approach problematizes both the public's understanding and valid scientific knowledge. It is a symmetric view of expertise. PUS studies reconstitute the public as a complex group of actors who interact with and judge scientific knowledges based on social factors—

factors broader than those assumed by the scientific community they come in contact with. The public may indeed need to be educated, but PUS studies remind us of the political meaning of such education.

It is the above understandings that I took with me into the field as I explored the restoration controversy ethnographically. I have spent two years as an ethnographer, videographer, and participant–observer in both camps of the debate. During this time, I volunteered many Saturday and Sunday mornings clearing buckthorn, pulling garlic mustard, spreading seed, and lopping brush as a VSN volunteer. I conducted in-depth interviews with twenty-two restorationists, eleven critics, and three individuals who considered themselves neutral. Most of the interviewees were open and honest and wanted to share with me their deeply held beliefs and experiences as players in the controversy. Some respondents were careful, almost calculated, in their discussions and attempted to enroll me as an ally. Others seemed to deliberately mislead me or avoid certain topics altogether. A few respondents refused to participate because they believed that their personal and professional lives might be too greatly affected by my use of their words, even if they were granted anonymity. It has been a difficult period for all of us, as we formed relationships in which I was frequently reminded of the responsibility I had in the future (re)presentation of my informants' words.

> My concerns are, first of all, that you look kind of like a restorationist. [laughs] That's really silly. It's true. The first time I met you, you were sitting with the restorationists. You did a very disruptive interview behind me during the meeting, which you should not have done. So you are a bad person. [laughs] . . . My concern is where you're getting your money from, because the Forest Service has given a huge grant to [the FPDCC]. They have a lot at stake to make the program look good, for better or worse. I'm also afraid of being misquoted because they misquote us all the time. . . . I was not going to do this because I have these concerns. . . .

Trust, what some define as the basis of good ethnographic work, was not something I comfortably had. As the research progressed and participants on both sides developed personal views of what they thought I was about, I found the restorationists to be somewhat more careful and distant in our relations, while the critics became more trusting and some even began to count me among their own.[3] This made the research more difficult because I had to negotiate a public appearance that would not project an alliance with the critics. It is a balancing act I continue today as I speak, write, and edit video presentations about my experiences, while trying to maintain many of the relationships formed during the research.

Asserting Expertise: Defining the Community of Experts and Nonexperts

This research is about social–political processes, not values. The Chicago restoration controversy is not simply a clash of values but a struggle over the social relationships that form the contexts in which these values are created and used. These social relations, not value orientations per se, are, in my view, the more important focus for sociological understandings of the conflict. Where many see value conflicts, conflicts about what nature is and should be in the county forest preserves, I see a particular sensitivity on the part of the critical public to its experiences of being on the consumptive end of expert practices. The critics have a keen awareness of the position they hold within the social structures that result from, and form the context of, local conservation practice.

> . . . I got angry and I stood up and when I was finally called on I said, "What's so special about prairies?!" [laughs] The young man next to me said, "Shut up and sit down! You don't know what you're talking about!" Well, that galvanized me! Nobody tells me to shut up and sit down. I am a citizen. I have a right to say what I feel. . . . I do not think the public is as stupid as [the FPDCC] think. At least they like to tell us we're stupid and don't know what we're talking about, which is what got me into this. . . . They feel that the public is too dumb to understand how great this is.

The initial controversy may have begun over different visions for the future of the forest preserves near critics' homes: a preference for dense woodlands over more open savannas or, perhaps, the critics' philosophical commitment to "nature knows best." However, it has grown into a conflict over the processes of negotiating nature and science in Cook County.

"How are these amateurs experts?! They have no formal training or credentials!" reads a small leaflet pinned to a display at a Trees for Life meeting. It is the same question asked about volunteer restorationists at an earlier time by the scientific-academic community. During that painful growth period, when the VSN attempted to establish themselves as expert "knowers" of the land, criticism was focused on just what made these lay volunteers favored members of the public who could create privileged stories about the local landscape's condition and needs (Helford 1999). Restorationists countered those arguments by claiming to have developed an intimate knowledge of the flora that made up the ecological communities of the region and a long-term relationship with the sites where they practiced restoration—the type of knowledge and relationship that few members of the academic ecology community or general public had achieved. While there is still some concern today within the scientific community over the place of volunteer restorationists, the harshest critiques now come from the lay public that has not embraced the grassroots recruitment efforts of their restorationist neighbors.

Defending themselves against these new lay critics, restorationists present impressive evidence of their scientific discoveries and examples of volunteers who have attained esoteric knowledge of nature. These stories attempt to demonstrate how the intimate relationships restorationists have with the landscape lead to a different yet more powerful expertise than that of the more formal scientist.

> I certainly think that one of the interesting stories that I remember, for example, was at the restoration in Madison. They wanted to check on how their seeding was going and they had to go and get Ms. A., who was doing some early work in restoration and growing native plants, to come to check to see how the seeding was going because none of the academics knew what the plants looked like as seedlings! That is a very real difficulty. If you're focused on something very narrow, you probably know how all of the different chemicals cause the plant to grow this way or grow that way or bloom, but you may not know what the plant looks like when all it has is cotyledons. So, there is a different relationship with the plants. . . . I think that's the real difference. The difference is that you can take a volunteer and the volunteer can actually go out and collect the seed and cut the buckthorn and pull the weeds. Whereas we don't need the Ph.D. doing that. . . . I think that's actually one of the additional pieces of expertise that the volunteers can now bring back to the whole scene.

Establishing this relationship as part of the expert practice of volunteer restoration meant that citizens who didn't venture out on workdays and spend time with the landscape, as regular VSN members did, could not be expert knowers of the land or be in a position to justifiably pass judgment on restoration science. In the words of one prominent restorationist:

> Just driving by in your car or riding the bike trails does not give you an understanding of these landscapes. They just don't know what is happening in here.

Restorationists' expertise appears to require weekend workdays and perhaps years of tending a site and learning to understand the complexities of these "recovering" ecosystems. It is the "getting inside the preserves" that many of the restorationists spoke of that separates a knower of nature from other limited and distant observers.

> That is, when you work with areas and you watch how plants respond to different treatments, y'know it's not scientific in the sense that we've taken detailed measurements and so forth, but you do see different responses in different species and responses to different kinds of management approaches. That's very valuable information.

One critic angrily told me of her

> 40 years of walking my dogs and taking my children in these woods. I can tell you when the trillium come up or how many more or less oak trees are here and which birds are declining. I know the woods. I have lived with these woods my whole life! Now these people come here and tell me I don't know what is going on in my forest preserve?!

Many of the critics shared with me similar concerns that their experience of the preserves didn't count for much. Yet their experiences were not restoration experiences. Most in the restoration community, while appreciative of the ways in which the critics have used and understood the preserves, do not recognize the critics' views as complete or necessarily useful when deciding the fate of the preserve's plants and animals. This seemingly simple point is critical for understanding the controversy.

Restoration is not simply the management activity required to recover the ecological health of a preserve; it is the ongoing development of an expertise based on a specific relationship to the land and the lay public. A volunteer cutting brush on Sunday morning doesn't see her work as establishing the boundaries of expertise for Chicago's community of expert knowers of nature. Few of us are ever forced to see the professional work we do as more than just the work itself. Yet the controversy brings these issues out clearly to the sociological observer. The everyday practice of restoration does establish for the restorationist an ideological framework for recognizing whose views of nature count and whose don't. None of the restorationists I spoke with saw this boundary work as part of their restoration activity. Some said "the political stuff" was done by others, usually leaders of the VSN or TNC, and wanted little to do with it. It was hard for them to see their work or their identity as restorationists as ideological. But for those outside the boundaries of expert or conservationist, it was a difficult political identity indeed. Many of the critics were painfully aware that these were "made" boundaries, boundaries they believed kept them from being participants in an important dialogue. Many critics took this exclusion as a personal attack, and believed that they were being judged without any real understanding of who they were.

> How do they know what my version of nature is? How do they know what books I've read, where I've been, where I have spent my entire life—which consists of the University of Illinois as an undergrad and also graduate school there at the U of I? What makes [someone] with a bachelor's degree better science than my science? My degree wasn't in biology, but why are his studies more accurate or more truthful than my science? Who's to say what is good . . . who can judge? How can you cast judgment on something when you don't know what my view of nature is?

In defending their privileged status, many volunteer restorationists employed traditional representations of expertise and authority. The members of the public are consumers, in this rhetoric, of what experts prepare for them.

> . . . I think it is important to remember that we do not manage our public lands by majority vote. We also don't manage the National Gallery of Art by majority vote, and we don't manage Cook County Hospital by majority vote. Why not—why don't we put every acquisition at the National Gallery up for public referendum, or every procedure used at Cook County Hospital up for a vote? We are not dumb or incompetent people, we can learn about art and medicine and natural resources, but we can't all be experts. I love trees, but I am not schooled in tree biology or plant pathology. So I rely on the expertise, judgment, and experience of professionals. I have heard professionals say that our forest preserves are degraded and ill, even if they may not look that way to our unschooled eyes. I heard them say we need to use a variety of treatments to assist our precious natural heritage back to health. Of course, we should ask our professional land managers to tell us why they make such a diagnosis. But I don't think it is fair for us to second-guess or denigrate them.

For many critics of restoration, second-guessing experts is considered a central component of appropriate and effective political practice, especially when dealing with environmental concerns. Several of the critics I interviewed had been active in political challenges against the use of DDT nearly thirty years before the restoration conflict. These critics wondered why activity deemed "heroic" back then was not respected now in the case of restoration. The land management agencies and their experts, argued the critics, must not only answer the public whose land they manage in trust, but also listen to and incorporate these public concerns. Many critics believed that public land use and management depended upon a set of social relationships under which the public was a nearly equal partner in the overall management of these lands. When these beliefs proved false, several critics angrily declared that the very meaning of the word public in the term "public land" was threatened as issues of land use were separated from management and policy by political boundaries of expertise.

Many critics responded to the restorationists' rhetoric of expertise by describing different credentials that they believed were necessary to be eligible to comment on the future of nature in these public preserves. Some of these responses confused me at first because they were not defining scientific credentials; rather, these critics valued credentials that were more explicitly moral or political in character. Having used the public preserves, or even just having had the potential to have used them, was all the expertise that critics required to participate in the dialogue about management of the forest preserves. Here critics drew a much broader boundary that required a different sort of intimacy than that described by restorationists. Most importantly, these credentials were not defined by any special knowledge or ability to produce truths about the preserves. Simply put, the preserves are public spaces, so the public should govern them. It is the everyday use of them that entitles one to be a credible and welcome participant in their management. The following quote is not atypical of the responses to my question, "So who is qualified to decide what is best for the preserves?"

> *Respondent:* It's our land. It was set aside initially to be protected and preserved. Probably 90 percent of the people in Chicago believe it's still being protected and preserved. They believe that when they have their union picnic out in Western Springs— that when they get there it's gonna look the same as it did last year. They're still gonna have a ball field, they're still gonna have a forest, they're still gonna have a river where the kids can go down and do what kids like to do. They really trusted their officials, unfortunately, that this area was going to be protected. They tell their children, as I did my children, "Don't pick the flowers, don't pull up the . . . don't disturb it—just enjoy it."
>
> *Interviewer:* So there aren't any credentials . . . just people who use it?
>
> *Respondent:* Yeah, it's our land!

It is interesting to consider these competing definitions of expertise and public involvement, especially when we take into account the specific history of the volunteer restorationist in Cook County. At one time it was these volunteers who challenged established authority in order to extend the value and meaning of their work beyond simple management activity to that of scientific authority (Helford 1999). Employing this rather conservative notion of expert authority belies the historical grassroots, "citizen–scientist" ethos of the volunteer restorationist. The ways in which these conservationists describe and defend their work have changed as they have grown in authority and gained new political associations within the region's conservation establishment.

Attempts at Educating a "Deficient" Public

In response to initial complaints, some restorationists took Trees for Life members on tours of the preserves and invited them out to workdays to educate and immerse them in the contexts that these restorationists saw as necessary to understand the preserves accurately. For restoration stewards, recently burned woodlands are beautiful sites, "finally opened up so that the native understory could return." For critics, they are "virtual wastelands where the soil is sterile and nothing but charred stumps remain." For one group it is an exciting and promising sight; for the other it is a sad and scary portent of the future of the FPDCC land. It was commitments to these quite different views of nature that led restorationists to call for greater public education. In addition, these experiences introduced the possibility to the restorationists that the critics had another, perhaps even sinister agenda because they couldn't be so stupid as to not "get it" after all the evidence of the value of restoration that they had been presented with.

> *Respondent A:* I think there is some other agenda that I'm not aware of that's going on. I know that there are people who have been taken out on trips and who have seen things and, I think, understand that a lot of what's going on is good and right, and they're still not budging.

> *Respondent B:* There's a political agenda. [laughs]

> *Respondent A:* Right. There's something else going on. I just know that there are people that I've taken out and shown what we're doing, and they get it. On the other hand, I've taken out people like [a Trees for Life board member] who are very intelligent, and she *could* get it, but . . .

> *Respondent B:* The other thing, actually, on the Community Advisory Council, there are three people there who have been exposed to all kinds of information, data, scientific studies—you name it, they've had it, had access to it. Yet they continue to make claims about what's happening that are simply foundationless.

Attempts to "educate" critics were often painful failures. Some VSN site stewards told me that they felt "stabbed in the back" by critics whom they'd taken to their sites to show what restorationists really did—only to find their words turned into propaganda meant to make restoration look unsuccessful, unscientific, and dangerous. Only a few of the restorationists I spoke with felt uncomfortable with the idea of "educating" the critics. Most felt that the basis of the whole controversy was an uneducated citizenry, yet few reflected on what it meant to educate. I often posed the question "Where is the line between education and indoctrination?" to both sides of the debate. Rarely did restorationists see their education work as ideological. It was science for most—facts and basic ecological truths. Critics, on the other hand, were quite sensitive to any attempt at education. One educator and naturalist who was critical of restoration told me he viewed attempts to educate the "unenlightened" critics as advocacy, "plain and simple."

> Then it becomes an educational problem: "People aren't educated." I like to read that. So that's why they send these [holding up restoration brochure] out to educate people. It's not an educational process. It's just not. So when somebody on either end of the spectrum says, "Well, what we have to do is educate people," that's their own demise too, because to educate people you have to educate yourself. To just say, "I am going to educate these people here" is such an ego trip. . . . As soon as you tell people you're gonna teach them something, it's advocacy.

Some restorationists saw the critics' failure to accept the scientific evidence of restoration's value as a sign that they rejected the scientific method altogether. Some portrayed the critics as people who couldn't distinguish between real flaws in one's understanding of nature and simple disagreements that happen along the way in the development of any good scientific theory or understanding. A few restorationists lumped critics in with other "anti-science" groups such as animal rights activists and creationists.

> This is the single issue that has troubled me more than anything else in the whole restoration controversy. My anger about it isn't about restoration per se, it's about the [critics'] abuse of science and the scientific process. This is not a legitimate scientific disagreement that we're having here. This is about people who want to sway opinions, sway policy, and they don't care about the facts. It's like the evolution debate. If you look at the type of evidence that was used in the evolution debate, every legitimate scientific disagreement was twisted to mean that evolution wasn't really true. They're arguing very much the way creationists argue against evolution.

In response, some critics tried to explain why more than just scientific information is needed to make decisions about the forest preserves.

> It is at the very nature of what science is. A true scientist understands the tenuous hold on truth that science has—that it is no better or worse than any other system of truth finding. In fact, science is much better off if they stay away from "truth" and try to stick to the facts. They also know that their facts change. It's the reliance on science as the only vehicle to find ultimate truth that allows something like [facts changing] to go on. . . . There are other values besides those of science. . . . People are attached to nature and have a broader view of nature than restorationists have.

Is It Science or a Social Movement?: The Complexities of an Activist Science

The critics' charges of advocacy as opposed to objective attempts at education lead us to another story about challenges to ecological restoration. It has to do with the dual identity of the VSN restorationist. Restorationists are not simply expert knowers of local nature preserves, nor are they just a collective of concerned citizens drawn from the grass roots. They are both. They scientifically define local ecological issues and educate the public about them, while at the same time they politically organize action to address the problems and physically attempt to solve them. Restorationists describe their work as urgent and warn of the dire consequences of losing plant and animal species forever. Restoration science can't look like other basic scientific research, they claim, because it must save nature at the same time it strives to study it. Its immediate goals are moral, according to restorationists. Nature is dying and we need to do something now to save it.

> I would say that science—that monitoring, the studying, the research—has always been very important, but given limited resources there's always a struggle between where do you devote your resources. And if you see the system going down the tubes, research is not going to save it in the short run. . . . I think the difficulty with not just restoration but conservation is [that] you're not gonna have all the questions answered, but you have to do something. You reach a point where you look at the land and you see everything dying and the soil washing away and you don't know everything at that point, but you know you have to do something.

The VSN is a social movement, and in this controversy it has proven difficult to present the politics of this movement as separate from the unbiased work of their science (see also Hull and Robertson in this volume). Critics are aware of this, and for some of them it is the most frightening aspect of the ecological restoration in Cook County. David Takacs (1996), in his book *The Idea of Biodiversity: Philosophies of Paradise,* describes the beauty and danger of this dual identity:

> Science is commonly thought of by the public and portrayed by its practitioners as an objective, cold, nonpartisan, value-neutral enterprise. Scientists discover facts, mediate truths about nature: on this image their prosperity is thought to ride. Yet a group of biologists have been as partisan as can be in their attempts to preserve biodiversity. . . . They weave sensuous word tapestries in books meant to seduce readers to love biodiversity and therefore join biologists in their attempts to sculpt the political, physical, and normative landscapes to its needs. They profess to be experts on an array of economic, ecological and even aesthetic and spiritual values of biodiversity that would seem to stretch the limits of what we normally consider to lie within scientists' expertise. Hence the tension: biologists jeopardize the societal trust that allows them to speak for nature in the first place (3–4).

The controversy has been difficult for many restorationists because they now see a separation of their ecological work from the politics of its promotion. Many have described to me their feelings of loss due to the controversy.

> It no longer has the purity it once had. I don't have the same joy in doing it that I used to. I have to think now before I cut a sapling and wonder if I am making a mistake or if someone is watching me.

A certain confidence in the rightness of their work has been damaged. I have been moved during interviews as I watched these restorationists pause, often looking down or holding their face in their hands, as they recount the experiences of the controversy that have forever tarnished the joy and simplicity of doing their restoration work. This sense of loss speaks to the importance of the concepts of purity and good science for the identity of restorationists as restoration activists.

> A lot of people got into this because they didn't like the political end of the environmental movement. I got so tired of the "pollution du jour." I've terminated my membership in a num-

ber of environmental organizations because of that, because of
bad science.

Restoration simply and purely serves the natural communities of the
FPDCC, restorationists argue. Critics, of course, see restoration work very differently. For them it is clearly a social movement, and they have had to confront it as such. The VSN's ability to mobilize hundreds of people to attend
public hearings and support its work stands out in the minds of many critics.
Claimed one critic when she tried to explain how the VSN outnumbered the
critics at public hearings by as much as six to one:

> They are a well-oiled machine. They've had twenty years to cre-
> ate this movement. . . . I was raised Catholic. I used to have to
> go to catechism class. "Who made us?" "God made us." "Eco-
> logical restoration facts." [reads pamphlet] "Why do some trees
> get cut or girdled during restoration?" Paragraph of a fact. This
> is so they can hand these out to all their stewards and [the stew-
> ards will] give the same reply. When I went to the hearings for
> the [FPDCC] I was amazed. . . . They all said the same thing
> because they had read their little fact sheet. . . . I'm not criti-
> cizing it that much, but the clear-cut way it's going to be a
> fact. . . . In that aspect there is an evangelicalism. It's a move-
> ment. It's a religion.

The possible danger of public mistrust of scientific authority that Takacs
(1996) warned about proved to be reality in the Chicago restoration controversy. The work of seamlessly blending science and ideology in the activist
restoration of the VSN no longer served to maintain the authority of restorationists in this debate as the seams began to split. The critics, in seeing restoration as an ideological movement based more on moral commitment than on
impartial scientific analysis, have pursued the scientific evidence with an eye
for the faddish, the misinterpretation of results, and the hiding of research
unbecoming to the goals of the VSN. It was noted earlier that some restorationists dismissed the critics' attacks on "legitimate scientific disagreements" as
anti-science. However, I think the critics' challenges are best understood as
reasonable responses to the unraveling of the two strands of the restoration
movement, strands that critics believe must be kept separate if truth about
nature is to be found. It is not an anti-science sentiment but a commitment to
a very traditional notion of science that informs the critics' exploration of
every disagreement or unclear finding.

> . . . what is going on in Chicago is going on at such a break-
> neck speed without careful evaluation of the feedback we're

getting on it. If it turns out to be something that the scientific community is going to agree maybe we shouldn't be pursuing, there's going to be a tremendous amount of damage done . . . and I heard the term zealots used . . . they feel as though Chicago is going too hard, too fast, and trying to do too much, without really putting in the necessary safeguards—the checks and balances. . . . The problem is . . . you come up with a theory, and then you need to be really objective enough to be able to alter your theory based on the results you're seeing.

Another critic of restoration added,

You come out against Chicago Wilderness right now and if you're a restoration manager, I think you can probably forget about getting another job. So they start talking about science? No, that's politics. They start talking about science? There's values.

Especially disconcerting for critics is the use of promotional literature and language to discuss the supposedly scientific work of ecological conservation and restoration. The work of TNC and the CRBC in promoting the Chicago Wilderness project and restoration involves the production of brochures, posters, magazines, and public events. Public and private funds must be obtained, individual contributions are courted, and new partners in the CRBC are solicited to maintain the work of Chicago Wilderness. It is a political and financial reality that this work must continue around the activities of the restorationists and land managers. For all of the restorationists I talked to, this work was easily separated from their work on the landscape, even though they may participate in both activities.

They were composing a publicity piece, and one of the species that was on the preserve we were promoting was called the prairie dandelion. Well, no one is going to get too excited about the conservation of a dandelion, even though this was a rare species. They changed the name to "prairie lion's tooth" to avoid it sounding like a weed. We just laughed about it. It doesn't really make a difference for anything.

Critics, however, do not make the distinction between the fund-raising and promotional efforts of the CRBC organizations and the scientific and management work of the VSN in Cook County. Brochures describing restoration work in terms designed to appeal to the general public appear as just public relations "spin" to critics, who see the two activities as inextricably connected in the restoration movement. Many critics believe that the "sugar-coated" descriptions of restoration work and its benefits are designed to hide what the public would consider abhorrent practices.

> I think there has been a concerted effort to spin this in a certain way without telling people the nuts and bolts of what is actually going on. For instance, it sounds wonderful to say, "We're going to restore these woodlands," and call things "degraded woodlands." Restoration doesn't sound like "We are going out to cut down 158 black cherry trees." . . . Most people wouldn't interpret that as that. So the people . . . the public needs to know, "This is what we're calling it, but here is how we are going to accomplish it. It includes girdling trees. It includes cutting trees. It includes burns that create pollution. It includes the loss of some wildlife from those burns. It includes herbicides that you may be exposed to. It includes a lot of things that are going to directly affect your life."

Other critics of restoration point to the glossy magazines and the beautiful pictures of the forest preserves as misleading advertisements that give a false view of nature. Surprisingly, these critics don't wish for the "Bambi-like" nature stories that many restorationists accuse them of preferring over reality.

> It's that massive aesthetic view of what restorationists have. It's the aesthetic view. I'm so tired of The Nature Conservancy magazines, and in Chicago Wilderness publications now you see this fantasy view of what nature looks like: four or five neatly spaced trees, and you've got every possible wildflower growing. It's a proverbial Garden of Eden! Isn't nature nice! You can walk through and just smell the flowers. Boy, this is beautiful! Part of the nature experience is getting stuck by the hawthorn patch. It's like they didn't exist before? Thorn Creek Woods was named by settlers—I think there were thorns in there. Thorn Grove? Thornton? It sounds to me that thorns were part of the presettlement conditions also.

Contextualizing Science and Nature

At public hearings and meetings, critics have paid much attention to the ways in which restorationists define ecosystems and native and nonnative plants, and the ways in which concepts such as canopy cover, for example, are interpreted and used. The critics believe that restorationists leave themselves room to "fudge" in their scientific definitions so they can cover themselves when they are wrong or to prevent critical outside examination of their work.

One of the biggest problems I have with the restoration effort is that they have a tendency to define things and make new definitions for old words and define things in their meaning of the term. Savanna: if you look it up in the dictionary, it says "treeless plain," but they're using it to mean 10 percent to 70 percent tree coverage. Well, that's fine except . . . scientifically, if you say it means 10 percent to 70 percent . . . that's not a description at all. There is so much room in that description that you are describing something from a heavy woodland all the way down to something that really resembles a prairie.

Restorationists deny this, and heated discussions occur between critics and restorationists over seemingly minute details of how a land management plan is worded or how community types are described.

The problem stems, in part, from the very different contexts within which each group makes sense of these definitions. As described earlier, restorationists view their restoration activities as urgent. There is a need for flexible definitions and understandings that make sense in the changing realities of the field. These definitions are based on restoration practice, the on-the-ground physical activities of cutting, burning, and seeding. Most words and ideas used come from traditional ecological science, but some are transformed in use by the restorationists. Admittedly, say restorationists, they make mistakes and change ideas about community types and their floral makeup or alter management techniques as they watch a site respond. But, they argue, that is the normal process of discovery required in the saving of native species by restoration.

The critics, on the other hand, see the manipulation of definitions and concepts as the political process of restoration as a social movement. Critics demand a more mature, precise science that restoration ecology is not. Most critics have difficulty understanding the context of restoration practice, in which these apparently fuzzy definitions and classifications make sense and are appropriate. Operating from expectations based on very traditional notions of science, critics have trouble accepting that restorationists would dare present these fuzzy definitions and flexible classifications publicly to describe and defend their work. Restorationists often struggle to translate why they know what they are saying is "right," and such struggles confirm for the critics that these people are untruthful, defensive, and not sure of what they are doing. Neither side can step outside the limits of its commitments to differing concepts of appropriate science. Such failures of self-reflection on both sides have so escalated the debate that in this region, the future of restoration as both a social movement and an applied science is in doubt.

Conclusion: Restoration as a Reflexive Practice

One of the founders of the Chicago-area restoration movement once said to me that the value of ecological restoration was not only in its ability to restore the region's native flora but also in the way it could initiate public dialogue about nature. He believed that restoration challenged traditional ways of thinking about nature and engaged people in discussion about what nature is and what relationship humans should have with it (see also the philosophical discussion about this topic in the first section of this book). I thought the restoration controversy was going to be that dialogue. I had hoped that the initial anger and mistrust would be replaced by attempts at listening and discussion. Instead, there is just more anger and mistrust. The controversy has spawned an all-out war to win on both sides. Restorationists and their critics have failed to learn enough about each other, and themselves, for dialogue to begin. According to the critics, this is because the restorationists never really wanted a dialogue. They wanted to persuade the public and teach but not listen. For the restorationists, the failure of a public discussion is due to the critics' dishonest refusal to accept the region's ecological peril and their desire to destroy the restoration movement with exaggeration and lies on behalf of some unrelated political agenda. It is unfortunate that these small segments of Cook County's population, both of whom actively concern themselves with the ecological health of the forest preserves, continue to fight over whose concern is best.

In this chapter, I have sought to demonstrate that the work of ecological restoration is political. Restoration gains broader political meaning in its reception by the larger public. The example of the Chicago restoration controversy clearly demonstrates that the response of land-managing authorities to such public definitions, even ones they disagree with or don't understand, further defines the politics of their conservation practices. The social and political meaning of restoration is defined not only by the changes in the floral composition of a particular site but also by the ways in which restoration practices establish the place of restorationists and their knowledge in relation to the public. Restoration activities carry with them assumptions about the best way to see and interact with the landscape. These assumptions privilege certain understandings of nature and, as is the case in Cook County, draw boundaries that exclude many of the lay public's experiences as invalid, inappropriate for contributing to a dialogue on the management and care of the public preserves.

Certainly, we must have criteria to determine the best course for the management of public natural areas, but we must carefully reflect on the ways in which these criteria are determined and the meaning they may have for those beyond the circle of experts who create them. This is especially important when conservationists are dealing with public lands and are reliant on the public to support their work (see Ryan, this volume).

The concept of the volunteer restorationist that was developed on the FPDCC lands may be one of the great success stories of U.S. grassroots environmentalism and conservation. The VSN is recognized as having set the standard for the organization of citizen participation in the work and science of ecological restoration. The VSN is a successful social movement, but can it also be a successful scientific authority in the eyes of the nonrestorationist public? In the Chicago controversy, the VSN struggles with maintaining this dual identity. It is this struggle that has made attempts to resolve the conflict by use of the restorationists' own scientific evidence so difficult. Restorationists can't be trusted, say critics, to do the unbiased scientific study necessary to prove the value of their work. This is a most difficult problem to solve. Some have argued that eventually our culture's notion of science will change and allow the seeming contradictions of restoration science to be understood as good science (Jordan 1997, Siewers 1998). I don't think restoration in the Chicago area is really about reconstructing the whole society's views of objectivity and authority. The political work of the volunteers I spoke with is much more parochial and immediate.

I hope that the experience of the Chicago-area restorationists encourages local conservationists to begin considering a new practice of ecological restoration—a practice that recognizes rebuilding natural systems on local preserves as necessarily the rebuilding of local social relationships as well. These relationships must be as important a responsibility to restorationists as is the responsibility already assumed for the alterations made upon the natural communities they restore. But let me be clear about which social relationships I am referring to. Certainly, they include those created through the recruitment and training of volunteers, the cultivation of support from local politicians and landowners, and the development of financial support from public and private sources. They may also include those social relationships affected by the broader project of redefining the human relationship with nature. These are some of the key activities of ecological restoration as a social movement and are changes in social relationships that are openly acknowledged by restorationists. But it is the subtle structuring of the social relationships of power that goes unrecognized by many restorationists. It is these relationships that position restoration as an objective science and privileged practice on public preserves designed for multiple use and interpretation. Restorationists involved in Chicago Wilderness often fail to take responsibility for establishing these relationships—relationships that structure how the preserves and their natural components will be valued, interpreted, and acted upon by the local community.

This active concern for how one's scientific practice creates the social arrangements that support the political agenda of its practitioners, often at the expense of competing agendas, is what social scientists call reflexivity. Reflexive practice for me requires that I pay careful attention not only to the biases I bring to the research as an individual but also to those inherent in the seemingly objective practices of sociological data collection and analysis, theoretical reflection, and writing. This chapter has elements that reveal my attempt to reflexively pursue this analysis of the Chicago restoration controversy. Not only have I tried to explain the theoretical agenda that guides my perception of the controversy, but I have also allowed the reader a glimpse of the politics and problems of doing and presenting the research itself. My assumptions, and those inherent to the sociological practices I employed, were pointed out rather forcefully by many of the people I interviewed. These challenges proved to be important data with which I improved and altered my later practice and analysis. The challenges of restoration critics could serve as similar data for ecological restorationists. But it will require listening and learning about one's own practice and politics through the experiences and sometimes angry voices of others. Of course, restoration is not ethnography, and it probably shouldn't be. Yet restoration can be, and in my opinion should be, a reflexive conservation practice.

Before the conflict in Chicago can become a productive dialogue between restorationists and their critics, there will need to be a dialogue among restorationists. The controversy provides a critical opportunity for the restoration community to explore the ways in which reflexivity can be incorporated as a means for addressing problems central to the perpetuation of the conflict. There is no one model for defining a reflexive practice. It would be foolish and possibly destructive for restoration science to simply copy the model from the social sciences. Yet in conjunction with social scientists, restoration practitioners and land managers can begin to define this new practice locally, as it meets the needs and problems of their particular landscapes and communities. In the long run, restorationists must become sociological strangers as well as scientists, land managers, and politicians. The work of ecological restoration should be more than just the interpretation of nature's needs; it must be the discernment of the needs of nature's publics as well.

Notes

1. I do not attribute any of the quotes in this chapter by name. While most of the respondents gave me permission to include their names, I have chosen to maintain the anonymity of all respondents out of respect to the few who wished to remain unacknowledged. In addition, I have removed the names of those persons

mentioned within the quotes. As the NEPA lawsuit continues, I believe this to be the most prudent method for protecting the respondents. A complete list of the interviewees whose comments are used in this analysis can be obtained from the author.

2. One notable exception is the work of USDA Forest Service social scientist Paul Gobster. His analysis (Gobster 1997) simply and clearly describes the specific critiques and concerns of local restoration critics. Unfortunately, most restorationists dismissed even this effort. Speaking about the article, a TNC employee remarked to me, "It wasn't very useful. He is giving credibility to these people!"

3. Those who have studied similar public controversies argue that such events are attempts to enroll the researcher on their side (Scott et al. 1990). Some have argued that symmetric, constructivist accounts of scientific controversy inevitably appear to be written from the side of the underdogs or critics of established authority, and thus are not symmetric (Mulkay et al. 1983). I would suggest that while this is a valid concern, it is often true that much can be learned about a controversy from the bottom up—from the perspective of those whose challenges to the established hierarchies make clear the social practices and relationships that are central to understanding these conflicts.

References

Bloor, D. 1976. *Knowledge and Social Imagery.* London: Routledge and Kegan Paul.

Gieryn, T. 1983. "Boundary-Work as the Demarcation of Science from Non-science: Strains and Interests in Professional Ideologies of Scientists." *American Sociological Review* 48: 781–795.

Gieryn, T. 1994. "Boundaries in Science." In *Handbook of Science and Technology Studies,* edited by S. Jasanoff, G. E. Markle, J. C. Petersen, T. Pinch. Thousand Oaks, CA: Sage.

Gobster, P. 1997. "The Chicago Wilderness and Its Critics, III. The Other Side: A Survey of the Arguments." *Restoration & Management Notes* 15: 32–37.

Helford, R. 1999. "Re-discovering the Presettlement Landscape: Making the Oak Savanna 'Real.'" *Science, Technology, & Human Values* 24: 55–79.

Irwin, A. 1995. *Citizen Science: A Study of People, Expertise and Sustainable Development.* London: Routledge.

Irwin, A., and B. Wynne. 1996. *Misunderstanding Science?: The Public Reconstruction of Science and Technology.* Cambridge: Cambridge University Press.

Jordan, W. 1997. "Foreword." In *The Tallgrass Restoration Handbook for Prairies, Savannas, and Woodlands,* edited by S. Packard and C. Mutel. Washington, DC: Island Press.

Mulkay, M., J. Potter, and S. Yearley. 1983. "Why an Analysis of Scientific Discourse is Needed." In *Science Observed: Perspectives on the Social Studies of Science,* edited by K. Knorr-Cetina and M. Mulkay. London: Sage.

Scott, P., E. Richards, and B. Martin. 1990. "Captives of Controversy: The Myth of the Neutral Social Researcher in Contemporary Scientific Controversies." *Science, Technology, & Human Values* 15: 474–495.

Schutz, A. 1964. "The Sociological Stranger: A Essay in Social Psychology." In *Collected Papers,* edited by A. Schutz. The Hague: Nijhoff.

Siewers, A. 1998. "Making the Quantum-Culture Leap: Reflections on the Chicago Controversy." *Restoration & Management Notes* 16: 9–15.

Takacs, D. 1996. *The Idea of Biodiversity: Philosophies of Paradise.* Baltimore: Johns Hopkins University Press.

Wolpert, L. 1992. *The Unnatural Nature of Science.* London: Faber and Faber.

❧ Chapter 7 ❧

PUBLIC VALUES, OPINIONS, AND EMOTIONS IN RESTORATION CONTROVERSIES

Joanne Vining, Elizabeth Tyler, and Byoung-Suk Kweon

Ecosystem restoration efforts are increasing throughout the United States and in many places around the world. Many of these efforts are undertaken with the support and cooperation of local residents, interest groups, and government agencies. However, some restoration efforts are meeting with public resistance, and conflicts between various individuals and groups are resulting in controversies about whether and how ecological restoration should be carried out on public lands.

The Chicago restoration controversy, described in the Introduction and Helford's chapter in this volume, is a case in point. Conflicts over the management of public forest preserve lands in the Chicago region have evolved into a highly contentious debate, pitting public land managers and ecological restoration volunteers against restoration critics. The controversy temporarily halted restoration activities in two counties, and, as this is written, it is still having major effects on how, where, and to what extent activities can proceed in some areas.

As is the case in many controversies, the conflict inherent in the Chicago situation is multifaceted. Our understanding and ultimate resolution of it requires examination by different disciplinary and methodological perspectives within the social sciences and humanities. In the previous chapter, Reid

Helford examines the dimensions of expertise and activism within restorationist and opponent groups from a sociological perspective, using ethnography and participant observation to understand the conflicts experienced by those directly involved in the controversy. In this chapter we take a psychological perspective by examining the values and perceptions that give rise to controversial ecosystem restoration activities, as well as the emotions that result from such controversies. Within this context, we use a survey-based approach that employs a scenario of a hypothetical restoration controversy to understand how average metropolitan residents (i.e., those not directly involved in the controversy) perceive, value, and react to conflicts concerning the restoration and management of urban natural areas.

We begin by placing the study within a more general psychological framework of environmental values and value conflict. We then describe the results of an analysis of news articles and other public documents that we conducted, looking specifically at the Chicago restoration controversy to develop a comprehensive list of value-based arguments for and against restoration. We apply this knowledge to our survey of a random sample of Chicago metropolitan residents, and we describe and discuss the methods and findings related to participants' decisions and emotions, opinions about human interventions in ecosystems, and opinions about restoration practices and policies. We conclude with some general suggestions for dealing with issues raised in the Chicago controversy and other cases involving conflicts over environmental values.

Values and Emotion in Environmental Conflict

Recent research efforts have identified and explored the environmental values held by various members of the public as a means of understanding the basis for their specific environmental concerns and conflicts, improving management decisions for public lands, and finding areas where competing users may have common values (Kellert 1996, Kempton et al. 1995, Vining and Tyler 1999).Vining (1992a, 1992b) argues that emotionality is a necessary and commonplace characteristic of public involvement in issues of environmental values, for a number of reasons. Psychologists have discovered that emotion is not easily separated from cognitive processes. Emotion is stored along with other information in memory and helps us interpret, summarize, and organize information. Emotion is also an effective motivator, often spurring individuals to speak out on issues of concern to them. In addition, emotion performs a highly effective communicative role through facial expression, body posture, and voice tone—means that are in many ways more expressive than verbal communication. Finally, emotion helps to reveal value conflict. When discrepancies between actual and desired values arise, emotion results.

Historically, public land managers have tended to discount the importance of value-laden and emotional responses of the public to land management plans and projects (Vining and Tyler 1999). But managers are now beginning to understand the importance of values and emotions as rational motivators for the public to become involved and to voice their concerns. After all, if people did not care about an issue and feel somehow threatened by the decision at hand, they would not express their concerns with great emotion (Creighton 1983, Vining 1987, 1992a, 1992b).

Values, Emotions, and the Chicago Restoration Controversy

Within this general psychological framework, we began to look closely at the environmental values and emotions being expressed in the Chicago restoration controversy. Informed by work by Gobster (1997), and Schroeder (1998), both of whom were studying aspects of restoration and restoration opposition in Chicago (see the Introduction and Schroeder's chapter in this volume), we undertook our own analysis of the controversy as expressed by the media and the public in hearings and other forums. Our purpose in this analysis was to develop a list of value-based arguments for and against restoration to include in our survey.

In our analysis we found that one of the most common concerns raised by restoration opponents was the cutting and clearing of existing mature trees. Residents and visitors complained about seeing rows of stumps instead of groves of trees and about the resulting changes to their community's character. As one nearby resident said of a restoration project at Belleau Woods in DuPage County, "[T]here's been an awful lot of cutting. It's nice woodland there. It was always nice to have that claim to fame" (Zalusky 1996). But restoration supporters had a different perspective. One of the forest managers said that "cutting trees is only one small part of it. . . . The overall aim is to increase plant and animal diversity with more native growth that can sustain a balanced system far into the future" (Coffey 1996). Thus, both supporters and opponents of restoration wished to have natural environments in the metropolitan area. However, nature meant different things to different groups. Supporters of restoration preferred prairies and savanna as they may have existed in pre-European-settlement times, while opponents preferred the contemporary urban forest.

Restoration supporters contended that instead of only a few kinds of wildlife, vegetation, and habitat, there would be millions of wildflowers, hundreds of birds, and dozens of native animals. Opponents perceived the likely outcome differently, refusing to believe that biodiversity would or should result from restoration. "This is nature's process of eliminating certain species. If that were not the case, we'd still have dinosaurs" (Hodson 1996).

Restoration supporters emphasized the necessity of using prescribed fire and herbicides in controlling exotic plants and stressed the safety precautions taken in their application. Opponents asserted that using fire to maintain prairie and savanna would worsen the problems of asthma sufferers, endanger houses and property, and harm animals, and worried that the types and concentrations of herbicides being applied were toxic to birds, fish, mammals, and humans.

The cost of restoration projects was also at issue. Opponents of the DuPage County Natural Areas Management Plan objected to spending taxpayers' money to cut down trees. A Burr Ridge resident argued that "it needs to be scaled back and slowed down; $11.6 million is a lot to spend for what nature does for free" (Hodson 1996). In contrast, restorationists in DuPage and elsewhere cited the substantial cost savings through volunteer stewardship efforts, along with the many other personal benefits restorationists received through participation.

Cutting of trees was also an important aesthetic and land value issue for nearby residents. Existing trees and brush helped to buffer unpleasant scenes such as traffic and commercial buildings that were considered eyesores. Residents claimed that cutting trees and brush would remove this visual buffer and lower their property values. In contrast, restoration supporters argued that restored prairie and savanna ecosystems had a unique beauty and that restoration helped to reclaim an important part of Illinois's natural heritage as the Prairie State.

These and other arguments that we documented through our analysis formed the basis of the value-based statements for and against restoration that appear in Tables 7.1 and 7.2. By developing concise summaries of these arguments, we hoped to provide the social context for participants to understand ecological restoration and respond thoughtfully to our survey questions.

Method

The purpose of the study reported here was to examine Chicago-area residents' perceptions of restoration practices, as well as their decisions and emotional reactions regarding a restoration scenario based on the Chicago controversy. We were particularly interested in the reactions and concerns of residents who were not directly involved in the restoration controversy, but who may have learned enough about resource conflicts to develop beliefs about the importance of natural areas and the role of government in providing such areas. We were also interested in perspectives on management goals and priorities for publicly owned natural areas and in the respondents' own ideas about conflict resolution in the political process.

A questionnaire was prepared to address public responses to an environmental restoration scenario. The scenario, presented in the accompanying boxed text, described a hypothetical controversy surrounding a restoration. Such scenarios are often used in research on reactions to environmental issues

Hypothetical·Situation

The fictional town of Hillendale is a suburb of a large Midwestern city. Its population is 38,000. As an older suburb, Hillendale is largely developed and is surrounded by other suburban communities. However, years ago Hillendale's founders and others in Forsythe County set aside open space reserves for preservation and for the recreational use of the public. These preserves include Shady Woods, which offers nature trails, picnic areas (including the Rustling Picnic Grove along the Babelin River), playgrounds, and a nature center.

The Shady Woods Preserve is almost a square mile in size. It is used as the site of a day camp during the summer months. The Rustling Picnic Grove is a favorite place for company and service club picnics. During the springtime, the Hillendale Birds n' Bees Club uses Shady Woods for bird watching and nature walks.

Portions of Hillendale located near Shady Woods are considered to be among the best neighborhoods in the community. Residents of the neighborhoods near Shady Woods have easy access to its playgrounds and nature trails (see map).

Ecologists at the nearby Learned Community College recently discovered some maps from the early 1800s that indicate that much of Forsythe County was a prairie with oak savanna areas along its creeks and rivers. Savanna is a grassland with scattered trees or clumps of trees. Both prairie and savanna are fire-dependent plant communities that have diminished due to human settlement and fire suppression.

Environmental groups have become alarmed by the almost complete loss of prairie and savanna habitat in the state and the endangered status of many prairie/savanna species. Based upon these old maps and the presence of remnant species found in the area, a group from a local environmental club called Grasslands Forever determined that the Rustling Picnic Grove would be an excellent site for savanna restoration.

In recent years, Shady Woods has been affected by a fast-growing nonnative shrub species known as thornybush. The thornybush has taken over large portions of the preserve, making many areas impassable and crowding out native tree species of the area. The mature native trees in the preserve are reaching the end of their natural lifespans. Foresters believe that these trees will disappear without human help because the thornybush and other species prevent them from becoming established on their own.

Representatives of the local open space management agency (which owns and manages the Shady Woods Preserve), working along with several volunteers from Grasslands Forever, began savanna restoration efforts at the Rustling Picnic Grove in the late 1980s. These restoration efforts included thinning of native trees, removal of nonnative trees and brush, periodic controlled burning of the undergrowth, application of herbicide on the hardy thornybush plants, sowing of savanna/prairie plant seeds, and planting of savanna/prairie grasses and flowers.

The efforts of the agency and Grasslands Forever over the past several years have been slow but sure. The savanna at the Rustling Picnic Grove is returning, and last spring volunteers were excited to find a small population of the endangered native sundarter orchid in the restoration area. The restoration effort at the Rustling Picnic Grove began to attract attention from elsewhere in the metropolitan region. The restoration effort was even featured in the national magazine *Ecology Today*. Volunteers reported that their participation in the restoration efforts had given a positive focus to their lives. They felt gratified by the visible changes to the area and by the camaraderie of working with other volunteers for a common cause.

But not all of Hillendale was as pleased. Visitors to the grove noticed fewer trees and bushes. Those who had previously enjoyed walking their dogs in the Rustling Grove area were faced with trail closures due to restoration efforts. Some residents said that their favorite trees had been lost or harmed. Many of the neighbors wanted to know why they did not get to vote on whether and where restoration took place. Some felt that their local tax dollars could be put to different use.

A group of neighbors organized themselves into a group called Save the Grove. They opposed the restoration efforts, as did a group of citizens against local taxes, animal rights activists, and two ecologists who disagreed with the restoration methods being used. The efforts of the Save the Grove alliance received extensive favorable coverage in one of the local newspapers. An influential alderman for Hillendale championed the alliance's cause as an effort to protect property values and to reduce possible impacts from controlled burning and herbicide use.

The two sides began to battle in the local press and to stage protests and counter-protests. There were threats of lawsuits, political revenge, and ballot initiatives. The arguments that were used by each side are shown on the next two pages (see Tables 7.1 and 7.2).

The city council of Hillendale and the board of directors of the Open Space Agency want public input. Alternative solutions being considered include:

1) stopping the restoration efforts permanently
2) continuing the restoration efforts as currently conducted
3) placing a moratorium on the restoration efforts until a thorough study of the issues can be conducted
4) expanding the restoration efforts to encourage further recovery of savanna and prairie environments
5) other compromise solutions, not yet identified

and serve to ensure that research respondents have information on the issue in question. Like the arguments for and against restoration discussed in the previous section, the scenario used in this research was developed through extensive review of public documents on the Chicago restoration controversy. Although it is a hypothetical description of a restoration controversy, it was modeled very closely after the events in Chicago.

Respondents were asked to read the scenario and the list of arguments for and against restoration (Table 7.1, Table 7.2) and write a brief essay on how they would address the controversy. Listed at the end of the scenario were five possible solutions that participants could use in part or whole as the basis for

Table 7.1. Summary of Arguments in Favor of Restoration

Argument	Explanation
Ecological Purity	Restoration can return an ecosystem to a state closer to what it was prior to European settlement or to a state prior to more recent changes in species composition.
Species/Ecosystem Diversity	Restoration can improve species and ecosystem diversity. This can be accomplished by removing competing nonnative species and by introducing the desired species.
Reclaim Threatened Ecosystems	Restoration can reintroduce or strengthen ecosystem types that may be threatened and diminishing in distribution or quality.
Stop Degradation	Restoration efforts can help stop or retard degradation in plant or animal species composition or in species health, and can ameliorate erosion.
Reclaim Natural Heritage	Restoration may return an area to a prior historic or prehistoric condition, for purposes of preserving environmental heritage.
Preserve for Future Generations	Restoration may ensure that certain ecosystems or species types are present in a particular area for future generations to appreciate.
Educational	Restoration may provide examples for community education or for seeking scientific study.
Benefits to Volunteers	Restoration volunteer efforts provide profound psychological and social benefits for the volunteers.
Beauty of Restored Ecosystems	Restored ecosystems, such as prairies and wetlands, have a certain beauty or aesthetic aspect that is appreciated.
Remove Invasive or Troublesome Species	Restoration can remove or minimize the effects of plant or animal species that are nonnative, extremely invasive or aggressive, or otherwise troublesome. Examples include the kudzu vine, pampas grass, and European buckthorn.

their written decision. After writing the essay, respondents were asked to answer a series of closed-ended questions dealing with the emotions they experienced during the reading and decision-making process, their perceived importance of different reasons for attempting restoration, and their opinions on various restoration practices. Other questions asked respondents about their experiences with restored areas, perceived scenario bias, and various personal characteristics.

Questionnaires were mailed to a sample of 200 residents of Cook and DuPage Counties, the two counties at the locus of the restoration controversy. We selected respondents from directories of the two counties using a stratified random technique. Those who did not respond to the first mailing received a postcard reminder and up to three repeat mailings. We offered payments of $5

Table 7.2. Summary of Arguments Against Restoration

Argument	Explanation
Tree Removal	Cutting or damaging mature trees is objectionable because of the visual, microclimatic, and biological benefits they provide.
Animal Harm	Removing, harming, or killing animal species (through extermination efforts, herbicide use, loss of preferred habitat, or controlled burns) is objectionable.
Let Nature Take Its Course	Restoration efforts get in the way of how outdoor environments would develop on their own. People should not disturb nature and should just let it take its course.
Change to Wooded Areas	Change to wooded areas (due to prairie, savanna, or woodland restoration) is objectionable because these are valuable areas in their own right and have recreational, visual, and microclimatic benefits. Homes near wooded areas may also have higher property values.
Change in Recreational Opportunities	Restoration efforts interfere with recreational opportunities while restoration is under way. The restored environment may be less useful for some recreational purposes, such as hunting and camping. Other recreational uses, such as horseback riding, may not be permitted in restored areas.
Fire Hazard	Controlled burns associated with restoration efforts may present a fire hazard to nearby property.
Air Pollution	Smoke from annual controlled burns and increased dust during plant removal and planting efforts result in temporary local increases in air pollutants.
Health Hazard from Herbicide Use	Use of herbicides to suppress invasive species may be harmful to humans or other animals coming in contact with these chemicals.
Financial/Resource Limitations	Despite the use of volunteers, restoration efforts can be costly, inefficient, and time-consuming. Public funds would be better spent acquiring additional open space lands or in addressing other needs.
Aesthetics	During certain stages, restoration efforts may result in a visually unattractive area.
Scientific Uncertainty	Ecologists and other scientists often do not agree on what an environment should be restored to and how this should be done.

for return of the completed survey and included business reply envelopes with each questionnaire.

This procedure resulted in a final response rate of 33 percent ($N = 66$). In a telephone follow-up, the majority of the seventy-five nonrespondents we were able to reach said they did not respond to the mail survey due to a lack of time or interest. Six people we contacted in this manner volunteered to complete the survey by phone (minus the scenario). We found no statistically significant differences between their answers and those of people who completed the survey by mail, so we combined their responses with those of the mail sample in the appropriate subsequent analyses. Although this comparison was one indication that our sample did not suffer from nonresponse bias, thirteen individuals in the phone follow-up also stated that they had not responded due to the length of the questionnaire. The length and demanding nature of the survey may have biased the sample in favor of more educated respondents, as 85 percent indicated having at least some college education. Readers thus should weigh these factors in interpreting the study results.

Results and Discussion

Despite our attempts to be as unbiased as possible, we recognize there is no truly neutral information. We asked respondents to rate the amount of bias they perceived to be present in the hypothetical scenario (1 = pro-restoration bias to 7 = anti-restoration bias). The mean of the respondents' ratings was 3.6 (SD = .97, N = 66), indicating that the scenario description was perceived to be a fairly unbiased source of information about a restoration controversy.

Nearly 80 percent of the respondents said they were unaware of the controversy surrounding ecosystem restoration in the Chicago area before completing the questionnaire. This seems somewhat surprising given the media coverage of the controversy. However, 49 percent of the respondents reported visiting restoration sites, and 6 percent reported having participated in restoration activities. Only 3 percent were members of environmental organizations. As a whole, these results indicate that the respondents were moderately aware of restoration activities but not the controversy, and that they appeared to have no overwhelming interest in environmental issues in general.

Decisions and Emotions

Respondents were given a page on which to write their solution to the hypothetical environmental restoration controversy, but most of their solutions averaged a paragraph or two in length. The sample excerpts below capture the diversity of participants' responses:

> There is no reason to keep the prairie. It is a terrible environment. Trying to recultivate it is a waste of money. And to take forest preserves and parks for this purpose is taking away the only cultivated beauty in the state of Illinois.

> Stop the restoration efforts permanently and immediately. From what I have seen, these so-called restoration efforts are criminal.

The removal of mature trees and shrubs have been harmful to wildlife, not helpful.

When at all possible mature trees should be left alone. "Thorny-bush," however, would probably be okay to remove. . . . While native prairie might be ecologically pure, times have changed—like it or not. Europeans have arrived and become well-settled. A restoration area is a nice addition to a community but it shouldn't be allowed to expand beyond a reasonable limit. Many others would view a landscaped park setting as preferable to a prairie.

We should try to restore the natural environment but we have to look at the implications. We should avoid harming animals, avoid starting forest fires, avoid herbicides. But if damage needs to be repaired we need to do it but the community should be brought in and their views should be heard. More research should be done in order to avoid harming people. Remember the land belongs to the people, but people also tend to destroy nature.

In this instance, perhaps a vote before anything was begun should have been considered. Since that is not the case and there are viable arguments both for and against restoration, I believe a moratorium should be set up to determine next steps. As an individual I would vote to save and restore the habitat to its natural beginnings; as a member of a democratic community, the people must ultimately collectively speak for common areas.

I agree with [alternative solution] #4—expanding the restoration efforts to encourage further recovery of savannas and prairie environments. I strongly believe [in] this alternative because every day we use cars, sending carbon monoxide to the air, polluting it more and more every day. And now nature needs help and it can't possibly survive without our help, so you have to do something to save it!

We classified the written decisions using the set of five solution options that appeared at the end of the scenario. The results of this analysis, presented in Table 7.3, further demonstrate the wide range of participants' suggested solutions to the hypothetical problem. About a third of the respondents favored a moratorium on restoration activities while further study was done, which was a strategy employed in the actual Chicago controversy. Only one in ten respondents felt that restoration efforts should be halted, and 21 percent thought that restoration should be continued.

After writing down their decisions, respondents indicated which of several

Table 7.3. Solutions to a Hypothetical Restoration Controversy Offered by Participants

Proposed Solution	Percentage[1]
Place a moratorium on restoration until a thorough study of the issues can be conducted	35
Continue restoration efforts as currently conducted	21
Other compromise solutions, not yet identified	15
Stop restoration efforts permanently	12
Expand restoration efforts to encourage further recovery	2
Other	15

[1]N = 66

emotions they experienced while reading the scenario and deciding what should be done about the controversy. The frequencies of reported emotions are presented in Table 7.4. The active negative emotions of anger and disgust were reported with relatively less frequency than the passive negative emotions of sadness and fear. A fifth of the respondents reported being happy during the consideration and decision-making process.

The proportion of respondents who stated that they experienced various emotions seems somewhat high given the fact that they were considering a hypothetical rather than a real restoration scenario. Additionally, the balance of passive and active negative emotions indicates that emotions such as anger and disgust that usually drive controversies were relatively less important in the response to this problem. In real situations, however, it takes only a small number of concerned and emotional citizens to generate a controversy. Nonetheless, these results from our scenario indicate that a significant proportion of the broader public may experience negative emotions while considering an ecosystem restoration problem.

Previous studies (e.g., Vining 1987, 1992a; Vining and Schroeder 1987) have shown that negative emotions are often associated with decisions to preserve the environment. We tested this relationship in our present study by

Table 7.4. Frequencies of Self-Reported Emotion Evoked by the Hypothetical Controversy

Emotion	Percentage[1]
Sadness	24
Happiness	20
Disgust	15
Fear	14
Anger	6

[1]N = 66

cross-tabulating respondent data on emotions with the categories used to classify their decisions regarding the hypothetical controversy. These analyses indicated that there were no systematic relationships between any of the emotions and decision categories. Since there was demonstrably a great deal of emotion involved in the actual Chicago controversy, these results indicate a need for further examination of the relationship between environmental restoration activities and emotional responses of the public.

Opinions about Human Intervention in Ecosystems

In another question, respondents were asked to indicate the importance of a variety of reasons that humans might intervene in nature. These reasons and their mean importance ratings are listed in Table 7.5.

Two reasons for intervening in nature—to produce material goods and to reap private economic gain—rated as lowest in importance, while human health and ecosystem health were rated as the most important reasons. The relatively low importance given to economic and material gains may reflect a social desirability bias among respondents, in that personal gain is not generally considered to be a socially acceptable reason for exploiting anything (or anyone). These attitudes may not be consistent with behavior, however, as many individuals espouse environmental conservation ethics while engaging in behavior that is inconsistent with those values (e.g., Ebreo et al. 1999). Also, these questions did not require realistic trade-offs between the protection of nature and economic welfare. If preservation of old-growth forests, for example, required personal sacrifices of building materials, it might not be so easy to dismiss economic or material gain.

It is noteworthy that promoting ecological health was placed ahead of most of the other reasons for intervening in nature, including preserving

Table 7.5. Importance of Reasons for Human Intervention in Ecosystems

Reason to Intervene/Restore	Mean Rating[1]	Std. Dev.
To provide for improved human health	3.4	0.8
To improve an area's ecological health	3.2	0.9
To provide food for humans	3.1	0.8
To improve the appearance or beauty of an area	2.6	1.1
For national security	2.6	1.0
To provide a place to live for humans	2.4	0.9
To improve recreation	2.3	0.8
To provide material goods	2.1	0.9
For private economic reasons	1.6	0.8

[1]$N = 72$; Rating scale: 1 = weak reason, 4 = strong reason

national security and providing homes for humans. This finding appears to coincide with the reasons restorationists themselves often give for why they engage in restoration—that is, "to help the environment" and "to protect nature" (see chapters by Schroeder and by Grese et al. in this volume).

While participants' emphasis on intervening in nature to provide human health benefits seems at odds with their emphasis on protecting nature from human activities, these joint health concerns are entirely consistent with the messages many environmental organizations are using to urge the protection of natural areas. There is widespread interest, for example, in protecting rain forests and other natural areas in order to search for plants and animals that could provide medications for humans. The endorsement of ecosystem health as a reason for intervening in nature may provide a useful communication strategy for future restoration projects. Although the improvement of ecosystem health was probably the single most important reason the Chicago-area restorations were conducted, this may not have been communicated to the public clearly enough or early enough.

Opinions about Restoration Practices and Policies

Respondents were asked to indicate the extent to which they agreed or disagreed with a series of seventeen opinion items about restoration practices and policies. These items and the mean ratings for them (1 = disagree strongly to 5 = agree strongly) are presented in Table 7.6 in descending order of agreement.

Respondents strongly endorsed items indicating that local residents should be fully informed and involved before restoration efforts are begun. Conversely, they disagreed with the statement that restoration should be done despite opposition. These findings are fully consistent with the literature on public involvement and democratic theory, and with the experiences of many land managers over the past 40 years (Knopp and Caldbeck 1990, Mohai 1995). From the clearcutting controversies of 1960s and 1970s to the present day, land managers and members of the public have repeatedly clashed over the proper use and management of public lands. Land management practices are undertaken by professionals who take pride in their training and work, and who may not believe that members of the public have appropriate expertise (Tipple and Wellman 1989; see also Helford, this volume). Members of the public, on the other hand, behave in accordance with the belief that public lands are in some sense their own and that they have a right to say what should be done on them. This conflict of values has resulted in repeated land management controversies and is at the heart of the restoration controversy in Chicago. Given the generally positive reaction toward restoration, especially when it is conducted for preservation of species diversity and ecosystem health, it is possible that the Chicago controversy might have been avoided or

Table 7.6. Participants' Opinions about Restoration Policies and Practices

Opinion Statement	Mean Rating[1]	Std. Dev.
Local residents should be fully informed before restoration efforts begin in their communities	4.5	0.6
Restoration efforts should be used to help recover plant and animal species that are rare and endangered	4.1	1.0
The public should have a say about whether and where restoration takes place	4.0	0.8
Restoration efforts should try to improve the appearance of an area	3.8	0.9
Restoration work should be done only by professionals or scientists trained in environmental management	3.7	1.2
Controlled burning to regenerate growth is acceptable, even near developed areas	3.7	0.9
I would support savanna restoration efforts in a wooded area near my home	3.4	1.1
Herbicides should never be used in restoration efforts	3.4	1.1
Restoration techniques should be used even if the ecological health of an area cannot be returned to what it was in pre-settlement times	3.4	1.1
Ecosystems are the same thing as nature	3.3	1.0
Large trees should never be removed in restoration efforts, even if they are not native to an area	3.3	1.3
Environmental restoration should be done only in cases of extreme environmental degradation	3.1	1.3
We should allow natural areas to evolve as they will without any intervention	3.1	1.3
Public funds are better spent on acquiring additional natural lands or open space than on funding restoration efforts	3.0	1.2
Restoration efforts should try to bring our natural areas back to a condition as close as possible to pre-European settlement (what it was like when the land was inhabited only by Native Americans)	3.0	1.3
Removal of nonnative or invasive species is acceptable, even if some desirable species are hurt in the process	3.0	1.2
There will always be people who oppose restoration, so it is best to do it regardless	2.8	1.3

[1]N = 72; Rating scale: 1 = strongly disagree, 5 = strongly agree

minimized by the implementation of a good public information and involvement program.

Respondents also endorsed the idea that improving the appearance of an area was a worthy goal of restoration projects. This finding has implications for the methods in which restoration activities are conducted. In the real controversy, opponents objected strenuously to what they considered a clearcutting of the nature preserves. Although the rapid removal of alien species and other trees may be the most efficient means to restore a savanna ecosystem, it is objectionable visually. This issue again echoes the land management controversies of the 1960s and 1970s that led NEPA to require consideration of the aesthetic consequences of land management practices. A more gradual phasing of restoration activities combined with an aggressive public involvement program may have been helpful in this respect (for more on this idea, see Ryan's chapter in this volume).

There was moderate support for the use of controlled burns in management of restored areas, but respondents also felt nearly as strongly that herbicides should never be used. Here again, a clash between the values of the public and those of the restoration advocates can be seen. In the actual controversy, restoration advocates believed that the use of herbicides, as with the cutting of trees, was an important means to a worthy end. Conversely, while supporting the general notion of ecosystem restoration, members of the public appeared to be more likely to question the means by which this is achieved.

The credibility and credentials of the individuals or groups carrying out the restoration activities were also important to our research participants. Respondents agreed that restoration work should be done only by professionals or scientists trained in environmental management. This issue became a very important one in the real Chicago controversy, where restoration activities were carried out by Nature Conservancy volunteers working in association with Forest Preserve District officials. Volunteers carried no identification and did not wear uniforms or T-shirts identifying them as representatives of either The Nature Conservancy or the Forest Preserve District. Thus, what forest preserve visitors and neighbors saw was what appeared to be other members of the public cutting down trees and removing large quantities of brush from the forest preserves. It is not surprising that this was objectionable, and eventually volunteers were required to carry identification, wear identifying clothing, and be supervised by a uniformed representative of the Forest Preserve District. While better credentials may have eliminated important objections that opponents had about restoration, it is uncertain whether they would have prevented the controversy from happening. For additional thoughts on this topic, see Andrew Light's discussion of the certification of restorationists in the following chapter.

The acceptability of attempting to return areas to pre-European-settlement conditions was assessed by two items. Respondents gave these items nearly neutral mean ratings, neither agreeing nor disagreeing that the goal of restoration should be to return areas to pre-European-settlement conditions. This reflects the difficulty of the issue of establishing and communicating ecosystem restoration goals. The pre-European-settlement criterion is problematic even for restoration advocates and ecosystem scientists—suggesting, for one thing, that Native Americans were a part of the natural ecosystem while European settlers were not. In the actual controversy, the restorations in question took place in an existing urban ecosystem. Residents were used to thinking of the forest preserves as wooded recreational areas, parts of the urban "human habitat." Residents probably did not think of these areas as prairies or savannas invaded by alien species. Thus, restoration activities, however well intended, were perceived as drastically changing the familiar and cherished urban forest.

Conclusion

Controversies result when values conflict. Respondents to our scenario of a hypothetical restoration controversy expressed a strong belief in public involvement, reflecting one of the principal issues raised by restoration opponents and acknowledged in retrospect by restorationists and land managers in the real Chicago restoration controversy. In this way, the Chicago restoration controversy is reminiscent of the clearcutting controversies over national forests (Dana and Fairfax 1980). In both cases, environmental changes were made in line with decision-making processes and criteria that were neither communicated to members of the public nor agreed upon by them. In today's society, failure to involve the public in decisions regarding management of public lands is generally regarded as unacceptable. The negative consequences of closed-door decision making have been played out enough times over the past thirty years that public involvement is now a mandate for virtually every American land management agency. There is also growing recognition that public involvement not only helps to prevent (or at least lessen) controversies, but also can improve the decision-making process (Creighton 1981, 1983, Gericke et al. 1992).

Our results indicated that nearly 80 percent of respondents were not familiar with the controversies raging over the Chicago restoration activities. However, respondents did report significant amounts of negative emotions after reading and deliberating over a hypothetical restoration scenario based on the actual Chicago situation. It is reasonable to speculate that many members of the public would be upset about the restoration activities had they witnessed unidentified volunteers removing trees and large amounts of brush from forested areas. Emotion, especially negative emotion, is a strong motivator, and it is plausible to expect that any individual witnessing the restoration activities without prior notice or understanding of what was going on would be upset enough to take action. This is exactly what did happen with neighbors and visitors who knew of the activities, and the scale of the controversy likely could have been much greater had more individuals witnessed the brush and tree removal.

Previous studies have shown that negative emotions are often associated with preservation decisions (Vining 1987, 1992a, Vining and Schroeder 1987). In the present study, the issue of preservation is very complex. Nature preserves can be viewed as areas that are both natural and unnatural. They are invaded by human-introduced species and are not good representations of the area as it was before European settlers arrived. At the same time, these areas represent precious islands of nature in an environment dominated by human constructions. It will continue to be a challenge for environmental managers, activists, and researchers to understand this relationship.

A solid majority of our respondents advocated compromise solutions to the hypothetical restoration scenario. Moreover, there was considerable explicit support for judiciously proceeding in conducting restorations and resolving restoration controversies, as well as enthusiasm for the concept of restoration in general. These moderate responses seem at odds with the highly polarized and contentious debate that has taken place in Chicago. Again, we emphasize the importance of public involvement in resolving controversies before they begin. If county and Nature Conservancy officials had, at a minimum, conducted a social impact assessment, they would probably have discovered that there was cautious support for restoration as a concept and for restoration actions on the ground. These sorts of data can not only inform the process by which restoration should occur, but also provide a measure of the broad base of support among county residents for the restoration activities. There is almost always tension between the interests of local residents and members of the broader public, and good public involvement techniques are instrumental in identifying and resolving these value conflicts.

We did not assess the values of restoration volunteers directly. However, it is clear from several of the other chapters in this volume that the volunteers valued doing restoration work so highly that broad-based public involvement may have been a secondary concern at best, deemphasized altogether if it involved political decisions about whether, how much, and where restoration should take place. Restoration activists are fond of referring to themselves as members of grassroots movements (Stevens 1995), and thus may have assumed that their values did represent those of the public. Schroeder (this volume) and Grese et al. (this volume) found that volunteers on restoration projects took great pride in their work and accrued other psychological benefits as well. It is worth considering the idea that greater involvement of members of the public in restoration plans and activities might have given others a sense of pride and accomplishment as well.

The results of this study suggest that ecological restoration specialists, public land managers, decision makers, and social scientists interested in human-environment interactions have a lot to learn from average citizens. Survey respondents strongly identified the need to inform and involve the public in restoration activities, to frame compromise solutions, and to proceed judiciously. At the same time, the global issues of both human and nonhuman health and survival clearly emerged. In many ways the Chicago restoration controversy is a microcosm that reflects our broader concerns about the character of human habitats and our place in the natural order.

Acknowledgments

We are grateful to the USDA Forest Service, North Central Research Station, Evanston, Illinois, for providing support for this study.

References

Barro, S. C., and A. D. Bright. 1998. "Public Views on Ecological Restoration: A Snapshot from the Chicago Area." *Restoration & Management Notes* 16(1): 59–65.

Coffey, R. 1996. "Half Million Trees May Face the Ax: Du Page Clears Forest Land to Create Prairies." *Chicago Sun-Times* May 12.

Creighton, J. L. 1981. *The Public Involvement Manual.* Cambridge, MA: Abt Press.

Creighton, J. L. 1983. "The Use of Values: Public Participation in the Planning Process." In *Public Involvement and Social Impact Assessment,* edited by G. A. Daneke, M. W. Garcia, and J. Delli Priscoli, 143–160. Boulder, CO: Westview Press.

Dana, S. T., and S. K. Fairfax. 1980. *Forest and Range Policy: Its Development in the United States.* New York: McGraw-Hill.

Ebreo, A., J. Hershey, and J. Vining. 1999. "Reducing Solid Waste: Linking Recycling to Environmentally-responsible Consumerism." *Environment and Behavior* 31: 107–135.

Gericke, K. L., J. Sullivan, and J. D. Wellman. 1992. "Public Participation in National Forest Planning." *Journal of Forestry* 90: 35–38.

Gobster, P. H. 1997. "The Chicago Wilderness and Its Critics, III. The Other Side: A Survey of the Arguments." *Restoration & Management Notes* 15: 32–37.

Hodson, J. 1996. "Restoration or Devastation? Forest Board Rethinks Plan to Help Turn Back the Clock to Save Land." *Daily Herald,* May 17.

Kellert, S. R. 1996. *The Value of Life.* Washington, DC: Island Press.

Kempton, W., J. S. Boster, and J. A. Hartley. 1995. *Environmental Values in American Culture.* Cambridge, MA: MIT Press.

Knopp, T. B., and E. S. Caldbeck. 1990. "The Role of Participatory Democracy in Forest Management." *Journal of Forestry* 88: 13–18.

Mohai, P. 1995. "The Forest Service Since the National Forest Management Act." *Policy Studies Journal* 23: 247–251.

Schroeder, H. W. 1998. "Why People Volunteer." *Restoration & Management Notes* 16(1): 66–67.

Stevens, W. K. 1995. *Miracle Under the Oaks: The Revival of Nature in America*. New York: Pocket Books.

Tipple, T. J., and J. D. Wellman. 1989. "Life in the Fishbowl: Public Participation Rewrites Public Foresters' Job Descriptions." *Journal of Forestry* 87: 24–30.

Vining, J. 1987. "Environmental Decisions: The Interaction of Emotions, Information, and Decision Context." *Journal of Environmental Psychology* 7: 13–30.

Vining, J. 1992a. "Value Conflict, Emotion and Forest Management." In *Ecosystem Management in a Dynamic Society*, edited by D. C. Le Master and G. R. Parker, 26–35. West Lafayette, IN: Purdue University Department of Forestry and Natural Resources.

Vining, J. 1992b. "Environmental Emotions and Decisions: A Comparison of the Responses and Expectations of Forest Managers, an Environmental Group, and the Public." *Environment and Behavior* 24: 3–34.

Vining, J., and H. W. Schroeder. 1987. "The Effects of Perceived Conflict, Resource Scarcity and Information Bias on Emotions in Environmental Decision-making." *Environmental Management* 13: 199–206.

Vining, J., and E. Tyler. 1999. "Values, Emotions, and Desired Outcomes as Reflected in Public Responses to Forest Management Plans." *Human Ecology Review* 6: 21–34.

Zalusky, S. 1996. "Man vs. Nature: Another Forest Preserve Plan Has Activists Up a Tree." *Press Publications* May 17.

❧ *Chapter 8* ❧

RESTORATION, THE VALUE OF PARTICIPATION, AND THE RISKS OF PROFESSIONALIZATION

Andrew Light

Efforts to professionalize restoration include the regulation of restoration projects, the certification of restoration volunteers, and the creation and accreditation of restoration degree programs. By increasing the expertise and authority of restorationists, professionalization offers a potential mechanism to reduce the conflict that seems inherent in many restoration projects. However, professionalization may have significant costs. Professionalism will likely close the content of the language of restoration by controlling how concepts, terms, and practices of restoration are defined and delimited. This control may make restoration less participatory and degrade the unique democratic potential of restoration projects. I will address these issues using as an example the conflict created by the numerous restorations known collectively as the Chicago Wilderness project. In the first section I will explain and establish the democratic values of restoration projects. In the second section I will describe how professionalism threatens these democratic values. I will conclude with an illustration of these issues using the Chicago Wilderness restoration controversy.

The Democratic Potential of Restoration[1]

In previous work I argued that the practice of ecological restoration contains an inherent democratic potential (Light 1995, Light and Higgs 1996). By this claim, I meant that at its best the activity of ecological restoration preserves the democratic ideal that public participation in a public activity increases the value of that activity. This value in restoration is brought out most effectively by those projects that unite local human and natural communities, and that increase the level of local participation in those restoration projects. Here I wish to revisit the arguments I have made on the value of participation and extend them further. I hope that this exercise will help readers think through the advantages and disadvantages of professionalization by providing a moral and political foundation for the practice of restoration, the participation in which could be hindered or helped by moves toward increased professionalization.

William Jordan, one of the most influential writers on ecological restoration and the editor of one of the two main journals in the field, has tried with some success to articulate a coherent restoration ecology paradigm. Included in his program are cultural, social, and political elements. In a nicely evocative metaphor, Jordan helps open up the discussion of the connection between democratic participation and restoration. In his discussion of the fifth element of his ecological restoration paradigm, "change and adaptation," Jordan claims: "What is involved [in ecological restoration] is a continual dialogue rather than a program, paralleling in our dealings with the biotic community the dialogue that sustains a democratic society and makes it adaptable to change" (Jordan 1994a, 24). One of the things Jordan has in mind is the sense in which restorations are organized around communal activities for communal concerns. In what Jordan takes as the best examples of restoration, people tend to participate by and large as equals, creating an egalitarian framework within which restorations are performed. As such, ecological restoration should connect us to a process that is integrated into a close communal connection with the land. Our activity with nature is analogous to our activity with each other in a democratic society. I would argue that compatible with Jordan's view is a claim that the values we should seek in the practice of restoration should compare to the things we value in a democratic society, such as equal participation. Again, while such a claim may go a bit further than Jordan's comparison, it is at least compatible with the overall sensibility of his views.

Comparing the values at work in a good participatory restoration with the values of a participatory democracy is very useful. But we have to be careful not to go too far with such a comparison. It would be a mistake to go from this analogy to claim that acts of restoration are inherently democratic. The only way to get such a conclusion would be to overly stipulate what counts as a restoration: restoration is democratic by definition because only fully participatory and egalitarian restorations count as restorations. But, of course, there is no reason why democracy or egalitarianism inheres in the simple act of restoring a landscape unless the act necessarily must be prescribed within a certain context. If we were to do that, then we would have to be prepared to argue that certain acts are not restorations by definition, specifically those performed under undemocratic conditions. For example, we would have to be prepared to say that a restoration produced by slave labor was not a restoration.

But the problem with such stipulations is that there would be no reason to question such a restoration on purely technical grounds. We can imagine a case where a restoration produced by slave labor resulted in a wonderfully diverse and healthy ecosystem. Something other than technical criteria would be needed to establish that such a practice couldn't possibly be an ecological restoration (or at least couldn't count as a good one). Such criteria would have to show that all restorations share a common character that necessarily omits nondemocratic practices as good restorations regardless of the results. And while the example I have given may encourage our intuitions that a practice undertaken with slave labor cannot be "good" in any sense, simply stipulating democratic conditions as a criterion of restoration won't achieve a shift in our understanding of what counts as a good restoration. An argument is needed for why there is a democratic potential in restoration and for why that potential should be preserved. It is philosophically insufficient to simply assert the priority of democracy to restoration, and practically unsound to expect that because this condition can be analogously implied it will be followed in practice.

My claim will be that restoration is not inherently democratic but that it does have an inherent democratic potential that can be either lost or preserved in any act of restoration. The problem is not just to identify this potential, but to make a case for why it is part of the criteria for what identifies restoration as a good environmental practice. To explain more fully the participatory potential in restoration, it may help to briefly compare what happens in an act of restoration of nature as opposed to what happens in an act of preservation of nature, from a standpoint where we consider the range of values that are produced or protected in such acts. Both types of acts produce some sort of value; each token of each type of practice contains its own evaluative content. But the character of the two values generally produced by the two practices is quite different. And as we will see, the relationship between content and character in both acts is distinct. Understanding this distinction, however, requires further argument.

As far as I can tell, no new natural value is produced in an act of preservation of nature because it preserves only the values that existed before the act of preservation, however one wishes to identify the nature of those natural values.[2] Since no new value in or for nature is created in acts of preservation, no value is actively produced by the agents engaged in acts of preservation. They are doing something good, without a doubt, but they are not producing a value in the way that a restorationist may when she restores some bit of nature that has been degraded. The act of restoration is different from the act of preservation. It is unique as an environmental practice that makes value—a value that, so far as we know at any point in time, wouldn't be produced otherwise. It is a unique quality of the act of restoration that it produces this value, and part of what we value in acts of restoration is the uniqueness of this form of value. Let's call this unique aspect of the value-producing properties of restoration its character.[3] In addition, we can say that this valuative character is tied to the person or community that performs the act. Without someone engaging in a restoration, the value produced by the restoration never appears. The character of restoration is thus one that (1) produces a unique value—that is, one that will not exist otherwise—and (2) is necessarily tied to a participatory act by a human.

Criterion (2) also gives us an insight into a crucial part of the content of each act of restoration. If (2) is true, then each act of restoration produces a value whose content is shaped, perhaps even determined, by the profile of its participatory elements. The content of a value can be either good or bad (or, more accurately, can exist on a scale of positive and negative values). Because (2) ties the values at work in restoration to the humans producing the restoration, the way that humans produce a restoration will shape the positive or negative profile of the content of the value of any act of restoration. In the example above, it should be clear that a restoration performed by slaves has a bad content when examined according to criterion (2). When we tie the evaluative content of a particular restoration to the participatory character of the value, we are entitled to say that the content of the value of a restoration performed by slaves is always negative because the value of the thing produced by slaves is implicated in the disvalues associated with slavery.

Now let's go back to the broader question of the differing character of the values produced by preservations and restorations. While the content of acts of preservation is variable, and an existent value in nature is preserved in each act, the value preserved is not unique (criterion 1) because it could occur without any act of preservation, nor is it intimately tied to the human practice of preservation. The character of preservation is therefore quite different from the character of restoration. One can imagine a situation in which a bit of value in nature is preserved without any preservationist needing to do the preserving. For example, an act of preservation could occur by accident if a bit of land changed ownership and the new (very wealthy and distracted) owners simply forgot about it, inadvertently leaving it protected and untouched. Or more simply, the inaccessibility of the land could be the condition that leads to its preservation. In such cases the mere change of ownership or inaccessibility of the land is not an act of preservation per se but rather the maintenance of a value based on contingent events. Such a case is distinguishable from one in which a bit of land is intentionally preserved through a public political process. In this way, acts of preservation do not fit criterion (1) above of acts of restoration. More importantly, in different cases of intentional and contingent preservation, although the value of the nature preserved is the same, the value of the act that produced the preservation is not. One case involves an intentional human action and can be praised or critiqued as such, while the other does not involve such an action. Thus acts of preservation do not share criterion (2) of the character of the values at work in restoration because the content of the value of an act of preservation is not necessarily tied to the character of the act (whether or not an act occurred). This does not mean that restorations are better than preservations, just that they are normatively different.

Back to restorations. If criterion (2) ties the content of a restoration to its character, then we need to say more about what counts as a better or worse content of restorations. Most restorations are not produced by individuals acting alone, so an assessment of restoration as a practice must assess the act as a value for the community engaged in the restoration and the product as a value for nature, not separate from but intrinsically bound to the community producing the value. While the value to the community and the value to nature can be assessed separately (each partner in the practice—humans and nature—has different needs), as a practice these values are produced together. But what is the nature of this value for the community? Although I have discussed at length the potential values for nature in my other contribution to this volume, what can we say more precisely about the nature of the value of restoration for the restorationists themselves?

To begin, it seems that because of this unique combination of value for nature and value for the community involved in the practice of restoration, the content of the value of any restoration can be assessed as good or bad in terms of its participatory elements. At its core, as I argued earlier in this volume, restoration is public participation in nature; it is a restoration not only of nature but also of the human culture of nature. Presumably, if the value of participation in democratic activities in the public sphere is positive, then the value of participation in restoration activities is also positive for similar reasons. The more participation the better, therefore, especially if we take seriously the analogy to democratic practices that Jordan had in mind. Restoration can have a democratic and communal content, as Jordan suggested, just not a necessary democratic component. The potential for that component has to be actively embraced. This potential for creating valuable democratic forms of participation is there for any restoration, even if the scale and complexity of some restoration projects may restrict or even prohibit public participation. The content of the values produced in a restoration may vary and be hard to discern, but no matter what particular values are produced for nature or the human community in any particular act, some part of the evaluative content of restoration will always be tied to the participatory character of restoration.

We know that the character and the content of the value of a restoration can be evaluated negatively. I maintain that a restoration that lacks community participation, when there is no good reason for that lack, will have a bad content in this view. A restoration that is not participatory loses the values of participation that could have been produced under more democratic conditions. This loss in value is uniquely felt at the local level. Where a restoration has been slated for a particular place, and where the local community contiguous to that place does not participate in the restoration of it, then the community loses a chance to create value for itself and for the nature around it. Because I consider cultures of nature as beginning (but certainly not ending) at the local level, and because I think restoration involves a unique opportunity to restore that culture (see my other contribution in this volume), then losing an opportunity to participate at a particular site is a loss first for the community closest to that site. This is the community that most importantly needs to develop or expand its relationship with its proximate nature. This is also the community that needs to develop or expand its long-term interest in preserving and protecting that bit of nature into the future. Restoration as a practice that helps to engender that relationship between a community and the nature proximate to it is thus tied to local participation as the best content for a particular act of restoration.[4]

Before moving ahead, I should address what may be an obvious concern about my comparisons between restoration and preservation: it may appear that I have simply stipulated a difference between the values produced in restorations and those produced in preservations, thus contradicting my earlier rejection of stipulative definitions of the character of restorations. I do not think that this is the case. One could argue that my suggestion that restorations, unlike preservations, could not occur accidently (or as I put it before, contingently) risks being stipulative? But using the term restoration to refer to something that could occur without intentions would be a mistake. Suppose, for example, that the point of a particular restoration project is the restoration of a wetland that had been destroyed to create a parking area. If that restoration is scrapped and a wetland reappears at the site a hundred years later, we would not call the new wetland a restored wetland but, more properly, a spontaneously regenerated wetland. The fact that restorations require intentional processes is not a problem for my argument about the differences between the differing values of restoration and preservation; it is the reason why these values can and should be distinguished. Again, I do not claim that a preserved site is of lesser value than a restored site but that its value must be evaluated in different terms because of the different kind of project it is. In contrast to a restoration, we do not generally have any problem describing something as a preservation if it does not contain a human factor. For example, we often speak of things having been preserved by unintentional processes. I can say quite legitimately that an ancient artifact or fossil has been preserved by its burial in a desert (without any person needing to bury it) or that a forest has been preserved by virtue of its remoteness and inaccessibility.

In principle, there seems nothing wrong with my pointing out how the values of restoration and preservation differ as long as the analysis of the characterization of the values at work in each project is not used as a basis for critiquing one form or another of environmental practice. Just pointing out the differing character of the value of restoration and its connection to the content of the value of a particular project is not to argue that restoration is superior as an environmental practice. It is, however, to argue that some kinds of values can be produced by a restoration that cannot always be produced in other kinds of practices. Surely people can participate in acts of preservation, but participation is not an issue uniquely at stake in all preservations. In contrast, participation is always an issue in a restoration, as are other evaluative criteria for good restorations, such as technical rigor, historical continuity with previous ecosystems at the site, and so forth. As I point out in my earlier contribution to this volume, we are remiss if we box ourselves in to evaluating restorations only at the level of their natural value. We must also consider the value of participating in projects that bring humans into relationships with nature. Although I had previously restricted my claim about the value of human participation in restoration to a methodologically pragmatist approach to restoration, here I can claim that considering this larger arena of values in restoration, participation is justified on a much broader ground. When compared with other environmental practices, restoration has an evaluative component involving participation that cannot be ignored without risking counterintuitive conclusions (a restoration performed by slaves is a good restoration) or dismissing the intentional components of restoration.

One last issue to consider in this general line of argument: in my view there is no inherently undemocratic potential in restoration.[5] To not fulfill the democratic potential of restoration is a failing of a restoration project and, as I will argue below, can be used as part of an overall consideration of criteria of what counts as a good ecological restoration.[6] If I am right that a democratic potential exists in each act of restoration, and it is true that some forms of environmental practice are inherently undemocratic (like slave labor), then restorations performed using those undemocratic methods are not living up to their potential. In my view, these are bad restorations in the same way that a restoration that fails to achieve its technical goals can be called a bad restoration.

But clearly we don't have to worry too much about the specter of restorations performed by slave labor. In other work, I have argued that particular kinds of restorations—like those performed by corporations—carry a very high burden of proof that they are not a waste of the democratic potential of restoration (Light and Higgs 1996). But this critique applies to only a very small category of restorations, and it does not necessarily demonstrate for us how this general criterion of preserving the democratic potential inherent in restorations affects the practice of all restorations. I will now consider an example of a worrisome parameter of restoration that may threaten the democratic character of all restorations.

Certification and the Restriction of Meaning

The example I want to look at is the sometimes discussed proposal in restoration circles to at least encourage, and at most require, the certification of practitioners of ecological restoration. Such certifications could take a variety of forms, everything from a certification only for use of fire or herbicides (which has been put in place in some areas) to formal degrees for site stewards or project leaders from a school or academic department specializing in ecological restoration (see Harris 1997). Certification is a curious issue in ecological restoration. Certification has to start with an understanding of what ecological restoration amounts to, accept some institutionalized form of that understanding, and then pass on that understanding to a core of specialists who would further revise and possibly make official the status of that understanding. While I have concerns about certification that I will discuss below, it should be clear that in principle certification could involve some tasks friendly to my approach to thinking about the value of restoration, namely a willingness to think hard about the meaning and implications of the practice of restoration, both in the abstract and for the larger community of restorationists.[7]

But more than an analysis of the value of restoration, certification would require more precise definitions of the practice of restoration. Where else to start with such a project but with definitions of the practice so that the field to be certified can be individuated from others? Definitions of a practice are not in themselves a problem, as we will see below. The deeper concern is whether moves toward defining restoration that are more ambitious than those I have offered here will stifle the democratic potential inherent in restoration. Given my comments above about the importance of preserving the value of public participation in restoration, it should be clear why I would be concerned about a framework for thinking about restoration that pushes us toward certification: if certification becomes required, then public participation could be chilled. Imagine, by analogy, the case where all democratic participation required a citizenship test for all citizens, regardless of whether they were foreign born. Requiring such a certification for participation in every-day democratic practices (like voting) would plausibly reduce participation in those practices even more than we see today. Finally, as we will see, the interest in moving toward certification and greater professionalization of restorationists may increase when volunteer restorationists are scapegoated in controversies over restoration. We need to avoid the temptation to move to greater professionalization just because volunteers become an easy target for the opponents of restoration.

Let's assume for a moment the plausibility of my previous arguments about the inherent democratic potential of restoration. Once we bring into this setting the possibility of certification of practitioners, the problem becomes walking the fine line between creating professional practitioners and maintaining the participatory structure of restoration that we currently find in many of the best examples of restoration. In the Chicago Wilderness project, for example, while participants are encouraged to take courses at the Prairie University (a virtual university comprising courses related to restoration practices, natural history, biology, and other topics, held at area schools and sponsored by volunteer organizations), they are not required to do so. Most learning, as Stephanie Mills (1995) and Reid Helford (this volume) point out, occurs in the field in the course of everyday restoration practice.

If participatory values are important for good ecological restorations, then certification at worst changes part of the essential character of the activity by creating an official hierarchy of practitioners (no matter how benignly it may be administered), rather than a de facto apprenticeship relationship as Mills describes in the Chicago case. If participatory values are an inherent potential for restoration, then should we preserve this part of the activity over the advantages certification might bring (e.g., systematization, rigor)? One concern is the extent to which certification would require formal definition of the practice and ends of ecological restoration. To explore this concern, we need to consider what happens when concepts or practices are overly defined. I will argue that terms can have an open or closed content; each kind of content has different implications for the issues at hand here. But this distinction requires further explanation.

Open content, with respect to language in general, refers to the sense in which terms can sustain different sorts of meaning by different people or communities in such a way that variability of reference of a term is understood as part of the term. The relative open content of much of language is what makes semantic drift (the process of words changing meaning over time) intuitively plausible. For instance, although it is always susceptible to being appropriated (or of being thought to have been appropriated by a particular community), the term God/god is relatively open with respect to content. Many of us now understand and largely accept that not everyone using this term means the same thing when they use it, and a growing number of people do not appear to be terribly disturbed by this state of the language. When someone says, "I think of God as _____," and then describes something wholly foreign to us, we accept that "God" is one of those terms whose meaning can be radically different for lots of people. We can disagree with someone else's description of God and yet possibly agree that some things are common to our differing descriptions, such as "God" referring to a being that is omnipotent and omniscient.

Closed content, on the other hand, means that a term, or a whole vocabulary of related terms, has had its meaning determined to the point where alternative uses can be deemed objectionable. When the state backs up closing the meaning of terms, bad things can happen. For example, in Germany in the 1930s, it was difficult to talk about nature without implying a reference to a big part of Nazism because the Nazi party used a particular conception of the human-nature relationship as a foundation for racial and sexual prejudice and eventual genocide. Proto-Nazis at the turn of the century embraced a nature philosophy (focusing on a particular Nordic conception of the place of the healthy human body in nature), which later the Nazi movement, then the party, and eventually the state used to secure a monopoly on the public perception of a range of related concepts—such as nation, nature, health (including a version of ecosystem health), and fitness. All these terms came to have clear political content. To challenge the dominant interpretation of nature was to incur the wrath of the state.

In a much less extreme form, certification risks closing the content of the meaning of a practice by authorizing a specific vocabulary about that practice. The American Medical Association (AMA) provides an example of the sorts of concerns that are justified about some aspects of certification. Certification and accreditation of doctors gives the AMA authority to determine how some kinds of practices meet the association's prescriptive views of such things as medicine, health, and fitness, and others do not. In general this is a good idea because it serves the public interest of having a community of competent doctors and reliable institutions that train medical professionals. Doctors must receive their degree from an AMA-accredited school to practice medicine or else go through an extensive review process. The political nature of certification is distinctly revealed when this system is challenged. The AMA has, for example, used its status as the certifier of medical education to quash the legitimacy of chiropractors by withholding accreditation from medical schools that offer courses in chiropractic medicine. Why? Cynics would argue that the dispute is less about what counts as good medicine, and more about who gets paid to heal the nation's back pains. Regardless, with certification comes authority over practices, and that authority may not always be fairly exercised. The same is true for any practice, but if a practice is uniquely situated to encourage a participatory culture of the practice, which I believe medicine is not, then certification risks attributing authority by closing the content of the meaning of the practice.

I want to suggest that part of what sustains the participatory character of ecological restoration is the open content of its vocabulary. What nature really is and what it represents in a larger sense is not necessarily prescribed by any authority in ecological restoration, as health and medicine are by the AMA. To try to overly prescribe the act of restoration would run against the participatory potential of ecological restoration that Jordan recognized and that can be further explicated as I have tried to do here. If open content is an important part of the democratic potential of ecological restoration, and certification is a move toward closed content, then certification can threaten the egalitarianism of ecological restoration.

One may reasonably find this last claim at odds with an important part of my earlier analysis: distinguishing restoration from preservation. Additionally, several of the arguments I make against Eric Katz's views in my earlier contribution to this volume rest on distinguishing restoration from other practices such as wetland mitigation. Why isn't the stipulation of a more formal definition of restoration, either as part of or as separate from a move to certification of practitioners, consonant with the distinctions I used in my earlier work? On the face of it, I would reply that identifying a practice as different from other practices in itself does not necessarily close the content of the meaning of a practice such as was the case with the AMA example. Surely a very thin line is being drawn here. But in cases where we must set policies for one kind of practice rather than another, such distinctions are important. For example, when the Bush administration set its "no net loss of wetlands" policy, it did not distinguish between restorations of destroyed wetlands as a substitute for lost wetlands and mitigation of wetland loss through the creation of new wetlands where none had existed. As a result, many "restored" wetlands were actually ecologically inferior mitigations. Definitions for directing policy may then be simply required ends for policy making and do not always imply closing the content of the meaning of a term. Schiappa (1996) uses the controversy over the definition of what counted as a wetland in the Bush policy to come to a similar conclusion: "To claim that one definition is superior to another because it captures what is 'really and truly' a wetland simply avoids the pragmatic question of *what ought to count* as a wetland for the purposes of federal regulation" (224, emphasis in original).

Following Schiappa, I would argue that the extent to which distinguishing one practice from another closes meaning is determined by the ends or purposes of the act of defining or distinguishing one thing from another. If the definitional process is designed to narrow or restrict meaning or create grounds for institutionalized hierarchies, we should be skeptical about its legitimacy. If the end is to create a space to more fully understand the richness and depth of the term or to prescribe policy in the face of conflicting demands, then we can worry less. But there is no firm dividing line here. Each act of defining or distinguishing a term needs to be looked at individually. In the end, it is crucial to remember that we cannot simply sit in our armchairs and speculate about the result of defining or prescribing a practice. We need to be prepared to gather empirical data to see what results from such a move. Perhaps this is the best argument against required certification, at some level, for all restorationists: if we institutionalize definitions of restoration by creating ambitious certification programs, then it becomes harder to back away from the institutions we create if they wind up restricting the evolution of our practices. Imagine how difficult it would be, for example, to dismantle or disempower the AMA.

In this way, certification risks restricting the language of ecological restoration. Perhaps only those who do not see the inherent moral and political elements of ecological restoration would not see how certification threatens its participatory character. For those who would argue that restoration works within a morally and politically neutral vocabulary, and can be evaluated only in scientific terms, then certification will no doubt seem uncontroversial. But if ecological restoration contains any inherently participatory potential, then it has a moral and political content, and if that participatory element is eroded, then that political content will be threatened by an anti-participatory, even anti-egalitarian content. Any act of ecological restoration is either (at least) participatory or not, and any vocabulary of ecological restoration either contributes to its participatory framework or does not. In either case the vocabulary of ecological restoration cannot be politically neutral. Following from this claim, and I hope by now some shared intuitions, it seems that closing the content of ecological restoration through certification (or some other means) is inconsistent with a robust description of the values at work in ecological restoration. Or, more precisely, any attempt at certification or definition must overcome the presumed hurdle that it risks closing the content of restoration.

With this last revised claim, the question remaining is whether any move to define ecological restoration, and any consequent move to certification, must threaten the democratic potential of ecological restoration. We can imagine moves to define and certify programs that did not threaten the democratic potential of ecological restoration, but only if such moves self-consciously addressed this worry. Part of the importance of including the democratic component of restoration in our evaluation of specific acts of restoration is to emphasize the value of keeping the vocabulary of ecological restoration open with respect to its content. A healthy tolerance of how people talk about ecological restoration ought to be encouraged within the bounds of preserving restoration's distinctiveness as a participatory practice.

Participation and the Chicago Wilderness Controversy

I am not suggesting here that restorations should be performed only by untrained, well-intentioned volunteers. Professional scientists, resource managers, and site stewards are absolutely needed to direct the efforts of volunteer restorationists. But do all directors need an official pedigree? One could argue, following my claims above, that especially if what counts as a good restoration goes beyond natural scientific criteria—for instance, if it embraces the democratic criteria I have introduced—then perhaps we do need to train restorationists in order to make sure they understand all of these criteria. At least in the case of the democratic criteria discussed above, however, this intuition runs head-on into its own justification. If certifying restorationists cuts against the grain of restoration's democratic potential, then to use that same democratic potential as a justification for certifying restoration is contradictory.

Still, there is an interesting point here. How do people learn about the democratic potential of restoration? Why will they value it? Do they learn it by being taught? I don't think so. I think it comes out in the practice—or the performance, as Jordan would say—of restoration. Thus, even though I can offer a philosophical justification for the democratic potential in all restoration projects, that potential is more often something that emerges or is realized through the practice of restoration itself (this claim seems consistent with Mills's [1995] understanding of the Chicago experience). For this reason, I understand why Jordan was tempted by the analogy between restoration and democratic culture. Jordan's understanding of the participatory character of the activity came from his participation in some of the most ambitious and longest-running restoration projects of late, and then later reflection on that participation. Ecological restoration and democratic values need not be forced together; they are cut from the same cloth. To separate these two is to harm the biotic community made up of restorers and the restored.

If we don't define restoration and don't certify restorers, however, we risk two immediate problems: (1) restoration may be defined for us from the outside (for example, by anti-environmentalists in some sort of wise use scenario) and (2) we may run into trouble when we do not have accepted experts on restoration available to be trotted out before the media and at oversight hearings to spar with opponents of restoration. The case of the Chicago Wilderness project and the related controversy over restoration in the Chicago-area forest preserves is a good place to investigate point (2). In 1996, following outcries by local critics, a partial moratorium on restoration activities was declared in two of the county forest preserve districts included in the project. As a result, a nineteen-year partnership between volunteer restorationists and public agencies ground to a halt. (For more details on the project and the controversy, see the Introduction and chapters by Helford and Vining et al. in this volume as well as articles by Shore 1997 and Gobster 1997.) As is well documented by Ross (1997) and by Schroeder in this volume, restoration activities conducted under the umbrella of the Chicago Wilderness project have realized their democratic potential and remained largely volunteer efforts, ensuring preservation of the participatory values in restoration. This has been done without mandatory certification.

But the focus on volunteer labor, even with such participatory benefits, was surely an important part of the restoration controversy in Chicago. For example, in the coverage of restoration efforts by the Chicago press, it was often pointed out how integral volunteers were to the maintenance and completion of the restorations. Claims that "volunteers were running amok without supervision" definitely hurt public reception of the project. Mark Brown (1997) of the *Chicago Sun-Times* reported that "Mary Lou Quinn, a leader of the Edgebrook residents who had complained, said the volunteer management should be eliminated entirely." Perhaps if some of the volunteers had had degrees to show reporters to prove they were certified to carry out these restorations, the project would have been less susceptible to such criticisms.

Certainly the response of Cook County Forest Preserve Board President John Stroger fueled the concern that the volunteers needed supervision by experts and that such supervision was lacking. Stroger lifted his September 1996 moratorium on restoration activity in Cook County on February 5, 1997 (except for the preserves near the Edgebrook community just mentioned), only after stricter guidelines for restoration activity were approved, including creation of a citizen advisory council to oversee the projects and restriction of many restoration activities unless a county employee was present to oversee the work (Carmody 1997). In one of the most extreme instances of enactment of the new county rules, volunteers were not allowed to pull garlic mustard from the Hidden Pond Prairie Forest Preserve because the county employee assigned to supervise the work did not show up. Volunteers, of course, were dismayed. The response of the restorationists was reported in an interview in the *Daily Southtown*: "'It's crazy to require that a [forest preserve] district employee be present for pulling garlic mustard or white sweet clover,' said Keller, the volunteer steward who coordinates restoration work at Hidden Pond Prairie near Hickory Hills. 'I used to go out three to four evenings per week when my schedule permitted, and others did too, but that's now impossible'" (Carmody 1997).

It is tempting to think that certification of volunteers and stricter definition of acceptable restoration practices could have stopped this set of problems. After all, if the restorationists were experts, then they could not have been so easily made scapegoats. One could argue that a certification program for restorationists, or even less reliance on volunteer labor to begin with, would have stood in the way of such a response to, and later restriction of, restoration activities. But there is good reason to be skeptical of such a suggestion. There is no reason to believe that the Chicago restoration controversy would have been avoided if volunteers had not participated, or if they had all been certified in some way. The same opposition likely would have occurred even if restoration activities had been carried out by 3,800 clones of project founder Steve Packard. Opponents of restoration were upset over a host of issues (for example, killing exotic trees and endangering animals), not just by the participatory elements of the process. So the values of participation captured by the Chicago Wilderness project neither stood in the way of the success of the project nor uniquely hindered it. While we can imagine how the existence of a cadre of certified supervisors would have taken the edge off some of the criticisms, it would not have deflected the worst political response to the criticism (the moratorium) or the results of the controversy.

Still, to be fair, one can see how the culture of experts plays an undeniable role in situations like this one (see Helford, this volume). In a story about the creation of the citizen advisory council, membership in the council is described as including "Edgebrook resident Petra Blix, a Trees for Life member [one of the neighborhood groups opposing the restorations] who also holds a doctorate in biology" (Keenan 1997). Certainly Blix's Ph.D. in biology is supposed to be noteworthy. Would it help to have someone with a doctorate in restoration ecology to counter Dr. Blix? Perhaps, although if the degree came from the Prairie University, its legitimacy would likely be challenged.

Rather than regarding more precise definitions of restoration and increased calls for certification as the solution to such controversies, we, as a community of restorationists convinced, I hope, of the necessity of creating avenues for public participation in restorations whenever possible, should consider other alternatives. As I said before, it is certainly fine to have project managers, botanical and biological experts, site stewards, and other leaders on a project. But before jumping to certification as a further level of making such leadership positions professional, we should instead focus on accepting as a community the value and importance of maintaining the participatory elements of restoration projects because of the unique democratic values we may capture in such projects. I will not stoop to trite sayings such as "Our leaders should also be followers," but will instead argue that our leaders must acknowledge the full range of values at work in assessing a good restoration— from the scientific to the moral and political—to be worthy to lead our projects. Already, this is a characteristic of many of the great restoration site managers in our midst, since many of them either started out or continue on as volunteers. It will be up to the full community of restorationists to ensure that this characteristic of leadership is expected from all site managers and other experts working on such projects.

Of course, we can do other things as well to help ensure that the participatory values of ecological restorations will always be potentially present. One idea (which I will develop in a future paper) is to propose legislation or policies requiring any restoration project that receives public money to offer local communities the right of first refusal to undertake these projects, where the scale and complexity of the project permit public participation. If local communities accept this offer, then public funds can be used to hire experts and managers to provide technical expertise to direct the work of the volunteers. As such, voluntary participation will be one of the foundations of the project from the start. Where scale and complexity prohibit widespread voluntary participation, then efforts will have to be made to involve the local community in smaller tasks that contribute to the larger project. In the end, though, those restoration projects that contain more public participation will be, all things considered, better than those that contain less.

Notes

1. This portion of my argument draws from some of my original contributions to Light and Higgs (1996), but has been greatly revised and should supersede the argument made there about Jordan's views on the democratic potential of restoration and my own argument for the values inherent in restoration. Although my more recent views here should be taken as an update of my previous work in this area (which goes back to Light 1995), I cannot say whether Eric Higgs would prefer this version of the argument or the one that we published jointly in 1996. I continue to be grateful to Eric for conversations that have helped me sharpen and revise these arguments.

2. This assumes, of course, that the value of the land is not simply reducible to the value given to it by a valuing agent. Most environmental philosophers assume that the value of nature must be articulated nonanthropocentrically. See my other contribution in this volume for a description of the basis and function of such arguments.

3. The question of whether or not the value produced in a restoration is natural value is philosophically up for grabs and beyond the scope of this chapter. Here it should be permissible to separate out the disagreements over the value of restoration such as those that may be stimulated by the work of Robert Elliot (1997) and Eric Katz (1997), except for Katz's claim (which he makes inconsistently) that all restoration produces disvalue in nature by dominating nature. See my other contribution in this volume for a full explication of Katz's claims and an answer to the harshest of them. If my arguments against Katz there are persuasive, then my argument here should at least not suffer from a concern about whether or not restorations can produce positive natural value. I maintain in my previous chapter in this volume that even if restorations cannot produce natural value per se, they can produce value for nature.

4. At this point my argument about the locality of the values at work in restoration follows part of the logic of Eric Katz's (1997) claims about how restoration results

in the domination of nature. Part of Katz's position relies on the argument that restorations replace whatever nature would have been eventually produced on the site where the restoration takes place. As such, for Katz, even if a restoration would produce a better ecosystem (for surrounding fauna, for example) than a naturally evolved system, the restoration still counts as an act of domination over nature. While I reject Katz's claim, my logic here is structurally similar: if all acts of restoration include an inherent democratic potential, then to produce a restoration undemocratically necessarily excludes the potentially democratic restoration that could have occurred at that particular site. Just as Katz's argument is about local disvalue of restoration, my argument also locates potential disvalue at a particular site. Here, however, I see no countervailing positive value (morally or politically speaking) that could outweigh this disvalue, even though some technical constraints to the restoration (scale and complexity) could certainly be used to rule out wide-scale local participation.

5. There is the nagging question of whether restoration can be connected with fascism, either metaphorically through the idea of rooting out exotics, or through some more direct historical connection. Bill Jordan (1994b, 113) provides a good answer to the question of the metaphorical connotations of restoration in an editorial, "The Nazi Connection." Donna Haraway (1995) voices concern over the direct connection in a brief exchange with me reprinted in *Society and Space*. For reasons I will not go into here, but which I do discuss in Light (2001), I do not think that charges of fascism in relation to restoration are sound.

6. For a more complete argument describing the qualities of a good ecological restoration, see Higgs (1997).

7. Harris's (1997) suggestions for mandatory certification are certainly motivated by concerns friendly to my interests. Anyone familiar with his editorial on this issue, however, will see where my objections to his proposals would begin, especially if one is sympathetic to the concerns I will raise in this section of this chapter. While Harris's proposal is not fully developed (it is, after all, a one-page editorial), his intentions are quite clear: certification of restorationists that would be "backed by a professional body with moral and legal liabilities and procedures" (5). The Society for Ecological Restoration (SER) and Jordan's nascent New Academy are indicated as bodies that could back certification and carry out the programs necessary to make it work. But as I argue below, using the example of the American Medical Association, investing authority for certification in a body like the SER comes at a price and a high risk, especially with respect to the issue of what understanding of restoration, in terms of both its practice and its ends, is codified in the process of certification. And while I am very sympathetic with Harris's worries over shoring up the lines of responsibility for what counts as a good restoration, I am not so sure that the actual on-the-ground controversies over restoration would be ameliorated all that much by a process of certification. I say more about this issue in the next section. (Harris and I might just be talking past each other, of course; he might not advocate certification for volunteers, just for project managers. His editorial is unclear on this point, something that we can surely forgive given the requirements of brevity for editorials.)

I want to state clearly that I am not against better, more robust interdisciplinary education for restoration professionals or the creation of something like the New Academy; I just do not believe these efforts are a panacea for the problems of restoration identified by Harris and by me here. One can have education without certification, as is currently the case with the Prairie University (more on this virtual campus below).

I will not take up here the specifics of Harris's or any other certification proposal. My purpose in this chapter is only to provide some cautionary tales about defining restoration and certifying restorationists in relation to the value of public participation in restorations. As the reader will see below, I don't rule out certification writ large, although I would put some constraints on the values that it would have to engender and the relative authority of certified restorationists in the field. No doubt some will find my lack of analysis of specific proposals frustrating; I can only hope that those readers will wait until I have an opportunity to explicate my concerns about particular proposals in another forum.

References

Brown, M. 1997. "Stroger Proposes Closer Supervision of Forest Restoration Work." *Chicago Sun-Times* (Online Edition) January 8.

Carmody, K. 1997. "Unruly Nature: Rules Sideline Conservation Volunteers." *Daily Southtown* June 27.

Elliot, R. 1997. *Faking Nature.* London: Routledge.

Gobster, P. 1997. "The Chicago Wilderness and Its Critics, III. The Other Side: An Analysis." *Restoration & Management Notes* 15(1): 32–37.

Haraway, D. 1995. "Nature, Politics, and Possibilities: A Debate and Discussion with David Harvey and Donna Haraway." *Society and Space* 13: 523–524.

Harris, J. 1997. "Certification for Responsible Restoration." *Restoration & Management Notes* 15(1): 5.

Higgs, E. 1997. "What Is a Good Ecological Restoration?" *Conservation Biology* 11: 338–348.

Jordan, W. 1994a. "Sunflower Forest: Ecological Restoration as the Basis for a New Environmental Paradigm." In *Beyond Preservation: Restoring and Inventing Landscapes,* edited by A. D. Baldwin, Jr., J. De Luce, and C. Pletsch, 17–34. Minneapolis: University of Minnesota Press.

Jordan, W. 1994b. "The Nazi Connection." *Restoration & Management Notes* 12: 113.

Katz, E. 1997. *Nature as Subject: Human Obligation and Natural Community.* Lanham, MD: Rowman & Littlefield.

Keenan, K. 1997. "Silvestri Seeks 9th Advisory Council Volunteers." *Elmwood Park Elm Leaves* July 16.

Light, A. 1995. "Hegemony and Democracy: How the Inherent Politics in Restoration Informs the Politics of Restoration." *Restoration & Management Notes* 12: 140–144.

Light, A. 2001. "What Is an Ecological Identity?" *Environmental Politics* 10, forthcoming.

Light, A., and E. Higgs. 1996. "The Politics of Ecological Restoration." *Environmental Ethics* 18: 227–247.

Mills, S. 1995. *In Service of the Wild.* Boston: Beacon Press.

Ross, L. M. 1997. "The Chicago Wilderness and Its Critics, I. The Chicago Wilderness: A Coalition for Urban Conservation." *Restoration & Management Notes* 15(1): 17–24.

Schiappa, E. 1996. "Towards a Pragmatic Approach to Definitions: 'Wetlands' and the Politics of Meaning." In *Environmental Pragmatism,* edited by A. Light and E. Katz, 231–250. London: Routledge.

Shore, D. 1997. "The Chicago Wilderness and Its Critics, II: Controversy Erupts over Restoration in Chicago Area." *Restoration & Management Notes* 15(1): 25–31.

✤ *Part III* ✤

MAKING RESTORATION HAPPEN: PROCESS AND IMPLEMENTATION

❧ Chapter 9 ❧

NEGOTIATING NATURE: MAKING RESTORATION HAPPEN IN AN URBAN PARK CONTEXT

Paul H. Gobster and Susan C. Barro

Is nature "out there" or in our heads? Recent debates in the humanities and the physical and social sciences provide convincing arguments on both sides (e.g., Cronon 1995, Rolston 1997, Soulé and Lease 1995; see also chapters by Brunson and by Hull and Robertson in this volume). But despite which side people may lean toward, most would agree that as we turn our focus from wild landscapes toward ones that are dominated by humans, "objective" indicators of nature and naturalness that can guide restoration and management efforts become more and more ambiguous.

Urban parks are places where such ambiguity reigns. In many urban parks, historic conditions of soil, hydrology, microclimate, and vegetation have been so severely modified by past human activity that even the use of the term restoration sometimes seems inappropriate (Raffetto 1993). Landscape fragmentation and adjacent land uses can also limit how well the structure and function of an ecological community can be restored and ecological processes like fire successfully reintroduced (e.g., Kline 1997). Add to these physical and biological conundrums social and political constraints such as divergent values and uses of urban parks, and the prescription for restoring and managing nature becomes a very blurry one indeed (Gobster 1997).

Yet despite these challenges, people's desire for interaction with urban

185

nature is stronger than ever. Studies in urban settings have shown that nearby nature fulfills many important restorative functions, from stress reduction (Ulrich 1981) and temporary mood improvement (Hull and Michael 1995) to opportunities for inner growth and change (Kaplan 1995). Demographic analyses project that as the population becomes older, more diverse, and more urban, demand for urban nature activities like bird watching will increase significantly (Dwyer 1994). And environmental educators are increasingly advocating programs that bring urban children into contact with nature in the course of everyday experiences (Simmons 1994).

The typical landscape of urban parks—an expanse of mowed turf studded with trees—constitutes nature of one sort, especially in contrast to the surrounding cityscape. Through the process of restoration, however, these settings could offer much more in the way of wildlife habitat, species diversity, or other valued natural qualities. The question then becomes, "What form should urban nature take in a particular setting?" Despite the strong desire and appreciation for urban nature, the diversity of people's ideas and values often makes it difficult for managers to identify the kinds of nature and nature experiences people want in a given area. This diversity of ideas and values was one of the main problems in the controversy over restoration of the Chicago-area forest preserves described in the Introduction and chapters by Helford and Vining et al. in this volume. One might guess that for an urban park the range of views could be at least as diverse.

In writing about the interaction of culture and landscape ecology, landscape architect Joan Nassauer (1997) has called the resolution of this dilemma one of "placing nature":

> Where nature *should be* in settled landscapes to improve their ecological function is a critical question for which landscape ecology suggests answers. Where nature *can be* in the enormously complex but fundamentally pragmatic cultural process of making places is equally fundamental. Science may give us normative criteria for new landscape patterns, culture will give us the realized design (5–6, emphasis in original).

Thus, even if ecologists can provide theoretical and technical input to answer questions about what goes where and how to accomplish it, the ultimate success of such efforts relies on cultural acceptance. And what constitutes acceptability makes the management of urban natural areas a real challenge. When, in the course of a planning effort for a large Chicago park, an opportunity became available to study people's concepts of nature, we saw it as a means of answering some of these questions.

A second area we sought to examine was how a participatory planning and design process was being used to arrive at socially acceptable ways for defining, restoring, and managing nature.

Many models of participatory planning and design exist and have been described and critiqued elsewhere (e.g., Arnstein 1969, Francis et al. 1987, Innes 1996). The approach used in the case study we examined most closely parallels what landscape architect Randolf Hester and others have called "participation with a view" (Francis 1999, Hester 1999). In this approach, proactive designers and planners take a pivotal role in helping to guide the process, working together with stakeholders to achieve a synthesis of goals and a more holistic and inclusive vision. This role goes beyond that of the advocacy planner, who uses his or her expertise to reach an equitable solution for the groups involved. As will be seen in our case study, expertise is a relative concept (see also Helford, this volume). Many stakeholder groups hold higher levels of knowledge about particular restoration issues than do planners or designers leading the process, and outside experts can often provide fresh perspectives from other places and experiences. The role of participatory planners and designers also goes beyond that of a rational planner, who just synthesizes expert information from these diverse participants into a logically acceptable solution. As our study also shows, expert information often is built upon an ideological foundation, in this case strong emotional attachments to place, and thus opposed groups are not always swayed by rational solutions. As a result, participatory designers and planners must also be advocates to successfully motivate change. Finally, participatory planners and designers as envisioned by Hester and others must go beyond the role of the facilitator or conflict mediator, who may be able to work out an acceptable compromise among ideologically opposed groups but may end up with a product that lacks a unified vision and spirit. Instead, making complex decisions about which nature might be chosen among a number of alternatives requires the ability to identify stakeholder goals and knowledge about the particular aspects of a place that they value, as well as the leadership to integrate them within a broader vision of what urban nature can be. Understanding just how this process of negotiating nature can most effectively work can thus be a key to the successful implementation of restoration and management projects.

In the sections that follow, we describe our research, done within the context of an ongoing effort to provide a broad spectrum of nature experiences within a large, heavily used urban park. We first characterize the effort, including the park context and the stakeholders involved. We then describe the process of how park stakeholders are attempting to place nature and negotiate appropriate ways to design and manage it at one site within the park. From these findings, we attempt to draw some conclusions and implications for urban park and forest restoration efforts. It is our hope that this account of our experiences will provide insights that others might use in their attempts to work with diverse stakeholders toward the development and implementation of restoration goals.

Montrose Point Case Study

The context of our work is Lincoln Park, a 1,200-acre park along the shore of Lake Michigan, stretching north from downtown Chicago for six miles. Managed by the Chicago Park District, it is the largest city park in the Chicago region and one of the largest in the country. In recently completed plans, several areas within the park were identified as having a high potential for enhancement to attract wildlife and to more closely mirror the structure and species diversity of landscapes that existed in the region prior to urbanization (Chicago Park District 1997, Chicago Park District and Lincoln Park Steering Committee 1995). Based on these assessments, funds were secured to study four sites within the park in more detail and to develop plans and policies for their restoration and management. In this chapter, we focus on the largest of these sites, Montrose Point, and on a cooperative research effort with the Lincoln Park Advisory Council (LPAC) called the Montrose Point Restoration Project.

Montrose Point is an eleven-acre section near the park's northern end. Although from an ecological restoration perspective the natural and social history of the point might seem unusual, in many ways it captures the range of issues and conditions faced by restorationists in urban settings. Like much of Lincoln Park, Montrose Point is an entirely artificial creation. Constructed from landfill that was removed for new harbor and subway development and placed into the lake, Montrose Point allowed for the extension of Lake Shore Drive and development of new parkland for the expanding metropolis. Construction of the Montrose Extension began in 1929, and a landscape plan for the site was developed in 1938 by Chicago Park District landscape architect Alfred Caldwell (Nathan et al. 1991). Caldwell was a contemporary of Jens Jensen, often referred to as the dean of the Prairie School of landscape architecture.

Following the Prairie School ideals promoted by Jensen and others, Caldwell's design plan for Montrose Point used native plants in a stylized arrangement that emulated the diverse Midwestern landscape of prairie, savanna, and woodland (Domer 1997, Grese 1992). The central feature of the plan was an open, meadowlike "room" enclosed by multilayered masses of wildflowers, shrubs, and trees. From the meadow, openings through these masses toward the lake were to create a sense of the infinite. On the landward side, a similar opening was planned to create a sense of mystery about what lay beyond. In Prairie School parlance, this was known as the long view. As an abstraction of the native prairie, the meadow was to be of mowed grass, to facilitate recreational use and to act as a neutral ground plane to lead the eye toward the key views. A path around the perimeter of the site would lead parkgoers through this alternating series of densely planted masses and open views and out to a beachfront promenade (Figure 9.1).

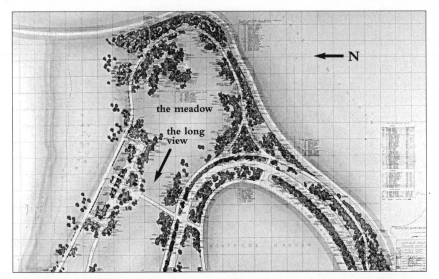

Figure 9.1. Original Alfred Caldwell Design for Montrose Point Showing Location of the Meadow and the Long View (1939). (Chicago Park District)

While this plan had a great deal of aesthetic and ecological merit, little of it was ever implemented. Shortly after its completion, the point was taken over by the U.S. Army and fenced off for use as a World War II radar station, and in the 1950s it was more fully developed as a Nike missile base as part of the Cold War strategy to protect Chicago. To screen structures and operations from park users, a row of honeysuckle shrubs was planted along the Cyclone fence, separating the site from the park proper. When the site was finally reclaimed as park space in the 1970s and the fence and other structures were removed, the landscape consisted of scattered trees—some of which may have been planted according to the original Caldwell plan—and the honeysuckle fencerow (Figure 9.2). The perimeter pathway was widened to allow automobile access to the tip of the point for fishing and picnicking, but no strategy was developed for dealing with Montrose Point until the late 1980s, when the Chicago Park District began a master planning process for the park as a whole.

But in that period between the early 1970s and the late 1980s something happened. Partly due to benign neglect of the point and partly because the point juts into the lake and away from active use areas, the row of honeysuckle became a virtual magnet for birds. This scruffy mass of vegetation became known as the Magic Hedge to birders, who regularly counted more than 200 different species there during spring and fall migrations. With the cooperation of the Park District, Chicago-area birding groups began augmenting the Magic Hedge in the 1980s by planting additional shrubs and trees, mainly nonnative honeysuckle and mulberry, to attract more birds. Also in the inter-

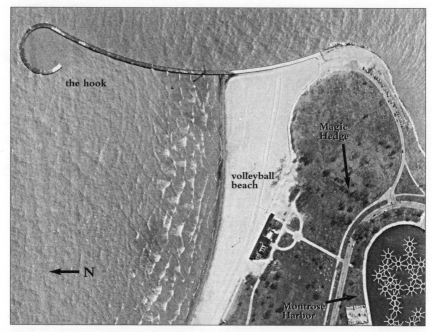

Figure 9.2. Aerial View of Montrose Point Prior to Master Planning Efforts Showing Location of Key Landscape Features (1990). (Chicago Park District)

est of accommodating the migrating birds, the Park District in the last decade has instituted a no-mow policy for the point. This policy has provided more insects and better cover for the birds and has resulted in a look distinctly different from the groomed grass found in the rest of the park. Publicity given to these habitat improvement efforts has also helped to attract birders, and today the Magic Hedge draws birders from far and wide.

With completion of the Lincoln Park Framework Plan in 1995, it became clear that Montrose Point and the Magic Hedge served unique roles in the park and that much more could be done to improve them, not only for birds but also for this expanding group of birders. At the same time, however, the planning process provided an opportunity to hear from other stakeholder groups so their views could be considered in the decision making for the point. If a more nature-oriented future was to become a reality, any implementation strategy for the plan would need to address the concerns of all stakeholders.

Stakeholders

A wide range of stakeholders have an interest in Montrose Point and its management. The two groups most directly involved in the Montrose Point

Restoration Project are the Chicago Park District and the Lincoln Park Advisory Council. Under the 1995 Framework Plan, the Park District was directed to "[e]xpand wildlife habitat with additional planting near the Magic Hedge" and "[r]estore historic landscape in manner consistent with original Caldwell landscape plan" (Chicago Park District and Lincoln Park Steering Committee 1995, 33). The Lincoln Park Advisory Council (LPAC), a nonprofit organization representing community interests in Lincoln Park, is the lead entity in the Montrose Point Restoration Project. In its formally established role as an advisory council for Lincoln Park, LPAC works with and makes recommendations to the Park District on planning and other activities. Working with a team of consultants that it established for the project, LPAC pursued its charge of directing and coordinating design, planning, and public involvement efforts. As part of the public involvement process, LPAC identified and sought input from the following three major categories of public stakeholder groups: environmental, historic preservation and design, and recreational interests.

Environmental interests. As previously mentioned, the Chicago-area birding community is an important environmental interest of Montrose Point. Composed of several organized groups and many nonaffiliated individuals, this community is focused on protection and enhancement of the Magic Hedge and its surroundings for bird habitat and birding. Environmental interests are also represented by a loose coalition of individuals from established restoration, citizen-forestry, and adjacent yacht club groups. These individuals formed the Montrose Point Stewardship Group in 1996 with the goal of ecological enhancement of the point. Their interest in the point is much more recent than that of the birder group.

Historic preservation and design interests. A chief proponent of historic preservation and design interests in park restoration has been the Chicago Park District itself. The Park District has sought to restore significant parks in their system that exemplify the Prairie Style, Naturalism, and other important movements in landscape architectural history (Chicago Historical Society 1991). Other individuals and groups such as the Landmarks Preservation Council of Illinois have joined the Park District in achieving this goal, and see restoration of the Caldwell plan for Montrose Point as a unique opportunity.

Recreational interests. As in most of Lincoln Park, recreation at Montrose Point and its surroundings can be characterized by a high level of diverse uses (People, Places & Design Research 1991). The long, unmowed grass of the central part of the point both encourages and discourages certain recreational users; in addition to birders, a variety of passive users such as walkers, dog walkers, and picnickers frequent this wilder portion of the park. The perimeter areas of the point cater to a variety of other specialized recreational interests. In summer, league volleyball players use the beach along the north shore of the point, and yacht club members concentrate at Montrose Harbor, just west of the point. Anglers form one of the major recreational interests at Montrose; the harbor and the breakwater hook extending out from the point are the most popular and productive pedestrian fishing areas along the entire Lake Michigan shoreline in Illinois (Brofka and Marsden 1997).

While not included as a separate stakeholder group in the discussions, another key type of interest includes individuals and groups who see Montrose Point as a place to actively engage in experiencing and restoring nature through volunteering. These participatory interests include the Montrose Point Stewardship Group mentioned earlier, as well as a subset of the birding community that has organized under the Bird Conservation Network to work on bird habitat conservation and monitoring. Another group is focused on education and has developed an experiential learning program called Nature Along the Lake to bring elementary school children to Montrose to learn about terrestrial and aquatic ecosystems. Finally, there is the Montrose Point Youth Program, which involves high school students in hands-on projects to learn about the natural environment and its design and management in an urban context. All of these groups have a stake in the future design and management of Montrose Point and are seeking active involvement in the implementation of the Montrose Point Restoration Project.

Placing Nature at Montrose Point

The planning and design process began with a series of focus group discussions that were held to get a better idea of how different individuals and groups felt about the prospects of restoring the natural and historic qualities of Montrose Point. Focus groups were conducted with six stakeholder groups in the fall of 1997. Individuals for the angler and passive user groups were recruited on site. Participants for the other four groups—environmental, historic preservation and design, volleyball, and yacht club—were recruited through personal contacts with their organizations. The focus groups, ranging from two to twelve people each, were held at the yacht club adjacent to Montrose Point and were moderated by a professional facilitator. Each session began with a tour of the point followed by a guided discussion lasting about one hour and covering the following topics related to Montrose Point: uses and values, problems and concerns, and rehabilitation and change.[1]

Agreement about Nature

When asked why people valued Montrose Point, focus group participants widely agreed that nature was a key element in their use and appreciation. As these quotes exemplify, individuals of diverse affiliations see Montrose as a special natural place that provides the kinds of recreation opportunities and experiences not available elsewhere in Lincoln Park or the city:

> *Environmentalist/Birder:* I can go out there and feel like I'm completely separate from the city, that there's nothing out there that—there's no lights. There's no aspect of any part of the city. It's just the trees and the birds and the water, just a very nice, isolated place to be.

> *Passive user:* I appreciate the area much more since it's become naturalized. And it does offer a certain spiritual retreat from the rest of the park. It's quite removed from that.

> *Angler:* [Besides the fishing], it's such a nice experience to come here because of the other things, the landscaping. You know you're not fishing below the generating station. There's some "fishing intangibles" here that you don't find in other places.

Accommodating Specific Uses

Within this natural context, however, most of the groups also wanted to see Montrose Point designed and managed so that their uses could be accommodated and that other uses did not conflict with their own interests. Sometimes the conflicting use was nature itself. For example, a few birders felt that the natural environment should be managed to maximize opportunities for bird viewing:

> I don't know that there should be a mania for native plants here. Maybe the mania should be for what's going to feed and attract birds.

Similarly, anglers who were dismayed by the removal of an asphalt road along the southern perimeter of the point in the fall of 1996 strongly felt that any design and management plan should restore access to the breakwater hook for fishing:

> Keep part of the nature intact, but still have a good area, easily accessible, parking, and still have it primarily for fishing.

Individuals in other groups also voiced concerns about the prospects of managing the site as a natural area in relation to their interests. Volleyball players, for example, found restoration activities acceptable as long as the portion of the beach they used for court space was not jeopardized. Yacht club members felt that increased popularity of the point as a natural area could make access and parking for harbor users more difficult and worsen an already serious safety conflict between cars and bike path users. Individuals in the group of historic preservationists and designers were concerned about the unique historic qualities of Montrose Point and how these could be compromised by such a diverse set of activities:

> When it becomes an historic landscape it's got museum quali-
> ties but then it also has to function as a space that on the week-
> ends in the summertime is trampled on, used, and abused. . . .

Negotiating Nature

The focus groups were invaluable for understanding how the various interests felt about the point and how they would like to see it managed. While there was a general agreement on seeing the natural qualities of Montrose Point enhanced for plant and bird species, there were equally strong feelings about balancing concerns for nature with those for human use and enjoyment. The issues raised in the focus group sessions helped begin a process of negotiating the kind of nature that will be present at Montrose Point, a process that is still ongoing.

Development of Design Alternatives

During the winter of 1997–1998, landscape designers from the LPAC con-
sulting team worked on initial concept plans for Montrose Point. Three design alternatives were developed. Each design followed the general layout of the original Caldwell design—a central meadow surrounded by masses of multi-
level vegetation and a main gravel pathway along the perimeter and out to the base of the breakwater. The alternatives varied in the treatment and species composition of the central meadow and the presence of built structures such as picnic areas and council rings (a circular arrangement of stone benches, a signature element of Caldwell's and Jensen's Prairie School designs). For discussion purposes, these three alternatives will be referred to based on their treatment of the central meadow as follows: the prairie meadow, the prairie/mowed meadow, and the mowed meadow.[2] One notable exception to the Caldwell design in all three plans was that the Magic Hedge would be maintained and expanded, even though its location does not correspond to the tree and shrub masses in the original design.

A public meeting was held in the spring of 1998 to involve stakeholders in a discussion of the three alternatives. Although notices of the meeting had been sent to all interested groups, birders made up a large proportion of attendees. In the course of the meeting, the designers for LPAC, consistent with their participatory role, endorsed the plan featuring the prairie meadow, which they felt maximized the natural values of the point and minimized use con-

flicts. They felt the other two plans, featuring some form of mowed meadow, would invite active uses into the area that would be incompatible with the values people were seeking at the site. The majority of the attendees also favored the prairie meadow plan, but were averse to including any built structures on the point—council rings, picnic groves, or shelters—as they felt these, too, would attract incompatible users and uses.

Park District Responses

One of the main stakeholders in the negotiation process, the Chicago Park District, remained fairly silent until after the public meeting. At that time, however, they decided that holding a focus group with their own employees could be beneficial. The Park District focus group was composed of ten staff members representing the range of Park District interests, from landscape architecture, forestry, and historic preservation to engineering, operations, and administration. Despite the diversity of interests represented, these members of the Park District staff were in broad agreement with each other and with the public interest stakeholders on many issues, including promoting nature and wildness as a primary theme for the point and accommodating appropriate uses and levels of access within that theme.

One important topic for this group concerned the balancing of restoration goals at Montrose between improving wildlife habitat and implementing the original Caldwell design. Some Park District participants, especially the historic preservation interests, differed substantially from the public interest stakeholder groups and LPAC on this issue:

> Person 1: Well, I'm concerned about retaining the historic integrity of the landscape. And even though the landscape is kind of in a state of decline . . . the basic essence of Caldwell's design is still pretty much there, which is an open meadow enclosed by planted edges with certain areas that provide specific views. . . .

In the course of this discussion, it became clear that there were two main issues where the Caldwell design and the prairie meadow plan, favored by LPAC and some public stakeholders, were in conflict. The first point of contention was related to the Magic Hedge and its location with respect to Caldwell's plan:

> Person 2: [The Magic Hedge] seems to interrupt the long view. But yet, in part I sense [the hedge] is what triggered us to do [this plan], and so I think there's kind of an interesting contradiction going on here. And in reality, it sounds like we are going to want to make the argument to remove the Magic Hedge and open the long view, which seems ironic to some degree. . . .

The second issue concerned the height of plants in the meadow:

> *Person 1:* The thing that concerned me was that I saw a plan
> where there would be a lot of tall grasses and other kinds of
> plant materials in the center. And to me, it seems like they'd be
> much more appropriate on the edges . . . if there's tall grasses
> and other plant materials in the middle, then obviously you
> don't have a view.

A subsequent Park District working session was held in the early fall of 1998 to follow up on issues raised in the Park District focus group and to develop an internally consistent position for dealing with the design and development of Montrose Point. Participants in this larger group generally reaffirmed ideas advocated in the Park District focus group to favor elements of the Caldwell plan, in apparent opposition to some of the other groups. The general consensus was that the Magic Hedge would not be expanded; additionally, it was suggested that an opening be created at midpoint in the hedge to allow for the long view as intended by Caldwell. Likewise, the meadow would be maintained as mowed grass in the center, with taller grasses and perennials forming a transition to the perimeter masses of shrub and overstory trees (similar to the prairie/mowed meadow plan). Park District staff believed these perimeter masses would in effect create additional Magic Hedges throughout the point, deemphasizing the unique importance of the original hedge for birds.

Resolving the Conflicts

By the close of 1998, much progress had been made in placing nature at Montrose Point in terms of defining appropriate access, use, and other issues. Yet stakeholder positions regarding the central meadow and the Magic Hedge seemed further apart than ever. Part of the problem, participants agreed, was that up to this point much of the discussion had occurred within groups, with little direct interaction between groups. To help remedy this situation, a workshop was held in early 1999 to address the integration of historic preservation and nature enhancement goals for Montrose Point.

Four respected outside speakers were recruited to provide some ideas and perspectives for consideration in the Montrose plan from their fields of expertise in landscape architectural history, restoration ecology, conservation biology, and botany. Each speaker gave a short presentation at the beginning of the workshop. This was followed by a facilitated discussion focusing on questions about (1) the general structure of the landscape, (2) what to do about the Magic Hedge, and (3) how the meadow should be managed. Key individuals from Park District staff, the environmental group (largely birders), and the historic preservation and design group worked through each of the three issues with guidance and input from the speakers and from LPAC's designers.

With respect to the general structure of the landscape, the issue of the significance of the Caldwell landscape was at the center of the discussion. Birders wondered why the Park District wanted to manage the area to be consistent with Caldwell's plan:

> What are you managing for, why Caldwell? Why is he so important? This is an expensive proposition, and if there's no particularly absolute reason to use Caldwell, couldn't you do something cheaper that's just as good?

In response, one Park District historian likened the Caldwell landscape at Montrose Point to

> having the *Mona Lisa* in your backyard. If somebody handed you a Leonardo da Vinci painting, would you say, "Let's just paint over this?"

As for the Magic Hedge, stakeholders presented information and made use of knowledge provided by the outside experts about plant species, bird behavior patterns, and site sustainability to argue for its preservation or dissolution. A discussion of seasonal changes in leaf cover and height variations in native shrub palettes suggested that there might be a resolution that would accommodate coexistence of the hedge and the long view. It may be possible, for example, to achieve a continuous hedge with a section of low shrubs that would afford a type of long view (albeit somewhat obstructed), especially during the leaf-off part of the year.

Above and beyond these debates, however, was the value that birders placed on the Magic Hedge. For instance, one birder spoke of the hedge as

> an icon. It's a cultural icon that's so powerful you can't even imagine it. I can't talk for all birders, but lots of birders hold it sacred. You do something to the Magic Hedge, anything other than augment it I mean, I've got bail money set aside, I mean, I'll chain myself to a tree and lots of other people will, too.

In the course of this discussion, it became clear that one root of the conflict between the Magic Hedge and the Caldwell design is that both had attained the status of cultural icons among their respective interests.

The final topic of discussion, the meadow, also concluded without a clear consensus on direction but with a tendency to favor a modified version of the prairie/mowed meadow plan. Here, however, many participants, including some birders, saw the mixture of no-mow turf and low forbs described in the restoration ecologist's presentation as an attractive alternative to mowing.

From Negotiation to Policy

Following the workshop, LPAC drafted a set of policy and implementation recommendations for further discussion. The general consensus of public and Park District stakeholder groups on issues of overall management philosophy, appropriate recreational use, facilities development, and access made these recommendations relatively clear cut. Regarding vegetation management at Montrose, LPAC made the following statement:

> Specific components of the landscape at Montrose Point are deeply appreciated by many people. Some view these components as cultural icons; change is not wise or needed. LPAC strives to reach consensus on issues that impact the park and park users. Consensus is not always possible. It is LPAC's method to hear as many sides of an issue as possible and make recommendations that take into consideration all sides of an issue.

Based on this philosophy, LPAC worked with the Park District over the following months to develop what both entities felt would be a final conceptual plan that all stakeholders could generally agree on. They recommended that the basic design intent of the Caldwell plan be applied to Montrose Point with several caveats: The council ring would stay out of the plan, and the plant palette would be modified to achieve sustainability, habitat, and biodiversity goals within the general, multilayered structure laid out by Caldwell. As for the Magic Hedge, the policy would be to keep it at the same location but allow modification and expansion along each end of it—replacing the dying honeysuckle, adding native plants that provide food and cover, and removing invasive weeds. Other recommendations by LPAC and the Park District followed suggestions that came out of the workshop discussion and included: select and manage shrubs within a section of the hedge to afford a long view of the landscape in leaf-off conditions; use a short grass mixture in the central meadow along with a selection of low-growing forbs to allow views across the site; surround the central meadow with bands of taller grasses and forbs contiguous to the tree and shrub masses; and provide a gravel path to the hook suitable for disabled access and smaller, mowed paths through the site for use by birders and other users of the point (Figure 9.3).

LPAC also recommended management responsibilities for areas within Montrose Point. The Chicago Park District would install and manage the central meadow, and maintain the mowed grass access paths. For the other areas, LPAC called for active participation from volunteer organizations and individuals. As mentioned in the introduction to this case study, numerous stakeholder groups are interested in actively participating in hands-on projects to implement the plan for the point, and LPAC and the Park District recognize

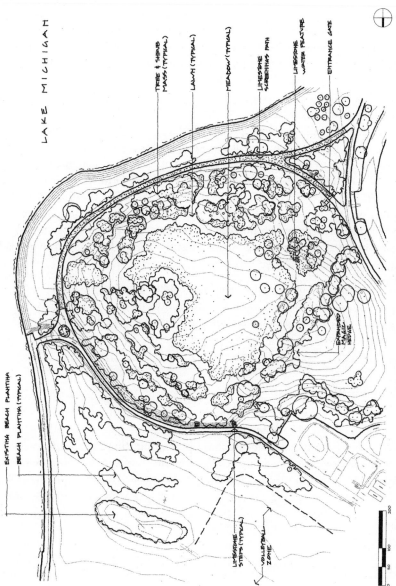

LAKE MICHIGAN

EXISTING BEACH PLANTING

BEACH PLANTING (TYPICAL)

TREE & SHRUB MASS (TYPICAL)

LAWN (TYPICAL)

MEADOW (TYPICAL)

LIMESTONE SCREENINGS PATH

LIMESTONE WATER FEATURE

ENTRANCE GATE

EXPANDED HAWK HEDGE

LIMESTONE STEPS (TYPICAL)

VOLLEYBALL ZONE

0 50 100 200

Figure 9.3. "Final" Design Proposed for Montrose Point (1999). (Wolff Clements and Associates, Ltd.)

that the cooperation of these groups is critical to the plan's success. Birders would take primary management responsibility for the Magic Hedge. The perimeter plantings would be designed as subunits to be planted and maintained by other stewardship groups and youth education programs. The overall landscape program would be supervised by the Park District. Both LPAC and the Park District see long-term management and monitoring of changes as a collaborative venture, and are looking to formalize the Montrose Point Stewardship Group as the primary entity through which volunteer efforts can be coordinated.

The conceptual plan was presented at a well-attended public meeting organized by LPAC in the late fall of 1999. There was broad agreement among the audience as to the direction of the plan, with the understanding that a task force of stakeholder representatives would be assembled to work with LPAC's designers and the Park District to hammer out the many details with regard to plant species mixes, signage, and the like. While support was not unanimous, the broad agreement and enthusiasm for the conceptual plan was summed up by one meeting participant, an angler from the earlier focus group who had also been a student of Alfred Caldwell:

> I'm excited by what I've seen presented here tonight, and as a former student of Caldwell's I'm confident that your plan is moving in the right direction, one that parallels the tradition established by Jensen and Caldwell.

Discussion

In examining this process of negotiating nature over the last two years, we observed a continual focusing and refocusing of issues as stakeholder discussions moved from broad concepts about preserving nature to specific proposals and solutions for providing for appropriate types of use, development, access, and vegetation management. In the early stages of discussion, there was general agreement among a broad range of public stakeholder groups—environmental interests, historic preservation and design interests, passive users, volleyball players, yacht club members, and anglers—to maintain and enhance the natural qualities of the environment. Beyond this general goal, several of these groups were not interested in the details of the plan except as it would affect their ability to use the point for their principal recreation activity. This was especially true of peripheral groups like the volleyball players and yacht club members, whose interests were literally on the periphery of Montrose Point—the beach and the harbor, respectively—and who were not so much concerned with what happened on the point itself. When they felt that their needs and desires would be accommodated by the plan, these groups no longer sought an active role in the negotiation process.

The anglers were another peripheral group, but one with a greater stake in the point since they were trying to regain a higher level of access that had been lost when the road to the breakwater hook was removed. As this is written, this group seems to have acquiesced to the idea of having an improved pedestrian path to the hook, with a somewhat closer parking area for anglers who are disabled. It will be important to continue the dialogue with this and other public stakeholder groups through the task force process that is being established, to ensure that their interests receive consideration as the plan's details are finalized.

The most problematic issues in placing nature at Montrose Point are related to vegetation, particularly with regard to what should be done with the Magic Hedge and how the central meadow should be managed. Here, discussions with environmentalists (mostly birders) and historic preservationists and designers (including individuals from public interest groups and the Park District) showed that there would be no easy resolution of conflicting ideas, and that science and other expert information were limited in what they could do to guide decision making. Rather, ideology was the overriding reason for the lack of consensus; the Caldwell plan and the Magic Hedge had become cultural icons to their respective interest groups, who remained steadfast in their quests to see Montrose Point restored as their sacred site. While this realization was a valuable outcome of the negotiation process, without a clearer idea of how to embrace these factions and move forward, the stakeholders appeared to be headed for gridlock.

According to Hester (1999), this gridlock in the planning and design process is increasingly a consequence of participatory planning, in which empowered interest groups preserve their ideologies by blocking each other's goals. A typical strategy of planners and designers is to mediate such conflicts by "dividing the pie" among the most vocal interests. The alternative chosen by LPAC was to take a more proactive approach with its recommendations for policy and implementation. From the inception of the process, LPAC and its consultant team have maintained an open yet interested stance in guiding a vision for Montrose Point. In the spirit of the original policies brought forth from the 1995 Lincoln Park Framework Plan, they continued to emphasize nature and historic preservation as the two key themes for the Montrose Point Restoration Project. These themes were generally in sync with stakeholder values. However, when stakeholders differed, LPAC took a leadership role in arguing for a direction that would uphold the integrity of these goals while attempting to meet diverse values and uses.

This "participation with a view" (Francis 1999, Hester 1999) was evidenced in LPAC's decisions to provide pedestrian and disabled access to the breakwater hook rather than restore road access, and to keep facilities on the point to a minimum. On the issues of the hedge and meadow, LPAC and its designers and planners did not simply divide the pie by giving the hedge to the birders and the meadow to the historic preservationists. Instead, it appeared that their decision was informed by expert information received by stakeholder groups and the outside experts during the workshop. By understanding how certain plants and plant mixes might meet various aesthetic, historic, biodiversity, bird habitat, and sustainability goals, the planners and designers came to the conclusion that the available options were not as black and white as they might have originally been cast by stakeholder groups. This put them in a better position to advocate vegetation management policies for the hedge and meadow that they felt would respect both historic preservation and ecological/birding goals.

Finally, it should be emphasized that the participatory process employed by LPAC and the Chicago Park District was one that would evolve through the course of planning and design and into actual management. In this respect, the framework for collaborative management and monitoring proposed through the Montrose Point Stewardship Group holds promise. Volunteer-based projects would be phased in over a period of years, giving the site and the concerned groups time to reflect on changes and adapt designs to better suit goals and objectives. The group itself would be an amalgamation of diverse stakeholders and thus would provide a forum for continued negotiation as well as an interface with the Park District as management and design implementation progress.

Implications for Restoration and Management Programs

Since the process of negotiating nature as it is being applied at Montrose Point has not yet come to an end, advocating its wholesale adoption by other restoration and management programs may be premature. Yet when looking at its elements in relation to those at play in the Chicago restoration controversy described in the Introduction and other chapters in this book, we see some contrasts worthy of exploration.

First, the Montrose Point Restoration Project followed from a framework plan for Lincoln Park that was grounded in a diverse set of research studies and a comprehensive planning and design process. A subsequent natural area rehabilitation plan further supported ecological restoration goals. From these efforts came the dual mission to expand wildlife habitat at the Magic Hedge and rehabilitate the historic design of Alfred Caldwell. In the Chicago restoration controversy, ecological restoration projects began and expanded throughout the Cook County forest preserves based on individual site plans and prescriptions developed by volunteer stewards in consultation with the district.

While these may have provided a vision for restoring individual sites and groups of sites, development of a formal guiding plan was still in progress at the time the controversy erupted.

Second, there was a long history of public involvement established under the Lincoln Park Framework Plan, with an open process for participating in committees and a broad-based appointed steering committee set up from the very beginning. In this way it was a more natural evolution for established and new stakeholders to be included in the Montrose Point Restoration Project; multiple ideas and perspectives could be taken into account, not only in the planning and design process but also in project implementation. In the restoration controversy, the Forest Preserve District's Citizens Advisory Council was a step in the right direction, but its timing of implementation and its composition of members may have destined it to become more of a reactive group than a proactive one. As Helford notes in his chapter in this volume, the council was not established until well after the controversy had erupted, and then was composed of appointed participants who in many cases represented polar opposites in the debate. These factors, according to Helford, have often served to increase the distance between factions rather than reduce it.

Third, as a primary stakeholder in the Montrose Point project, the Chicago Park District recognized that it, like its public constituents, was made up of a diverse range of interests. By bringing its various staff interests into the process, the Park District helped identify a broader range of considerations than would have occurred with only one or two staff from the obvious professions assigned to the project. In the Forest Preserve District of Cook County, principal involvement has been by staff whose primary responsibility is restoration and forestry. Noticeably lacking in the effort has been involvement from staff in landscape design and recreation, who play major roles in other land planning and management activities in the Forest Preserve District.

Fourth, in the Montrose Point project there was a greater diversity of stakeholders who were accepted as experts than in the Chicago restoration controversy. Planners and designers within LPAC held expertise as keepers of the vision and worked with a variety of specialists in the Chicago Park District to ensure that the dual goals of wildlife habitat and historic preservation enhancement were upheld. The environmental and historic preservation and design interest groups brought their own expertise to the table, as did outside experts who were invited to the workshop, and the critical information they provided about bird habitat, plant species suitability, and the like helped form the basis for subsequent designs and management policies. The expertise of the birders and historic preservation stakeholders, however, may have also given these groups a measure of privilege beyond those of the other stakeholder groups, which were perceived as being more solidly recreational in nature. Thus, while the interests of the various public stakeholders appear to be accommodated in the final design and policy for the point, the privileges of expertise as discussed in Helford's analysis of the Chicago restoration controversy may have parallels in the Montrose situation in determining whose views count and whose don't.

There might be other reasons why the process at Montrose Point has progressed more smoothly than the Cook County restoration program. The Montrose Point Restoration Project is an eleven-acre site in a 1,200-acre park, while the Cook County restoration program covers dozens of sites in a countywide system of forest preserves comprising more than 67,000 acres. Additionally, the process for Montrose began before many decisions about land management and design had been made, while in the forest preserves some restoration efforts had already been in progress for twenty years. Yet many of the issues discussed here are independent of the scale, physical complexity, or timing of restoration efforts under consideration. For Montrose Point, the Cook County preserves, and many other urban and wildland sites where natural area restoration and management is being undertaken, the most vexing issues are social ones dealing with how different groups see nature and how these visions can be brought into a common focus. In these respects, we think that the lessons learned from the Montrose case study can be applied in Cook County and elsewhere.

Conclusion

The ultimate success of the Montrose Point Restoration Project and other restoration and management programs in urban and wildland areas will rely on how diverse values of humans and nature are integrated with one another. By keeping the process of negotiating nature open and by guiding it with the appropriate combination of vision and leadership, it seems possible that we can develop new and more inclusive concepts of restoration than those that hold to a single disciplinary focus. Ideas of nature conceived by ecological restorationists, historic Prairie School landscape designers, and current recreational users at Montrose Point seem highly compatible, and could form the basis of a model for restoration that is not only suited to an urban park context, but is perhaps also applicable in other locations and situations.

Acknowledgments

LPAC involvement in the Montrose Point Restoration Project was guided by Elizabeth Altman, Brett August, Robert Nauert, and Charlotte Wheeler. The consultant team for LPAC included designers Ted Wolff and Joel Baldin of Wolff Clements and Associates, project coordinator Kathleen Dickhut, workshop and focus group facilitator Bruce Ives of the Metro Chicago Information Center, and focus group field tour leader Nadine Zelle. Chicago Park District involvement was guided by Julie Gray and Mary Ellen Messner. Workshop speakers included Dave Egan, *Ecological Restoration*; Robert E. Grese, University of Michigan; Douglas Stotz, Field Museum of Natural History; and Gerould Wilhelm, Conservation Design Forum. We thank these individuals and the many stakeholder groups and individuals who have given their time and energy to help plan and carry out the restoration of Montrose Point.

Notes

1. Focus group transcripts served as the basis for analysis in this part of the case study. Each investigator independently read text passages (e.g., paragraphs) for each focus group and identified a set of preliminary themes, which were then compared and discussed until an overall coding scheme (with twenty-four different themes) was agreed upon. We then independently recoded the text passages for one or more themes and tallied the number of times each theme occurred per focus group. This process helped to organize information and guide analysis. This analysis did not include the focus groups with the volleyball players and yacht club members because no transcripts were available. This same procedure was used for the focus group with the Park District.

2. In the prairie meadow plan, the entire central meadow would be planted in tall prairie grasses and forbs and maintained by fire. A band of mowed grass between the central meadow and perimeter plantings would act as a firebreak and allow for pedestrian circulation. A council ring would be positioned on the eastern edge of the meadow for education, volunteer, and other programs. An open-air shelter at the base of the hook would serve as a storm refuge for anglers. In the prairie/mowed meadow plan, the middle of the central meadow would be mowed, with taller meadow grasses and forbs at its outer margins becoming extensions of the Magic Hedge and other new masses of trees and shrubs. A picnic area would be located on the eastern edge of the point inside the circular path. In the mowed meadow plan, the entire central meadow would be mowed. A large council ring would be located on the eastern end of the point. This plan is most like the original Caldwell plan.

References

Arnstein, S. R. 1969. "A Ladder of Citizen Participation." *Journal of the American Institute of Planners* 35: 216–224.

Brofka, W. A., and J. E. Marsden. 1997. *A Survey of the Sport Fishing in the Illinois Portion of Lake Michigan* (Tech. Rep. 97-7). Zion: Illinois Natural History Survey.

Chicago Historical Society. 1991. *Prairie in the City: Naturalism in Chicago's Parks 1870–1940*. Chicago: Chicago Historical Society.

Chicago Park District. 1997. *Ecological Rehabilitation Plan: Lagoons and Natural Communities within Twenty-four Parks of the Chicago Park District.* Chicago: Chicago Park District.

Chicago Park District and Lincoln Park Steering Committee. 1995. *Lincoln Park Framework Plan: A Plan for Management and Restoration.* Chicago: Chicago Park District.

Cronon, W., ed. 1995. *Uncommon Ground: Toward Reinventing Nature.* New York: W. W. Norton.

Domer, D. 1997. *Alfred Caldwell: The Life and Work of a Prairie School Landscape Architect.* Baltimore: Johns Hopkins University Press.

Dwyer, J. F. 1994. *Customer Diversity and the Future Demand for Outdoor Recreation.* USDA Forest Service General Technical Report RM-252. Fort Collins, CO: Rocky Mountain Forest and Range Experiment Station.

Francis, M. 1999. "Proactive Practice: Visionary Thought and Participatory Action in Environmental Design." *Places* 12(2): 60–68.

Francis, M., R. Moore, D. Iacofano, S. Klein, and L. Paxson. 1987. "Design and Democracy: An Introduction." *Journal of Architectural and Planning Research* 4(4): 273–281.

Gobster, P. H. 1997. "The Chicago Wilderness and Its Critics, III. The Other Side: A Survey of the Arguments." *Restoration & Management Notes* 15(1): 32–37.

Grese, R. E. 1992. *Jens Jensen: Maker of Natural Parks and Gardens.* Baltimore: Johns Hopkins University Press.

Hester, R. T. 1999. "A Refrain with a View." *Places* 12(2): 12–25.

Hull, R. B. IV, and S. E. Michael. 1995. "Nature-based Recreation, Mood Change, and Stress Reduction." *Leisure Sciences* 17(1): 1–14.

Innes, J. E. 1996. "Planning through Consensus Building: A New View of the Comprehensive Planning Ideal." *Journal of the American Planning Association* 62(4): 460–472.

Kaplan, S. 1995. "The Restorative Benefits of Nature: Toward an Integrative Framework." *Journal of Environmental Psychology* 15: 169–182.

Kline, V. 1997. "Planning a Restoration." In *The Tallgrass Restoration Handbook for Prairie, Savannas, and Woodlands,* edited by S. Packard and C. F. Mutel, 31–46. Washington, DC: Island Press.

Nassauer, J. I., ed. 1997. *Placing Nature: Culture and Landscape Ecology.* Washington, DC: Island Press.

Nathan, J. A., J. C. H. Lee, J. Sniderman, W. W. Tippens, B. H. Rycksbosch, and members of the Lincoln Park Historic Preservation Task Force. 1991. *Lincoln Park Restoration and Management Plan Historic Preservation Analysis.* Chicago: Chicago Park District, Office of Research and Planning.

People, Places & Design Research. 1991. *Recreation and Leisure Time Study Concerning the Users and Non-Users of Lincoln Park.* Northampton, MA: People, Places & Design Research.

Raffetto, J. 1993. "Perceptions of Ecological Restorations in Urban Parks." In *Managing Urban and High Use Recreation Settings,* edited by P. H. Gobster, 61–67. USDA Forest Service General Technical Report NC-163. St. Paul: North Central Forest Experiment Station.

Rolston, H. III. 1997. "Nature for Real: Is Nature a Social Construct?" In *The Philosophy of the Environment,* edited by T. D. J. Chappell, 38–64. Edinburgh: University of Edinburgh Press.

Simmons, D. A. 1994. "Urban Children's Preferences for Nature: Lessons for Environmental Education." *Children's Environments* 11(3): 194–203.

Soulé, M. E., and G. Lease, eds. 1995. *Reinventing Nature? Responses to Postmodern Deconstruction.* Washington, DC: Island Press.

Ulrich, R. S. 1981. "Natural versus Urban Scenes: Some Psychophysiological Effects." *Environment and Behavior* 13(5): 523–556.

❧ Chapter 10 ❧

A PEOPLE-CENTERED APPROACH TO DESIGNING AND MANAGING RESTORATION PROJECTS: INSIGHTS FROM UNDERSTANDING ATTACHMENT TO URBAN NATURAL AREAS

Robert L. Ryan

Urban natural areas are precious resources. As illustrated by the Chicago Wilderness project, many urban natural areas are treasure troves of biodiversity (Ross 1997). Substantial research (Kaplan 1983) has found that the presence of nature holds a strong appeal for urban dwellers. In the natural environment, people can find a connection with something that is both larger and more timeless than themselves; nature can provide spiritual sustenance for their souls, physical relief for their bodies, and psychological restoration for their minds. And when people are drawn to natural areas and experience them, they may develop an attachment to these places.

Considering the draw that nature has for people, it is not surprising that urban areas have been the setting for much environmental restoration work. In the Midwest, degraded urban open spaces are increasingly being transformed into vibrant prairie, wetland, and savanna ecosystems. Much of this work is being carried out by cadres of dedicated volunteers under the direction of professional natural area managers and ecologists. Chapters by Schroeder and

by Grese et al. in this book talk about some of the important psychological benefits that these volunteers seek and receive from their restoration of
nature.

Unfortunately, restoration does not always receive this same high level of
enthusiastic response from the wider public. The Chicago restoration controversy is a good case in point. For more than twenty years, natural areas located
within the system of county forest preserves throughout metropolitan Chicago
have been the home of cutting-edge efforts in ecological restoration, conducted by a collaboration of volunteers, public agency staff, and nongovern-
mental environmental groups. These efforts, however, have come under recent
attack by neighborhood residents and local groups, in part because of practices
such as tree and brush removal that have been done to restore more open
prairie and savanna ecosystems. These issues are discussed more fully in the
Introduction to this volume [see also chapters by Helford and by Vining et al.
in this volume and articles by Gobster (1997) and Shore (1997)]; suffice it to
say, the controversy has caused a great upheaval in the restoration community
and a reassessment by public officials about both the ends and means of restoring urban natural areas. And while the Chicago controversy has been a touchstone for discussion in this book, restoration efforts have also come under
attack in areas as diverse as the Florida coastline, New York City's Central Park,
and the wine country of California (Shore 1997).

Why are there conflicts over environmental restoration projects? After all,
it appears that for the most part, volunteers and staff involved in these projects
have the best intentions in their efforts to restore degraded landscapes, promote biodiversity, and teach urban people about their native ecosystem. Some
insights into the origins of these controversies may come from studying the
relationships between people and the natural environment. Central to the
argument presented here is the concept of place attachment and its multifaceted nature. In other words, while many people can be attached to an area,
their attachment may be expressed in diverse and even contradictory ways.

Place attachment can be developed by experiencing a place. However,
people experience an urban natural area in many different ways—they may
use it for active recreation such as walking or jogging, they may visually experience it from the windows of their homes or cars, or they may physically
work on a landscape to restore the native ecosystem. We propose that people's
attachment to place may vary depending on how they use or experience it.

Environmental expertise is also likely to influence reactions to natural areas
and their restoration and management. Landscape preference research has
shown that knowledge about topics related to natural areas can cause people
to look at nature differently (Anderson 1978, Gallagher 1977, Kaplan and Herbert 1987). These different views of nature can be the source of conflicts
between experts and laypeople about the design and management of urban

natural areas, such as those in the Chicago controversy described in Helford's chapter in this volume.

Restoration designers and managers caught in the cross fire of controversy need to know how to respond in a manner that respects the attachment that people have for urban natural areas. How can restoration projects be designed in a manner that is appreciated by the public at large? How can management decisions maintain and improve the quality of experience for a wide range of users? This chapter will present suggestions for restoration design and management gleaned from a case study of natural areas in Michigan and from an extensive literature on people-centered design and planning.

Case Study

The study involved surveying more than 300 natural area users—including staff, volunteers, neighbors, and visitors—about their attachment, use, environmental knowledge, and attitudes toward the management of three urban natural areas in Ann Arbor, Michigan. The study sites, which included areas within two city parks and a university arboretum, were chosen because they are actively managed by volunteers and staff to restore the native prairie and riparian forest ecosystems. The study used both photos and written questions to ask participants about their attachment to the study sites.

We were particularly interested in finding out if participants differed in their responses according to how they used these natural areas. Therefore, participants were categorized according to their type of involvement with the natural area: conceptual (i.e., staff), actively working on the site (i.e., restoration volunteers), actively traversing the site (i.e., walkers, bikers), and passively using the site (i.e., viewing the site from the window of their homes or while driving by in their cars). These groups were then used to compare participants' attachment, preference, and attitudes toward management. (A more in-depth description of the research sampling, methods, and results can be found in Ryan 1997.)

Understanding Attachment

In the first part of the study, we were interested in understanding the degree to which participants had an attachment to urban natural areas and how this attachment manifested itself in their feelings and actions. As might be expected, we found that people had a strong attachment to the nearby natural areas in our study. This attachment was revealed in many ways; natural areas were participants' favorite places, places that they were eager to show others, and places that they would miss if they moved away from the area.

Often, people don't realize how much they love a place until the place changes—for example, when a favorite woods is cleared for development. Participants in our study said they would experience a very real sense of personal loss should changes occur that they felt would harm their natural area. Furthermore, their attachment to these sites revealed itself in their willingness to take action to protect their special natural areas. Thus, restoration designers and managers, who are often the catalyst for change within urban natural areas, need to understand whether their proposals are perceived by users as having any negative effects. The following sections summarize the results of our study that addressed this issue by looking at how different user groups perceived the physical features and management of these urban natural areas.

The Effects of Place: Physical Features

It is important for natural area managers and designers to know if there are certain landscape types or physical features of natural areas to which local people are strongly attached. If so, any changes proposed through restoration or management should proceed, if necessary, only with extreme caution and sensitivity. We found that within the three study sites, scenes of the wooded riverside area within the arboretum site received significantly higher attachment ratings from its respective users than did the nearby restored prairie area. For those interested in managing and restoring particular types of natural areas in the regional context of this study, this result suggests that people might be more sensitive to changes in landscapes that include such features as moving water and large trees because these areas generate stronger attachment than areas such as prairies with wide expanses of tall grasses. However, it is important to note that among the study sites, the presence of water alone did not always increase attachment. A large artificial pond at one of the parks received only moderate attachment ratings.

On the other hand, we found that users strongly appreciated changes that gave the sites a more natural appearance. Landscape features perceived as incompatible with natural settings, such as chain-link fences, power lines, and modern concrete benches, lowered users' feelings of attachment.

The Effects of Experience

We found that the frequency and type of environmental experience were important factors in differentiating participants' attachment and attitudes toward management of these natural areas. The more frequently participants used a site (i.e., recreated, volunteered), the greater their attachment. Moore and Graefe (1994) had similar results in their study of rail-trail users. This lends credence to the hypothesis that attachment is built through experience.

Our study used the notion that environmental experience is a multidimensional concept. People's involvement with urban natural areas comes in many ways. They may be passive users, viewing a natural area from the window of their home or office, or even while passing by on their daily commute.

They may be active users, walking along the trails of a nature preserve, jogging through on their morning exercise routine, or enjoying an early evening bike ride. Active involvement also includes management activities, such as brush clearing or mowing, that change the physical characteristics of a site. Often such transformations are conducted with some larger conceptual goal in mind, such as converting a degraded urban habitat into a more naturally functioning ecosystem. Individuals who guide restoration activities through their design and management efforts might be said to have a conceptual involvement with a site. They view places through the lens of the expert; their knowledge and understanding of the theories of a particular discipline, such as parks and recreation management, restoration ecology, or landscape architecture, frame the way they perceive the landscape.

An important finding of our study is that these different types of involvement—passive, active, and conceptual—lead to different types of attachment. One type of attachment is a place-specific attachment; the other is a more conceptual attachment to a type of landscape, such as a prairie.

Place-specific attachment. Both passive and active users tended to have a place-specific attachment. But while both groups' attachment was focused on a particular natural area, they expressed a range of opinions about the management of that area. Passive users were more concerned that these areas exhibit refined management, that is to say, more traditional park maintenance such as mowed areas, picturesque plantings, and developed paths. Active users, on the other hand, were more in favor of minimal management, reducing management interventions and letting nature take its course. Active users also expressed a greater willingness than passive users to protest negative changes to these natural areas. Because of this, active users, especially those who used the natural areas frequently, along with passive users who were nearby neighbors, were more disturbed by proposed actions that might create additional development or increase the number of visitors. For these groups, buffer management might be advocated in some areas to screen development and uses like parking lots.

Conceptual attachment. Staff and volunteer restorationists expressed a more conceptual attachment; they were attached to a particular type of natural landscape such as a prairie rather than to a specific place. For these study participants, seeking another site would be an acceptable option if the one they were working on might change in a negative manner. This lack of place dependency suggests a substitutability of natural areas that is not shared by the other users.

The idea of conceptual attachment is further supported by the positive attitudes of these groups toward more intensive management strategies that promote native species (i.e., cutting exotic trees and brush, burning, using herbicides) and by their negative attitudes toward minimizing management activities or creating a more refined landscape. Because the staff and volunteers appear less dependent on place, it is reasonable to assume that they would push for this type of management even in places they had never visited. Similarly, these participants expressed a willingness to become environmental advocates to protest changes even where they may have had little or no personal experience.

It is important to note that people may actually experience both types of attachment, place-specific and conceptual. For example, natural area volunteers may have a favorite prairie site that they frequently use and at the same time may strongly support the preservation of all prairies.

Environmental Expertise, Attachment, and Management

Environmental expertise (i.e., natural history knowledge) proved to be an important underlying construct that influenced the development of a conceptual attachment. Those who used an area for nature-based activities were more strongly attached to sites devoted to native ecosystems, such as prairies and wetlands, that had a more wild or undeveloped appearance, than they were to sites that appeared more refined or traditionally parklike in character. These results suggest that a higher degree of natural area knowledge may allow these experts to more comfortably experience these places and consequently develop an attachment to them. This hypothesis is supported by the fact that these natural area experts, both women and men, expressed the least fear (i.e., the most comfort) in using these natural areas. In contrast, nonexpert users, particularly women, expressed significantly more fear of some of these wilder natural areas, and some commented that these areas appeared overgrown. Comments such as these reinforce the idea that not all participants appreciate native ecosystems that appear to be in their wildest, least developed form.

These results imply that those whose primary landscape involvement is visual are more likely to feel that a natural area should exhibit attributes of a more refined landscape. These results are supported by Nassauer's research (1993, 1995), which showed that residents of suburban neighborhoods were more accepting of native landscapes that included some refined management (e.g., mown areas within an otherwise native grass front yard).

Conversely, those with the greatest conceptual understanding of these natural systems and the volunteers committed to restoring them to a more native ecosystem were less accepting of having refined landscapes within a natural area. They showed significantly lower attachment to a traditional turf landscape and developed area around a park reservoir. Active users (e.g., walkers and bikers), on the other hand, appreciated this developed area with its seemingly incompatible dam structure and powerhouse as much as the nearby native prairie ecosystem. At the root of these differences are participants' visions of what is appropriate within a natural area.

Case Study Discussion: Attachment and Conflict

The results of this study suggest that people care deeply about urban natural areas and that their appreciation deepens the more they use these areas. People's attachment to natural areas also makes them more concerned about the future of natural areas and more willing to actively protect these areas.

But attachment also makes people sensitive to environmental change, and can result in a very real sense of personal loss or grief when favorite natural areas are changed or threatened by change. The loss of a special tree, changes in management, or increased development are some examples of natural and human-created changes that can have a negative effect on people who have an attachment to natural areas (Dwyer et al. 1991).

This loss or grief is not always verbally expressed. However, sometimes the environmental changes are significant enough that people with a strong attachment to an area will voice their opposition in the public arena, often to the astonishment of well-intentioned managers or designers who thought that their changes would be indisputably good for the particular natural area.

The results of this study suggest that at the root of some of these environmental conflicts are differences in attachment. For those who passively view natural areas from nearby streets and homes, the visual characteristics of these places are very important. These people appear to appreciate a more refined, parklike landscape, and may not be particularly concerned about whether the plants there are natives or exotics. In contrast, volunteers and staff members see these natural areas as the last bastions of native ecosystems within the heavily developed urban fabric. Their attachment may be fueled more by such concepts as ecosystem integrity, wildlife habitat, and species diversity than by the actual place itself. The active users (walkers and joggers) seem to form a middle ground. They appear to be more accepting of a wilder, less developed appearance, perhaps because they feel that this is the result of letting nature take its course. To many of them, any tree or shrub, regardless of species, has a place in these natural areas and should be allowed to grow undisturbed.

With these different viewpoints of the same place, it is not surprising that conflicts over natural areas occur. The removal of exotic tree species to bring these areas closer to the concept of a native ecosystem may be viewed with horror by active users and neighbors, who see existing trees as integral parts of the natural area that they have grown to love. This conflict is further exacerbated by the fact that those interested in promoting native ecosystems appear to have an attachment that is less place dependent, so restoration volunteers and staff may be surprised that others (whose attachment is very place specific) may not share their universal love for native landscapes such as prairies.

The results of this case study have direct implications for the Chicago restoration controversy mentioned earlier and for other situations where conflicts have developed among expert and user groups over the restoration and management of urban natural areas. Our study showed that while staff and volunteers may think alike about management issues, their viewpoints may be extremely different from those held by active users and neighbors. But it is also important to add that, as in the Chicago controversy, conflicts can also be heightened when public groups are not involved in restoration and management decisions. For instance, volunteers and staff may be unaware of how the changes brought by restoration and clearing invasive exotic species may negatively affect other users. Involving citizens in the decision-making process is thus an essential step in reducing conflicts over environmental restoration. The next section elaborates on ways that public viewpoints can be included in design and management decisions for urban natural areas.

Insights for Restoration Design and Management

One goal of natural area managers is that people will develop an attachment to the urban natural areas that are provided and, because of these feelings, will help protect existing areas and support efforts to acquire new ones. The second half of this chapter applies the insights gained from our study and from those of other researchers to illustrate ways to design and manage urban natural areas in a manner that respects people's attachment and attitudes. These suggestions are presented as steps in the design and planning process for natural areas where restoration activities are being considered.

Step One: Identify Sensitive Areas and Features

Managers must be sensitive to the fact that in many urban natural areas there may be people who have a strong attachment to the existing landscape. Therefore, the first step in a more people-sensitive design process is to conduct an inventory and analysis of the site to identify areas and features that may be special to particular user groups. Restoration managers should involve a wide variety of users, including public and expert groups, to identify and understand the breadth of areas and features considered to be especially important. The photo-based technique used in our study proved valuable in this respect [see Kaplan et al. (1998) for further suggestions on eliciting public input].

The results of our study identified several key areas for special management consideration. The first area to analyze is the perimeter of the natural area. Sections of a natural area that are visible from nearby homes and neighborhoods are particularly sensitive areas, because management decisions can have an impact on the beloved views that neighbors have of these natural areas. Since urban natural areas are also important to those who drive (or walk) by them, views from adjacent streets are another sensitive area to delineate.

The next area of study is the travel corridors that run through a natural area. The areas adjacent to popular walking and biking trails are important to identify, because the view from the trail is the way that traditional recreational users experience the landscape (Kaplan et al. 1998, 93). Areas adjacent to canoe trails or other waterborne transportation should also be identified. In larger natural areas, entry drives into the area may be other important corridors to identify.

The next things to identify are the special places and positive features of the natural area. Our study identified a riverside area with large trees as a particularly special area for users. Our findings suggest that waterfront areas may be special to users in other natural areas as well. However, not all waterscapes are perceived equally. Although a large body of research has shown water to be a preferred natural setting, waterscapes that are overgrown, eroded, or unkempt tend to be much less appreciated (Ellsworth 1982, Kaplan 1977, Ryan 1998). Natural area managers need to discover from their users which areas are most beloved to them.

The role of trees as important landscape features should not be underestimated. In addition to our research, numerous other studies have shown that people have a strong affinity for trees, especially large ones (Barro et al. 1997, Dwyer et al. 1991, Getz and Kielbaso 1982, Sheets and Manzer 1991). Understanding this relationship helps to explain why the removal of large trees as part of ecological restoration projects is especially controversial (Shore 1997). The conversion of a forest to a prairie should not be taken lightly. The results of our study confirm this notion that large trees are one of the special features to respect when planning a restoration project. Not only did participants in our study appreciate the large trees near one riverside area, they also bemoaned the fact that managers had removed a row of trees at the periphery of the site, which opened up views to adjacent power lines.

And while it is important for planners and managers to know which areas are appreciated by users, it is equally important for them to identify the detracting areas and negative features. Comments from participants in our study suggest that landscape features such as chain-link fences, power lines, and adjacent buildings are considered incompatible with these natural settings and should be screened from view.

Step Two: Develop a Balanced Management Plan

The second step in the planning process for restoration involves creating separate management zones that can respond to the opportunities and constraints identified in the previous phase. The results of our study show the need to balance the type of management that occurs in urban natural areas to respond to the different attitudes held by users. The periphery of a natural area, which is visible to nearby roads and homes, should be zoned for more refined management (e.g., mowing grass along the edges of walks and trimming dense shrubs) to make it more acceptable to key users of those areas. Within this zone, managers and designers should work together to maintain native plant material in a more obviously designed manner.

Areas near unsightly views of nearby commercial areas, power lines, or other incompatible features should be zoned for buffer management. Working with users, a planner may have identified aesthetically unpleasant views that are currently not screened. These zones should be targeted for future plantings of native trees and shrubs to improve the visual quality within the natural area.

For many users, letting nature take its course is a preferred management approach. It is important for planners and managers to recognize that certain sections within a natural area should be zoned for minimal management. This is especially true for undisturbed areas, such as woodlands, for which users may have indicated a strong attachment. For managers, this type of strategy may be easier to adopt in natural areas that are less open to the threat of exotic species.

Intensive management activity to promote native plant species, such as prairie burns or shrub removal, may be more acceptable if zoned for areas that are less visible from adjacent roads, homes, or popular trails. If managers need to use intensive techniques to promote native species, they will have stronger support from people if they also manage these areas with people's preferences in mind. The next section describes design and management strategies for restoring landscapes in a manner that people prefer.

Step Three: Develop Site-specific Design and Management Strategies

The third step in a more people-centered approach to ecological restoration involves detailed decisions about natural area design and management. This section is broken down into two parts: the first part presents strategies for encouraging the use of urban natural areas, and the second part discusses strategies for designing restoration projects within these natural areas that will be appreciated by a broader constituency.

Encourage use. An important insight from our study of natural area users is the strong relationship between natural area use and attachment. As people's use of these areas increases, so does their attachment. Building these connections between people and the natural environment is essential for creating advocates for natural area restoration and preservation. Designers and managers need to look for opportunities to increase people's use of urban natural areas while at the same time protecting the fragile ecosystems. Physical access provided by new trails and boardwalks is one way to encourage use of urban natural areas. Another is to improve visual access to these areas for both nearby residents and passersby.

Designers and managers need to be aware that while providing physical access to natural areas can lead to increased use and attachment by some groups, access can also negatively affect the attachment of other groups. For example, neighbors may object to the increase in the number of users because they consider these natural areas to be an extension of their backyards. At the physical level, these concerns may be addressed by being sensitive to location—in this case, locating improvements away from nearby homes. It is important to note, however, that in our study, nearby neighbors did not object to the increased access provided by new trails and boardwalks, presumably because these improvements would also facilitate their own use of these areas.

Naturalists and other experts who have a conceptual attachment to natural areas see these areas as important in protecting the regional ecosystem and as symbols of urban wilderness. Our study found that improved access that brings more people to these natural areas may be perceived by these experts as incurring damage both to the environment and to the notion of urban wilderness. While sensitive trail design and the use of boardwalks can alleviate some of the environmental impacts of increased access, designers and managers should also strive to preserve some wilderness character. Strategies to accomplish this include limiting improved access to certain sections of the natural area; providing visual access to sensitive features, such as bogs and marshes, while limiting physical access; and screening developed trails and other improvements from wilder areas.

Designers and managers should also be aware that visual access is important for some user groups. The results of this study showed that passively viewing a natural area from one's home or car was related to a feeling of attachment for it. Adjacent neighbors are especially dependent upon their views because these views are an integral part of their residential setting, one that is less fluid than that of the passerby or recreational user. Therefore, designers and managers must be attuned to opportunities to provide visual access to natural areas from adjacent homes and roads, instead of presenting neighbors and those passing by with an impenetrable screen of trees and shrubs. Off-site users can be provided with glimpses of marsh or prairie areas by creating openings in a dense row of trees.

Directing people's attention to key views of natural areas should be accomplished through landscape design rather than through signage. For example, refined plantings at key viewing areas (such as mowing the turf and pruning shrubs) can be used to contrast with less manicured plantings. Another strategy is to capture and direct people's attention by framing views with flowering plants or distinctive plant forms. To increase compatibility with the surrounding landscape, native plant species should be selected for this use. It is also important that these views be engaging; instead of showing a panoramic view of a marsh, it would be more effective to provide a partial or obscured view that allows for the recognition of landscape features but hides most of the landscape from view. This creates a sense of mystery and allows people to conjure up their own image of what lies beyond. Furthermore, deciduous plants can be used to create seasonal effects, so that viewers can see a different section of the landscape at different times of the year.

While providing visual access for the passerby is important, it must not compromise the view of the active user. For example, permitting panoramic views from off-site may create undesirable views of adjacent roads and houses from nature trails. Therefore, to avoid detracting from the natural feel that active users want in these urban natural areas, existing vegetation should be preserved and supplemented to screen incompatible views from trails.

Design and manage for preferred settings. Providing physical and visual access to urban natural areas is only part of the strategy in increasing use and, consequently, attachment for these places. Natural area users also need to enjoy their experience in the landscape. They need to find these restored settings to be aesthetically pleasing and engaging enough to explore, yet coherent and understandable enough to make the experience feel safe and enjoyable. Research has shown that people's preferences for landscapes that fulfill these human needs are remarkably predictable and consistent (Kaplan and Kaplan 1989, Kaplan et al. 1998). Our study also indicates that attachment to urban natural areas is related to landscape preference. Preference may be especially important for luring first-time visitors into exploring natural areas. In other words, there needs to be something along the trail to entice people to use it. Furthermore, people need to be confident that they can find their way around these areas. If the initial experience is both comfortable and rewarding, visitors may repeat the experience and in time develop an attachment.

The following section provides some insights from landscape preference research about landscape features and configurations that visitors may find interesting and understandable. Some of the topics that may be particularly important in developing attachment involve perceptions of safety, landscape aesthetics, and familiarity. This discussion draws heavily from the ideas presented in my 1998 book, *With People in Mind: Design and Management of Everyday Nature,* co-authored with Rachel and Stephen Kaplan.

ENHANCE VISITORS' PERCEPTIONS OF SAFETY ALONG TRAILS. Participants' comments in our study suggest that it is very important to ensure adequate visibility so that visitors feel safe within urban natural areas. If people feel unsafe in a natural area, they are unlikely to use it. Dense vegetation, such as tall grass or shrubs, that blocks views along trails is especially problematic (Kaplan and Kaplan 1989, Schroeder and Anderson 1984). Managers should strive to keep vegetation pruned along trails that go through areas of dense growth. This involves keeping sight lines open to allow views down the trail. In tallgrass prairie settings, long-distance views could be created through strategic planting of shorter growing species along trails and periodic mowing or burning.

In dense woods or other heavily vegetated settings, visibility can be improved by clearing some shrubs and trees to allow a more open understory, especially along trails. It should be emphasized that we are not suggesting a wholesale removal of all understory vegetation, but rather the strategic pruning of large shrubs that block views at eye level, while retaining the overstory tree canopy and lower-level groundcover vegetation. Research has shown that people prefer the more open woods that results from such management strategies (Kaplan and Kaplan 1989, Kaplan et al. 1998). Restoration activities can aid in this effort. Clearing exotic shrubs that have invaded the forest understory can serve the dual purpose of improving the habitat for native woodland plants while enhancing visitors' perceptions of trail safety.

INCORPORATE AESTHETIC "CUES TO CARE." While the importance of providing visibility within natural areas should not be underestimated, too much visual access—for example, wide-open prairies or lawn areas—can also create nonpreferred settings (Gallagher 1977, Talbot et al. 1987). To many people, such areas are considered too hot, visually monotonous, and intimidating to cross. Visitors need to see enough to find their way around, but not so much that they are not engaged to explore the area further. Drifts of trees or shrubs that break up large open areas give people more to look at while offering them a sense of the extent of the area. Although it is important to be able to see the landscape, it is more interesting not to see it all at once. Native trees and shrubs can be used to create a savanna landscape that improves both natural and visual diversity.

Nassauer's research (1993, 1995) has shown that suburban homeowners are more accepting of native plants when they are used in more refined configurations, where "cues to care" within the front yard plantings tell other neighbors that this is an intentional, managed landscape. Gaining the public's acceptance for native plantings in larger natural areas also means using more flowering plants and bold patterns, and keeping distinct boundaries between different plant masses. Landscape features such as paths, walls, or bird feeders can also be integrated with native plantings to provide additional cues to people that this landscape is well cared for. New improvements must be compatible with the vision that people have for the landscape. This includes using visually compatible materials that harmonize with lines, forms, colors, and textures of the natural settings. Comments from participants suggest that they prefer more rustic elements that blend with the natural surroundings; consequently, designers should consider using on-site materials for improvements. For example, a fallen log or boulders found on site can be used for informal seating areas.

Our research study also found that native prairie plantings with mown edges along the trails were more preferred by the general public. In addition to mowing the edge of a prairie, bordering it with well-maintained fences is another technique for creating a more refined and appreciated landscape. All of these signs of human intention convey the message to those who are unfamiliar with native plants that restored landscapes are part of an intentional management plan.

The importance of showing signs of human care within the landscape should not be underestimated. For many inner-city dwellers, urban natural areas can be perceived as wild, unsafe areas (Bixler and Floyd 1997, Talbot and Kaplan 1984). The addition of familiar landscape cues such as mown grass (native or nonnative) is one way to help ease the fears of those who are unfamiliar with native landscapes; the following section describes some other strategies for increasing familiarity.

ENHANCE FAMILIARITY. Environmental knowledge is an important factor in increasing people's appreciation of wilder-looking native landscapes (Gallagher 1977, Kaplan and Herbert 1987, Nassauer 1993, 1995). Our research showed that while experienced people expressed high levels of attachment to native settings (i.e., prairies), these settings were less preferred by inexperienced groups. Of course, natural areas need not be entirely made up of highly preferred settings, but to get the uninitiated to visit those areas, designers and managers may need to include some preferred settings along the way. Locating trails near the edges rather than through the middle of wide-open settings such as prairies or marshes can provide exposure to and increase preference for these less familiar landscapes in ways that do not intimidate the new visitor. When trails do go through large, open areas, adding a few native trees or mowing a border along the trail edge may also increase users' sense of familiarity and preference. The idea is that if we use preferred cues to introduce newcomers to these less familiar settings, they can over time develop the necessary experience or expertise that will make them comfortable or appreciative of these wilder ecosystems. It may sound contradictory to say that we have to develop a natural area to preserve it, but winning long-term public support for natural area restoration and management often begins first with designing and managing areas the public finds attractive and enjoyable to use.

Step Four: Allow and Plan for Incremental Change

Implementation is the final phase in a more people-centered restoration planning process. The results of our research indicate that the public does not appreciate drastic changes to the natural areas they use and love. Therefore, designers and managers wishing to avoid conflicts should consider strategies that gradually introduce change to the landscape. Below we discuss four factors that are critical to fostering incremental landscape change.

Scale. Scaling down restoration efforts gives managers the ability to gauge public responses in a less confrontational manner. Restoration projects should be viewed as small experiments (Kaplan 1996) in which the feedback gained from a small investment of time and money can greatly enhance the final outcome. This idea is a key ingredient behind the adaptive management principles discussed by Hull and Robertson in this volume, and has parallels to the reflexive management Helford calls for in this volume.

Timing. The proper timing of ecological restoration efforts can hasten the recovery of the landscape from planned management activities, thus softening the visual impact for users. For example, winter removal of exotic deciduous woody shrubs when the shrubs are dormant and leafless creates a less dramatic impact than removal during the summer season. Likewise, because of the spring rains, a tallgrass prairie will regenerate more quickly after an early spring burning than after a fall burning.

Phasing. By phasing in restoration efforts, managers can give people time to become gradually accustomed to the changes in the native landscape. An example of implementing these ideas comes from conflicts that have erupted over the removal of trees within urban natural areas. Imagine a manager who is intent on restoring a particular area to a more native ecosystem. Unfortunately, the area is bordered by a row of nonnative trees that screen it from unsightly urban land uses, such as utility lines. Immediate removal of these trees may spark an outcry among those who use the site, because many people oppose the removal of trees, particularly when they find the resulting landscape inherently less preferable. Instead of removing the trees immediately, the manager might be better advised to first plant a screen of fast-growing native trees in front of the existing ornamental trees. When the new trees reach sufficient maturity, a gradual removal of existing exotic trees may be more acceptable to people, especially if managers are careful to state why they are removing the trees and to get people's input concerning the removal process.

Information. Informing the public about proposed restoration activities is critical so that they can be involved in the decision-making process before implementation. The importance of an open decision-making process for restoration planning and implementation should not be underestimated. The perception that tree removal in Chicago's forest preserves had been done in a secretive manner was one of the reasons behind opposition to restoration efforts (Helford, this volume; Shore 1997).

Educational material may also be helpful in addressing some of the public's negative reactions to the initial landscape changes that result from ecological restoration (Kearney 1996). Public information in the form of signs and brochures can describe the rationale behind work efforts and include pictures of the landscape at different stages of work, along with a view of the ultimate landscape that managers are trying to achieve. For example, signs showing a scorched prairie immediately after a burn and the healthy, flowering prairie that will result from this type of management have already been successfully used by the parks department in some of our Ann Arbor, Michigan, study sites. It is important to note, however, that public support for aggressive restoration activities such as tree clearing and prairie burns may be stronger when the target landscape is a setting the public prefers (Kearney 1996). That is to say, managers cannot expect environmental education efforts to change people's landscape preferences; the landscape that ultimately results from an incremental management strategy should still strive to create a preferred landscape setting (as described in the previous section).

Conclusion

Our study has shown that natural areas play a vital role in the lives of urban residents. The river outside one's window, the prairie one is helping to restore, and the woods one sees on a daily walk are all important to people. The attachment that people have to urban natural areas can be a powerful force for restoring nature within the city. It is important for designers and managers to understand and respect the landscapes to which people have an attachment before undertaking ecological restoration projects. Such projects can drastically alter the existing landscape and destroy the very qualities of places that many natural area users may love, leading to public outrage over restoration efforts. Thus, an underlying theme in our design and planning recommendations is the need to involve the public in planning restoration projects.

People view natural areas through lenses of different experiences, resulting in attachments to different qualities of these places. Natural area managers, volunteer restorationists, and landscape architects must be cognizant of the different viewpoints that are held by each group when proposing changes affecting special natural areas. The challenge is to accommodate a range of stakeholder attitudes in a plan that balances the need for intensive restoration activities with other, equally valid viewpoints about natural area management, including minimizing management or managing for a more refined landscape. Therefore, we propose developing a balanced management plan that creates different management zones relating to the concerns of particular user groups identified in this chapter.

It is important to recognize, however, that natural area users often have conflicting viewpoints about how the same place should be managed. The case study described by Gobster and Barro in this volume is a good example of this type of conflict. In cases like these, negotiations between stakeholders must become a key part of the planning process. Our study, while focusing on physical design strategies for resolving these conflicts, did not address the public participation process per se. Nevertheless, in applying these strategies, managers and designers need to know when to involve the public, how to make the public's participation useful and meaningful, and how to resolve conflicts when different user groups have opposing viewpoints. Restorationists interested in improving public involvement in restoration planning are advised to look at other case studies in this book as well as the extensive body of public participation research [including Fisher (1981) and Kaplan et al. (1998)].

People's interest in protecting urban natural areas often comes from their attachment to these places. We learned from our study that this attachment is developed through repeated use of a special natural area. Through ecological restoration, designers and managers have the opportunity to build this connection between people and their local natural areas. An important insight from our study is that use can be encouraged not only by improving physical access such as trail design, but also by managing the views from nearby streets and homes. Highlighting positive views and mitigating negative views can expand the perceived boundaries of a natural area and build a more diverse group of natural area advocates that goes beyond the traditional recreation user.

The results of our study show that expertise (i.e., the degree of knowledge people have about natural systems) plays a major role in support for restoration efforts and in appreciation for the wilder native landscapes that can result from these efforts. But we also found that this appreciation is not universally shared by the broader constituency of natural area users. To avoid the conflicts that can occur because of these different viewpoints, restoration must occur in a manner that is also culturally sustainable, that is to say in a manner that people appreciate and understand. As described by Joan Nassauer (1997, 81), "Landscapes that evoke the sustained attention of people—that compel aesthetic experience—are more likely to be ecologically maintained in a world dominated by humans." Design and management strategies to create a more culturally appreciated landscape include addressing concerns over safety along trails, incorporating visible signs of human care into the landscape, and enhancing unfamiliar landscapes.

Designing restoration projects in a manner that a broad spectrum of people will appreciate provides the opportunity to expand restoration efforts beyond the boundaries of designated nature preserves. Opportunities abound for creating new native landscapes within corporate campuses, on school grounds, and even in one's own front yard (Hough 1995, Nassauer 1997, Sauer 1998). Incorporating native landscapes and ecological processes into the everyday lives of urban residents multiplies the opportunities for increased understanding and appreciation of urban nature.

Since many natural area experts, including designers and managers, appreciate native landscapes in ways different from the broader public, ecological restoration projects of any scale must involve the potential users. One strategy suggested earlier in this chapter involves having the public identify the special places and features within an area that is slated for restoration. Gobster and Barro (this volume) also used this strategy in their planning process for a Chicago lakeside park. Another strategy is to implement restoration efforts in a more incremental fashion that allows for more gradual landscape change and can facilitate an ongoing dialogue between managers and the public. In other words, rather than seeing public involvement as being limited to initial planning efforts, successful restoration projects require continual and long-term involvement of local stakeholders as management decisions respond to the dynamic natural landscape.

The bottom-line message from our research is that those concerned with natural area preservation need to take as much care in developing open, diverse forums for public participation as they have in preserving and restoring native ecosystems. Public participation in design and management decisions is necessary to restore and enhance urban natural areas and people's attachment to them. Natural area managers and restorationists must realize that focusing on this critical connection between people and place is essential for the survival of these vulnerable pieces of urban nature.

Acknowledgments

I would like to thank the USDA Forest Service, North Central Research Station, Evanston, Illinois, for their help in funding this research. My grateful appreciation goes to Rachel Kaplan for her help in designing this research and reviewing this chapter. Thanks also go to Donna Erickson, Stephen Kaplan, and Raymond DeYoung for their keen insights during this study.

References

Anderson, E. 1978. *Visual Resource Assessment: Local Perceptions of Familiar Natural Environments.* Ph.D. Dissertation, University of Michigan, Ann Arbor.

Barro, S. C., P. H. Gobster, H. W. Schroeder, and S. Bartram. 1997. "What Makes a Big Tree Special? Insights from the Chicagoland Treemendous Trees Program." *Journal of Arboriculture* 23(6): 207–217.

Bixler, R. D., and M. F. Floyd. 1997. "Nature Is Scary, Disgusting and Uncomfortable." *Environment and Behavior* 29(4): 443–467.

Dwyer, J. F., H. W. Schroeder, and P. H. Gobster. 1991. "The Significance of Urban Trees and Forests: Toward a Deeper Understanding of Values." *Journal of Arboriculture* 17(10): 276–284.

Ellsworth, J. C. 1982. *Visual Assessment of Rivers and Marshes: An Examination of the Relationship of Visual Units, Perceptual Variables, and Preference.* Master's Thesis, Utah State University, Logan.

Fisher, R. 1981. *Getting to Yes: Negotiating Agreement without Giving In.* Boston: Houghton-Mifflin.

Gallagher, T. J. 1977. *Visual Preference for Alternative Natural Landscapes.* Ph.D. Dissertation, University of Michigan, Ann Arbor.

Getz, D. A., and J. J. Kielbaso. 1982. "Inner City Preference for Trees and Urban Forestry Programs." *Journal of Arboriculture* 8: 258–263.

Gobster, P. H. 1997. "The Chicago Wilderness and Its Critics, III. The Other Side: A Survey of the Arguments." *Restoration & Management Notes* 15(1): 32–37.

Hough, M. 1995. *Cities and Natural Processes.* New York: Routledge.

Kaplan, R. 1977. "Preference and Everyday Nature: Method and Application." In *Perspectives in Environmental Design: Theory, Research, and Applications,* edited by D. Stokols, 235–250. New York: Plenum.

Kaplan, R. 1983. "The Role of Nature in the Urban Context." In *Behavior and the Natural Environment,* edited by I. Altman and J. F. Wohlwill, 127–161. New York: Plenum.

Kaplan, R. 1996. "The Small Experiment: Achieving More with Less." In *Public and Private Spaces: Proceedings of the Twenty-Seventh Annual Conference of the Environmental Design Research Association,* edited by J. L. Nasar and B. B. Brown, 170–174. Edmund, OK: EDRA.

Kaplan, R., and E. J. Herbert. 1987. "Cultural and Sub-cultural Comparisons in Preference for Natural Settings." *Landscape and Urban Planning* 14: 281–283.

Kaplan, R., and S. Kaplan. 1989. *The Experience of Nature.* New York: Cambridge Press. (Republished by Ulrich's, Ann Arbor, MI.)

Kaplan, R., S. Kaplan, and R. L. Ryan. 1998. *With People in Mind: Design and Management of Everyday Nature.* Washington, DC: Island Press.

Kearney, A. R. 1996. *Public Attitudes and Preferences Regarding the Indian River.* Research report submitted to USDA Forest Service, North Central Forest Experiment Station, East Lansing, MI.

Moore, R. L., and A. R. Graefe. 1994. "Attachments to Recreation Settings: The Case of Rail-Trail Users." *Leisure Sciences* 16: 17–31.

Nassauer, J. I. 1993. "Ecological Function and the Perception of Suburban Residential Landscapes." In *Managing Urban and High-use Recreation Settings,* edited by P. H. Gobster, 55–60. USDA Forest Service General Technical Report NC-163. St. Paul: North Central Forest Experiment Station.

Nassauer, J. I. 1995. "Messy Ecosystems, Orderly Frames." *Landscape Journal* 14(2): 161–170.

Nassauer, J. I. 1997. "Cultural Sustainability: Aligning Aesthetics and Ecology." In *Placing Nature: Culture and Landscape Ecology,* edited by J. I. Nassauer, 65–83. Washington, DC: Island Press.

Ross, L. M. 1997. "The Chicago Wilderness and Its Critics, Part I. The Chicago Wilderness: A Coalition for Urban Conservation." *Restoration & Management Notes* 15(1): 17–24.

Ryan, R. L. 1997. *Attachment to Urban Natural Areas: Effects of Environmental Experience.* Ph.D. Dissertation, University of Michigan, Ann Arbor.

Ryan, R. L. 1998. "Local Perceptions and Values for a Midwestern River Corridor." *Landscape and Urban Planning* 42: 225–237.

Sauer, L. J. 1998. *The Once and Future Forest: A Guide to Forest Restoration Strategies.* Washington, DC: Island Press.

Schroeder, H. W., and L. M. Anderson. 1984. "Perceptions of Personal Safety in Urban Recreational Sites." *Journal of Leisure Research* 16: 178–194.

Sheets, V. L., and C. D. Manzer. 1991. "Affect, Cognition, and Urban Vegetation: Some Effects of Adding Trees along City Streets." *Environment and Behavior* 23: 285–304.

Shore, D. 1997. "The Chicago Wilderness and its Critics, II. Controversy Erupts over Restoration in Chicago Area." *Restoration & Management Notes* 15(1): 25–31.

Talbot, J. F., and R. Kaplan. 1984. "Needs and Fears: The Response to Trees and Nature in the Inner City." *Journal of Arboriculture* 10(8): 222–228.

Talbot, J. F., L. V. Bardwell, R. Kaplan. 1987. "The Function of Urban Nature: Uses and Values of Different Types of Urban Nature Settings." *Journal of Architecture and Planning Research* 4: 47–63.

❋ Chapter 11 ❋

MANAGING NATURALNESS AS A CONTINUUM: SETTING LIMITS OF ACCEPTABLE CHANGE

Mark W. Brunson

This chapter explores a concept that many readers might consider an oxymoron: the management of naturalness. One can easily argue that naturalness—a term that for most people implies the absence of human intervention in ecological processes—is antithetical to the manipulations of nature that we call management. Yet I will argue that this apparent contradiction is an artifact of an outmoded and inherently dangerous distinction between human society and the natural world. If we see humans as part of nature rather than apart from nature, those behaviors that we call management can be modified to fit our ideas about what is natural. Planning tools similar to the Limits of Acceptable Change (McCool and Cole 1998, Stankey et al. 1985) can be used to incorporate humans into natural area management and will be presented later in this chapter as a means to help reduce conflict and sustain or restore ecosystems.

The idea that one can manage for naturalness is pertinent to a discussion of restoring nature for several reasons. It confronts the arguments of Elliot (1997) and Katz (this volume) that ecological restoration is fundamentally artificial or unnatural because it belies nature's meaning as a product of evolution apart from human intervention. Moreover, it acknowledges the troubling likelihood that human technology now influences every inch of the Earth, without adopting the despairing tone taken by McKibben (1989) in his argument that we are witnessing the "end of nature." And, perhaps most importantly, it proposes a framework for decision making about the manner and extent to which human influence will be considered appropriate in natural places during and after restoration.

The ideas expressed in this chapter grew out of three separate but parallel explorations of the relationships between humans and nature in the context of public land and protected-area management. The first of these was an annual meeting of the Natural Areas Association in Portland, Oregon, in August 1997. The theme of that conference was "Bridging Natural and Social Landscapes," and its plenary session featured a series of presentations by historians, philosophers, conservation biologists, and natural area managers on the topic of the linkage (or lack thereof) between nature and culture. As a social scientist who studies human dimensions of nature and its management, my role was to play devil's advocate—maybe even to annoy my hosts—by suggesting that the central idea of the Natural Areas Association is inherently flawed even if the goal that flows from that central idea is noble and good.

The Natural Areas Association exists to promote both the acquisition of scientific knowledge and the development of management strategies that help us sustain the environmental conditions necessary for species and ecosystems to persist through time in the face of ongoing and accelerating anthropogenic change. Public opinion research suggests that this is a goal valued by most of American society (Kellert 1996, Steel and Lovrich 1997). However, underlying that goal are assumptions that (1) there are such things as natural places that are critical to the existence of most species of plants and animals, and (2) these places are demonstrably different from those that are strongly influenced by humans. The second assumption is the one that I am calling into question.

A second inspiration for this chapter was work completed in 1997 by U.S. and Canadian wilderness managers and scientists (McCool and Cole 1998) who sought to assess and fine-tune the Limits of Acceptable Change (LAC) planning system, which has become the framework for management of legally designated wilderness areas in North America. The LAC system was developed in the early 1980s (Stankey et al. 1985) as a means of resolving an inherent contradiction in the Wilderness Act, which stipulates that wilderness areas "shall be administered for the use and enjoyment of the American people in such manner as will leave them unimpaired for future use and enjoyment as wilderness, and so as to provide protection of these areas [and] the preservation of their wilderness character" (U.S. Code, Title 16, Chapter 23, §1131a). Since the very fact of human use and enjoyment can impair the preservation of the wilderness character of these areas, LAC essentially gives managers a means for deciding how wild a place that is used and enjoyed by humans must be if it is to remain wilderness. My role in the 1997 LAC project was to describe how the process can or should be applied in places outside of designated wilderness (Brunson 1998). Restored natural areas are one such type of place because the process offers a means for deciding how natural—i.e., how much it remains unaffected by humans—a place must be to remain a natural area.

The third leg on which this chapter stands is my continuing study with colleague Bruce Shindler of the social acceptability of forestry practices and the conditions they produce in managed forests. We have found that much of what people like or dislike about forests and forestry is tied to their beliefs about what is a natural environment (Brunson 1993, Shindler 1998, Shindler and Brunson 1999). Since a tenet of contemporary forest management is that timber should be produced via silvicultural systems designed to mimic natural disturbance processes (Hansen et al. 1991, Logan and Fletcher 1996), foresters are, in effect, trying to manage for an increased degree of naturalness in timber-production forests.

And that brings us back to the apparent oxymoron that opened this chapter: Can one actually manage for naturalness? What I try to do in this chapter is to present a framework for answering that question. After first discussing why many people say that nature (and thus naturalness) is a product of culture rather than an absolute state, I describe how the concepts of nature and culture can be seen as complementary rather than dichotomous, and how naturalness can be seen as a kind of continuum that describes the form of the nature–culture relationship at any given place. Finally, I suggest how we might use the LAC process as a framework for developing public dialogues about the location along that continuum that is most appropriate for the places we care about and want to restore.

Cultural Constructions of Nature

In 1995, environmental historian William Cronon published *Uncommon Ground,* an edited volume of essays about nature in the modern world. The book's subtitle, "Toward Reinventing Nature," set many readers' teeth on edge. It was partly this book that sparked the Natural Areas Association's interest in the nature-culture interface. Yet despite its provocative title, the book is founded on a premise that is difficult to dispute. As Cronon notes:

> The work of literary scholars, anthropologists, cultural historians, and critical theorists over the past several decades has yielded abundant evidence that "nature" is not nearly so natural as it seems. Instead, it is a profoundly human construction. This is not to say that a nonhuman world is somehow unreal or a mere figment of our imaginations—far from it. But the way we describe and understand that world is so entangled with our

own values and assumptions that the two can never be fully separated. What we mean when we use the word "nature" says as
much about ourselves as about the things we label with that
word (Cronon 1995, 25).

Cronon's argument is consistent with those of many social scientists who
argue that individuals define nature in terms of cultural templates, formed
from the constant flow of texts and images we receive from childhood onward
(Fine and Christophorides 1993, Greider and Garkovich 1994, Swidler 1986).
These writers do not deny the reality of soil, water, plants or animals, nor do
they mean to suggest that human actions don't have the capacity to drastically
transform those entities. However, they argue that in order to interpret what
we observe, we transform natural things into symbols and organize these symbols into self-constructed descriptive frameworks that allow us to understand
our environment.

A principal function of any culture is to promote communication and
exchange of information among its members (Kroeber and Kluckhohn 1952).
And to do that, the culture must both construct and promote a shared descriptive framework—a commonly expressed way of categorizing and organizing
the world, whose meanings are recognizable to members of that culture
through verbal and nonverbal behaviors, but are not necessarily shared by
other cultures (Robbins 1993). Such descriptive frameworks must be relatively
constant, since the distinctions between frameworks help to maintain cultures
as discrete entities over time; yet they are also dynamic, changing and evolv-
ing over time within cultures.

Three Constructions of Nature

Fine (1997) has identified three constructions of nature that have predominated in Western worldviews at different times in our history as a culture. He
identifies these as humanist, protectionist, and organic constructions. Each has
different implications for the way we manage for sustainable environments.

Humanist view. Also called the utilitarian or dominionistic view, this construction of nature sharply differentiates culture and nature, suggesting that nature
exists primarily to be a vast storehouse of potentially useful goods for human
society. This view predominated in Middle Eastern, European, and Euro-
American societies for millennia (Nash 1967, Worster 1985), and is most
closely associated with the Judeo-Christian cultural tradition (White 1967)
although it also exists in other cultures in somewhat different forms (Saito
1992). Some societies that have held a humanistic view have seen nature as
tainted or evil, something to be tamed or transcended. But a more prevalent
view in modern times sees nature as mildly positive or benign, something to

be desired insofar as it affords benefits to people. Similarly, a natural area is worth protecting as long as it sustains something we might need, even if only because we find it aesthetically pleasing.

Protectionist view. In what Fine (1997) calls "the standard strong environmental position," nature is seen as authentic and uncontaminated, and thus distinct from human life. Nature and culture are as sharply divided in this view as in the humanist orientation, but nature is worth preserving not because it benefits humanity, but because it is purer than humanity (e.g., Commoner 1972, Manes 1990). This doesn't mean nature cannot have benefits for humans, but those benefits are not the reason for protecting nature. Some adherents equate the protectionist view with non-Western cultures, which they see as less exploitative than our own, but it is more properly identified with the Romantic philosophy of Rousseau and later Thoreau, which has found its full flower in postwar Europe and America (Nash 1967).

Many people who hold a protectionist view of nature reject the idea that natural areas can be managed in any way, because that entails human contamination (e.g., Sagoff 1985). Katz's argument (see this volume) that restoration is simply another form of human domination of nature might also be characterized as a protectionist view. Protection means letting nature find its own way, preferably with no human influence at all. Implied in this approach is an almost religious faith in stable climax states such as ancient forests, and in the inherent self-restorative ability of nature.

Organic view. This is both the oldest and the newest orientation toward nature. In this view, the line between nature and culture is seen as blurred if it exists at all. The postmodern essayists in Cronon's (1995) book largely embrace this view, but so have non-Western tribal ideologies, as in this statement attributed by Stegner (1992) to a Sioux chief, Luther Standing Bear: "Only to the white man was nature a 'wilderness,' and only to him was the land 'infested' with 'wild' animals and 'savage' people. To us it was tame. Earth was bountiful and we were surrounded with the blessings of the Great Mystery" (118).

Not only does Standing Bear's statement describe a nature-culture relationship that is holistic rather than dualistic, but modern Americans can read into it a Romantic vision of a benign and benevolent (unless provoked) nature that also underlies the protectionist view (Ritvo 1987). This may be why people associate the protectionist view with indigenous and traditional cultures; however, it might be more correct to say that such cultures typically treated nature as a vital part of their home places, tending or taking from it as needed or desired. Raish's chapter in this volume examines more fully the relationship between traditional cultures and nature.

If nature and culture are inseparable, then any place might be a natural area. One can easily see a danger in that view. It's exemplified in questions such as this posed by Robert Nelson (1990): "If the lion is not to be condemned morally for wanton acts of cruelty against other creatures, why should mankind be judged harshly for making practical use of the natural world?" (57). If most of society held this view, there would be no need to restore ecosystems to natural conditions because whatever environment we create would be natural by definition. Alternatively, however, if nature is seen as part of the human environment, humans might be motivated to treat it as carefully as they do their own properties.

Clearly there is evidence that humans have influenced natural systems for longer than once supposed. This is part of what Cronon (1995) meant when he wrote that nature "is not nearly so natural as it seems." One example comes from the theory that North America's Pleistocene megafauna—giant sloths, mastodons, saber-toothed tigers, and the like—were hunted into extinction by humans that crossed the Bering land bridge from Asia. For more than a century, anthropologists have debated whether human hunting caused the destruction of whole species of giant mammals in North America, or whether extinctions should be blamed on climate change at the end of the Ice Age. Paleontologist Peter Ward (1997), citing recent evidence from study of growth rings in mammoth tusks, concludes that "this particular murder mystery is solved. We know 'whodunit.' We did it. Our species, our kind—humanity—armed only with stone-tipped spears, caused the extinction of the great mammoths and mastodons and perhaps that of many other large megamammal species" (220).

It has been suggested that some of our most desirable natural communities are, in fact, the result of human activity. Kay (1997) argues that the Rocky Mountain aspen type was maintained largely by Native American burning, and that we will lose this highly desirable plant community unless we maintain it through anthropogenic means. If so, it would make little sense to establish natural areas to maintain aspen communities and then protect those places by excluding most human activities.

Cultural Constructions in Natural Science

Despite scientific evidence that humans have long been part of natural landscapes, many natural scientists have been slow to abandon the dichotomous view of nature and culture. Perhaps this is because modern Western culture typically sees scientific inquiry as yielding truth that somehow rises above the interpretive variability associated with the social sciences. An atom is an atom, a plant is a plant, and saying it differently cannot change that circumstance. In reality, however, the natural sciences are as subject to evolutions of meaning as any other cultural constructs. A relevant example comes from the science of taxonomy.

Taxonomy strongly influences the work of conservation biologists, who are among the more vocal proponents of ecological restoration. Conservation biology has little meaning if we do not agree on what biological units to conserve. In the case of species conservation, we must agree that there are distinct categories of organisms whose genetic material cannot be shared with others outside those categories, and whose genetic makeup must therefore be maintained. Thus, we must believe that taxonomic classification describes reality; if not, there would be no reason to preserve individual species or distinct populations.

Yet taxonomy changes—not necessarily as a result of biological evolution, but because of the evolution of the meanings that scientists assign to taxonomic categories of organisms. An illustration comes from the taxonomic journey of the great-tailed grackle (*Quiscalus mexicanus*), a common blackbird of the south-central United States. In the past 100 years, this bird was demoted from a separate species (Coues 1892) to a subspecies of the morphologically similar boat-tailed grackle (*Quiscalus major*) (American Ornithologists' Union 1931), and then promoted back to its own species after Selander and Giller (1961) showed that the two grackles do not interbreed in Gulf Coast states where they are sympatric. During that same period, the bird has moved from the genus *Quiscalus* to a new genus, *Cassidix,* then back to *Quiscalus*; and from the family Icteridae, the blackbirds and orioles, to a much larger family, Emberizidae, which also includes New World warblers and sparrows.

In part, these changes resulted from the acquisition of new knowledge that changed old conceptions about the relationship between two similar-looking songbirds. But they also reflect a more fundamental change in the criteria of taxonomic classification. No longer do scientists rely primarily on observations of successful interbreeding. Instead, they focus on what electron-microscopic examination tells them about genetic variation.

As all these changes were taking place, the genetic makeup of the great-tailed grackle stayed the same. What changed was how scientists organized their constructions of the natural world. Differences between birds may be quite real, but taxonomy is a cultural construction. And changes in that construction affect natural areas and their management. If a natural area has a slightly variant population of a common species, that species may not be a high priority for the manager. But if a geneticist somewhere discovers that the local variant is more variant than we thought—that it's actually a separate (and quite rare) species—priorities suddenly change. The manager may decide to try to maintain a different kind of natural habitat or seral stage. In effect, the local definition of the natural area must change to match the change in taxonomic definition.

The Naturalness Continuum

If humans have been major agents of environmental change for millennia, and if Cronon (1995) is right that nature is a cultural construction, this should not mean that protecting and restoring nature is unnecessary. Nor should it mean that humans no longer have a moral and ethical obligation to maintain conditions that we might call natural because those conditions are critical to one or more of the organisms with whom we share our Earth. What it may mean is that we shouldn't waste much time drawing a clear line between what is natural and what is not, because that line is a cultural construct rendered less valid by recent scientific evidence. In drawing that line, we ultimately reject the biocentric view that *H. sapiens* is just one citizen of an infinitely interconnected Earth. We separate ourselves from the rest of what is ethical and natural.

Jordan (1994) suggests that "the real challenge of environmentalism is not to preserve nature by protecting it from human beings or rescuing it from their influence, but to provide the basis for a healthy relationship between nature and culture" (21; see also his chapter in this volume). One step toward doing so is to acknowledge that nature can't be as easily distinguished from culture as we pretend it can be. The line between nature and culture is very much blurred. But that doesn't mean there aren't important differences between places that can be described in terms of the direction, rate, and intensity of anthropogenic change. There is utility in the concept of naturalness. However, it is not an either/or proposition.

Instead, we might define naturalness as a relative quality—a continuum that can be defined by the characteristics of its polar extremes, but generally existing in some middle ground that is best measured by comparisons rather than absolutes. In line with the contemporary construction of nature, the poles of the naturalness continuum might be described by a ratio of indigenous to nonnative species, the similarity/dissimilarity of the landscape mosaic to pre-settlement conditions, the degree to which nonanthropogenic disturbance is allowed to proceed, or similar criteria. Such a concept offers a more reasonable basis for developing management strategies, and in fact natural resource managers regularly use tools based on relative qualities of this sort (e.g., recreational crowding, scenic beauty).

At the same time we must recognize that this continuum, like all models, is an oversimplification. Science is full of examples of models acknowledged as oversimplified yet valued as conceptual aids: e.g., Newtonian physics or Bohr's model of the atom. To cite another example that is especially relevant to the issue of restoration, natural scientists frequently describe ecological processes in terms of the simple facilitation model of succession proposed by Clements (1916, 1936), in which ecological disturbance is said to be followed by a series of successional stages leading to the inevitable establishment of a stable climax community that remains in place unless a catastrophic disturbance occurs. Even though subsequent study has shown that successional processes are much more complex and variable than the facilitation model allows (e.g., Connell and Slatyer 1977, Walker and Chapin 1987), it is often used as a conceptual aid because it is simple enough to be useful in discussions with laypersons, and because it usually does a good job of explaining or predicting what happens in the systems we seek to sustain and manage.

Conversely, the facilitation model may be partially responsible for some of the ongoing conflict over natural resources. Disapproval of old-growth forest management in the Pacific Northwest seems partly rooted in a belief on the part of many environmental activists that late-successional forests represent a stable climax that will remain indefinitely in the absence of anthropogenic disturbance. Although scientists now believe these forests have been subject to periodic nonanthropogenic disturbances at various scales, many of which were severe enough to bring about conversion to earlier successional states (Franklin and Hemstrom 1981), the persistence of belief in the simpler model can lead to a faulty conclusion that all disturbances in old-growth Douglas-fir forests are unnatural and thus undesirable. Therefore, it is crucial, when employing models, to take care that they do not lead logically to contrafactual arguments about the management of nature.

This caution is surely valid for our models of naturalness. For example, a key principle of ecosystem management suggests that a given place is more natural than another place if it contains more of the species, in approximately the same proportions and supported by the same mix of habitats and seral stages, as existed in similar locations prior to some reference period, e.g., frontier settlement (Swanson et al. 1994). But this implies that anthropogenic change of eighteenth- or nineteenth-century European origin is somehow less natural than anthropogenic change of earlier Siberian origin. Is that conclusion logically supportable? How do we know that our selected reference period is truly representative of conditions that existed over a longer time frame that has greater relevance from an evolutionary standpoint?

The answer is that we *don't* know. We've made a cultural construction, and we've agreed to adhere to it until society decides that a different cultural construction will achieve a more desirable result. Embracing Fine's (1997) organic perspective of nature means we acknowledge that nature is a cultural construction—merely one of the infinite number of ways to organize and understand our world. A key principle of contemporary public land management (i.e., ecosystem management) is that humans are part of systems, and that socioeconomic imperatives, as well as biophysical imperatives, must be considered in making natural area management decisions (Endter-Wada et al. 1998). By separating humans from nature—even if to achieve the honorable goal of protecting natural systems—we run the risk of creating a society that obtains its natural experience solely from the high-tech depictions of ecosystems that Orr (1996) calls "virtual nature" (see also Foster, this volume). Even more threateningly, when we divorce humans from all other species, people may tend to see those decisions as us-versus-them conflicts, and the ultimate loser of all such conflicts is nature.

Managing along the Continuum

The concept of naturalness has been useful in defining conditions at one end of a spectrum of conditions characterized by the degree of anthropogenic change. However, as we have seen, anthropogenic change may be inherently natural, and at any rate is an inevitable consequence of human existence as a part of nature. Moreover, we know that intimate contact with nature has benefits to the human psyche that cannot be ignored. This is not a new idea—indeed, it is the central theme of writers like Thoreau, who certainly did not argue that humans can best serve nature by keeping as much distance as possible. On the contrary, Jordan (1994 and this volume) argues that participation in nature through the practice of restoration is a new environmental paradigm that allows humans to resolve difficulties in the nature-culture relationship. If so, one of the tasks of a natural area manager would be to maintain a dynamic tension between two human values: the value associated with a natural world that is not unduly transformed by society's activities, and the value derived through direct interaction with the natural world.

Public land management in North America already offers a management framework that deals with those ambiguities: the Limits of Acceptable Change (LAC) planning process. At the root of the LAC concept is an idea that natural resource management represents a dynamic tension between two seemingly contradictory objectives: the legal and moral obligation to protect natural systems, and the legal mandate to provide opportunities for primitive and unconfined recreation experiences (McCool and Cole 1998, Stankey et al. 1985). As long as recreational access to wilderness is guaranteed by law, anthropogenic change is inevitable. What management can do is try to direct, divert, or diminish the rate of change that occurs as a result of wilderness recreation.

Cole and Stankey (1998) describe the conceptual core of LAC as a six-step process leading to management strategies that can hold anthropogenic change within agreed-upon limits in the face of specific challenges:

1. Agree that two or more goals are in conflict. Typically, one goal is to maintain current conditions that are presumed to be influenced primarily by nonanthropogenic forces. The other may be to provide wilderness recreation opportunities, graze livestock, protect adjacent nonwilderness lands against fire, or support a similar beneficial human use.
2. Establish that all goals must be compromised to some extent. If one goal legally cannot be compromised (as in protection of endangered species), there is no dynamic tension to be maintained.
3. Decide which conflicting goal will ultimately constrain the other goal. One goal, typically the protection of wilderness quality, is given priority over the other. This ultimate constraining goal is the one for which a limit of acceptable change is established. The other, called the initial constrain-

ing goal, can be achieved only insofar as it does not cause the limit to be exceeded.

4. Establish indicators and standards, as well as monitor the ultimate constraining goal. Through a process that ideally entails some collaboration with wilderness constituencies, managers determine how to tell if the ultimate constraining goal remains within an agreed-upon standard of acceptability. They then monitor the wilderness to ensure that these standards are maintained.

5. Allow the ultimate constraining goal to be compromised until a bottom line is reached. Recreation or other uses are allowed to continue or even increase as long as they do not cross the limit of acceptable impact.

6. Compromise the initial constraining goal so the ultimate constraining goal's minimally acceptable condition is never violated. Although some degree of degraded condition is accepted without imposing restrictions on use, regulatory action is imposed if monitoring shows that it is necessary to avoid exceeding the limit of acceptable change.

In other words, wilderness managers manage wildness as a continuum that describes the degree of anthropogenic change that may occur. The LAC process is a way to help managers determine where along the continuum we should be. Ideally this happens through consultation with wilderness constituencies, although nothing in the six-step process makes this mandatory.

In the context of LAC, the term wildness refers to the extent to which wilderness areas remain untamed or untrammeled by human action. Similarly, naturalness refers to the extent to which ecological processes are uninfluenced by some or all forms of human action. Elsewhere I have argued that LAC not only can be applied to nonwilderness lands, but in fact offers one of the best ways to incorporate the human dimension into ecosystem management (Brunson 1995, 1998). An obvious area for doing so is the management of natural areas, including making decisions about whether and how to attempt to restore natural conditions, as well as making the somewhat easier decisions about how to allow human use without undue intrusion upon the ecological conditions that are to be maintained.

Applying LAC to Decisions about Naturalness

Decisions can be based primarily on expert scientific judgment, and natural area managers have long made such decisions. For example, federal waterfowl refuges are managed to offer nature-based recreation experiences, but refuge managers are empowered to decide whether, and for how long, to exclude human use in order to minimize disturbance during the nesting season. In such a case, the ultimate constraining goal is to provide habitat conditions that will ensure continued production of waterfowl, while the initial constraining goal is to provide opportunities for people to view waterfowl in those habitats. These goals are set by law (since the refuges are designated by Congress), guided by years of experience in waterfowl production, and affirmed by the consent of the public that benefits from waterfowl production.

However, in the case of ecological restoration, there may be neither a statute that sets the goals nor a history of scientific expertise on which to base decisions about where to draw the line between nature and culture. The process of setting goals (and perhaps standards as well) must therefore entail an ongoing dialogue with constituents. This is especially true if we are to support the idea that restoration is a participatory endeavor. Jordan (1994) asserts that ecological restoration requires "an ecological relationship with these systems . . . that entails a genuine exchange of goods and services between ourselves and the natural community. This must be reciprocal, or, as Aldo Leopold and others have said, mutually beneficial, involving both taking and giving back" (18). Collaborative discussions between natural area managers and other stakeholders, typically part of the LAC process, are an appropriate forum for determining which goods and services can be taken and which must be given.

Constituents of a natural area—whether it is an urban Midwest arboretum, a waterfowl refuge, or part of a national forest managed under tenets of ecosystem management—would most likely be involved in several steps of the planning process. Since the poles of the continuum are not set by law (except perhaps when threatened or endangered species are affected), it may be necessary to negotiate definitions of the initial and ultimate constraining goals. Similarly, there may be a need to collectively work out disagreements about scientific underpinnings of a proposed restoration: e.g., what the pre-settlement conditions might have been (and whether those provide the most appropriate benchmark for restoration; see Hull and Robertson, this volume, for a discussion of selecting benchmarks); what tools might be employed to achieve the goals; and what protections are needed to buffer against the uncertainty inherent in restoration processes.

Yet while science is necessary to guide restoration strategies, it is not sufficient to ensure socially viable decisions. For example, some scientists believe intervention is needed in western forests to restore the distribution of tree species and age classes that existed prior to the arrival of settlers from the East. This is most efficiently done through silvicultural manipulations that guide the disturbance and subsequent regeneration of forest stands without the risks associated with nonanthropogenic disturbances such as fire or insect outbreaks. But to many people, restoration that entails the use of chain saws cannot be called restoration at all. LAC offers a framework for deciding the extent to which silvicultural approaches can be used in restoring a pre-settlement forest mosaic. In this example, the ultimate constraining goal is to maintain places where nonanthropogenic ecological processes continue to function unimpaired, while the initial constraining goal is to reshape the forest mosaic to conform to our contemporary scientific understanding of forest health or biotic integrity. In other words, both sides can claim to have science on their side.

At other times, LAC may provide an appropriate framework for deciding the extent to which science, rather than cultural preferences, should guide the choice of an ultimately constraining goal. For example, the USDA Forest Service recently established the Midewin National Tallgrass Prairie in Illinois with the primary objective of restoring the prairie ecosystem that existed before European settlement and that was maintained by frequent fires. European settlers altered the prairie ecosystem by planting not only crops but also shrubs such as lilac and Osage orange, which were shaped over decades into a lattice of living, flowering fences between fields. These more recent cultural features have become an important symbol of place for residents, which is now part of the outer edge of metropolitan Chicago.

Now that Midewin is managed as a natural area, there are several opportunities for constituents to participate in setting the naturalness continuum. One involves the restoration of fire to the prairie ecosystem. It should not be difficult for constituents to agree that prescribed fire is an acceptable part of the natural system. However, due to concerns about smoke and adjacent private property, managers and neighbors may agree that restoring fire is the initial constraining goal that ultimately must be compromised to protect public health and safety.

Another continuum might define the extent to which nonnative fencerows are allowed to remain (and even themselves be restored) in some parts of Midewin as a characteristic of the cultural landscape without unduly impeding the ultimate constraining goal of maintaining a prairie ecosystem. The decision about locations and proportions of shrub-retaining fields could be made as part of a collaborative process involving both natural area managers in the Forest Service and neighbors who have an interest in the future of the tallgrass prairie. By joining in those discussions, neighbors would become restoration participants, intimately involved in the giving and taking back that constitutes Jordan's (1994, and this volume) vision of restoration.

Conclusion

In this chapter I have sought to describe how a relatively simple tool, the Limits of Acceptable Change process, may be useful for resolving dilemmas over ecological restoration. While the tool may be simple, its application is not. Negotiations between constituencies with differing values and intellectual reference points are never easy, even if the groups share the goal of restoring nature (for further discussion of this issue, see Gobster and Barro, this volume). Yet the complexity of the task leads us to be guided by an alternative conception of natural area management—attempting to completely separate humans from natural areas—which is probably impossible to maintain and leads us to become preoccupied by intense political opposition.

I have suggested that the cultural construction of the term natural has changed over time. Conditions that may be considered equally natural from an ecological standpoint are not necessarily seen as natural by nonscientist observers. That's something we must not forget, because it is by and for those nonscientists that we are asked to manage protected areas. Ultimately, we manage nature because society wants us to do so—partly for selfish reasons, because if we foul the nest that is our Earth, we haven't the means to move to a new one; but just as importantly for moral reasons, because our culture has decided that humans have the unique ability and responsibility to act in ways that can control the rates and direction of anthropogenic change. History suggests that such responsible behavior may not be the natural way for a society to behave, but in contemporary Western society we seem to be moving toward a conclusion that it's the only option left to us.

References

American Ornithologists' Union. 1931. *Checklist of North American Birds, 4th Edition.* Lancaster, PA: American Ornithologists' Union.

Brunson, M. W. 1993. "'Socially Acceptable' Forestry: What Does it Imply for Ecosystem Management? *Western Journal of Applied Forestry* 8: 116–119.

Brunson, M. W. 1995. "The Changing Role of Wilderness in Ecosystem Management." *International Journal of Wilderness* 1: 12–15.

Brunson, M. W. 1998. "Beyond Wilderness: Broadening the Acceptability of Limits of Acceptable Change." In *Proceedings—Limits of Acceptable Change and Related Planning Processes: Progress and Future Directions,* edited by S. F. McCool and D. N. Cole, 44–48. USDA Forest Service General Technical Report INT-371. Ogden, UT: Intermountain Research Station.

Clements, F. E. 1916. *Plant Succession: An Analysis of the Development of Vegetation.* Carnegie Institution of Washington Publication 242.

Clements, F. E. 1936. "Nature and Structure of the Climax." *Journal of Ecology* 24: 252–284.

Cole, D. N., and G. H. Stankey. 1998. "Historical Development of Limits of Acceptable Change: Conceptual Clarifications and Possible Extensions." In *Proceedings—Limits of Acceptable Change and Related Planning Processes: Progress and Future Directions,* edited by S. F. McCool and D. N. Cole, 5–9. USDA Forest Service General Technical Report INT-371. Ogden, UT: Intermountain Research Station.

Commoner, B. 1972. *The Closing Circle: Nature, Man, and Technology.* New York: Knopf.

Connell, J. H., and R. O. Slatyer. 1977. "Mechanisms of Succession in Natural Communities and Their Role in Community Stability and Organization." *American Naturalist* 111: 1119–1144.

Coues, E. 1892. *Key to North American Birds.* Boston: Estes and Lauriat.

Cronon, W. 1995. *Uncommon Ground: Toward Reinventing Nature.* New York: Norton.

Elliot, R. 1997. *Faking Nature: The Ethics of Environmental Restoration.* New York: Routledge.

Endter-Wada, J., D. Blahna, R. Krannich, and M. Brunson. 1998. "A Framework for Understanding Social Science Contributions to Ecosystem Management." *Ecological Applications* 8: 891–904.

Fine, G. A. 1997. "Naturework and the Taming of the Wild: The Problem of 'Overpick' in the Culture of Mushroomers." *Social Problems* 44: 68–88.

Fine, G. A., and L. Christophorides. 1993. "Dirty Birds, Filthy Immigrants, and the English Sparrow War: Metaphorical Linkage in Constructing Social Problems." *Symbolic Interaction* 14: 375–393.

Franklin, J. F., and M. A. Hemstrom. 1981. "Aspects of Succession in the Coniferous Forests of the Pacific Northwest." In *Forest Succession: Concepts and Application,* edited by D. C. West, H. H. Shugart, and D. B. Botkin, 212–229. New York: Springer-Verlag.

Greider, T., and L. Garkovich. 1994. "Landscapes: The Social Construction of Nature and the Environment." *Rural Sociology* 59: 1–24.

Hansen, A. J., T. A. Spies, F. J. Swanson, and J. L. Ohman. 1991. "Conserving Biodiversity in Managed Forests." *BioScience* 41: 382–392.

Jordan, W. R. III. 1994. "'Sunflower Forest': Ecological Restoration as the Basis for a New Environmental Paradigm." In *Beyond Preservation: Restoring and Inventing Landscapes,* edited by A. D. Baldwin, Jr., J. De Luce, and C. Pletsch, 17–34. Minneapolis: University of Minnesota Press.

Kay, C. E. 1997. "Is Aspen Doomed?" *Journal of Forestry* 95(5): 4–11.

Kellert, S. R. 1996. *The Value of Life: Biological Diversity and Human Society.* Washington, DC: Island Press.

Kroeber, A. L., and C. Kluckhohn. 1952. *Culture: A Critical Review of Concepts and Definitions.* Cambridge, MA: The Peabody Museum.

Logan, R. S., and R. A. Fletcher. 1996. *Forest Ecosystem Stewardship.* Bozeman: Montana State University Extension Service.

Manes, C. 1990. *Green Rage: Environmentalism and the Unmaking of Civilization.* Boston: Little, Brown.

McCool, S. F., and D. N. Cole. 1998. *Proceedings—Limits of Acceptable Change and Related Planning Processes: Progress and Future Directions.* USDA Forest Service General Technical Report INT-371. Ogden, UT: Intermountain Research Station.

McKibben, B. 1989. *The End of Nature.* New York: Random House.

Nash, R. F. 1967. *Wilderness and the American Mind.* New Haven: Yale University Press.

Nelson, R. H. 1990. "Unoriginal Sin: The Judeo-Christian Roots of Ecotheology." *Policy Review* 53: 53–59.

Orr, D. W. 1996. "Virtual Nature." *Conservation Biology* 10: 8–9.

Ritvo, H. 1987. *The Animal Estate.* Cambridge, MA: Harvard University Press.

Robbins, R. H. 1993. *Cultural Anthropology: A Problem-based Approach.* Itasca, IL: Peacock.

Sagoff, M. 1985. "Fact and Value in Ecological Science." *Environmental Ethics* 7: 99–116.

Saito, Y. 1992. "The Japanese Love of Nature: A Paradox." *Landscape* 31(2): 1–8.

Selander, R. K., and D. A. Giller. 1961. "Analysis of Sympatry of Great-tailed and Boat-tailed Grackles." *Condor* 63: 29–83.

Shindler, B. 1998. *Using Qualitative Research to Examine Public Acceptance of Ecosystem Management: Six Important Factors in Forest Communities.* Portland, OR: USDA Forest Service, Pacific Northwest Research Station.

Shindler, B., and M. Brunson. 1999. "Changing Natural Resource Paradigms in the United States: Finding Political Reality in Academic Theory." In *Handbook of Global Environmental Policy and Administration,* edited by D. Soden and B. S. Steel, 459–473. New York: Marcel Dekker.

Stankey, G. H., D. N. Cole, R. C. Lucas, M. E. Petersen, and S. S. Frissell. 1985. *The Limits of Acceptable Change (LAC) System for Wilderness Planning.* USDA Forest Service General Technical Report INT-176. Ogden, UT: Intermountain Forest and Range Experiment Station.

Steel, B. S., and N. P. Lovrich. 1997. "An Introduction to Natural Resource Policy and the Environment: Changing Paradigms and Values." In *Public Lands Management in the West: Citizens, Interest Groups, and Values,* edited by B. S. Steel, 3–15. Westport, CT: Praeger.

Stegner, W. 1992. "A Capsule History of Conservation." In *Where the Bluebird Sings to the Lemonade Springs,* 117–132. New York: Penguin.

Swanson, F. J., J. A. Jones, D. O. Wallin, and J. H. Cissel. 1994. "Natural Variability— Implications for Ecosystem Management." In *Volume II: Ecosystem Management Principles and Applications,* edited by M. E. Jensen and P. S. Bourgeron, 80–94. USDA Forest Service General Technical Report PNW-318. Portland, OR: Pacific Northwest Research Station.

Swidler, A. 1986. "Culture in Action: Symbols and Strategies." *American Sociological Review* 51: 273–286.

Walker, L. R., and F. S. Chapin III. 1987. "Interactions Among Processes Controlling Successional Change." *Oikos* 50: 131–135.

Ward, P. D. 1997. *The Call of Distant Mammoths: Why the Ice Age Mammals Disappeared.* New York: Copernicus.

White, L., Jr. 1967. "The Historic Roots of Our Ecologic Crisis." *Science* 65 (March 10): 1203–1207.

Worster, D. 1985. *Nature's Economy: A History of Ecological Ideas.* San Francisco: Sierra Club Books.

✤ *Part IV* ✤

MAKING AND MAINTAINING RESTORED ENVIRONMENTS

Chapter 12

THE RESTORATION EXPERIENCE: VOLUNTEERS' MOTIVES, VALUES, AND CONCEPTS OF NATURE

Herbert W. Schroeder

The last several years have brought significant changes in the management of public lands and natural resources in the United States. As a result of debates over management practices, shifts in the goods and services demanded by the public, and developments in scientific knowledge, there has emerged a general, philosophical shift toward managing natural environments as integrated, dynamic systems. As part of this shift toward a more holistic perspective, there has been a growing recognition that people are an important part of ecosystems and that human values, behaviors, and experiences must therefore be integrated into the planning and management of natural environments (Christensen et al. 1996, Cordell 1997).

At the same time, because public agencies are faced with shrinking budgets for programs and services, people are being encouraged to contribute their time, energy, and skills in volunteer activities that benefit their communities. Even before President Clinton's April 1997 summit on volunteerism, many Americans were becoming involved in volunteer programs that they considered to be personally satisfying as well as beneficial to their communities.

These two trends—the shift toward an integrated view of ecosystems that includes human beings, and the increasing reliance on volunteer efforts to carry out programs to benefit communities—have come together in the volunteer ecological restoration movement. Thousands of people are now volunteering their time, energy, and skills to restore endangered native ecosystems in and near their communities (Ross 1994). In Illinois, volunteers interested in restoring prairie and savanna ecosystems have formed the Volunteer Stewardship Network (VSN), an association of restoration groups coordinated by the Illinois chapter of The Nature Conservancy. The members of the VSN are very motivated and appear to derive a great deal of satisfaction from their efforts. They are willing to spend long hours outdoors in physically demanding labor, sometimes under less than ideal weather conditions.

My goal in this research study was to learn more about these volunteers, what their work means to them, and what specific motives, values, and rewards have induced them to give so many hours of their free time to restoration activities. The primary source of material for this study was the periodic newsletters distributed by many of the individual stewardship groups. These newsletters, written and edited by the volunteers themselves, contain many passages that express who the volunteers are, what they are trying to achieve, why they are drawn to this kind of work, and what rewards they experience in the course of doing the work. By reading and systematically interpreting these passages, I hoped to gain insight into how the volunteers view themselves, their work, the sites they are restoring, and the natural world in general.

Methods

With the assistance of the Illinois chapter of The Nature Conservancy, I gathered copies of newsletters from several restoration groups belonging to the VSN in northern and central Illinois. The results reported here are based on a total of twenty-seven issues of newsletters published during the period 1991–1995, representing nine different volunteer groups.

My objective was to identify the main recurring themes in the newsletter text relating to volunteers' motivations, and to document the themes with illustrative quotes drawn from the original text. I used an approach for interpreting textual material that I had employed in two previous studies for analyzing people's written descriptions of special places (Schroeder 1991, 1996). The process involves building an outline of topics, cross-referencing each topic back to the original text, and then using the topic outline to compose a narrative of themes occurring in the text.

First, I read the newsletters and identified passages that pertained to the volunteers' goals, the rewards they experience from doing restoration work, and their values and concepts about the natural world. I typed each of these passages into a computer word processing file. Next, I divided each passage into smaller units of text. Each text unit consisted of one or more phrases or sentences that expressed a distinct idea or line of thought. Then I read each of these text units carefully and began developing an outline of topics that were being repeatedly mentioned across different articles in the newsletters.

As I continued reading the text, I elaborated upon the outline by adding more specific subtopics and by grouping topics together under more general categories. I cross-referenced each entry in the outline to the places where it occurred in the original text, so that I could easily refer back to and retrieve specific instances of each topic. My goal was to have each unit of text linked to at least one entry in the topic outline.

When I had finished reading, outlining topics, and cross-referencing the text, I reviewed the results by tallying the frequency with which each topic had appeared in the newsletter passages. My purpose in doing this was not to quantify the data in any precise way, but simply to get a general idea of which topics were appearing most consistently. Then, based on the topic outline and the tallies, I began writing a summary of how the volunteers who write in the newsletters view themselves and their work. In writing the summary, I referred back to the original text to find quotations illustrating the themes in the summary.

Results

This process of interpreting and summarizing resulted in nine main themes, each having two or more subthemes. The themes and subthemes are listed in Table 12.1 and briefly described below; each subtheme is illustrated by one or more quotations drawn from the newsletters. Thus, to a large extent, this summary of newsletter themes is presented in the words of the newsletter writers themselves. The themes and subthemes included in this summary represent the themes that occurred most consistently across the nine volunteer groups. Almost all of the subthemes were expressed in the newsletters of at least four of the groups. (Those subthemes that appeared for less than four of the groups will be identified as such when they are discussed below.) The reader should bear in mind that this summary reflects the views of a subset of volunteers— those who edit, contribute to, or are interviewed in the newsletters—and that their views are not necessarily identical to those of all other volunteers.

The Purpose of the Volunteers' Work

Preserve, protect, and restore nature. The basic purpose of the volunteers' work, as seen by the newsletter writers, is to preserve, protect, and restore nature. This goal is expressed with respect to the whole Earth; general types of ecosystems; and particular species, features, and sites within ecosystems. Preservation, protection, and restoration seem to be regarded as complementary goals. More than one of them is often mentioned in the same sentence or phrase.

Table 12.1. Themes and Subthemes Identified in Restoration Newsletters

The Purpose of the Volunteers' Work	Being surprised
Preserve, protect, and restore nature	Getting excited
Protect the original, native landscape	Having fun
Preserve and restore biodiversity	
	Social Dimensions of Restoration
The Current State of Nature	Socializing
Small, isolated remnants	Developing a sense of community
Development pressures	Feeling attached to the group
Nonnative plants	Admiring leaders
Struggle for survival	
Nature needs help	**Volunteers as People**
	Ordinary people
Metaphors of Invasion and War	Enthusiastic and dedicated
Science-fiction invaders	Hard-working
Army on the battlefront	Persevering
Making a Difference	**Feelings Toward Nature**
Acting locally	Aesthetic appreciation
Being part of a larger effort	Friendship with nature
Envisioning future outcomes	Attachment to their site
Benefiting future generations	Sense of loss
Personal Rewards of Restoration	**Sources of Ideas and Inspiration**
Having a satisfying experience	Literature
Seeing tangible results	Native Americans
Learning and sharing knowledge	Religion
Enjoying the outdoors	

> We have a need to exercise our right as stewards of this Earth, our home, to protect what is nature. . . . We want to make a positive difference in helping to restore our Mother Earth.

> Large tracts of woodland such as Cedar Glen are important today because they represent our best chance to restore and preserve this ecosystem.

Protect the original, native landscape. More specifically, the nature that these volunteers want to protect is the original, native landscape—the vegetation and the land of Illinois as they existed in the past, before the European settlers came.

> The DuPage Volunteer Stewardship Group is dedicated to preserving remnants of the original Illinois landscape.

> We [will] reclaim this land from farmland and turn it back to native prairie and woodland.

Preserve and restore biodiversity. One of the most important attributes of nature that the stewardship volunteers wish to preserve and restore is biodiversity.

They are pleased when they discover evidence that many varied species are surviving within the small area of one of their restoration sites.

> By returning the prairie to this area, Carpenter Park would become one of the most biologically diverse areas in Central Illinois.

> The final count of species should approach 600, a very respectable number for a preserve of 215 acres.

The Current State of Nature

Small, isolated remnants. The volunteers' efforts are motivated by their perceptions of the current plight of nature. The original landscape of Illinois now exists only in small, isolated remnants. The volunteers regard these remnants as precious because they harbor the last vestiges of many rare plants and animals.

> Indian Bluff Prairie—that tiny, isolated remnant of what was once a vast expanse of waving grasses and colorful flowers.

> At the fringes of the cliffs, one can see the last vestiges of the flora that once covered the ridge top.

Development pressures. These remnants of original nature are threatened by the pressures of development and land-use change that alter or destroy native landscapes.

> Because of the planned widening of a county road, many prairie plants will be destroyed unless we move them.

> [DuPage Volunteer Stewardship Group] is working to save remnants of the original Illinois landscape that are under severe stress from neglect and encroaching development.

Nonnative plants. Another threat is the invasion of nonnative species of plants, which crowd out the native vegetation.

> But invaders are taking over the ridgetops, shading out plants that depend upon full sunlight for survival.

> Buckthorn shades out potential competitors, and is easily and widely spread by birds. It is possibly also allelopathic, releasing chemicals to destroy competition.

Struggle for survival. Faced with these threats, native species and ecosystems are struggling for survival and are barely hanging on to their existence.

> Prairie species . . . struggle to exist.

[We came to] help it fight for its existence, before the battle—
and the prairie—are lost forever.

Nature needs help. In this fight to survive, nature needs help from human
beings. The volunteers feel called upon to aid nature in its struggle because
without the efforts of concerned people, endangered natural areas will be lost.

But this . . . is an expansive Forest Preserve area which desperately needs human care and appreciation.

The prairies need our help! Won't you give a few hours to a
worthy cause?

Metaphors of Invasion and War

The volunteers' sense of the current situation and their goals regarding nature
are sometimes expressed in metaphors of invasion and war. This is especially
the case with respect to exotic plant species, which constitute the most immediate and persistent threat that these volunteer groups must deal with on their
established sites.

Science-fiction-type invaders. Nonnative plant species are depicted (tongue-in-
cheek) as evil, science-fiction-type aliens—an invading menace that threatens
to take over the restoration sites if it is not destroyed.

You saw the first installment, and dread the next. Yes, it's
ALIENS! the fearful sequel to ALIEN. That's "Alien Weed Control."

Parts of Kibbe are being taken over by the alien invasion of the
black locust. . . . Cut down the scum, spray them with killer
herbicide. . . . How many locusts will die in one day?

Army on the battlefront. Volunteers use military metaphors, comparing themselves to an army on the battlefront: waging war, defeating the enemy, and
helping endangered ecosystems to fight back against the invaders.

From the Battlefront: I was . . . waging war against some aliens!
. . . If we don't fight back, they'll take over! . . . See these beau-
ties? If we hadn't defeated the enemy, none of these would be
here. . . . Along with many like us, we can join forces to defeat
the evil alien.

On this frigid March day, our small band of intrepid volunteers
went to war, armed with a rag-tag assortment of loppers, pruning shears, [etc.] . . . to help tip the delicate balance ever so
slightly back in favor of the little prairie, and help it fight for its
existence, before the battle—and the prairie—are lost forever.

Making a Difference

Acting locally. Volunteers find satisfaction in knowing that they are doing something about the problems described above. They believe that they can make a real difference by getting actively involved and putting their beliefs into practice in their own local area.

> Join us and make a difference for the last few remnants of native Illinois ecosystems . . . and the plants and animals that thrive there.

> Saving Antarctica or the Amazon rain forest is important, but we here in the Midwest can't do much about it. What we can do is to make a difference here in our own backyard.

Being part of a larger effort. The volunteers work locally in small groups, but at the same time they feel that they are contributing to a much larger effort that involves many other like-minded people and groups.

> Each group is not acting alone, but as part of a much greater enterprise.

> We are among more than 4,000 people statewide who volunteer their time to care for some 16,000 acres of significant natural lands.

Envisioning future outcomes. In their imaginations, volunteers look forward to the outcomes of projects now under way. Their ability to envision the future enables them to accomplish important goals. They hope and dream of a future when nature will be restored on a broad scale.

> There were many . . . who realized that a diversity of native plants still survived among the weeds. They had the vision to look beyond the wine bottles and garlic mustard to see the area as a safe and convenient nature preserve for the surrounding communities.

> It will be a land abundant in rolling prairie, interrupted only by an occasional creek and woodland. Where deer and buffalo roam.

Benefiting future generations. The volunteers believe that their efforts will benefit future generations, by preserving nature so that it will be there for others to enjoy.

> I want the world to know that a small group of dedicated people in the south suburbs are doing their part to see that future generations will have these beautiful places to enjoy.

I do this because I want future generations to be able to enjoy open lands. If we don't conserve them now, there won't be any in the future.

Personal Rewards of Doing Restoration Work

Having a satisfying experience. Volunteers find that getting directly involved in restoration work is a satisfying way of contributing to an environmental cause.

A few hours of time volunteered can be more rewarding than donating a few dollars to let someone else do the work.

Being a volunteer gives me a feeling of satisfaction and a sense of security that I am doing a little something to help.

Seeing tangible results. Volunteers take great satisfaction in seeing the tangible results of their labor. For the prairie and savanna landscapes of the Chicago region, even a small effort may produce a visible change in the landscape after one or two years. Seeing clear signs of progress is rewarding and motivates them to continue their work.

Just one year's work by a small group of volunteers has made a visible difference on the first ridge of Warnock Prairie.

We work hard and already see results of our continuous efforts. . . . It is both gratifying and rewarding to visualize these results and then see them happen right before your eyes.

Learning and sharing knowledge. Volunteers also enjoy learning and sharing knowledge about native plants and animals and about restoration techniques.

Workdays are also a time for learning about an area's native plants and animals and for gaining a better understanding of the delicate process of ecological restoration.

We can learn from this diversity, too, and use it to educate children as we take them on tours. . . . We can all learn more about the environment we live in just by taking a walk through one of Markham's sanctuaries of diversity.

Enjoying the outdoors. Restoration work gives volunteers a chance to get outside and enjoy the outdoors, the weather, and the wildlife. Restoration sites can also be settings for outdoor recreation activities such as canoeing, skiing, and bird watching.

The days set aside to come out and cut brush and assist in burns are called workdays, but are truly a time to come out and enjoy the weather, to bird watch, to learn of the natural plants and animals of these areas.

[Cedar Glen-Kibbe] can be a great place to walk in the winter. Some people even cross country ski there. The deer are easy to spot. Although some trails that lead to the eagle roost are closed, the rest is open for your enjoyment. It's a winter wonderland.

Being surprised. Volunteers enjoy being surprised by new, unexpected, or unusual things at restoration sites.

We came across some interesting creatures. . . . One of the joys of going into the woods is not knowing what you'll come across.

It seems each day that I work, a new plant or animal makes its appearance and the steward's excitement highlights its importance to the prairie.

Getting excited. Some aspects of restoration work provide excitement or thrills. This is especially true of prairie burns.

"Burn" days are especially exciting.

Now the fun—the head fire is lit along the southern edge of the prairie. Towering flames roar across the fields, engulfing the whole thing in less than fifteen minutes. Dense black smoke pours into the air.

Having fun. Aside from the more serious aspects of volunteering, being part of a restoration group can provide opportunities to just have fun.

All it takes is the desire to work those muscles a little bit (or a lot), to share the beauty of the Grove, and to have fun!

The butterflies were numerous and it was fun to name them.

Social Dimensions of Restoration Work

Socializing. Restoration work involves more than just working on the land. Making friends and taking part in social activities at workdays, meetings, and special events are also important parts of volunteering.

The workdays . . . always include a chance to make new friends.

Come a little early if you'd like to chat with other volunteers before the work begins. Occasionally, coffee and doughnuts magically appear from some thoughtful person.

Developing a sense of community. A sense of community develops among volunteers as they work together for a common cause.

> Steering committees from all regions meet periodically to discuss common concerns, and these meetings engender a spirit of community.

> We are a group of ordinary people . . . joined by a common concern for our environment.

Feeling attached to the group. Volunteers feel pride and affection toward their group and the individuals they work with.

> Personally, I feel proud of the accomplishments of my prairie Friends.

> I love what I do and love the people I work with.

Admiring leaders. They have respect and admiration for their leaders.

> Site stewards: . . . These folks do the hero's work and are responsible for the ecological management of sites in the Volunteer Stewardship Network.

> [He] was a leader of men . . . and women. . . . He was imbued with a determination that scared ordinary people into saying, "Yes. Yes. We love to say yes."

Volunteers as People

Ordinary people. The newsletters also reveal how the volunteers look at themselves. Volunteers see themselves as ordinary people. Advanced degrees in biology and ecology are not a requirement for doing this work. (This subtheme appeared less consistently across the groups than most, being expressed by only three of the nine groups.)

> We are a group of ordinary people—professionals, homemakers, students and retirees—joined by a common concern for our environment.

> We'd rather have your bright spirit than your transcripts. You don't need a degree in botany or a job as a naturalist. We don't care if you never won a research grant.

Enthusiastic and dedicated. Volunteers are enthusiastic and energetic. They show great dedication and commitment to restoration work. They give freely of their time and energy and communicate their enthusiasm to others.

VSN is the Volunteer Stewardship Network, an army of dedicated, energetic, knowledgeable people who handle the task of managing the lands acquired by TNC.

I got involved in the summer of 1985 through [the group's founder]. His enthusiasm was contagious.

Hard-working. Volunteers are hard workers. When necessary they will spend long hours doing physically demanding tasks.

Using loppers, bow saws, fire, and a lot of sweat, volunteers have made great progress in controlling these brush and weed problems.

We are justifiably proud to say that our volunteers are so conscientious in coming to workdays.

Persevering. They are willing to brave the elements and persevere under difficult or uncomfortable conditions.

The schedule of workdays, which looked so realistic last winter, will not meet this spring's muddy reality. . . . We must, however, remain steadfast in the muck, plan on working through the merry month of May, and possibly later.

Not wind or rain or snow or cold can dampen the spirit of a prairie lover.

Feelings Toward Nature

Aesthetic appreciation. Volunteers enjoy the aesthetic qualities of nature and the beauty of their restoration sites. Some volunteers are deeply touched and inspired by their encounters with nature.

The spring growing season looks good and there should again be a spectacular display of Shooting Stars on Dropseed Prairie. Come out and see the beauty of this natural area.

In autumn we are thrilled by Mother Nature's spectacular leaf displays which set our hearts afire. . . . We can hear the clarion call of fall and appreciate its beauty.

Friendship with nature. Some volunteers feel a special affinity for nature, the Earth, and native ecosystems. They personify ecosystems and nature, and feel friendship toward the plants and animals that live on their restoration sites. (This subtheme appeared in only three of the nine volunteer groups and was especially prominent in one of them.)

Each time I've greeted the prairie and her volunteers, I've felt a wonderful kinship with the Earth and humanity.

For five years these same birds have made a home on Paintbrush [Prairie]. . . . Like old friends, I look forward to seeing them there in the summer months.

Attachment to their site. Some volunteers develop a strong feeling of attachment to their particular site after they have worked on it for a period of time.

Although [her] tour of duty as steward of Schiller Woods is over officially . . . , she will continue to keep an eye on her woods as she has in the past. (Natural areas that you've worked have a way of getting in your system like that!)

She . . . says her life consists of family . . . work, and Funk's Grove.

Sense of loss. Volunteers feel distress and a sense of loss at the vanishing of native plants and animals and at the rapid urbanization of the landscape. This gives a sense of urgency to their work. They believe that if they do not act now, irreversible losses of natural sites and species will occur.

Unless something is done, we will witness the loss of the oak woodland . . . just as our forefathers witnessed the loss of the bison, elk, and open prairie.

These natural areas present a striking contrast to the development activities all around us. Seeing a cornfield turned into a shopping mall or a woods transformed into a subdivision seemingly overnight can leave us with a sense of loss. Having those changes envelop an entire county, as they have in DuPage over the last decade, can destroy our sense of place.

Sources of Ideas and Inspiration

Literature. Volunteers draw ideas and inspiration from a variety of books, poems, talks, and other sources. Quotations from well-known environmental writers and speakers are used to elucidate the philosophy behind restoration work.

As Aldo Leopold wrote, stewardship is right when it increases the integrity, stability, and beauty of the land.

"All things by mortal power / Near or far / Hiddenly / To each other linked are, / That thou canst not stir a flower / Without troubling a star." . . . [by] Francis Thompson.

Native Americans. For some volunteers, Native Americans are a source of inspiration and provide an example of a traditional land ethic. (This subtheme occurred for only two of the groups and was especially strong for one of those groups—the same group for whom affinity with nature was a strong theme.)

> From Onondaga Chief Oren Lyon's Long Island University lecture: "When you sit in council on the welfare of your people, you must council with the seventh generation in mind." The wisdom behind it rings ominously true in our current time of ecological crisis.

> In spite of incredible cruelty and greed, the indigenous people survived. Their survival can be our hope for restoring the ecosystems of the earth.

Religion. Some volunteers derive religious inspiration from contact with nature at restoration sites, or base their land ethic on a particular religious tradition, e.g., Judeo-Christian or Native American. (This subtheme appeared for only two groups, again including the same group that expressed affinity for nature.)

> I hold in my sight thrilling variations of plant forms, whose structures boldly proclaim (to my eyes) praises to their Architect. . . . I see the fluidity of fascinating adaptation as it is channeled securely within definite guidelines of divine design.

> We need to learn the ways of those who . . . lived a life that was respectful of and spiritually rooted to the land. . . . Chief Seattle: "Every part of this soil is sacred in the estimation of my people." Chief Joseph of the Nez Perce: "The earth and myself are of one mind. The measure of the land and the measure of our bodies are the same."

Discussion

The results of this research study can help those who manage and coordinate volunteer ecosystem restoration activities to understand why certain volunteers become highly committed to restoration work. Based on the themes identified in the newsletters, I believe that the high level of motivation and enthusiasm of these volunteers stems from three interacting factors. First is the sense of urgency and immediacy they feel about the fragility of nature and the impending loss of native sites and species. They sense that something precious is slipping away and will be irretrievably lost unless immediate action is taken. Second is their belief that they can make an important and real difference in preventing this loss. By getting actively involved, volunteers see the possibility of actually changing the course of things and achieving a better outcome for the future. Third is the ability to see tangible progress from their efforts in a fairly short time span. The effects of volunteers' interventions in the prairie and savanna ecosystems in which they focus their efforts may become visible in as little as one year, reinforcing that their actions really are making a difference.

These three factors combine to create a powerful incentive and reinforcement for the volunteers' work. Therefore, managers and coordinators of restoration programs might help maintain the motivation and enthusiasm of their volunteers by highlighting the importance of restoration to the future of the local, regional, and global environment, and by providing frequent opportunities for volunteers to see the tangible outcomes of their work. In addition to these three important factors, the newsletters also reveal a diversity of other pleasures and rewards that ecosystem volunteers experience in their work. By building opportunities for learning and sharing knowledge, enjoyable outdoor activities, and social events into their programs, volunteer coordinators can help make the volunteering experience still more engaging and rewarding.

These conclusions parallel, at least in general terms, the findings of other studies of volunteers and their motives. For example, the themes of "making a difference" and "social dimensions of restoration work" in this study of newsletters parallel the categories of purposive benefits and solidarity benefits found by Caldwell and Andereck (1994) in a survey of members of the North Carolina Zoological Society. Manzo and Weinstein (1987) found that active members of the Sierra Club were motivated by a desire to make the world a better place, perceptions of the efficacy of citizen action, feelings of having been personally harmed by environmental problems, and friendships with other club members. These are similar to the themes of "making a difference" and "social dimensions" and the subthemes of "seeing tangible results" and "sense of loss" found in the restoration newsletters. Corresponding to the newsletter subtheme "attachment to their site," Ryan (this volume) found that park users (including volunteers) had developed feelings of attachment to urban natural areas in Michigan.

Grese et al. (this volume) found four factors that motivate volunteer ecosystem stewards. Their strongest factor, "helping the environment," includes several items similar to the "preserve, protect, and restore nature" subtheme and the "making a difference" theme in this study. A factor they label "exploration" appears similar to the "learning and sharing knowledge" subtheme in the newsletters. Grese et al. also found a "spirituality" factor that contains items similar to the "enjoying the outdoors," "friendship with nature," "sense of community," and "religion" subthemes from the newsletters. Finally, Grese et al.'s "personal and social" factor includes items similar to the "social dimensions" theme as well as the "seeing tangible results" subthemes in the newsletters.

The results of this study may also provide some insight into how volunteers' definition, purpose, and philosophy of restoration differ from how restoration is discussed in the academic world. In that world, scholars often treat restoration and preservation as conflicting or mutually exclusive goals, so that choosing one means rejecting the other (Baldwin et al. 1994). The main argument in the debate between preservation and restoration is clearly articulated in the philosophy section of this book. In this debate, preservation is interpreted as a hands-off policy that precludes active intervention of the type taken by restorationists. Judging from how the concepts of preservation and restoration are used in the newsletters, however, these volunteers do not seem to see any conflict or contradiction between preserving and restoring natural areas. In fact, their fundamental purpose (as they state it) is the preservation of nature. They view restoration as a means to that end, because it offsets the disruptive impacts of civilization and helps nature to function as it originally did.

Another philosophical question that has been debated recently concerns the status of restored ecosystems as either natural or artifactual. Eric Katz in this book and elsewhere has argued that restored ecosystems should be considered artifacts rather than natural entities, because they are the result of deliberate, intentional actions of human beings. (See chapters by William Jordan, Andrew Light, and Cheryl Foster in this volume for other views on this question.) The newsletters I examined in this study never explicitly discussed this issue, but the results of my analysis suggest that the newsletter writers would not agree with the assertion that restorations are human artifacts. These volunteers seem to regard nature as that which existed in the landscape before European settlement. Remnants of this nature still exist in places, but in a greatly damaged and diminished state. The volunteers' goal is to counteract the forces that have destroyed and altered these natural landscapes, thus freeing nature to once again function in the way that it would have if the damage had never occurred. Thus, these volunteers would most likely regard the restoration sites they work on as being more, rather than less, natural than before the restoration efforts began.

Both of the philosophical points discussed above are illustrated in the following newsletter quote:

> For the last fifteen years, the role that these volunteers have had in realizing those early dreams of preserved natural sites is inestimable. Without people out there cutting buckthorn and honeysuckle, and pulling garlic mustard and sweet clover, these "natural areas" would become Hansel-and-Gretel-type deep, dark woods, overgrown with Eurasian exotics.

For the author of this quote, the goal of "preserved natural sites" is achieved through the cutting and pulling of nonnative plants, with the implication that unchecked proliferation of exotic species would lead to sites that are neither preserved nor natural.

The results of this study may have implications for understanding why the Chicago restoration controversy described in the Introduction to this volume and elsewhere (e.g., Gobster 1997; Helford and Vining et al., this volume) has been so contentious and difficult to resolve. Of particular interest in this regard are the warlike metaphors sometimes used by volunteers to describe their work.

On the one hand, this metaphorical likening of restoration work to war has the positive effect of reinforcing the volunteers' commitment, dedication, and willingness to sacrifice for their cause. It seems that for some volunteers, restoration work is in fact "the moral equivalent of war."[1] Unfortunately, once the conflict over restoration in the Chicago area emerged, this martial view of restoration work may have intensified the controversy and made it more difficult to resolve. All the newsletters quoted in this chapter were published before the controversy emerged. Thus, it seems that restoration volunteers were already predisposed to view themselves as combatants in a war to save nature. When people raised objections to restoration projects, it was then easy to view these people as enemies of nature. The immediate impulse was to fight and try to defeat these enemies, rather than to try to understand their objections and look for ways to negotiate and compromise.

Of course, as with most controversial issues, combative individuals can be found on both sides of the restoration argument. It is not my purpose to identify one side as being more intransigent than the other. I am simply pointing out that, while metaphors of battle and war help evoke intense motivation and commitment to a cause, they probably do not make it any easier to resolve conflicts such as the one that has arisen in Chicago.

As in any research study based on written text, the source of the text and the intent of the writers must be taken into account when interpreting these results. The newsletters are produced independently by each of the individual stewardship groups, and they seem to serve several functions. They inform volunteers about upcoming events and workdays. They present technical information on ecology, restoration, and species identification. They help create a sense of identity and community for the group and encourage volunteers to become more actively involved in the group's activities. They also provide an outlet where volunteers can express and share their significant experiences, goals, and values.

The newsletter writers and editors are active members of the group and seem to direct their writing toward other members and potential members of their own group, as well as toward the larger community of restoration volunteers. It could be argued that the newsletters serve as a public relations tool and, as such, present a biased or idealized view of the volunteers. The newsletters do have a consistently positive tone. Most of the articles are upbeat and do not dwell on less pleasant topics like volunteer burnout, disagreements between group members, or failed restoration projects—all of which probably do occur from time to time.

On the other hand, because the newsletters are local, grassroots publications, they probably contain less calculated posturing and deliberate public-image manipulation than might be found, for example, in the national newsletter of a large organization. My impression is that, in writing for the newsletters, these volunteers are sincerely expressing their own experiences and understandings of the positive benefits and motivations that keep them coming back to work on the restoration sites. Most of the themes discussed above occurred consistently across many of the groups, and may represent common values and meanings that are shared broadly in the volunteer community. One exception was a cluster of themes having to do with a feeling of affinity with nature, spiritual or religious associations, and Native American views of nature. These themes were less widely expressed and appeared to be especially strong in one group. They may represent the perspective of the individual or individuals who are the most involved in producing that group's newsletter.

Of course, the volunteers who write for the newsletters are not a random sample, and their views do not necessarily correspond to those of all volunteers. The volunteers who write for the newsletters are probably among the more highly motivated members of their groups. Volunteers who are less motivated or more casual about their involvement in restoration work, or who disagree with some aspects of their group's activities, are probably less likely to have their experience of restoration work represented in the newsletters.

Thus, the summary of newsletter themes provides a glimpse of the volunteer groups and their work as seen through the eyes of some of their more highly motivated members. Additional research, such as a representative survey or in-depth interviews with the VSN membership, would help to expand upon the information in the newsletters. No single research approach can tell the whole story of what motivates the volunteers. The newsletters, however, contain authentic and spontaneous expressions of some of the most important goals, values, and rewards involved in being an ecosystem restoration volunteer, and as such they tell an interesting part of that story.

Note

1. The expression "moral equivalent of war" was first used by William James (1984, originally published in 1910) in a speech calling for a national public service program. James believed that such programs would help prevent war by providing an alternative means to satisfy the human drive for honor, discipline, and commitment to a higher cause.

References

Baldwin, D. A., Jr., J. de Luce, and C. Pletsch, eds. 1994. *Beyond Preservation: Restoring and Inventing Landscapes.* Minneapolis: University of Minnesota Press.

Caldwell, K. L., and K. L. Andereck. 1994. "Motives for Initiating and Continuing Membership in a Recreation-related Voluntary Association." *Leisure Sciences* 16: 33–44.

Christensen, N. L., A. M. Bartuska, J. H. Brown, S. Carpenter, C. D'Antonio, R. Francis, J. F. Franklin, J. A. MacMahon, R. F. Noss, D. J. Parsons, C. H. Peterson, M. G. Turner, and R. G. Woodmansee. 1996. "The Report of the Ecological Society of America Committee on the Scientific Basis for Ecosystem Management." *Ecological Applications* 6(3): 665–691.

Cordell, H. K., ed. 1997. *Integrating Social Science and Ecosystem Management: A National Challenge.* USDA Forest Service General Technical Report SRS-17. Asheville, NC: Southern Research Station.

Gobster, P. H. 1997. "The Chicago Wilderness and Its Critics, III. The Other Side: A Survey of the Arguments." *Restoration & Management Notes* 15(1): 32–37.

James, W. 1984. "The Moral Equivalent of War." In *William James: The Essential Writings,* edited by B. W. Wilshire, 349–361. Albany: State University of New York Press.

Manzo, L. C., and N. D. Weinstein. 1987. "Behavioral Commitment to Environmental Protection: A Study of Active and Nonactive Members of the Sierra Club." *Environment and Behavior* 19: 673–694.

Ross, L. 1994. "Illinois Volunteer Corps: A Model Program with Deep Roots in the Prairie." *Restoration & Management Notes* 12(1): 57–59.

Schroeder, H. W. 1991. "Preference and Meaning of Arboretum Landscapes: Combining Quantitative and Qualitative Data." *Journal of Environmental Psychology* 11: 231–248.

Schroeder, H. W. 1996. *Voices from the Black River: Obtaining Information on "Special Places" for Natural Resource Planning.* USDA Forest Service General Technical Report NC-184. St. Paul: North Central Forest Experiment Station.

Chapter 13

PSYCHOLOGICAL BENEFITS OF VOLUNTEERING IN STEWARDSHIP PROGRAMS

Robert E. Grese, Rachel Kaplan,
Robert L. Ryan, and Jane Buxton

"Volunteers are a priceless resource without which your organization would cease to exist." So reads a tip sheet called *The Care and Feeding of Volunteers,* provided by the Citizen Forestry Support System (undated). The tip sheet suggests that the success of tree programs needs to be measured not in the funding available to hire staff to maintain the trees, but in the ability to "attract and involve hundreds of volunteers." Volunteers are essential to ecological restoration efforts. They help with monitoring, clearing invasive plants, collecting seeds, planting, and many other activities that are directly involved with land stewardship. In addition, numerous volunteers perform services that are less directly tied to the land, including disseminating information (via newsletters, for example) and maintaining databases.

With the efforts of volunteers so important to the ecological restoration mission, it is appropriate to ask why so many people contribute their precious time to such work. One could easily imagine the countless reasons why people would choose not to spend their time in such activities. Complaints about lack of discretionary time are endemic, and the choices for ways to spend such time are not in short supply. Why, then, do some people volunteer to do stewardship activities? What benefits do they derive from such efforts? These questions are the focus of the research described here. While some benefits are likely to be common to volunteering in general, other benefits presumably reflect the particular choice of activities, namely environmental stewardship.

Handbooks and guidelines produced for recruiting and managing volunteer efforts suggest that the reasons for volunteering are as diverse as the people who participate and the types of work they do (e.g., Ellis 1994, Gaskell 1991, National Park Service 1988, Ross 1994). From this literature, we learn that volunteers have a strong desire to make direct, tangible, positive impacts on the environment. They also seem to value the social component of volunteering (being part of a team, developing new friendships). Furthermore, volunteers value the opportunities to learn about the environment and explore career options.

Newsletters that stewardship programs produce for their members provide many indications of volunteers' motives for participation. "Having fun" and "seeing the changes" are benefits that are mentioned quite often (e.g., Gingrich 1994, McCarthy 1991). Drinkin (1996) reflects on "What Kept Me Going" in *The Volunteer Monitor* (a national newsletter of volunteer water quality monitoring). Among other motivations for persisting in her leadership role, she mentions several social factors—the sense of being part of a larger community of volunteers, the friendship, and the attention. Using material offered by newsletters of volunteer groups in the Chicago area, Schroeder (this volume) provides an in-depth analysis of the personal and social values that ecological restorationists bring to their work.

Schroeder's work is one of the few studies that have specifically addressed environmental restoration activities. Fisk (1995), also studying the psychological effects of involvement in ecological restoration, found that "developing a relationship with nature" was the common theme in her interviews. This benefit involved a whole host of themes including "communal work in and for nature," an "expanded sense of identity as both a part of nature and a protector/nurturer of nature," and "reciprocal connection to other life." Both Westphal (1993, 1995) and Still and Gerhold (1997), in their studies of urban forestry volunteers, found that volunteers have strong inclinations to help the environment, especially in their own neighborhoods.

Our approach to studying motivations for and benefits derived from volunteer stewardship efforts was to gather data directly from those involved in such activities. The main objective of these surveys was to identify major types of benefits that volunteers derive from their stewardship activities. We expected to find several discrete themes, including social dimensions (e.g., meeting new people), educational interests (e.g., learning about plants), feelings about the land (e.g., feeling connected), sense of purpose (e.g., making a difference), and spiritual dimensions (e.g., peacefulness, aesthetic pleasure). In addition, we wanted to explore whether volunteering and recreation activities fulfill similar patterns of needs, because both claim people's precious discretionary hours.

Methods

We used a variety of strategies to gain information about volunteerism in restoration activities. We started with four interviews of Chicago-area participants in the Volunteer Stewardship Network. To help us understand how ecological stewardship programs organized their volunteer efforts, we also interviewed the leaders of several volunteer programs in Michigan. These interviews helped us develop a survey instrument that was distributed to volunteers of different organizations. The rest of the chapter focuses on these surveys.

Survey Samples and Participant Background

Study participants included volunteers in a variety of ecological stewardship programs. Several approaches were used to ask volunteers to participate in the study. In some instances, a member of the research team attended a workday conducted by an organization and, with prior consent from the leadership, asked those who attended whether they would be willing to complete a survey and return it in the stamped envelope provided. In other instances, the organization's staff person who met with the volunteers asked those present to help out with the project. In still other instances, surveys were mailed to individuals who were on record as being volunteers for a particular organization. Given the variety of techniques used to access volunteers, we can neither assess the return rate for the surveys nor claim to have a random sample. We can say that the sample is drawn from diverse projects in a number of localities, representing individuals with differing amounts of experience.

The data reported here are based on 190 individuals, drawn from five distinct groups: a Michigan-wide chapter of a conservation organization ($n = 71$); a stream monitoring program in Michigan ($n = 45$); the Natural Areas Preservation Program within a Michigan municipal parks department ($n = 26$); a Toledo, Ohio, Metropark volunteer organization ($n = 22$); and a group of bank employees who also worked at the Toledo, Ohio, Metropark ($n = 26$). This last group might differ from the other groups in that the participants were not necessarily volunteers on repeated occasions, but rather employees of a bank that closed for a day to permit its workers to participate in local volunteer efforts.

The volunteers from these different groups worked on several types of projects and in slightly different modes. Those working in stream monitoring were involved primarily in assessment activities, evaluating stream conditions, taking water quality samples to determine stream health, and recording aquatic invertebrates and other stream biota. The program also had a cleanup component involving clearing logjams and trash out of the streams. Individuals in this group went through substantial training and worked primarily on their own. Some of the volunteers working with the Natural Areas Preservation Program also went through training for doing surveys of flora, frogs and toads, butter-flies, or birds and then worked on their own or in small groups. Many of the other activities with the Natural Areas Preservation Program, the Toledo groups, and the statewide conservation organization consisted of brush cut-ting, weed pulling, tree and shrub girdling, seed collecting, planting, and pre-scribed burning on organized workdays spent on prairie, fen, dune, and forest habitats. Training was generally limited to teaching volunteers how to identify plants to help in seed collection or exotic species control, although each work-day usually included a tour of the preserve site and discussion about its gen-eral ecology and the species and systems found there.

The sample included volunteers with a broad range of experiences that pertained to the volunteer stewardship efforts explored here. These experi-ences included professional involvement in work related to ecological restora-tion and a history of volunteering in such projects, as well as a history of serv-ing as volunteers in activities of various kinds. For each of these domains of experience, as well as knowledge pertinent to the restoration activities, the sample included the full spectrum—from those with minimal or no experi-ence to those whose volunteering activities were closely related to their jobs or had become a major part of their lives.

Survey Instruments

The survey consisted of three pages. On the first page, respondents were asked to rate each of twenty-nine items that assessed reasons for participating in vol-unteer projects. Using a five-point scale (1 = not at all to 5 = very much), they were asked to rate each item in terms of whether it described a benefit they derived from their involvement. The items were drawn from a variety of sources, including material in newsletters of volunteer organizations, responses from open-ended interviews with volunteers, and our own hypotheses about the benefits people derive from such activities. Items can be found in Table 13.1. The questions on the other pages of the survey differed for the Michi-gan and Ohio samples. For the three Michigan groups, there were questions related to knowledge and experience in areas related to the restoration activ-ities. For the two Toledo groups, the survey included questions to permit com-parison between a person's recreation and volunteer activities. All surveys included questions about the extent of the respondent's other volunteer activ-ities. Age, gender, and occupation were included as background questions. Throughout the survey there was room for providing additional comments.

The survey was produced in a self-contained format, already addressed and stamped on the fourth side so participants needed only to fold the material in half, seal it, and drop it in the mail. The surveys could be returned anony-

Table 13.1. Group Means and Factor Solution for Benefits from Volunteering

Factor Labels and Individual Scale Items	Conserv. Org.	Stream Monit.	Nat. Area Prog.	Toledo Volunt.	Toledo Bank Day
Helping the environment Causing good things to happen Feeling of doing something useful Protecting natural places from disappearing Making the world better for others Concerns about losing areas to development Feeling less helpless about what's happening to the world Spending time for a good purpose	4.09	4.08[a]	4.12[a]	3.98[a]	3.89
Exploration Learning new skills Learning new things Doing something that is fascinating Opportunity to try something new Learning specific plants/animals	3.56	3.96[a]	3.97[a,b]	3.71[a,b]	3.45[a,b]
Spirituality Contributing to my spirituality Feeling peace of mind Chance to reflect Chance to be outdoors Sense of oneness with the natural world Sense of community	3.25	3.31[b]	3.67[b]	3.46[b]	3.35[a,c]
Personal and social Feeling good about myself Doing something tangible, where you can see you've done something Chance to have leadership role Having something to tell other people A better outlook on things in general Meeting new people Putting skills I have to use Working with people I already know	3.02	3.16[b]	3.15	3.12	3.52[b,c]

Notes: The means represent the average within each volunteer organization of all the items in a factor. Items were rated on a five-point scale (1 = not at all a benefit, 5 = very much a benefit). Means with the same superscripts within a column (i.e., volunteer organization) are not significantly different from one another at $p < 0.05$. The items are ordered within each factor from highest to lowest factor loading.

mously. However, in response to the final question about their willingness to participate in future parts of the study, virtually all participants indicated their names, addresses, and phone numbers.

Results and Discussion

Rather than rely on our a priori themes that led us to generate the twenty-nine items, we used a statistical procedure known as factor analysis to determine how our study participants viewed the items. The factor analysis (principal axis factor analysis with varimax rotation) was based on the responses from the initial 142 volunteers (i.e., not including the Toledo samples). The analysis yielded four distinct factors (i.e., categories). The Cronbach alpha coefficients (assessing the internal consistency of the items constituting a factor) ranged between .82 and .86, suggesting that the categories are relatively reliable.

Table 13.1 shows the four factors, with the items in each factor listed from highest to lowest factor loading. Three items did not meet the criteria for inclusion in factors: two because their highest loading was less than .45, and one item ("sense of accomplishment") because its loadings were greater than .45 on each of two factors. All factors have eigenvalues greater than 1.0.

Benefits of Volunteering

Helping the environment. The items included in this factor reflect benefits that are especially relevant to ecological restoration activities, as opposed to other kinds of volunteer efforts. This factor showed the highest rating across the five volunteer groups (mean = 4.09 on a five-point scale). One of the items in this factor, "protecting natural places from disappearing," received the highest rating (4.50) of any of the twenty-nine items on the questionnaire. Many of the written comments participants added to their surveys also reflected their concern about protecting and preserving the environment. Thoughts about maintaining places for future generations were often expressed in personal terms:

> I recently became a grandmother, which has heightened my horror of the kind of world we're bequeathing to our children and grandchildren. I feel a need to stem the tide of environmental degradation.

Many other comments also expressed volunteers' desires to help make the world a better place. Here are some examples:

> I am very disturbed at the rapid rate of urban sprawl and the destruction of so many green spaces. It is time to start protecting and valuing these areas. I feel sad for the wildlife and plants we keep displacing.

> I feel good about personally being responsible for making changes. In today's society it seems that so many things are out of our hands/control.

Exploration. This factor received the next highest average rating (mean = 3.76). It reflects the satisfaction people get from learning new things. Volunteer activities differ in the learning opportunities they provide. For example, a volunteer working on stream monitoring added:

> I am a fisherman. I enjoy learning about habitat and foods fish eat and when, where, and why.

Other comments reflected a broader sense of exploration, such as connecting to family history in the area or becoming more connected to the natural world:

> I was curious what this land along the Raisin River south of Tecumseh was like as my father owned a farm along here from about 1927 to 1933 and I was born there.

> As I learn more about the richness and the diversity in nature, the more fascinated I am and the more I want to protect what is left.

Spirituality. The factor we labeled "spirituality" received a mean of 3.35. Items loading on this factor refer to a personal state of mind that restoration produces (e.g., peace, oneness, reflection). The item referring specifically to spirituality, as well as the one about "reflection," received somewhat unenthusiastic ratings (2.77 and 2.79, respectively). By contrast, the "chance to be outdoors," with a mean of 4.21, was one of the most highly rated items in the survey. Perhaps many of these volunteers are more interested in being active participants than reflective observers. Some comments on the surveys mentioned a love of the outdoors, but relatively few comments specifically described spirituality.

Personal and social. The final factor involves personal and social benefits. Several of the items refer specifically to social rewards, such as "meeting new people." Other items reflect feelings about oneself and the satisfaction gained from using one's skills. Our expectation had been that the personal and social benefits would be distinct rather than combined in a single factor. The mean for this factor (3.09) was slightly below the other three, right around the midpoint of the five-point scale. Open-ended comments written on the survey supported the social aspect of volunteering:

> . . . networking with natural resource people . . .

> Getting together with people whose environmental views are like mine; knowing others think that its important and fun to look at plants, insects, etc.

Other. The contribution of the volunteer stewardship activities to an individual's job or vocation emerged as a theme from respondents' handwritten comments but was not captured by any of the items in the survey. Several volunteers who are teachers mentioned how their volunteering might be useful in their teaching and how it allows them to use knowledge they acquired in college. In a few instances, volunteering inspired individuals to consider career changes. For example, one of the participants whose volunteer efforts were part of the bank's program wrote:

> Talking with a park ranger during my volunteer activity led me to ponder the possibility of . . . an environmental career.

Group Comparisons

The groups participating in our study were similar in the benefits they attributed to volunteering in restoration projects. The relative ranking of the four factors (see Table 13.1) was remarkably consistent. In all instances the mean rating for "helping the environment" was the highest (or statistically tied for highest). "Exploration" was in second place in the rankings, although for three of the five groups the average ratings for "exploration" and "spirituality" were not statistically different. For all but one group, the "personal and social" rating was the lowest of the four. The exception to this last finding was the group of bank employees whose volunteer efforts were part of their company's "make a difference" program. Their mean ratings for the "personal and social," "exploration," and "spirituality" categories were statistically equivalent.

Comparison of Volunteer Stewardship and Recreation

Volunteer activities and recreation have many features in common. Most importantly, they represent a choice in the use of discretionary time. To the extent that participants in ecological restoration programs consider their volunteering as recreational, it may help explain their willingness to commit a great deal of time and enthusiasm to such activities. The surveys completed by the two Toledo groups included fifteen items that explored this relationship. These participants were asked to rate the importance of each of these items when they considered their recreation activities and, again, when they considered their volunteering efforts. Analyses of their responses permit an initial exploration; a larger sample representing a greater variety of groups would be needed to understand the relationship between these activities more fully.

As would be expected, there are similarities between the benefits derived from recreational pursuits and those from volunteering pursuits. For example, "be outdoors" received top endorsement, and "a way to fill time" was rated lowest with respect to both contexts. There were also noteworthy differences in the way these participants viewed their volunteering and recreation activities. For example, "be useful, make a difference" was the highest-rated item with respect to volunteering, but rated far lower in the recreational context. The reverse was true for "family time" and "time to be by myself." Both of these items received below midscale ratings in terms of volunteering, but far higher endorsement in terms of their role in recreation.

Using the same procedures and criteria as we did with the benefits questions (i.e., principal axis factor analysis and varimax rotation) led to further insights about the contrasts between the two domains. The results of these analyses are three factors describing recreation activities (Table 13.2) and three for volunteer activities (Table 13.3). It is striking to see the same fifteen items grouped so differently in the two cases. While "time out" (a stewardship factor) and "restored" (recreation) share three items in common, the juxtaposition of the unique items gives each factor a different emphasis. The same is true for "impact" (volunteering) and "useful" (recreation). It is also pertinent that the

Table 13.2. Group Means and Factor Solution for Benefits from Recreation

Factor Labels and Individual Scale Items	Cronbach Alpha	Means	
		Park Volunteers	Bank Day
Useful	.77	3.94	3.71
Be useful, make a difference[a]			
Have a tangible outcome[a]			
Be outdoors			
Learn/try out new things			
Social	.77	3.43	3.88
Family time[b]			
Be helpful to others			
Time with friends[b]			
Do something with my hands			
Restored[c]	.79	3.15	3.65
Get away[b]			
Relax/get restored[b]			
A change from what I usually do			
Time to be by myself[b]			
A way to fill time			

[a]The mean for the item is significantly ($p < 0.05$) higher for the "stewardship" as opposed to the "recreation" domain.
[b]The mean for the item is significantly ($p < 0.05$) higher for the "recreation" as opposed to the "stewardship" domain.
[c]The difference between two groups is significant at $p < 0.05$.

Table 13.3. Group Means and Factor Solution for Benefits from
Stewardship and Other Volunteer Activities

Factor Labels and Individual Scale Items	Cronbach Alpha	Means Park Volunteers	Bank Day
Outdoors	.85	3.99	3.63
Be outdoors			
Do something with my hands			
Relax/get restored[a]			
Be physically active			
Impact	.83	3.91	4.00
Be useful, make a difference[b]			
Be helpful to others			
Have a tangible outcome[b]			
A change from what I usually do			
Learn/try out new things			
Time out[c]	.77	2.59	3.22
Family time[a]			
Health and fitness[a]			
Get away[a]			
Time to be by myself[a]			
A way to fill time			

[a]The mean for the item is significantly ($p < 0.05$) higher for the "recreation" as opposed to the "stewardship" domain.
[b]The mean for the item is significantly ($p < 0.05$) higher for the "stewardship" as opposed to the "recreation" domain.
[c]The difference between two groups is significant at $p < 0.05$.

social theme emerged as distinct in the recreational context but stayed merged with other benefits in the volunteering context.

Comparison between the two groups responding to these items provides some further insights that may be useful to explore in future research. One of these groups—the bank employees—may be more akin to the general public inasmuch as their participation was part of a work program and thus less reflective of their personal choice for use of discretionary time. For this group the three recreation themes were equivalent in their importance. The park volunteers, by contrast, indicated that it was more important that their recreation activities provide a chance to be useful than that they provide a social outlet or a chance to be restored. With respect to the volunteering themes, for the park volunteers, both being outdoors and having an impact were of great importance. Being outdoors was significantly less important to the bank employee group.

Implications

Faced with limited budgets, land stewardship organizations and agencies across the country are increasingly turning to volunteers as a way of carrying out the complex array of ecological restoration and monitoring activities involved in caring for urban and rural natural areas. For these organizations and agencies, attracting new volunteers and keeping their long-term volunteers satisfied is a continual challenge. Understanding the psychological benefits volunteers get from their stewardship activities will undoubtedly help these managers design their programs much more effectively. Results of this study suggest several important themes that managers ought to consider.

Helping the Environment

The volunteers surveyed in this study clearly indicated that "helping the environment" was one of their chief motivations for volunteering. Program organizers should not underestimate the power of this motivation. A common thread that appears in all of the items under this theme is the desire to make a tangible difference, to have a positive effect in protecting nature. Much of the available information on the global environmental crisis (e.g., habitat loss, global warming, rain forest destruction) can overwhelm people, making them feel helpless. At a local level, people see the loss of cherished wildlands in the face of urban sprawl and continually hear of the effects of pollution and fragmentation in degrading what habitat is left. Volunteer stewardship programs give people the opportunity to take tangible action to help their local environment. Such opportunities empower them with the notion that their actions do make a difference.

For some time, William Jordan and other proponents of ecological restoration have argued that restoration and similar activities can be seen as a "way of achieving and acting out a healthy, constructive and mutually beneficial relationship between ourselves and the rest of nature" (Jordan 1989, see also this volume). He suggests that restoration provides a way for people to deal with the frequent, negative environmental messages by taking positive action to repair and heal past ecological damages while building a positive relationship with a place. Results of this study support Jordan's contention that helping the environment can be a prime motivating factor for many volunteers.

What does this mean for the design of stewardship programs or specific workdays? Clearly volunteers need to be reminded and shown that their efforts are making a difference. It may be essential, for example, for volunteers to understand the larger goals and desired results of a restoration program and how a particular work effort fits into that program. While providing this bigger picture may sometimes be regarded as taking precious time away from more "constructive" work efforts, it may be time well spent for motivating and keeping volunteers interested in the program. Many organizers of volunteer workday efforts have incorporated tours of areas restored in previous seasons as a way of helping volunteers see the progress of their efforts. Similarly, volunteers can be involved in monitoring the changes that result from their activities. Photographs of areas before and after restoration treatments could be effective tools in recruiting new volunteers to the program, demonstrating to them that their activities will help in making positive changes.

Exploration

Another important benefit of volunteering is the opportunity to explore and learn new things. Here again, it is essential that volunteer programs provide opportunities for personal growth and learning in addition to the traditional task-oriented activities. While the temptation may often be to streamline volunteer efforts to get as much work done as possible, if this is done at the cost of providing opportunities for discovery, the result may be decreased interest and participation on the part of volunteers as well as a reduction in their satisfaction with the entire program. Efforts that integrate opportunities for learning can be relatively simple. For example, among the volunteers surveyed in this study, many received specific training for monitoring particular habitats or species. Such training in plant or animal identification is integral both for preparing volunteers for the tasks they will be asked to do and for helping them gain skills they might use in other ways. As indicated by our study findings, some volunteers view their work activities as a way of exploring new careers and gaining useful work experience.

Some larger volunteer programs have gone so far as to develop networked programs of courses and other learning opportunities that provide some level of certification of training. A good example of this is the Volunteer Stewardship Network in the Chicago area and their Prairie University listing of courses and other training opportunities available in the region. Some of the activities associated with stewardship efforts may also provide rather novel experiences for the volunteer that are not available in other contexts. For example, numerous land stewardship efforts in the Midwest involve some measure of prescribed burning. For many volunteers, learning about prescribed fires and participating in burns can provide an extremely memorable and stimulating experience.

Volunteer programs can also provide for exploration by varying activities and allowing volunteers to work on different sites. For some volunteers, their activities provide important opportunities for getting to know unique local habitats. When work is restricted to the same site over and over, such opportunities can be diminished. When working on different sites or different portions of the same site, learning can be enhanced by encouraging volunteers to observe similarities and differences and discussing the ecological factors that might be responsible for these variations from one site to the next. Similarly, many of the techniques used in ecological restoration are necessarily experimental, and learning can be enhanced by involving volunteers in testing and evaluating different approaches and techniques. Volunteers can often provide useful feedback on the adaptive use of tools, on more efficient ways of getting a job done, or on the long-term effectiveness of various management strategies. Such opportunities allow program-level learning as well as learning by the individuals involved, and they help volunteers feel they are contributing something useful.

Reflection and Restoration

The benefits associated with the factor we labeled "spirituality" were rated positively, but slightly below the previous two. Several issues may account for this result, some of which may be methodological. For example, our questions may not have adequately dealt with the issue or people might consider spirituality to be a private issue. Spiritual rewards may also be felt as a side effect of other concepts included in the survey, such as being outdoors, helping the environment, and personal growth, rather than as a primary motivation for getting involved in ecological restoration. Other explanations for the lower rating may relate to the choice of activities and time factors; people consciously seeking a spiritual goal would probably choose a more direct path to spiritual fulfillment. It is also possible that the spiritual aspects of ecological stewardship develop over longer periods of involvement than those reflected by the groups included in this survey.

Personal restoration and reflection have been shown to be important benefits of natural environment experiences (Kaplan and Kaplan 1989). Many environmental stewardship programs are structured around group activities, such as brush clearing or seed collection, that provide little opportunity for clearing one's head and experiencing a cognitive quiet that helps one reflect on life's priorities. For program organizers, this may suggest structuring volunteer restoration activities so that they can also be conducted by individuals at their own pace, allowing time for the solitude that may be necessary to achieve these benefits. Activities such as collecting seed, counting plants, or monitoring streams may be amenable to this type of flexible structure and may well be more comparable to other recreational pursuits.

Personal and Social Benefits

Personal and social benefits were not as strongly valued by participants in our study, but have been found to be important benefits of volunteer activities in other contexts. People value the chance to meet others who share similar interests; they also value the opportunity to develop and extend their social networks. Thus, one challenge for program organizers seeking to expand their volunteer ranks and attract newcomers might be to modify existing programs to increase opportunities for social interaction. For example, many corporations these days use community service projects as team-building exercises to strengthen cooperative skills. Customized outings aimed at first-time corporate groups may pay off in terms of adding people-power during times of extra need and may encourage some individuals to continue on as restoration volunteers. The singles scene is another promising market to which the social benefits angle might be emphasized. A Chicago-area organization, Conscience Connections, is drawing on the recreation-stewardship connection in advertising restoration outings, among other community service activities, "as a fun and uplifting way for single people to meet. . . ." Touting noncontroversial restoration activities like seed collecting, their advertisements explicitly promote social interaction and the other benefits that restoration volunteerism creates: "Every conscience connection offers a unique and fulfilling experience with a purpose that goes beyond finding a mate" (Conscience Connections 1999). Other stewardship activities, such as propagating native plants, might provide for social occasions for family and other multigenerational groups.

Volunteering and Recreation

The exploratory comparisons between recreation and volunteer activities by the two Toledo groups suggest that recreation seems to have stronger restoration and social components. Some leisure science researchers have suggested that volunteering be considered a recreational activity because it is a conscious use of one's discretionary time (Tedrick and Henderson 1989). Henderson (1984) found much agreement among 4-H volunteers in the way they viewed recreation and volunteering. For restorationists, learning more about the overlap between recreation and volunteering may help enlarge the sphere of people who may be interested in these activities. For example, although social reasons were not very important to those who were already volunteering in restoration activities, they appeared to be important to those who didn't regularly do so, as represented by the bank employee sample. If volunteer stewardship activities are perceived as legitimate recreation opportunities as well as a way of getting essential work done in urban and rural natural areas, they may well gain greater attention when park and other land management agencies are making budgeting and programming decisions. Clearly these relationships deserve more study.

Conclusion

This study is an initial investigation into the types of benefits volunteers derive from participating in ecological stewardship projects. Our results strongly suggest that programs should seriously consider how volunteer work is described and how these efforts are organized to provide volunteers with the kinds of benefits they say are important. Volunteers seem highly motivated by a desire to help the environment and to learn new things in the course of their volunteer activities. They also may benefit from opportunities to reflect and seek spiritual fulfillment as well as develop friendships and social networks. Programs that pay attention to these considerations may fare better in attracting and retaining volunteers, issues that are critical to the long-term success of any ecological restoration effort.

Acknowledgments

The work reported here was partially funded by the USDA Forest Service, North Central Research Station, under Urban Forestry Unit Cooperative Agreement #23-94-53. We also wish to acknowledge David Borneman, Gwen Christensen, Elizabeth Dell, Michelle Grigore, Joan Martin, Catriona Mortell, Diane O'Hara, Bill Schneider, and all the volunteers from the conservation organizations and agencies in southeast Michigan and northwest Ohio who participated in the study. Paul Gobster's and Bruce Hull's efforts as editors are also greatly appreciated.

References

Citizen Forestry Support System. Undated. *The Care and Feeding of Volunteers: Tip Sheet.* Washington, DC: Citizen Forestry Support System.

Conscience Connections. 1999. *Conscience Connections, Inc. Chicagoland: "A Feel Good Singles Experience."* Online material available at www.conscienceconnections.com.

Drinkin, J. 1996. "What Kept Me Going: One Volunteer's Story." *The Volunteer Monitor: The National Newsletter of Volunteer Water Quality Monitoring* 8(1) Spring: 13.

Ellis, S. J. 1994. *The Volunteer Recruitment Book.* Philadelphia: Energize, Inc.

Fisk, S. J. 1995. "Psychological Effects of Involvement in Ecological Restoration." *Dissertation Abstracts International* 56-06B: 3475.

Gaskell, J. 1991. "Why Volunteer? The Answers Are as Unique as the People We Talked To." *Newsleaf: Friends of the Arboretum Newsletter* (University of Wisconsin–Madison Arboretum) 8(4): April: 2–3.

Gingrich, L. 1994. "Palos Profile: Karen Stasky Does a Little Bit of Everything." *Palos and Sag Valley Acorn: Newsletter of the Palos Restoration Project Volunteers* Spring: 3.

Henderson, K. 1984. "Volunteerism as Leisure." *Journal of Voluntary Action Research* 13(1): 55–63.

Jordan, W. R. III. 1989. "Restoring the Restorationist." *Restoration & Management Notes* 7(2): 55.

Kaplan, R., and S. Kaplan. 1989. *The Experience of Nature.* New York: Cambridge University Press (republished by Ulrich's, Ann Arbor, MI).

McCarthy, W. 1991. "Cap Sauer's Holding." *Palos and Sag Valley Acorn: Newsletter of the Palos and Sag Valley Forest Preserves* Spring: 4.

National Park Service 1988. *Volunteers in Parks Guidelines.* NPS-7, Release No. 3, Washington, DC: U.S. Department of the Interior, National Park Service.

Ross, L. M. 1994. "Illinois' Volunteer Corps: A Model Program with Deep Roots in the Prairie." *Restoration & Management Notes* 12(1): 57–59.

Still, D. T., and H. D. Gerhold. 1997. "Motivations and Task Preferences of Urban Forestry Volunteers." *Journal of Arboriculture* 23(3): 116–130.

Tedrick, T., and K. Henderson. 1989. *Volunteers in Leisure: A Management Perspective.* Reston, VA: American Association for Leisure Research.

Westphal, L. M. 1993. "Why Trees? Urban Forestry Volunteers Values and Motivations." In *Managing Urban and High Use Recreation Settings.* USDA Forest Service General Technical Report NC-163, edited by P. H. Gobster, 19–23. St. Paul: North Central Forest Experiment Station.

Westphal, L. M. 1995. "Birds Do It, Bees Do It, But Why Do Volunteers Do It? A Look at Motivations." In *Proceedings of the Midwest Oak Savanna Conference,* edited by F. Stearns and K. Holland, 1–6. Available online at www.epa.gov/glnpo/oak/westpha.html.

❧ *Chapter 14* ❧

LESSONS FOR RESTORATION IN TRADITIONS OF STEWARDSHIP: SUSTAINABLE LAND MANAGEMENT IN NORTHERN NEW MEXICO

Carol Raish

Distinct notions of ecosystem restoration, conservation, and preservation are often defined in terms of a dominant, Western worldview built upon the conservation and environmental movements of the twentieth century. These notions may have little meaning among many indigenous or traditional peoples (Stedman-Edwards 1998, 74), such as American Indian groups or the traditional Hispanic farmers of northern New Mexico, who comprise the foci of discussion in this chapter. However, the worldviews, bodies of traditional knowledge, and resource management practices of these groups can offer important lessons for efforts to restore, conserve, and preserve nature.

Although it is hazardous to uncritically accept generalizations about any group, culture, or society, some scholars have noted that the ways in which many indigenous and traditional cultures view and interact with nature differ fundamentally from those of Western society, and may have important lessons for contemporary resource management. For example, Callicott (1982) argues that American Indian attitudes toward nature are not explicitly ecological or conservative in the modern scientific sense so much as they are moral and ethical—considering animals, plants, and minerals as equal with humans in the natural social order. Such a view, according to Callicott, can result in a land ethic that establishes a nonexploitative relationship between human groups and their nonhuman environment (Callicott 1982, 310–311).

In a somewhat different vein, the Hispanic, small-scale subsistence farmers and ranchers of northern New Mexico before U.S. conquest tended to view the land as a gift from God to be used to support their families and future generations. Small populations and isolated conditions seriously limited commercial development in the area, leading to an ethic that valued continuity, community, and land above monetary gain. These groups did not consider land as a commodity to be used for commercial profit, but as a source of subsistence opportunities and as a home (Rothman 1989, 198–200). Their culture generally was and is intimately tied to the land and to traditional land use practices (García 1996, Peña and Gallegos 1993).

Traditional land and resource use practices, conditioned by worldviews such as these and operating in groups with generally low levels of population and technology, tend not to have the environmental impact of high-population, high-technology, commercial systems (Rothman 1989, 210–211; Stedman-Edwards 1998, 35, 74). Thus, conserving and restoring landscapes and maintaining traditional, noncommercial economic and resource use systems can be highly compatible goals. A variety of factors including worldview, values, traditional knowledge, and population size combine to produce ranching, farming, and resource extraction methods that, in concept as well as practice, fit well with ideas of conservation, restoration, and stewardship. In these respects, traditional practices and practitioners can have much to offer land managers in terms of environmental stewardship practices and long-held bodies of environmental knowledge (Capp and Jorgensen 1997). To echo Hull and Robertson's call for a more public ecology (in this volume), these groups have an important role to play in developing a body of managerially relevant environmental knowledge.

The following discussion focuses on the role and importance of traditional environmental knowledge and management practices in producing sustainable land use systems. It examines the relationship between worldview, values, and traditional knowledge on the one hand, and ranching, farming, and resource extraction techniques among traditional and indigenous groups on the other. It argues that traditional practices, although often ignored, make a substantial contribution to the desired conditions of sustainable ecosystems.

The examples discussed in the following sections demonstrate that sustainable ecosystems can include active human use and management, and have done so for thousands of years. Humans have been a part of the ecosystem for several million years and have produced major landscape impacts and changes since plant and animal domestication 10,000 years ago (Barker and Gamble 1985, Cohen 1977). Human impacts and use cannot now be excluded from vast tracts of land, even if exclusion were desirable. An understanding of traditional knowledge and practices can assist contemporary land managers in designing environmentally sound stewardship programs that take into account human sociocultural values and needs as well as resource sustainability.

The Role and Importance of Traditional Knowledge and Practices

Traditional knowledge is based on observations, interactions, and systematic feedback from the natural world (Capp and Jorgensen 1997). It includes a framework of classification, a set of empirical observations about the local environment, and a manner of living in balance and harmony with all things (Thakali and Lesko 1998). It is usually expressed in spiritual and cultural terms, with rules that provide an ethical system for human behavior to sustain ecosystems for the generations that will follow (Capp and Jorgensen 1997). Many traditional peoples have developed socially embedded systems of taboos and prescriptions related to appropriate resource use that are often reinforced by religious beliefs (Gadgil et al. 1993, Stedman-Edwards 1998). Thus, the body of traditional knowledge forms the backbone of, and is in turn conditioned by, worldview and value systems. Among these groups, systems of land use and resource protection are so intimately linked to cultural institutions that conservation of valued environmental qualities (i.e., biodiversity) actually depends upon preserving and sustaining the traditional patterns of land and resource use.

Traditional knowledge is oriented differently from Western science in many ways. To mention only a few examples, it is transmitted orally and experientially through hands-on learning, as opposed to being written and taught in an abstract context, and it is holistic, nonlinear, and nonreductionist (Capp and Jorgensen 1997). It is nonetheless equally valuable in helping to manage and conserve natural resources. To quote from Capp and Jorgensen (1997), "Like Western Science, Traditional Knowledge provides an additional body of knowledge and another way to instill conservation ethics into others. It teaches conservation and ecosystem management. As Traditional Knowledge keepers continue to point out, you pay particular attention to things when those things keep you alive" (199).

A growing number of examples highlight the importance of traditional knowledge and management practices in contributing to contemporary land and resource management goals. These include several cases of Native Alaskan information on bird, fish, and sea mammal populations, discussed by Capp and Jorgensen (1997), that preceded and were later corroborated by Western scientific studies. In many of these instances, the traditional practitioners already possessed the knowledge sought by the scientific studies; however, their information was not heeded.

Another example of traditional folk wisdom that went unheeded for many years concerns the value of intentional light burning (discussed in de Buys et al. 1999). Many indigenous peoples in the American West allowed wildfires to burn and ignited fires to clear the forest understory of fuels and undesirable growth (Scurlock 1998, 268–269). This practice promoted a preferred forest condition by limiting competition and preventing severe, stand-changing wildfires, which are often dependent on heavy fuel loads. Intentional burning was strongly discouraged by the USDA Forest Service in the earlier part of the century as the agency attempted to eliminate wildfires in the nation's forests. Fire suppression in forested ecosystems has since been identified as contributing to catastrophic, highly destructive wildfires. Contemporary agency policy now allows certain wildfires to burn under close monitoring and favors intentional, or prescribed, burning of other areas under supervision to improve forest health (de Buys et al. 1999).

International evidence also points to the value of traditional bodies of environmental wisdom. According to a World Wildlife Fund study (Stedman-Edwards 1998, 31–38), a root cause of biodiversity loss and a major source of land loss and degradation is the breakdown of traditional resource management practices in response to growing populations, increasing production pressures on resources, and commercial agricultural enterprises displacing peasant subsistence farmers. Loss also occurs as commercial logging companies displace traditional communities of forest users, and when common property resources, such as grazing lands, are privatized or otherwise diverted from their original uses and sources of regulation. In these cases, local political arrangements that ensured equitable resource distribution and costs of conservation are replaced by uncontrolled and inequitable resource appropriation and use. Resource control is removed from the local people who are most concerned and knowledgeable about maintaining resource productivity and health (Stedman-Edwards 1998, 55, 58).

As an example, loss of common grazing lands and access to water supplies in western Rajasthan, India, came about as the result of a government development program involving land reform and privatization of common lands. Results included a breakdown in institutionalized controls for maintaining and regulating the use of the commons. Much of the land was unsuited for crop production but was put under cultivation anyway in response to declining controls and market expansion. Without the traditional mechanisms of regulation, the shrinking commons were overgrazed and poorly maintained. Soil erosion, declining fertility, and declining water supplies resulted from inappropriate and unregulated use of the area once longtime management practices and institutions were removed (Stedman-Edwards 1998, 76). These instances point to the importance of careful consideration when development or restoration projects are designed that alter traditional management practices and uses. They highlight the need for consultation and collaboration among scientists, managers, and traditional practitioners.

Fortunately, recent examples of successful collaborative projects, albeit on a relatively small scale, demonstrate a growing trend toward valuing the body of knowledge possessed by indigenous and traditional peoples. For example, a major collaborative relationship is ongoing between the Hopi Indian tribe and federal agencies in northern Arizona to develop a tribal cultural preservation office and cultural resource advisory task team. These groups are charged with identifying places important in maintaining tribal cultural identity. The team evaluates potential impacts to these sacred places and recommends ways in which land management projects on federal, state, and private lands might be carried out without damaging them. They also suggest projects, such as prescribed burning, to benefit wildlife and plant species important to the tribe (Thakali and Lesko 1998). Other examples include the work of staff at several California national forests with the Karuk and Washoe Indian tribes to incorporate indigenous knowledge on the best means of improving the growth and productivity of basketry materials like bracken fern, hazel, and beargrass. These methods also include prescribed burning and timber harvest (Thakali and Lesko 1998).

De Buys et al. (1999) argue that the opportunity currently exists to join federal and native resource management paradigms in ways that benefit the landscape. As they state, "Local occupants, whose sense of right and wrong about the habitat is linked to places and landscapes valued as homelands . . . can assist relative newcomers in adapting to the area. This requires respecting the validity of local knowledge, local needs, and attachment to the landscape."

Northern New Mexico Case Studies

Four specific cases from northern New Mexico demonstrate in greater detail the interplay of worldview, traditional knowledge, and traditional resource use practices among Indian and Hispanic farmers and ranchers. These examples also show the value of traditional knowledge and practices in sustaining and conserving natural resources for future generations. After a brief historical review, the case examples are presented to illustrate the ways in which traditional cultures are addressing issues relevant to restoration and management of natural areas.

Historical Background of Land and Resource Use

When the Spanish colonized what is now New Mexico in 1598, they found groups of relatively settled farmers located along the Rio Grande and its tributaries. These linguistically diverse groups shared the same farming, hunting, and gathering subsistence base and were referred to as Pueblos by the Spanish. New patterns of resource use developed as the Spanish settled in to farm among the Pueblos, introducing Old World technologies and many previously unknown domesticated plants and animals. Thus, the intensive irrigation agriculture and livestock herding of the Spanish replaced extensive farming complemented by hunting and gathering (Scurlock 1998, 82–100; Wozniak 1995). Although Pueblos and Hispanic settlers quarreled frequently over land, native population declines left sufficient land for both groups to engage in a subsistence, agro-pastoral economy based in small, scattered villages along the Rio Grande and its tributaries. Raids from nomadic Indian groups limited range expansion and the distance villagers traveled from their homes to engage in commerce and trade (Clark 1987, 19–23; Van Ness 1987). Their basic goal was to produce for local subsistence, not for competition in a commercial market. From the 1500s to the late 1800s, Hispanic and Puebloan lifestyles in much of the area changed very little. Both groups combined animal and plant production in a mixed farming system, with average households owning from fifty to a hundred head of all types of livestock (Van Ness 1987, 188–191). The irrigated agricultural plots were often very small, averaging from five to ten acres. However, since groups of kinsmen tilled their fields cooperatively and herded their animals together on large tracts of communally owned land, they were able to survive on these small farm plots (Van Ness 1987, 172).

Traditional grazing practices offered little rest for the land, but the generally small herd sizes and a comparatively large land base lessened the environmental impact (Rothman 1989, 197). Although there were areas of damage and resource depletion in locations close to long-term settlements in the central Rio Grande valley (Scurlock 1998, 331), pasture and forestland were generally in good condition in other portions of the valley. Throughout much of the area, low human populations, small herd sizes, and noncommercial operations minimized environmental damage.

Case Study 1: Commercial Versus Subsistence Land Use

During the Spanish Colonial and Mexican periods, land use and ownership were confirmed by grants from the Spanish Crown or the Mexican government (Van Ness 1987, 172). Significant changes in land ownership and use occurred when New Mexico became a United States territory in 1848 and eventually a state in 1912. Differences in American and Spanish land laws and unscrupulous land speculation resulted in the alienation of more than 80 percent of the Spanish and Mexican land grants from their original owners (Westphall 1965, 49). Often the villagers retained their house and farm plots but lost the community pasture and woodlands essential to the survival of mixed farmers. At the same time, the region moved from a subsistence farming economy to a commercial economy, which also negatively impacted many of the small-scale farming and ranching operations (Eastman et al. 1971, 4–5; Harper et al. 1943, 17–21).

The population of the territory grew tremendously during this period, fueled by in-migration from the United States. Many of these immigrants brought substantial capital for investment in large-scale, profit-oriented operations (Scurlock 1998, 121–136, 331, 387). Many viewed the value of land in different terms than the American Indian and Hispanic residents—seeing not subsistence opportunities but commercial ones, and regarding the land not as a place to make a home but as a commodity to be exploited for maximum profit (García 1996, Rothman 1989, 198–200).

An example from the Pajarito Plateau west of Santa Fe illustrates the environmental and social consequences of commercial development that ignores long-standing traditional use practices. Throughout the 1800s, local Hispanic and Pueblo residents of the surrounding valleys used the plateau as common property. They brought their small herds to the plateau for summer grazing, used the abundant timber resources for personal needs and small-scale ventures, and planted occasional summer crops. The small size and noncommercial orientation of these operations ensured that sufficient grass and forest resources were available for all who needed them (Rothman 1989, 192–194).

In 1885, a Texas cattle operation leased a large amount of land on the plateau and grazed over 3,000 head of cattle in an area that modern calculations estimate could carry around 300. This large operation affected the communal nature of range use on the plateau, driving off the small-scale Hispanic and Puebloan operations that had used the area for many years. The land could not provide for both commercial and subsistence economies simultaneously. The severe winter of 1886–1887 destroyed the large Texas enterprise, and eventually the small, local operators returned with their herds. However, the serious overstocking caused long-lasting damage to the fragile resources of the plateau (Rothman 1989, 200–204).

This damage was compounded by commercial timber operations that followed the failed cattle business. Clearcutting replaced small-scale timber and personal-use fuel wood harvest. Together, the commercial cattle and timber enterprises caused serious damage to the native grasses and removed much of the old-growth timber. Destruction of the grass cover and the spread of low-quality forage affected the subsistence of the people in the surrounding valleys. They were forced to pasture their animals farther away and compete among themselves for increasingly poor range (Rothman 1989, 203–204).

To deal with such problems of land degradation and resource overexploitation throughout the West, forest reserves were established in the late 1800s and early 1900s. In the northern and central portions of New Mexico these reserves later became the Carson, Santa Fe, and Cibola National Forests, including portions of various former land grants that were originally used by Hispanic and Puebloan villages as community range and forest land (de Buys 1985, 235–277; Eastman et al. 1971, 6–7).

The Forest Service attempted to protect the rangelands, but the agency policy of fire suppression limited the natural process of regeneration that depended on fire as a catalyst (Rothman 1989, 209). In the past, American Indians and Hispanic settlers had used fire as a management tool to create grazing areas, stimulate new grass growth, and suppress invading woody species (Scurlock 1998, 269). As a consequence of fire suppression, the damaged grasslands remained unproductive, leading to restrictions in the numbers of livestock that were allowed to graze on public land. Ultimately, limitations on herd sizes and access to rangeland forced many Hispanic and Puebloan ranchers off the land and into the cash-based economy of wage work (Rodríguez 1987, 381). Others maintained the ranching and farming tradition but were obliged to supplement their incomes with part-time wage work, significantly altering their traditional lifestyles.

Case Study 2: Contemporary Worldview and Traditional Knowledge

The worldview and values of the farmers and ranchers who remain in the small communities of northern New Mexico are still strongly linked to valuing and caring for the land as a home for the present generation and future generations to come. The farmers and ranchers view themselves as environmentalists and stewards of both their private land and leased federal land. Their attachment to land and place has been well described and documented (Kluckhohn and Strodtbeck 1961, Knowlton 1967, Liefer 1970). In a 1995 study, McSweeney (1995) interviewed northern New Mexico ranchers concerning their values and attitudes toward traditional land uses and wilderness. They stressed the importance of land and traditional land use practices in maintaining family and community. They saw their connections to the land as links to their ancestral heritage, stressing that the traditional life way "must be passed along and lived or it [the traditional life way] will die" (101).

In comparison to ranchers in other regions of New Mexico, Hess (1990) found that "ranchers in the northern part of the state envision prosperity and security of future generations in altogether different terms. Their future lies not in the mixture of individual labor with the land, but in integration of community with the surrounding landscape." He continued, "In northern New Mexico, community is the glue which binds individuals and families into a coherent social whole" (24).

In Hess's view, culture and tradition are more important than individual ambition. Ranching is a part of that tradition and is performed more for continuity with the past than for profit (Hess 1990, 24). In *Enchantment and Exploitation,* de Buys observed, "Few small-scale ranchers in northern New Mexico consider money to be the primary reward of ranching. What they gain is the pleasure of outdoor work and contact with nature and the opportunity to keep alive an ancient tradition of ranching on ancestral grounds" (1985, 272).

Although many of the northern New Mexico ranchers have university degrees, much of their knowledge about ranching is practical and traditional, deriving from both personal experience and the teachings of older generations (McSweeney 1995). In McSweeney's interviews (1995), many of the ranchers stressed that they tried to make decisions with consideration for the welfare of both the land and the animals, using knowledge learned from their elders. One rancher described how he was taught to maintain cows adapted to the local area, or *querencia* cows, because they would be familiar with the land. Another rancher explained that *querencia* cows are accustomed to the area and know where to find food and shelter and how to avoid toxic forage. This rancher said he applies this idea to his own life and work. "He has learned the characteristics of the area, the habits of the animals, the patterns of storms, the proteins of the grasses, and how to watch changes in the wind in winter" (McSweeney 1995, 102–103).

McSweeney found the concept of *querencia* to be the basis of northern New Mexico rural tradition. The word *querencia* comes from the verb *aquerenciarse,* which means to become fond of a place. While most commonly used in reference to animals, it can also be applied to the Hispanic and Puebloan ranching families of northern New Mexico. "They are at home in a place where they live and work and raise their families. This place provides them with the resources needed for survival, and, in turn, they feel a responsibility to care for that place. This is their *querencia.* It goes beyond the boundaries of legal ownership, beyond the promise of monetary return" (McSweeney 1995, 112–113).

Case Study 3: Contemporary Small-Scale Livestock Operations

Although herd sizes have declined over the years, the contributions of livestock to the traditional Hispanic and Puebloan families and communities of northern New Mexico continue to be very important. Most of the small-scale livestock operators no longer depend on their animals for their full support; they generally have outside jobs or are retired. They consider their animals as a means of savings, as "banks-on-the-hoof," which can be used in hard times. Animals serve as a backup resource for emergencies, for periods of unemployment, or for special needs like college tuition for the children. They also add to family security by providing meat for the family (William de Buys, personal communication 1995; Eastman and Gray 1987, 39–50). Cooperative work arrangements and participation in livestock-related community events such as branding and butchering also help to keep alive social cohesion in the community (William de Buys, personal communication, 1995; Eastman and Gray 1987, 39–50).

The majority of northern New Mexico ranches mirror the communal nature, small size, and relatively low technology of the subsistence operations of the past. They are not large and are often not commercial, since a minimum of a hundred head is generally defined as a commercially viable ranch (Eastman and Gray 1987). For example, operations with less than a hundred head account for 85 percent of ranches in Santa Fe County, rising to 96 percent of ranches in Taos County (Eastman et al. 2000, 536–537; U.S. Dept. of Commerce, Bureau of the Census 1992). Most ranchers have from ten to twenty head of cattle; fifty or more cattle are considered a large herd (Eastman and Gray 1987, 51–82).

Environmental conditions, combined with cultural and historical factors, strongly influence the nature of stock raising in northern New Mexico, producing ranching operations that have far less environmental impact than the much larger operations found in drier portions of the state. Much of the area is mountainous, providing greater rainfall and more abundant natural waters and forage. The rugged landscape is often incompatible with the motorized vehicles and mechanized tools common on larger operations in different terrain. Ranchers in northern New Mexico generally work their small herds on horseback, take advantage of geographic barriers as boundaries (so that less fencing is required), and rely on the natural waters of the mountain areas. A worldview that places a high value on the virtues of family, tradition, and cultural continuity with the past is evident among the ranchers in their pride in managing their operations as their grandfathers did (Hess 1990, 21). In his study of ranching on public land, Hess (1990) found that Forest Service Wilderness designation caused relatively few changes in the livestock operations of the northern New Mexico permittees (ranchers permitted to graze their animals on an allotment of public land for a fee), because the wilderness concept was compatible with ranching operations in the region.

Considerable local environmental knowledge guides these enterprises, and land managers would be well advised to acknowledge that fact. A case in point comes from the history of disagreements over herd size on the El Pueblo grazing allotment of the Santa Fe National Forest (discussed by Eastman and Gray 1987, 109–120; Eastman et al. 2000, 539–542). In the 1980s, the Forest Service considered the allotment to be understocked. Most of the nine permittees had permits for 22 cows, while one had the maximum permit for 110 cows (Eastman and Gray 1987, 109–115; Eastman et al. 2000, 540). The number of permittees and the herd size range reflected the traditional communal nature and small herd sizes of the ranching operations, which fit well with both the lifestyle and the environment of the region.

The Forest Service put pressure on the permittees to add more cattle and adopt more intensive grazing management techniques. Most had to borrow money for additional livestock and were not ready to adopt more intensive and time-consuming management strategies. Drought hit the allotment during the mid- to late 1980s, making it more difficult for the permittees to repay their loans; many were forced to sell out during this period [Eastman et al. 2000, 540–541; Jerry Elson, Santa Fe National Forest Range and Wildlife Staff (retired), personal communication 1997].

In 1997 there were three permittees, two of whom were new to the allotment, with herd sizes of 46, 140, and 374, for a total of 560 head—almost double the number of cattle in the early 1980s. The range staff's assessment in 1997 was that the allotment was probably not understocked to begin with and may be overstocked today [Eastman et al. in press; Jerry Elson, Santa Fe National Forest Range and Wildlife Staff (retired), personal communication 1997]. Whether rooted in an agency desire for fewer permittees and larger herd sizes or in ignorance of local culture, this disregard for local practices with respect to herd size and appropriate management techniques harmed permittees, forcing them to sell out and contributing to overstocking and possible damage to range conditions.

Policies concerning the allotment lent credence to Kutsche and Van Ness's (1981, 45) view that Forest Service administration favored larger-scale ranching that was often not compatible with the subsistence needs of local traditional communities (Eastman et al. 2000, 541). Inattention to the needs and traditional practices of the local culture, among other issues, has resulted in varying levels of protest from the Hispanic and Puebloan communities of northern New Mexico over the years. These protests have ranged from prolonged legal wrangles to outright violence (de Buys 1985, Rosenbaum 1981). At one point, the Forest Service even developed a special policy for dealing with the area (Hassell 1968, Hurst 1972), which stressed assisting local communities in maintaining traditional economic practices and lifeways. Although the policy is no longer officially in effect, many current Forest Service personnel perceive a greater agency awareness of the importance of meeting local cultural needs and a greater understanding of the value of traditional knowledge and practices in rangeland management [Eastman et al. 2000, 547; Jerry Elson, Santa Fe National Forest Range and Wildlife Staff (retired), personal communication 1997].

Case Study 4: Contemporary Acequia Farming

In many cases, the worldviews, values, and attitudes of the traditional irrigation, or *acequia,* farmers of northern New Mexico are the same as those previously discussed for the ranchers. They carry on the old pattern of farming small irrigated plots and pasturing small herds of livestock on communal lands or community allotments.

Rivera (1998, xvii–xviii) uses Worster's (1985, 31) discussion of subsistence water control to describe the earthen ditches, or *acequias,* and the communities that build, maintain, and depend on them. In these communities, water control relies on temporary structures and small permanent works that interfere minimally with stream flow. The diverted water is used to grow subsistence crops. Control of water distribution and management lies within the local community of users, who have the skill and expertise to build and maintain their system.

A study of New Mexico *acequias* by Eastman and King (1997) found that the most common crops on small-scale irrigated farms were alfalfa and pasture and that cattle were the most common livestock on those operations. "Since forage is so scarce, it is economical for landowners to devote most of their irrigated land to their livestock, which requires relatively little labor, and to spend their own time earning wages elsewhere" (Kutsche and Van Ness 1981, 36). An alfalfa pasture and cattle operation lends itself well to evening and weekend care. In contrast, producing fruit and vegetables for sale require more management and seasonal labor not easily found in many households. In spite of this, such operations are still found in various locales around the state (Eastman et al. 2000).

Despite demographic changes over the years, researchers have found that the traditional acequia farming institution maintains both sustainable human communities and desired landscapes (Rivera 1998, xiv–xviii). As social and governmental institutions, the acequia associations help integrate and preserve the historic villages of northern New Mexico. Since many of these villages are unincorporated, the associations often function as the only mechanisms of local government below the county level. The local knowledge and traditional practices required to administer, maintain, and repair the acequia systems bond the social life of the community, enforcing an ethic of sharing and mutual assistance. These associations foster a land ethic based on the knowledge that community survival depends upon stewardship of the water and watershed on which they all depend.

The environmental contributions of the *acequias* have long been understood by local practitioners and are now being examined by the Upper Rio Grande Hispano Farms Study under the direction of Devón Peña and Rubén Martínez (Devón Peña, personal communication 1998; Rivera 1998, 32, 211–212). The work in progress on this multiyear study demonstrates how traditional *acequia* irrigation farming benefits local plants, wildlife, and hydrology as well as human communities.

The *acequias* fit into the natural landscape and extend the riparian corridor with greenbelts that provide wildlife corridors and habitat. They replenish eroded topsoils, providing nutrients for the crops. The irrigation water spreads rich silt over the fields (Scurlock 1998, 114). In many cases, the *acequia* systems create anthropogenic wetlands. The earthen ditches promote soil and water conservation; the gravity flow systems return excess water to the source, while the seepage helps to recharge the aquifer. The seepage also nourishes cottonwoods and willows along the ditch banks.

In addition to alfalfa, many of the small, *acequia*-dependent farm patches produce a varied polyculture that preserves the genetic diversity of native plant races, while not requiring fossil fuels and making little use of herbicides and pesticides (Devón Peña, personal communication 1998). As stated by Rivera (1998), "This record of accomplishment runs counter to the notion . . . that the earthen *acequia* irrigation canals are wasteful, abusive to soils, inefficient, and antiquated. Moreover, the fact that *acequia* communities continue to support human and other habitats, without depleting the resource base, is testimony to the existence and practice of a conservation ethic long ago ingrained in the local value systems" (xviii).

Both large and small attempts to modernize and improve traditional irrigation systems, as well as growing commercial development, often ignore the traditional knowledge base and constitute threats of varying degrees to local village systems. These can range from small modernization and improvement programs to the creation of large water conservancy districts, which generally favor the larger commercial interests of the region. The following examples examine both types of threats.

Eastman and King (1997) discuss problems that occurred in federal agency attempts to assist *acequia* associations through the Federal Acequia Rehabilitation Program. These efforts were designed to improve and modernize ditches by constructing permanent diversion structures to replace traditional ones of stone, logs, and brush. The newer structures are supposed to be more efficient and require less labor intensive maintenance, but the modern technology is costly to local communities even with federal assistance. In addition, a number of the new permanent structures have failed, with repairs adding much to their cost.

Eastman and King (1997) discuss problems with diversion structures in a range of northern New Mexico communities, concluding that agency designers should pay more attention to local knowledge and input concerning specific hydrologic problems and time-honored community solutions to those problems when planning the replacement structures. They also suggest that traditional "disposable" structures work better in some situations. These structures seem to be especially suitable in wide valleys or floodplains where new channels are established by meandering and flooding, since substantial repairs must be made to diversion structures after every flood. As Eastman and King

(1997) state, "It may be less costly and more efficient to replace an essentially 'disposable' structure each year than to try to maintain a permanent structure in some particularly difficult settings" (7).

A more serious threat to the small *acequia* farmers comes from large-scale water diversion projects, with the creation of conservancy districts that often effectively usurp local control and impact local water supplies. Large diversion and modernization schemes require equally large assessments to finance them and often substantially raise property taxes. The higher fees may require farmers to consolidate properties and change cropping patterns from subsistence to commercial produce. In many cases, such changes are neither feasible nor desirable for traditional irrigation farmers. Creation of the Middle Rio Grande Conservancy District (MRGCD) in central New Mexico in the 1920s (Wozniak 1998) eventually led to bankruptcy and land loss for many small farmers in the central valley. They were unable to pay the conservancy assessments and higher property taxes associated with the new developments (Forrest 1989, 153–157; Harper et al. 1943; Scurlock 1998, 316, 321, 375, 388).

With lessons learned from the MRGCD firmly in mind, *acequia* farmers in northern New Mexico have been able to resist several large water diversion projects proposed for the region. By forming associations to publicize their concerns and protesting directly to the governor and the New Mexico congressional delegation, they were able to halt implementation of the projects. The Bureau of Reclamation stated that one of the projects was terminated because of the "overwhelming desire of the area citizens 'to retain their lifestyle to the maximum extent possible'" (Rivera 1998, 150–158, 155). These types of decisions also maintain a desired landscape condition that could not be maintained with resources typically available to land management or restoration efforts. Groups of *acequia* associations have also been able to successfully argue that customs and tradition pertaining to water division and sharing among irrigators should be honored and considered binding and lawful by the courts. This is a major step forward in maintaining local control by recognizing the importance of local traditional culture and knowledge in administering smoothly functioning, cost-effective systems.

The small-scale farming and ranching operations of northern New Mexico demonstrate the varied contributions of traditional knowledge and practices to maintaining desired, sustainable ecosystems as well as healthy, sustainable communities. As discussed by Peña and Gallegos (1993), rural Hispanic and Puebloan communities and cultures are land based, so protecting water and land also protects the local culture. Rancher and farmer Joe Gallegos speaks of this connection: "My family has been farming the land here for five generations. . . . The land responds when you are good to it. I want to share this knowledge with younger generations so that we can keep the land in good health, and in so doing, keep our community full of the vitality and cultural heritage that has made it unique" (quoted in Peña and Gallegos 1993, 159). These value systems, which stress continuity with the past and view the land as a living heritage for future generations, buttress traditional practices and knowledge systems. The noncommercial orientations and generally small size of these operations are also major contributing factors in their ability to provide for functioning communities and landscapes. The farmers and ranchers of northern New Mexico demonstrate the invaluable knowledge base and ethic of stewardship of those living close to the land. Their solutions to land use problems provide a store of knowledge for those who manage land in the area.

Conclusion

As these examples demonstrate, indigenous and traditional peoples who live on the land have strong motivations to maintain its health and productivity. They are not divorced from the land by distance or the competing values of urban life. Their cultures, livelihoods, and futures depend upon sustainable ecosystems. The worldviews, traditional environmental knowledge, and long-standing resource use practices of these groups combine to produce use and management systems that are often compatible with notions of ecosystem conservation and environmental stewardship. Their worldviews and value systems are also generally oriented toward noncommercial economic systems. This noncommercial orientation, combined with the low populations and relatively low technological levels of most of these groups, produces a lower environmental impact than high-population, high-technology commercial systems. Although it is impossible to turn back the clock to a world of subsistence hunters, gatherers, and farmers, contemporary land managers can profit from knowing and understanding the resource use practices of these groups, especially when it comes to managing our remaining protected areas. Restorationists can profit too, by learning how to integrate the management provided by local, traditional, and existing cultures with the goals of ecological restoration projects.

References

Barker, G., and C. Gamble, eds. 1985. *Beyond Domestication in Prehistoric Europe: Investigations in Subsistence Archaeology and Social Complexity.* London: Academic Press.

Callicott, J. B. 1982. "Traditional American Indian and Western European Attitudes Toward Nature: An Overview." *Environmental Ethics* 4(4): 293–318.

Capp, J. C., and C. Jorgensen. 1997. "Traditional Knowledge: Don't Leave the Future

Without It." In *Transactions of the 62nd North American Wildlands and Natural Resources Conference,* edited by K.G. Wadsworth, 199–209. Washington, DC: Wildlife Management Institute.

Clark, I. G. 1987. *Water in New Mexico: A History of Its Management and Use.* Albuquerque: University of New Mexico Press.

Cohen, M. N. 1977. *The Food Crisis in Prehistory: Overpopulation and the Origins of Agriculture.* New Haven: Yale University Press.

de Buys, W. 1985. *Enchantment and Exploitation: The Life and Hard Times of a New Mexico Mountain Range.* Albuquerque: University of New Mexico Press.

de Buys, W., M. Crespi, S. H. Lees, D. Meredith, and T. Strong. 1999. "Cultural and Social Diversity and Resource Use." In *Ecological Stewardship: A Common Reference for Ecosystem Management,* vol. III, edited by W. T. Sexton, A. J. Malk, R. Szaro, and N. C. Johnson, 189–208. Oxford: Elsevier Science.

Eastman, C., G. Carruthers, and J. A. Liefer. 1971. *Evaluation of Attitudes toward Land in North-Central New Mexico.* Las Cruces: New Mexico State Agricultural Experiment Station Bulletin 577.

Eastman, C., and J. A. Gray. 1987. *Community Grazing: Practice and Potential in New Mexico.* Albuquerque: University of New Mexico Press.

Eastman, C., and J. P. King. 1997. "Federal Acequia Assistance Programs: Good Intentions Gone Awry." Paper presented at the Western Social Science Association, 39th annual conference, April 23–26, Albuquerque, NM.

Eastman, C., C. Raish, and A. M. McSweeney. 2000. "Small Livestock Operations in New Mexico." In *Livestock Management in the American Southwest: Ecology, Society, and Economics,* edited by R. Jemison and C. Raish, 523–554. Amsterdam: Elsevier Science.

Forrest, S. 1989. *The Preservation of the Village: New Mexico's Hispanics and the New Deal.* Albuquerque: University of New Mexico Press.

Gadgil, M., F. Berkes, and C. Folke. 1993. "Indigenous Knowledge for Biodiversity Conservation." *Ambio* 22(2–3): 151–156.

García, M. T. 1996. "Hispanic Perspectives and Values." In *Nature and the Human Spirit: Toward an Expanded Land Management Ethic,* edited by B. L. Driver, D. Dustin, T. Baltic, G. Elsner, and G. Peterson, 145–151. State College, PA: Venture Publishing.

Harper, A. G., A. R. Cordova, and K. Oberg. 1943. *Man and Resources in the Middle Rio Grande Valley.* Albuquerque: University of New Mexico Press.

Hassell, M. J. 1968. *The People of Northern New Mexico and the National Forests.* Manuscript on file. Albuquerque: USDA Forest Service, Southwestern Region.

Hess, K., Jr. 1990. *The Wilderness Experience: New Mexico Ranches on National Forest Wilderness.* Las Cruces: NMDA. Special Report No.7.

Hurst, W. D. 1972. "Region 3 Policy on Managing National Forest Land in Northern New Mexico." Memo on file. Albuquerque: USDA Forest Service, Southwestern Region.

Kluckhohn, F. R., and F. Strodtbeck. 1961. *Variations in Value Orientations.* Evanston, IL: Row and Peterson.

Knowlton, C. S. 1967. "Recommendations for the Solution of Land Tenure Problems among the Spanish American." Paper presented at the Cabinet committee hearings on Mexican American affairs, October 26–28, El Paso, TX.

Kutsche, P., and J. R. Van Ness. 1981. *Cañones: Values, Crisis, and Survival in a Northern New Mexico Village*. Albuquerque: University of New Mexico Press.

Liefer, J. A. 1970. *Attitudes Toward Land Ownership and Usage in North Central New Mexico*. M.S. Thesis. Las Cruces: New Mexico State University.

McSweeney, A. M. 1995. *Views on Land and Nature: Conversations with Northern New Mexico Ranchers*. M.S. Thesis. Las Cruces: New Mexico State University.

Peña, D., and J. Gallegos. 1993. "Nature and Chicanos in Southern Colorado." In *Confronting Environmental Racism: Voices from the Grassroots*, edited by R. D. Bullard and B. F. Chavis, Jr., 141–160. Boston: South End Press.

Rivera, J. A. 1998. *Acequia Culture: Water, Land, and Community in the Southwest*. Albuquerque: University of New Mexico Press.

Rodríguez, S. 1987. "Land, Water, and Ethnic Identity in Taos." In *Land, Water, and Culture: New Perspectives on Hispanic Land Grants*, edited by C. L. Briggs and J. R. Van Ness, 313–403. Albuquerque: University of New Mexico Press.

Rosenbaum, R. J. 1981. *Mexicano Resistance in the Southwest*. Austin: University of Texas Press.

Rothman, H. 1989. "Cultural and Environmental Change on the Pajarito Plateau." *New Mexico Historical Review* 64(2): 185–211.

Scurlock, D. 1998. *From the Rio to the Sierra: An Environmental History of the Middle Rio Grande Basin*. General Technical Report RMRS-GTR-5. Fort Collins, CO: USDA Forest Service, Rocky Mountain Research Station.

Stedman-Edwards, P. 1998. *Root Causes of Biodiversity Loss: An Analytical Approach*. Washington, DC: Worldwide Fund for Nature, Macroeconomics Program Office.

Thakali, R., and L. Lesko. 1998. "Wisdom of the Ages: Traditional Knowledge and Forest Ecosystems." Manuscript on file. Williams, AZ: USDA Forest Service, Kaibab National Forest.

U.S. Department of Commerce, Bureau of the Census. 1992. *Census of Agriculture*. Part 31, New Mexico, Table 14, 264–266. Washington, DC.

Van Ness, J. R. 1987. "Hispanic Land Grants: Ecology and Subsistence in the Uplands of Northern New Mexico and Southern Colorado." In *Land, Water, and Culture: New Perspectives on Hispanic Land Grants*, edited by C. L. Briggs and J. R. Van Ness, 141–214. Albuquerque: University of New Mexico Press.

Westphall, V. 1965. *The Public Domain in New Mexico, 1854–1891*. Albuquerque: University of New Mexico Press.

Worster, D. 1985. *Rivers of Empire: Water, Aridity and the Growth of the American West*. New York: Pantheon Books.

Wozniak, F. E. 1995. "Human Ecology and Ethnology." In *Ecology, Diversity, and Sustainability of the Middle Rio Grande Basin*, edited by D. M. Finch and J. A. Tainter, 29–51. General Technical Report RM-268. Fort Collins: USDA Forest Service, Rocky Mountain Forest and Range Experiment Station.

Wozniak, F. E. 1998. *Irrigation in the Rio Grande Valley, New Mexico: A Study and Annotated Bibliography of the Development of Irrigation Systems*. Report No. RMRS-P-2. Fort Collins, CO: USDA Forest Service, Rocky Mountain Research Station.

❧ *Conclusion* ❧

WHICH NATURE?

R. Bruce Hull and David P. Robertson

For any particular place, many states of nature can be created or restored. Which nature should it be? Which nature is likely to succeed socially as well as ecologically? Which nature will keep restoration efforts on the land rather than in the courts? Which restored nature is most likely to be maintained and thus survive in the long term? Which restoration project is more important than other pressing environmental and social problems and deserves allocation of society's scarce resources? These are some of the big questions confronting, and in some cases stalling, restoration efforts. The natural sciences (e.g., ecology, paleoecology, biology, geology) alone are unable to answer these questions. Contributions from the humanities and social sciences are needed to help decide restoration goals, to justify them in a competitive social context, and ultimately to plan, implement, and maintain desired states of nature. The chapters in this book begin to address these issues.

Certainly one of the most important challenges facing the readers of this book is setting restoration and management goals. What is possible? What is acceptable? What can be maintained? And why do it? We will begin with the last question and work our way through the others.

Why Restore Nature?

Restoration projects require extensive social resources and political support. As such, they compete not only with other worthy environmental projects but also with programs that support human health, education, and welfare. The public support given to restore the Chicago Wilderness could have been used to accomplish many other desirable social goals, such as renovating a children's hospital. How do we justify one set of restoration goals, or one specific project, over other worthy projects? Insights from the humanities help us ask and answer these difficult questions about social priorities.

Enlightened self-interest is one among many reasons why restoration projects deserve public support. Human societies depend upon functioning ecosystem services that, it is estimated, are worth at least $33 trillion annually, several times the global gross national product (Costanza et al. 1998). It can be convincingly argued that human health and welfare are enhanced through restoration of damaged ecosystems, and that it is thus in our own best interests to do so. Pragmatic arguments supporting these utilitarian justifications can be found in the fields of environmental mitigation, ecological economics, and environmental risk assessment. The first section of this book, however, explores a less understood philosophical justification for restoration—a justification that is closer to the hearts of those who participate in the many ongoing efforts to restore nature. In this first section we find arguments and debates about the moral values (Jordan, Katz, Light) and aesthetic values (Foster, Jordan) produced by restoration projects and by restored settings.

It is argued that participation in volunteer restoration activities may generate rich aesthetic experiences. Through involvement with nature, restorationists come to appreciate the sensuous qualities that appear on the surface of the landscape as well as understand the scientific, historic, cultural, and mythological stories that lie beneath. Unlike the familiar Romantic script, which requires the natural setting to be pristine and humans to be visitors who leave no trace and do not remain, restoration experiences demand that people participate in the creation of nature. By way of actively tending nature, restorationists develop respect and concern for the environment as well as a vested interest in its future—a deeper meaning. If nothing else, the aesthetic experience of the passive observer might be improved and deepened simply by an awareness that the scenery has been created and maintained through a long process of human involvement and care.

It is also argued that restoration projects are valuable because they provide a moral compass to direct society's relationship with nature. By becoming involved in the celebration and the ritual of restoring nature, people learn to respect the complexities of nature, including society's dependence and effect on nature's dynamics. In addition, the negotiation of restoration goals and participation in restoration projects are inherently democratic activities and potentially promote and further the democratic ideals valued by American and other societies.

Our landscapes reflect our values. Looking at our surroundings, we see our priorities and concerns. We see whether we care as much about the future and the past as we do about the comforts of the present. We see whether we value other members of the land community for more than what they do to satisfy our needs and wants. We see the trade-offs we make between human desire and environmental quality. Two centuries ago the stump was an American sign of progress. European settlers found what they thought to be an endless bounty, there for the taking. Use, consume, develop, tame the wildness—the faster the better. Then, in the 1800s, came a cry to value nature in its wild, undeveloped state, to value it for more than the economic resources it provided. Parks, wildernesses, and an Endangered Species Act became signs of progress, symbols of how far civilization had matured in its ability to respect and value the nuances of its relationship with the land. Nature was set aside and protected in national parks, wilderness areas, and wildlife preserves. This preservation ethic has left us a magnificent legacy of natural areas, more than 100 million acres of federally designated wilderness alone. But today, in this book and elsewhere (Baldwin et al. 1994, Callicott and Nelson 1998, Cronon 1995), we hear a call for a new land ethic, a restoration ethic.

Restoration raises difficult questions about American society's relationship with nature. By exposing our own loss of innocence and in turn celebrating our own naturalness, a restoration ethic allows us to dance with rather than on nature. Restoration blurs the distinction between culture and nature. It makes an open continuum out of the more simplistic and polarizing human-nature dichotomy. Where the preservation ethic polarizes humans and nature as distinct and separate entities, a restoration ethic opens up a broad middle ground where it is acceptable for humans and nature to interact. It encourages us to look forward to the potential of nature rather than backward to what nature was in the past. It allows us to imagine an Eden with people living in the garden, caring for nature, rather than being banished and allowed to return only as temporary visitors seeking recreation experiences.

A restored setting is intentionally trammeled and tended. And tending is thought to be a good thing. A restoration ethic, it is argued, might be a more sustainable environment ethic. The act of restoration instills respect in us for the land. It builds into our culture an appreciation and respect not just for nature, but for our relationship with nature, and not just for wild nature but for all forms of nature from parks to parking lots.

Many of the philosophical issues discussed in the first section of the book are reflected in the later chapters that present studies of the reasons people give for volunteering in restoration projects (see chapters by Schroeder and by Grese et al.). These issues also dominate public discussions about the worth of restoration projects and, as we see in the second section of the book, appear time and again in the conflict and litigation that halts restoration efforts (see chapters by Helford and by Vining et al.). The restoration community must continue to develop and discuss its philosophical rationale. Arguments for public approval of restoration work, and for the public resources required to do it, are likely to become sharper and more focused in an increasingly pluralistic society.

Which Natures Are Possible and Acceptable?

Once we decide that society's scarce resources should be devoted to the restoration of a setting, we must then decide what quality of nature should be restored. Which nature do we want? Physical and biological sciences, especially ecology and paleoecology, can help us answer these questions by setting boundaries on what is ecologically probable for a given place during a given time. There are broad limits as to what has survived and what is likely to survive in a particular setting. A tropical rain forest, for example, is unlikely to survive on its own in a region currently supporting arctic tundra.[1] However, as many of the chapters in the second and third sections of this book argue, the natural sciences cannot objectively decide among the many possible, equally feasible, equally healthy natures that did or might yet exist at a place. The past is one guide for what nature can be, but it is not the only guide, nor is it necessarily the best or clearest guide. The selection of which nature to restore should depend as much on which nature is socially acceptable, socially valued, and socially sustainable as it should depend on which nature is ecologically plausible.

The controversy over restoration in Chicago clearly illustrates the need to openly negotiate a socially acceptable, valued, and sustainable nature. Some people value pre-European-settlement savanna-like conditions, while other people (who also consider themselves motivated by environmental concerns) prefer the now familiar and current forested conditions that have evolved in part as a consequence of European settlement. Failure to negotiate and accommodate these different visions of nature can result in administrative appeals, litigation, and an outcome nobody wants: the prevention of any and all environmental management and, worse, the frustration of the diverse stakeholders who have sincere environmental concerns. Chapters in the second and third sections of this book attempt to make sense of the conflict inherent in many restoration projects (Vining et al.), offer suggestions for the planning and implementation of on-the-ground manipulations (Brunson, Ryan), provide detailed illustrations of the different positions stakeholders might advocate (Gobster and Barro, Helford), examine the role of science in these decisions (Helford, Brunson, Hull and Robertson), and discuss the role of the language used to discuss restoration (Light, Hull and Robertson).

What role should scientific environmental knowledge (versus values, beliefs, and traditional or lay knowledge) play in all this conflict? The answer to such questions depends, in part, on how much confidence we have in the environmental knowledge that science generates. According to what has been loosely called the postmodern view of science, scientific knowledge about the environment is always both normative (i.e., it reflects a value system) and limited (i.e., it is based on assumptions: its validity, applicability, and generalizability are always contingent on assumptions that in turn are based on agreement within the scientific community). The belief that science does not produce a positive knowledge of external reality (i.e., one-to-one correspondence) has obvious implications for the role of science in setting policy for restoration efforts. If there are many ways of knowing the environment, if all of them are normative (value-laden), and if many of them are equally correct, then who has the authority to say what is right? Some of the conflicts that hinder restoration efforts result from controversies over which knowledge is best. Conflicts arise between lay experts and scientific experts (Helford), between traditional knowledge and scientific knowledge (Raish), and between public preferences and all experts (Gobster and Barro, Helford, Ryan, Vining et al.).

There are many competing visions of what makes environmental knowledge useful and acceptable. A challenge for the people motivated to make restoration happen is to create an environmental knowledge that is meaningful within ecological science, comprehensible to most interested stakeholders, appropriate to the political context, relevant to the specific place and time, and constructive in resolving conflict and promoting action toward desired goals. This is a significant challenge! Through careful science and political negotiation, we *can* actively construct environmental knowledge that has these necessary qualities. We can forge, through careful study and negotiation, an environmental knowledge that helps restore nature. To do this, we must respect and consider the many ways of knowing nature. In addition to the systematic, peer-reviewed, generalizable knowledge generated by science, we must respect the place-specific knowledge that lay experts earn through their years of careful attention to local conditions, as well as respect the many public preferences and expectations held and promoted by less systematic but equally concerned citizen-stakeholders. These alternative ways of knowing nature make important contributions to the environmental knowledge needed to restore nature.

Which Natures Can Be Maintained and Sustained?

Restoration requires extensive human resources. It takes many people to plan, implement, and maintain the desired environment. In fact, most current restoration projects rely extensively on volunteers to do the work of restoration. But even these volunteer efforts will not be enough to sustain projects now under way. Many desired states of nature require constant human intervention (i.e., cultural practices such as farming) to maintain them. Ideas are cheap. Restoration projects may look good on paper, and may even look good just after implementation, but they don't count unless they can be sustained on the ground, through time, over multiple generations. When negotiating the goals of a restoration project and when designing project implementation, restoration organizers must consider what motivates and sustains volunteering.

Implementation and maintenance are two different things. Implementation of restoration projects requires extensive coordination of diverse volunteers to engage in relatively short bursts of hard physical labor, often in adverse conditions. In heat, cold, rain, and sun, people must pull, drag, cut, and burn unwanted nature and then plant, water, and nurture desired nature. The efforts are focused, intense, and acute. Volunteers see change; they witness the fruits of their labors. They are motivated because they care about environmental issues and, through volunteering in restoration projects, they can make an obvious difference. But volunteers are motivated by much more than nature's sake. Sustained restoration programs will also need to provide the other benefits volunteers seek, such as expertise and personal growth, through training and opportunities to assume responsibility. Volunteers also value the social networks, friendship, and sense of community available through volunteering. Successful volunteering efforts must promote all of these benefits if they hope to sustain the critically needed interest and resources of volunteers.

Maintaining a desired environmental condition begins after implementation and requires extensive social resources. The work to maintain and sustain restored conditions may be less glamorous and the benefits less obvious than the work required to implement a restoration project. Few studies help us see how the long-term maintenance of desired landscape conditions might be achieved. Raish's study of traditional agricultural practices in the southwestern United States is one such study. She illustrates how traditional land management practices based on local knowledge serve to maintain diverse and valued environmental conditions. Raish also illustrates how vulnerable these practices and conditions are to land management agency policies that promote nontraditional practices and ignore traditional, local knowledge. Her conclusions provide a valuable link between ecological restoration and recent advancements in the areas of biocultural conservation and political ecology. Biocultural conservation is an emergent paradigm in natural resource management, and political ecology is an emergent interdisciplinary field of environmental research. Both are derived from hard lessons learned at the interface of international development and environmental protection (Adams and McShane 1992, Blaikie and Brookfield 1987, Ghimire and Pimbert 1997, Gomez-Pompa and Kaus 1992, West and Brechin 1991, Zimmerer and Young 1998). Like Raish, many of these scholars contend that the easiest and sometimes only way to maintain desired environmental conditions is to maintain the human culture that maintains the setting.

Pollan makes a case for biocultural conservation in his argument that the "middle landscape" of New England is being lost because the culture that created it is vanishing (Pollan 1991, 1998). Its rural fields, fencerows, small farm lots, and farm structures are idealized not just as part of New England but also as part of the pastoral image of America (Schauman 1998, Short 1991). Maintaining these landscapes that blend culture and nature requires much energy and time. In the past, the small farming practices that maintained these landscapes were rewarded by economic and lifestyle benefits. Society no longer rewards those behaviors, so the landscapes they produced are disappearing. Is restoration needed?

Organizations could form to maintain desired pastoral landscapes. But could programs succeed in motivating volunteers to sweat and grunt over landscapes that are as much cultural as they are natural? Clearly, the volunteers described by Schroeder and by Grese et al. in this volume are highly motivated by the belief that they are helping nature. Would they be equally motivated to maintain a cultured naturalness? Many people seem highly motivated to preserve historic buildings and battlefields and devote much energy to cultivating nature in the form of gardens and lawns. Perhaps a more clearly articulated ethic is needed that values these middle landscapes and serves as a guide for their restoration. Pollan (1991) has long advocated such a garden ethic, as have Dubos (1980) and Turner (1985, 1988, and 1994). It is an ethic that not just values previous natures that happen to have resulted from previous cultural practices but also values future natures that might exist, in harmony with humans, with respect for both humans and nature, with the intent of realizing the full potential of both nature and humans.

Many restorationists are likely to find these ideas unsettling if not simply absurd because they question the common assumption that a restored environment is a previous environment. According to the popular view, restoration means going back in time, to a former glory. Certainly past states of nature are valuable and worthy goals of restoration efforts. But the past need not be the only goal restorationists consider. There are as yet unrealized states of nature that can exist through some prolonged relationship with human society. They will be important because they are healthy, possible, productive, meaningful, and likely to be maintained. Which nature do we choose? It is ever more clear that the restoration and maintenance of desired states of nature is a complex and sensitive social phenomenon we are only beginning to understand.

The scholarship of restoration found in the chapters of this volume occurs at the intersection of the humanities, the social sciences, and the biological and physical sciences. Within this interdisciplinary space will be found key questions and many answers affecting the restoration and management of nature. Because of this interdisciplinary perspective, restoration is at the forefront of many environmental fields. Recent reviewers from the field of environmental management have criticized the limited influence that the physical and biological sciences have had on environmental management, policy, and litigation (Bryant and Wilson 1998, Norton 1998, Sagoff 1988, Shrader-Frechette and McCoy 1993, Wiener 1996). Recognizing that the environment and its problems are as much social as they are physical, these critics note that the study and resolution of environmental issues requires blending the physical and natural sciences with the social sciences and the humanities. The social sciences and humanities are grossly underrepresented in national environmental agendas and in funding priorities. The chapters in this volume provide just a glimmer of the potential and promise of future collaborations.

The social sciences can help us to identify what is socially acceptable and politically feasible, and to understand the social mechanisms and processes by which restoration and management occur. The humanities can help us justify our selection among the many ecologically possible and socially acceptable natures and place our decision in the context of what that decision says about humanity. Ultimately, the restoration and management of nature requires much collaboration from all fields of formal scholarship as well as a real and meaningful sensitivity to existing conditions, local knowledge, and the unique factors that make special, valued, and important each instance of society's relationship with nature.

Note

1. Although it might be possible to create and sustain a tropical rain forest in a place currently supporting arctic tundra, doing so would require enormous amounts of human resources. Megamalls, state-of-the-art aquariums, museums, zoos, and theme parks re-create at one location and in great detail ecosystem examples from around the world to attract, amuse, and educate visitors. However, the motivation and rationale of these projects seem inconsistent with the type of restoration projects discussed in this book. For more, see Cheryl Foster's chapter in this volume.

References

Adams, J. S., and T. O. McShane. 1992. *The Myth of Wild Africa: Conservation Without Illusion*. Berkeley: University of California Press.

Baldwin, A. D., J. De Luce, and C. Pletsch, eds. 1994. *Beyond Preservation: Restoring and Inventing Landscapes*. Minneapolis: University of Minnesota Press.

Blaikie, P., and H. Brookfield, eds. 1987. *Land Degradation and Society*. London: Methuen.

Bryant, R. L., and G. A. Wilson. 1998. "Rethinking Environmental Management." *Progress in Human Geography* 22(3): 321–343.

Callicott, J. B., and M. P. Nelson, eds. 1998. *The Great New Wilderness Debate.* Athens: University of Georgia Press.

Costanza, R., R. d'Arge, R. de Groot, S. Farber, M. Grasso, B. Hannon, K. Limburg, S. Naeem, R. V. O'Neill, J. Paruelo, R. G. Raskin, P. Sutton, and M. van den Belt. 1998. "The Value of the World's Ecosystem Services and Natural Capital." *Ecological Economics: The Journal of the International Society for Ecological Economics* 25: 3–15.

Cronon, W., ed. 1995. *Uncommon Ground: Toward Reinventing Nature.* New York: W. W. Norton.

Dubos, R. 1980. *The Wooing of Earth: New Perspectives on Man's Use of Nature.* New York: Charles Scribner's Sons.

Ghimire, K. B., and M. P. Pimbert, eds. 1997. *Social Change and Conservation: Environmental Politics and Impacts of National Parks and Protected Areas.* London: Earthscan.

Gomez-Pompa, A., and A. Kaus. 1992. "Taming the Wilderness Myth." *BioScience* 42(4): 271–279.

Norton, B. G. 1998. "Improving Ecological Communication: The Role of Ecologists in Environmental Policy Formation." *Ecological Applications* 8(2): 350–364.

Pollan, M. 1991. *Second Nature: A Gardener's Education.* New York: Delta.

Pollan, M. 1998. "Preserving a View: Should People 'Garden' a Nature Area to Preserve a Farm Look?" *Chicago Tribune* April 25.

Sagoff, M. 1988. "Ethics, Ecology, and the Environment: Integrating Science and Law." *Tennessee Law Review* 56: 77–229.

Schauman, S. 1998. "The Garden and the Red Barn: The Pervasive Pastoral and Its Environmental Consequences." *The Journal of Aesthetics and Art Criticism* 56(2): 181–190.

Short, J. R. 1991. *Imagined Country: Environment, Culture, and Society.* London: Routledge.

Shrader-Frechette, K., and E. D. McCoy. 1993. *Method in Ecology: Strategies for Conservation.* New York: Cambridge University Press.

Turner, F. 1985. "Cultivating the American Garden: Toward a Secular View of Nature." *Harper's* August, 45–52.

Turner, F. 1988. "A Field Guide to the Synthetic Landscape: Toward a New Environmental Ethic." *Harper's* April, 49–55.

Turner, F. 1994. "The Invented Landscape." *Beyond Preservation: Restoring and Inventing Landscapes,* edited by A. D. Baldwin, J. De Luce, and C. Pletsch, 35–66. Minneapolis: University of Minnesota Press.

West, P. C., and S. R. Brechin, eds. 1991. *Resident Peoples and National Parks: Social Dilemmas and Strategies in International Conservation.* Tucson: University of Arizona Press.

Wiener, J. B. 1996. "Beyond the Balance of Nature." *Duke Environmental Law and Policy Forum* 7(1): 1–24.

Zimmerer, K. S., and K. R. Young, eds. 1998. *Nature's Geography: New Lessons for Conservation in Developing Countries.* Madison: University of Wisconsin Press.

CONTRIBUTORS

SUSAN C. BARRO is research social scientist with the USDA Forest Service, North Central Research Station, Chicago. Her research has focused on people's beliefs and attitudes about nature and natural resource management. (sbarro@fs.fed.us)

MARK W. BRUNSON is associate professor of forest resources at Utah State University. He teaches and writes about the human dimensions of forest, rangeland, recreation, and wildlife management. His research focuses on the interactions between ecological knowledge, environmental attitudes and beliefs, and behaviors in both natural and political settings. (brunsonm@cc.usu.edu)

JANE BUXTON is a landscape architect who works with an open space preservation district in the San Francisco Bay area. She received her master's degree in landscape architecture from the University of Michigan. (janeyb1@juno.com)

CHERYL FOSTER is associate professor of philosophy at the University of Rhode Island, where she teaches and writes on topics in environmental philosophy, existentialism, and the philosophy of art. She currently serves on the board of directors of the North American Nature Photography Association. (cherylf@uriacc.edu)

PAUL H. GOBSTER is a research social scientist with the USDA Forest Service, North Central Research Station, Chicago, and also co-leads an integrated research program on midwestern landscape change. His research focuses on urban nature access, landscape aesthetics, and the social aspects of natural areas restoration. (pgobster@fs.fed.us)

ROBERT E. GRESE is associate professor in the School of Natural Resources and Environment at the University of Michigan. His research focuses on various aspects of ecological restoration and environmental stewardship as well as historical traditions in ecologically based design. (bgrese@umich.edu)

REID M. HELFORD is assistant professor of sociology and environmental studies at Whitman College in Walla Walla, Washington. His research interests center on issues of expertise, the public understanding of science, the possibilities of democratic science, and the use of ethnography as a tool in public environmental controversies. His research reported here was conducted as part of his doctoral work in sociology at Loyola University–Chicago. (helforrm@whitman.edu)

R. BRUCE HULL is associate professor of forestry in the College of Natural Resources at Virginia Tech. His research focuses on public understandings of nature and other human dimensions of natural resource management. He teaches a large introductory-level class, popular with students of all majors, that covers the changing relationship between nature and American values. (hullrb@vt.edu)

WILLIAM R. JORDAN III is editor of the journal *Ecological Restoration/North America* and president of the New Academy for Nature and Culture (2236 Commonwealth Avenue, Madison, WI 53705; 608-231-1083; newacademy@execpc.com).

RACHEL KAPLAN is professor of environmental psychology in the School of Natural Resources and Environment at the University of Michigan. Her research interests include public participation and the role of experts, the importance of the natural environment to well-being, and what makes for preferred environments. (rkaplan@umich.edu)

ERIC KATZ is associate professor of philosophy and director of the Science, Technology, and Society Program at the New Jersey Institute of Technology. He is the author of *Nature as Subject* (Rowman & Littlefield 1997) and co-editor (with Andrew Light) of *Environmental Pragmatism* (Routledge 1996). His primary research interests include environmental ethics, philosophy of technology, and Holocaust studies. (katze@admin.njit.edu)

BYOUNG-SUK KWEON is assistant professor in the Department of Landscape Architecture and Urban Planning at Texas A&M University. Her research interests include the physical, social, and psychological effects of urban green spaces, and social and psychological aspects of ecological restoration. (bsk@archone.tamu.edu)

ANDREW LIGHT is assistant professor of environmental philosophy and director of the Graduate Program in Environmental Conservation Education at New York University. He is the author of over forty articles, reviews, and book chapters on environmental ethics, philosophy of technology, and philosophy of film, and has edited or co-edited ten books, including *Environmental Pragmatism* (with Eric Katz); *Social Ecology after Bookchin*; *Race, Class, and Community Identity*; and *Technology and the Good Life?* He is also co-editor of the journal *Philosophy and Geography* and currently vice-president/president-elect of the Society for Philosophy and Technology. (alight@binghamton.edu)

CAROL RAISH is a research social scientist with the USDA Forest Service, Rocky Mountain Research Station, Albuquerque, and has also served as Heritage Resource (Archaeology) staff for the Jemez Ranger District, Santa Fe National Forest. Her primary research interest is examining the social, cultural, and economic contributions of small-scale livestock operations to the Hispanic families and communities of northern New Mexico. She is also studying cultural conflict among American Indians, Hispanic Americans, and Anglo Americans in northern New Mexico, with an emphasis on the role of domesticated animals in these conflicts. She has a bachelor's degree in Spanish and master's and doctoral degrees in anthropology/archaeology. (craish@fs.fed.us)

DAVID P. ROBERTSON is a Ph.D. candidate and research assistant in the College of Natural Resources at Virginia Tech. He holds a master's degree in landscape architecture from Virginia Tech. His research interests include public understandings of ecology, the role of human perception and cognition in environmental evaluation, and applications of environmental history to the design, planning, and management of landscapes. (PorterDR@aol.com)

ROBERT L. RYAN is assistant professor in the Department of Landscape Architecture and Regional Planning at the University of Massachusetts–Amherst. He has practiced as a landscape architect and planner in California and Michigan. A recent graduate of the Ph.D. program of the School of Natural Resources and Environment at the University of Michigan, he has focused his research on understanding how attitudes toward natural settings can help inform design and management decisions. (rlryan@larp.umass.edu)

HERBERT W. SCHROEDER is an environmental psychologist with the USDA Forest Service, North Central Research Station, Chicago. He received his doctorate from the University of Arizona in 1980, and since then has been doing research on people's perceptions, preferences, experiences, and values relating to natural environments. (hschroeder@fs.fed.us)

ELIZABETH TYLER is a community planner and a Ph.D. candidate in regional planning at the University of Illinois at Urbana-Champaign. Her dissertation involves the development of a comprehensive environmental values scheme based upon a number of qualitative data bases and other sources. (e-tyler2@uiuc.edu)

JOANNE VINING is associate professor of environmental psychology in the Department of Natural Resources and Environmental Sciences at the University of Illinois at Urbana-Champaign. She teaches courses in environmental psychology, public involvement, and human–animal interactions. Her research interests include emotion in environmental decision making, assessing and interpreting public input to resource management decisions, and interactions among humans and other animals. She is past president of the Society for Human Ecology. (j-vining@uiuc.edu)

INDEX